Coronation Baby Council House Kid 70s Soulboy

The raising and working life experiences
of a surburban soulboy.
A cultural, social and soulcial history
from the early 1950s.

Graham Clark

Coronation Baby - Council House Kid - '70s Soulboy

Author: Graham Clark

First Published in 2021

ISBN 978-1-915164-00-1 (Paperback)
978-1-915164-01-8 (Ebook)

Published by:
Maple Publishers
1 Brunel Way,
Slough,
SL1 1FQ, UK
www.maplepublishers.com

Cover Design and Book Layout by:
White Magic Studios
www.whitemagicstudios.co.uk

A CIP catalogue record for this title is available from the British Library.

INTRODUCTION

At the time of researching, compiling and starting to write these words, I had reached that age of 65, a step away from my 'three score years and ten' and now stop singing that Beatles lyric, 'When I'm 64', which I first heard in 1967!

Nostalgia* now seems to be part of my everyday thoughts, when walking the dogs, especially listening to music. Occasionally, I will re-visit the area and streets where I grew up, I am sure I can still hear the voices of children I knew, as we happily played out. Looking at my old house, in which I was raised and that I first entered as a new born baby, recalling many memories some good and a few not so.

Retirement, allows more time to think, considering the past, reconnect with people and what you have achieved during your working and social life over the last 60 years. It's just one of those milestones, along with receiving my State Pension, and the status of a Senior, hopefully healthy and with a reasonable lifestyle or even some genetic luck, you can still have at least 20 plus more years of life. Exacerbated for many, I am sure from March 2020, when Covid-19 hit, when thoughts became deeper and that loss of socialising.

Being born in 1953, the average life expectancy was strangely around 65 for a working class man, especially if it involved manual labour in which many were. An 'Old Age Pension' payment was about thirty shillings a week, after more than fifty years of work, a married couple would receive around fifty shillings. It is said, that someone of 65 years of age in the 1950s, had the health of an 85 year old today.

Retiring in these modern times, I consider myself very fortunate to be born in those early 1950s, eight years after WW2 and just five years after the inception of our great National Health Service. Fortunate enough to live in housing that was fit for human

*"*NOSTALGIA – a sentimental longing or wistful affection for periods in the past*".

habitation, along with modern conveniences, to have neighbours that were and treated you as part of their families when required. Very lucky, not feel the direct effect of two dreadful world wars or extreme poverty, fortunate to experience technology changes that literally changed our world and are still doing today.

Really privileged, to live in a small hamlet in a bow of the River Thames just 10 miles from the hustle and bustle of London Town's Marble Arch and Oxford Street, edged by the River Thames on one side and Richmond Park on the other, nestled in a green cushion of trees and many open spaces. Situated to the south of the A307 between two towns, literally cut off from any public transport, no railways, road bridges and not until later that buses stopped in the middle of the village. Just a short distance, a mile or two, from Kingston and the beautiful Richmond town, that sits on a lovely stretch of a meandering Thames, having an iconic clothes shop and music venues, that saw famous 1960's bands, who later dominated the record charts around the world and some still doing it, still singing and playing music, now septuagenarians.

Fortunate enough to gain entry to the best music clubs and concerts, that played the best in R&B, Soul and Reggae in the late 60's and of course through to The Funk and Jazz Funk times of the 70's. Just a 30 minute drive from a London that beckoned, its West End clubs opening their doors to our world and more great music venues all over The South of England and further afield. Late nights and meeting other lads and of course young ladies from the Home Counties, inner and outer London suburban conurbations and above all, so multicultural, multiracial and welcoming, all there just to enjoy ourselves.

So different, to a inherently British white and formerly agricultural village, in which I was raised in the 1950s and 60s. The 70s attracted me like a magnet to London and bought so much cosmopolitan excitement, even when I visited as a toddler and schoolboy to see my grandmother in Battersea and later Wandsworth.

Very fortunate to have a mother and an older brother who loved me, cared for me, protected me, supported me, guided me and kept us all together. Although, keeping some truths from me throughout my early years, it could have been all so different.

I am not unusual, talented or gifted, just your regular ordinary boy growing up, attending state schools, average intelligence and exam results – as you will notice in the grammar and punctuation on the following pages. My school reports read 'easily distracted, tends to chat, must try harder, has improved this term, a better year, must concentrate more, disappointing term' etc. Trying to complete education as soon as possible, as would many school leavers in the 1960's, just finding a job or hopefully taking up an apprenticeship of some form. Strangely, but perhaps because of circumstances and wanting to improve my lot, I had this compelling reason to speed things up, leave school, later home and to have some money in my pocket.

I ask myself now 'Did I like school?', my truthful answer is, I should have made more effort academically and listened, but on the whole, the answer is YES! I really enjoyed the experiences and social support that it bought, being around other boys and girls that were fun to be with, before returning to their own family homes.

As Mum reminded me often, 'Nothing comes easy son, get a good work ethic and things will work out, it won't come to you, it won't be delivered on a silver platter, nobody owes you anything, get out there and just try to do your best!'.

Growing up - like many thousands – surviving not conceding, trying to get from life, new experiences, thankfully throughout my teenage years and into my twenties – well, most of the time anyway! Hoping to eventually settle down, that I honestly thought I would never do on that journey, given my circumstances and the way my early life unfolded.

Everybody lives in and through their own a slice of time and place, we don't choose to start that timer, it just happens, we are born and we are raised within our own given environment by a parent, parents and sometimes for reasons not within our control, perhaps grandparents, a guardian, an institution, who then in turn hopefully just try to do their best, whatever gets in their way or what life throws at them.

People come and go, throughout our life, some we loved and still do and some we have loved and lost, some we didn't like or get on with, some we should have kept in touch with and regrets that we didn't make that effort. All these things add to our experiences and above all, those happy and some inevitable melancholic memories. That famous phrase, "If only...........?', is always in our thoughts.

Sadly, my mother passed away with vascular dementia in 2010 at 88 years of age, in some ways being thankful it was only a three year period. This made me realise, that I should have asked more questions, throughout my life, look at photographs, letters and documents from forty or fifty years earlier. Details about her life and ours growing up, her relationship with my father, his family and the times she lived through. Unfortunately, with the onset of that horrible disease it took a lot of those memories away and far too late for many details, I should have made the time. My own family history details seemed to just start and stop at my parents, it wasn't until sixty years later that I understood my origins and 'where I came from'!

Thinking now about my family history, was I not interested, too selfish, not bothered or didn't want to rake up the past and any sadness that would it would bring or involve, because it may hurt or be uncomfortable, or simply too busy looking forward? Believing, I am from an age where people didn't talk about any trauma, difficult times and any back-story, I have to assume that two world wars didn't help many in the 1940s and 50s anyway. Losing family and friends, some call those 1920-30s born, 'The Secret Generation' burying thoughts, emotions and things that were not mentioned, they told themselves and each other to "Just get over it, life goes on, you just have to get on with it.........!", rightly or wrongly, for many of us, this management of thoughts worked for some, sadly, for others it couldn't.

THIS IS MY STORY, the best part of the first thirty years anyway!

This book is dedicated to Daniel James Mahoney 1953-2021.......a lad that I first met at 8 years of age in Orchard School when he introduced himself to me in the playground of my new school, inviting me to play a game of football. Over the next twenty years, we schooled together, attended Cubs, Scouts, football, youth and music clubs, we holidayed and shared the best music, sometimes girlfriends and experiences, throughout the 1960s and 70s. He features a lot in the following chapters, we cried, laughed and even slept together when the occasion required it. Not always in touch, but we didn't need to call each other often – but when we did, we shared the memories, they seemed just like yesterday.

Rest In Peace Dan, not just mine but everybody's mate in our village of Ham & Petersham. Get the vinyl out and be ready matey, save me a place near the DJ!

CONTENTS

Chapter 1 – Life Begins

It's the early morning of Coronation Day June 2nd 1953, overcast and damp, Keith, a small six year old boy wakes up at home alone at 2 Murray Road, in a village called Ham, near Richmond, then in the county of Surrey. He rushes to his, what was the night before his heavily pregnant mother's bedroom, after she had tucked him up in bed with a goodnight kiss, it now lays empty, bedding pushed back and unmade.

He shouts at the top of his voice "Muumm!", running downstairs at the same time as pulling up his shorts up and t-shirt on, out of the door, jumping through the purpose made gap in the fence and crashes through the unlocked backdoor of the Smiths house next door, shouting "Auntie Mary, Auntie Mary!" – then we called all our close neighbours and our friends parents, Auntie and Uncle, a term of respect and endearment, kindness and a sort of love. She calmly explains that his mother had been taken to hospital earlier that morning and they are now waiting for news of the birth of your baby brother or sister. He is so excited; he closes his eyes and crosses his fingers wishing for a brother.

It's only eight years after World War Two, the nation's hero Winston Churchill is Prime Minister for a second time. Austerity and rationing on hold, excitement of the ascension of our young attractive new monarch, following the passing of her father George

VI, the year before in 1952. After the mourning period, Churchill decided that the people needed something to celebrate and they did on this day of June the 2nd 1953.

The country seems to go from black and white to colour during this period, TV cameras and newsreels were let into Westminster Abbey for the first time - after a very big debate in Government circles - broadcasting the event, the population welcomed, looked forward too and enjoyed the introduction of a New Elizabethan Age and a 26 year old Queen and her handsome young consort, Phillip of Greece and Denmark now the Duke of Edinburgh, marrying the 21 year old Princess Elizabeth in 1947, after first meeting her at age 13. Their children, Prince Charles, 5 years old and Princess Anne age 2 at this time.

That Tuesday was deemed a public holiday, despite the drizzle and rain that morning, the trestles and all sorts of other tables were carried out into streets, bunting and flags were hung from windows, street lamps and fences. The people just wanted to celebrate.

The streets in Ham village were mainly made up of relatively new council estates, families had now made a new home for themselves. Some from the local village, a bombed out London, from overcrowded accommodation, local towns or straight out of the armed forces after demobilisation. People loved their new home from two to five bedrooms or their flat, hot and cold running water, perhaps an immersion heater or Ascot water heater installed, back boiler fireplaces, maybe the luxury of a back and front garden, an inside toilet, a bathroom, a front or a back sitting room, uncrowded bedrooms, in some cases one each for their children! Some were initially offered prefabricated dwellings or Prefabs as we called them, which I understand, should have been temporary, but some families loved them. We had a small estate of around sixty in the middle of our village, being demolished in the early 1960s, to make way for new council homes.

Furnishing these new homes meant new items, if you saved, a trip to Courts Furniture Store, a chain that opened in 1850 and now from 1946, offering hire purchase, window shopping to look at soft and hard furnishings like a new suite, a sofa and two chairs were a must. However, a shortage of timber during the war from bomb damage repairs and construction, led to the introduction and development of Utility Furniture, available from a catalogue. Initially and exclusively for newlyweds for families that were bombed out and assigned a new council home – the styles were sturdy, simple in design and made use of scarce and rationed timber. Influenced by the Arts and Craft Movement, completely different to anything before that their families would have used pre-war. There was even a committee behind it, the scheme closed in 1952, when furniture rationing ceased. There was a huge black market in sales of this furniture and its availability. Mostly pine, stained to give it that light oak look. In our house we had a table, with a top that I thought was magic and extended to make two more places, - we played tennis table on it, with the net that you could secure to the top with thumb screws - four chairs and a long sideboard to match, they sat in our back room, that Mum called 'the dining room'. We still used them in our house until 1975, I still have two of the four chairs in a kitchen today, recovered and still in use.

The Coronation ceremony was spectacular, filmed in colour but televised in black and white, but I doubt that there was a TV in our street at the time. The highlight being the actually crowning, that was superbly captured by an enthusiastic young cameraman, Sydney Samuelson, who went onto later set up the very successful Samuelson Film Services. In 1991 he was appointed as the first British Film Commissioner, later receiving a knighthood in 1995.

That lunchtime and afternoon, parents and excited children wearing homemade hats or crowns, smiling, happy and determined to make it a great day to remember. Sandwiches, biscuits, celebratory cakes, jelly with Carnation or Nestles condensed milk, urns or giant teapots along with Camp coffee, people sharing and bringing their own crockery! The celebrations will go on all afternoon and in some cases into the evening, with older brothers and sisters looking after the young ones as adults migrate to the local alehouses, - having access to around six pubs in our small village - a pint for the men or perhaps a port and lemon for the ladies. Coincidentally that day, the news of the British Mount Everest Expedition led by Colonel John Hunt, Edmund Hillary and Sherpa Tenzing Norgay had reached the summit on 29th May reached London that morning.

With mother in hospital, my brother was invited to the street party in the care of nearby opposite neighbours Auntie Joan and Uncle Pop and will stay with them tonight, until his mother returns home. Their son, Ian, a friend, attends the same Orchard County Primary School, in the neighbouring village of Petersham, one problem though, my brother Keith lives in Murray Road, the party is being held in Stuart Road, although they are adjacent neighbours they are not the same streets, some people were not happy, that he is attending! It may be, just because there is not enough places, food to go around or because of his situation at home.

Stuart Road was in fact added to Murray Road and the urgent need of more housing in the Richmond and adjacent areas, a new building programme in Ham and Petersham was expanded and more houses were built, where a cul-de-sac was planned and continued the road to the edge of Ham Pits, its fencing and the drop to the water. There was never a 1 and 3 Murray Road, replaced by a 1 and 2 Stuart Road, even the building style and road surfaces were different, which later didn't help with roller-skating, chalking hopscotch and marbles, we had a concrete finish they had the much smoother black tarmac! It always created a bit of amusement for us youngsters, watching delivery men and any new postman confused by the door numbering, especially when someone had removed or covered the street signs!

My brother is physically sick that night after the celebrations, the adults are putting it down to the excitement of the forthcoming birth - but the truth was, he just ate too much cake, biscuits, orange squash and jelly at the street party!

For the next three nights young Keith is offered a bed at understanding kind neighbours, being fed and looked after by caring people, as there is no-one else at his own home.

My mother, now overdue and it's a shame I wasn't born on Coronation Day, she may have qualified and won a Silver Cross pram, offered by Wrights of Richmond - for local babies born on June 2nd - the department store was in nearby George Street Richmond.

I eventually arrive on the morning of the 6th of June, by coincidence, Auntie Mary has dropped into the maternity unit at Kingston Hospital, a former workhouse infirmary and now managed by the NHS, she has found out that my mother - Sylvia - has just given birth to a baby boy! Communicating then wasn't easy, telephones were rare in households, above all by affordability and lack of infrastructure. Sending young children with a message to neighbours and relatives was common, along with other errands.

Getting around and especially from Kingston Hill, would mean a walk or a change of buses and getting on the No.65 route at Kingston Bus Garage, for a ride along Richmond Road, passing Ham Common, Petersham Road and alighting at Sandy Lane, half way down avoiding the mud, after the cattle have just been herded to and from their cowshed around Back Lane - so called, because cattle are taken around the 'back', rather than onto the main village road of Ham Street, - she passes Wiggins Cottages, the clinic and boys club, through the alley, onto Stretton Road, left onto Murray then Stuart Road. The same walk that we all did for many years in all weathers, it took at least 30 minutes from alighting the bus at Sandy Lane to get home, it wasn't until the 1970's the 71 bus would stop in the centre of the village.

It's a Saturday, my mother friends, Joan, Rene, my brother and Mary driven by husband Pip in his big black, sloped backed late 1940s Standard Vanguard, visit the hospital to see the new baby – but there's a small problem though, my mother promised Keith, he would be the first to see me, the new born, letting him into the maternity ward first, to see his new little baby brother!

I was named for some reason, Graham!!!! Why!? Believe me, it's the most uncoolest names you could bestow on any child, you can't shorten it - Gra', Grage, - nothing works! Growing up, there was so many easier names like, Pete, Johnny, Paul, Mike, Mick, Tony, Andy, Bob, Terry, at a stretch even the name Nigel was slightly better – but only just - than GRAHAM! On my father and mother's side, the males carried on the family names, ours were Jesse, George, Frederick and Hal respectively, my brother was named Keith Hal and Jesse or Jessie was rejected for a boy in the late 1940s, for any connotations that may have had then and in later life. Calling someone a Jessie, was then a derogatory term along with queer or pansie for a homosexual at the time. My birth and six years later, Jesse was rejected again, for the same reason as the 1940s. My mother, seemed to believe that I may have been named after Graham Greene, who by the early 1950's, was regarded as one of the finest writers of that generation, The Third Man, Our Man in Havana, Brighton Rock and many others, published from 1921 to 1988, which would have been OK if our surname was Greene! I challenged my mother when I was about 8, after Graham that had now been replaced with many nicknames! When I entered senior school it seemed to make up some 10% of the intake in 1964, so might have been something in what she recalled, that year I did lobby again and ask to change it, when The Dave Clark Five knocked The Beatles, "I Wanna To Hold Your Hand" off the top of the charts with "Glad All Over", now Dave would have been a really cool name at that time!

During this period of discussing my name, she told me sit down and listen, in our front room we had two built in storage and an airing cupboard where you stored towels and sheets, in the lower part was the large copper tank that would get heated by either fire in our back room or front room, - called a back boiler, water would heat in the pipes behind the fire back and convection would push it to the copper tank, that would be enough for a hot bath, if everybody was careful.

My mother called our 'front room' posh names like "the lounge" or "the sitting room", used more frequently for best, like afternoon tea when relatives called using the best crockery, a children's party, friends or neighbours visiting or for a small get together. Opening the top airing cupboard under some neatly folded white linen sheets, she lifts out a shoe box, with some photos, a few personal childhood bits and bobs and a semi naked china doll dressed in a badly knitted cardigan and torn dress, the only items left from her childhood days in Manchester. Holding it in her arms, she says "let me introduce you to Pamela-Diane", I say "Pamela-Diane!?" she then explains that the doll, holds special memories as her father had given it to her and if I had been born a little girl, I would have taken that name! On hearing the story my big brother would now use it, if ever I cried from one of his 'dead legs', 'a kneeing', 'Chinese burn' or 'dead arm' jab, the name would be used as a verbal weapon and he would say "Aww.... what's up Pamela Diane?" and pinch my cheeks, annoyingly.

One saving grace though, two of our famous racing drivers Graham Hill and Jim Clark, made my name more palatable later and would always confuse the teachers, when calling me out to stop talking.

However my birthday, was always by older people remembered for the anniversary of D-Day in 1944 just 9 years earlier, when in the first 24 hours nearly 15000 allied troops were killed, wounded or went missing, not Coronation week 1953 understandably, as they remembered ascension year of 1952 more and the death of King George VI. Coincidentally, my mother's birthday fell on The Battle of Britain day of September 15th. Born a healthy 6lb 7ozs, my mother benefited from ten days 'free' confinement by the NHS, resting and taking to bed after the birth, it was needed, especially after her genealogical complications, which would unfortunately affect her health soon after and throughout the 1950's, after a surgical error.

Arriving home, it must have been very tough, although my mother had the support of neighbours and a willing little six year old boy, she would struggle to get post birth healthy. With the absence of any money coming in, a contingency had been made by saving a little money when possible, before going on any maternity leave, however recovery wasn't easy and initially she was unable to return to work for many weeks. Running low on money, applied for any benefits that may available, considering our situation. An assessment visit was made, initially it was suggested that her sons could or should go into care for a time and allow her to recover, she told the woman 'to leave and get out of my house!'. Another appointment was made and the visitor this time had been in a similar situation, being more empathic and was able to make a case and still keep us still together. It was just enough money, along with the small savings to pay for food, bills and of course the council house rent, which was paid weekly and was over half of the main outgoings. The rent was collected at our local Council Rent Office on the corner of Back Lane and Lock Road, shared with a small council yard and store. This office had a counter, where you would physically pay by cash to a rent collector who would initial the payment in your rent book and pass it back. If any payments were late, rent collectors were sent very promptly to the house to chase, always a few people pretending they weren't in to gain more time to get the cash together and sort their finances before being confronted again. However, rent arrears seemed to be far and few apart, tenants at the time really appreciated their council house accommodation, families would rather go hungry than risk losing their home. However, if you did miss payments the Council really did come down hard on people, eviction was always a threat, seeing houses empty for a short while and families just disappearing from the village. These houses were well built and in good condition, tenants treated them as if they were their own. You would often see the mothers of the household, cleaning outside windows, ledges and polishing door knockers and painting steps and sills with a tin of red Cardinal paint, digging over the front garden and planting rose bushes. There were even Council Housing Inspectors, who came around every so often to check how the tenants were looking after the property. Every seven years, they would authorise paint from a selection of colours or you could choose from a book of wallpaper and all this as part of the tenancy agreement. I think in the late 1960's, you were still given a choice of decorating yourself or gave you a onetime payment to help, I also believe local paints shops, like Warners on Ham Parade were involved.

My knowledge of my mother's generation and anybody born before and just after the two world wars, were driven to work hard, earn money to buy food, pay bills, have the occasional trip to the pub and budget well to make it last the week, generally down to the last penny. Hopefully save a few pennies or shillings for a treat now and again. This didn't take into account, any money for saving for a new items like a vacuum cleaner, a washing tub or any household appliance and before the NHS, to pay for any medical treatment that a member of the family may need.

My own experience of entering this now 'modern' world, we learned and respected that they had survived those dark days of war and now peace time was to be enjoyed. They now strive to raise a family, advise their children to the best of their ability, even when under any adversity or hardship. Many parents were too busy, to do any hand holding, making you often think for yourself, which means a certain amount of initiative would develop, all good grounding, useful when you enter the world of work or eventually leave home, hopefully learning from any mistakes you may have made on your journey.

Unbeknown to me at this time, my mother with the help of my big brother, dug very deep to keep all three of us together.

As a former cook in the army, when demobbed it made sense, after all that training and experience that she would to go into catering, so in the late 1940's she worked in food pre-preparation, working alongside the chef in a restaurant, called the Cafe Continental at No. 8 Hill Rise, Richmond and later another job as a cook at Richmond Club, located in Northumberland House, on Petersham Road, a grand gentlemen's club with fantastic views to Richmond Bridge and down towards the Ice Rink across the river and to the left and Petersham. This restaurant was where she met Mary Smith, becoming her best friend, a relationship that lasted for nearly 60 years, a waitress, living in substandard accommodation with twins, Brian and Jane, on Red Lion Street, Richmond at the time. Qualifying for a council house, they moved next door to us at 2 Stuart Road Ham in 1951.

It's now late autumn 1953, A 6 year old Keith, is in his second year at the new Orchard Primary in Petersham. There was always something special about going to a village school, with local children and even teachers, it's a time when walking to school was the standard, unless for religious reasons you travelled further. Your class had pupils that will know, move through primary and secondary until your work years commence, unless they passed their Eleven Plus of course or at that time emigrated to perhaps Canada, New Zealand or popular Australia on a '£10 Ticket', as Pommies, a name for a new pale skinned immigrant and supposedly a meaning a 'Prisoner Of Mother England' from the transportation of convict days.

For some reason and sometimes it was random, but Riverside Drive, our roads, Murray and Stuart were in the catchment area for many at the Orchard School in Petersham. Although Ham village had its local school, St Andrews on the edge of the wonderful Ham Common overlooking the pond and was for decades the only school, until the 1950s. This was before the council houses were built, it only needed one school from the age of 5 to 14 years, given now the post war growth, there is a large new school building programme on predictions of growth – the Baby Boomers born in the late 1940s, Primary (8-11 years old) Orchard was such one, Meadlands would be another along with Infants Schools (5-7 years old) of Petersham Russell and Oakfield. However it was twice the distance to walk for some pupils, sometimes you weren't sent to one nearest you.

With our mother working, Keith would have to get himself to and from school, from about six years of age, luckily the children walked in groups. With many from our street and it could take the best part of an hour, with 'mucking' about. Luckily there were enough as we had a street full of young families, siblings were roughly two to four years apart, the average seemed to be about three children, there were some big families in Ham and Petersham, but that meant there was always someone to walk to school with. My brother's school piers were Brian Smith, Bill Smith, Peter Leonard, Dennis Botwright, Barry Cook, Barry Ashfield, Ian Whitaker, Pete Leonard, Mike Timms, Mike Sossick, living yards from each other's front gate. Around 8am, the front doors would start to open, firstly the 'man of the house' mounting his bicycle to go to his workplace, nearby factories, workshops and secondly the children in their school uniforms waiting or knocking for their schoolmates. Cars were few and getting a lift to school was rare and unheard of, except if their parent was a teacher.

Mother and myself now a few months old, I was told, would leave home around 7.30am, after preparing a breakfast for Keith and then plating some tea for him after school. He would leave at about 8am, to start walking to school, before the bell went at 8.45am for assembly.

Mother would wrap me up, ready for the journey and the state nursery in Parkshot, Richmond, a building near the Victorian swimming baths at the time. In the winter she would prop me up in a second hand pushchair, for that walk along Sandy Lane, through a muddy section and at some stages with no pathway or tarmac to the bus stop on the Petersham Road, alight at Richmond Station and drop me off at the nursery, here I would stay till about 4pm and the journey back and finishing her two jobs some days.

The following summer, and with the ability to sit up, my mother would strap me in a child seat over the back mudguard of an old black bicycle, she would pedal that same route, cycling on the main Petersham Road with cars, buses, motorbikes and lorries overtaking her, - up until the weather changed in late October, all to save spending on bus fares and convenience - one of my earliest memories at about three is holding on tight, to the sides of the rusty childseat and freewheeling downhill, the wind swirling around my mother's backside and her coat flapping in my face, leaning slightly outwards, speeding past The Dysart Arms and Petersham Gates at the bottom of The Star and Garter Hill and around the 'dangerous bend' and Petersham Road.

Chapter 2 – How Did I Get Here?

Like many couples, fate and the war bought my mother and father together and many from different parts of the country, my parents were married at St Andrews, Ham Common in August 1946.

My mother Sylvia Percival, born in 1922 in the backstreets of Moss Side, Manchester, the youngest of three children, with two older brothers Hal and Fred. Life was tough, her father Frederick b.1890, a music hall artist - his stage name being Percy Val - appeared at theatres around the North West of England and was even part of Fred Karno's Circus at one stage. Enlisting for The First World War in October 1914 after training was immediately posted to Egypt and later France, documented that his music hall experience allowed him to entertain the troops, before they embarked for the Dardanelles and their ill-fated battles in Gallipoli. We have a newspaper cutting from Manchester Evening News telling his story about those times.

Surviving the war and on returning to civvy street, theatre work was now scarce, he enlisted again to help out on the railways to repatriate prisoners back to Germany. Suffering a head injury after an unexploded bomb that was triggered in some railway sidings, just outside of Calais in 1919, medically discharged for 'Feeble Mindedness' in 1920, according to his army record. He came home, found little work or unable to be an entertainer again, eventually suffering from mental health issues before being admitted and passing away in an asylum in 1937 at just 47 years old. In 1934, my mother, who loved singing and dancing was enrolled into the Eileen Rogers Stage School, age 11, being schooled while touring. Mary Percival b.1884 d.1964, her mother, needed to earn in the early 1930s, became a 'bookies runner', to make ends meet and was sometimes paid in alcohol, generally gin, you can imagine all the issues and consequences that would bring later and raising a young family and a husband with no money coming in.

Aged 17 in 1939, my mother worked in a shoe shop in Piccadilly, Manchester, her older brother Hal had left home, brother Fred, already in the Territorial Army Royal Engineers, was sent off overseas to North Africa before war was even declared.

Manchester was frequently bombed, throughout 1940 and 1941, wanting do her duty, but more needing to escape, enlists in the women's Auxiliary Territorial Service (ATS) and after training at Catterick, near Richmond Yorkshire, takes up the profession of a Cook Private. Early 1942 saw her posted down to The South and to Richmond Park, where she was billeted at the army camp, consisting of rows of semi-cylindrical huts, prefabricated structures developed by Major Peter Nissen of The Royal Engineers in the First World War and extensively used in WW2. These buildings although useful, were damp and cold in the winter and hot and humid in the summer.

Carrying out her catering duties, just within Kingston Gate, providing meals for soldiers, life was strangely slightly easier. So different to the back to back rundown Victorian housing, after moving nearby to Greenheys, Manchester after her father died. Away from nightly bombing raids, fire, smoke, destruction and walking in and around rubble most days, to her workplace. Now she was living, albeit an Army Life in a rural, clean environment, Richmond Park must have been so interesting and a million miles from the Mancunian slums, even though gun placements were nearby. This is where one of two placements of Anti-Aircraft ack-ack guns were positioned to protect London and I believe the Leyland tank and truck factory on the nearby Ham/Kingston borders. The Luftwaffe would fly down the Thames Estuary, follow the path of the river to London targets. Pinpointing the church roof at Teddington, bank over Kingston and The Park, dropping any unused ordnance before their return to France, which sometimes fell on Ham village – civilian families were affected in Ham. Some losing their lives, a high explosive bomb dropped on the 23rd November 1940 on Mead Road, sadly killing Louisa Spiers and her visiting two year old great nephew, Michael Jux.

Obviously working in a field kitchen or cookhouse, would lead to the odd mishap or accident. My mother, had the top of her right index finger missing, many of us will remember those meat mincers that we had in our homes in the 1950's, that we clamped onto the kitchen table to make our own lamb or beef mince. If you can imagine one, three times bigger and motorised, making cottage or shepherd's pie one busy morning while on duty. As she was pressing the meat into the receptacle her hand slipped, resulting in the top of her finger being cut off! As a small child sitting on her lap and holding her finger, it always caught my interest and I would always ask her to tell me the story again, with a mischievous wry smile, as nothing was wasted during the war and meals had to be made, she would always add that the severed tip along with the nail was never recovered from the freshly minced meat, the pie must have been served and someone may have eaten it!

Coming from Manchester, my brother and I would chuckle at the way she said her A's, in the South we put an r in bath, but her dialect made the A sound like a toddlers A for Apple when learning. The other thing she used was North Country expressions, for example when surprised would say 'Well, I'll go to the foot of ou' stairs!' and 'You daft ape'th', which always bought quizzical looks! Good old Mum and her Manc' accent, that wasn't at all Queens English in the 1950s, not that mine was either, when she corrected my slang!

⁂

My father, Keith George Jesse Clark, a third generation Ham village boy, his grandfather Jesse Slater was born illegitimately in Steventon, Oxfordshire in 1869, to a Sarah Buckle b.1850 from the nearby village of Drayton and Jesse Slatter Snr b.1846, eventually marrying her three years later, unfortunately Sarah died in 1875, I have his birth certificate, which Sarah had signed with a 'cross', obviously illiterate.

The majority of the work available in the area at the time was farm and seasonal agricultural labouring, presumably unable to look after a 6 year old, with no mother, the Buckle family took Jesse Jnr in and he forged a lifelong relationship with Sarah's sister Priscilla's son, his cousin Thomas Buckle, who was a little younger. Interestingly Thomas was born in 1871, strangely in Ham and it's where my connection with the village starts. Jesse Snr returned to Steventon and took a room with his young son Jesse now aged 11, the 1881 census indicates that he is a farm labourer. He later marrying Sarah Slade in 1885, 17 years his younger, they went on to have four more children. The village of Steventon Oxfordshire, uncannily looks and feels like Ham Common and its surrounding area.

Jesse Jnr and Thomas Buckle, not surprisingly became agricultural labourers after leaving any education that they may have had. Eventually leaving Oxfordshire, to look for work opportunities or casual farm labouring. Going their separate ways, working in various farms or other occupations, to earn a wage as most fathers and siblings did, to save themselves, their families and any young children possibly from The Workhouse.

It's now the late 1880's and with the Agricultural Revolution in its latter stages, a UK population tripling to 35 million and efficiencies with seeding, crops, livestock and mechanisation replaced many manual workers. Finding just labouring agricultural work, became increasingly difficult, so with a growing London, the migration was in the direction of the capital to find more opportunities and a wage. Thomas Buckle came via Chertsey and then Egham, securing a job as a cowman in Ham – later a market gardener - working on the Dysart estate or farms, returning to his birthplace of Ham and lodging on the borders with Petersham with his related Buckle family at Swann Cottage, on the Petersham Road.

Near to London and its growing need for fresh produce, dairy and flowers, migrant agricultural workers wrote to their families back in rural villages to say labour was required on the farms on the Dysart Estate. Thomas Buckle located his cousin Jesse and got him a job on the as a farm labourer.

When Jesse arrived in Ham, the population was around 1400, when Jessie Jnr passed away in 1944 it was just under 3500, at the time of my birth in the 1950's it was around 4000. Today the last census shows the population of nearly 11000, with some ward changes. Reading the 1911 censuses for Ham and Petersham and looking at birthplaces and where they were born indicates all parts of Southern England and surrounding counties, during this period.

Interestingly, before the building of social housing in Ham, in the 1920's there were twice as many men as women in the village, 90% of males being employed in agricultural and related work, 80% of women working 'in service' and domestic occupations - my great grandmother being a starchier - employed by and in many large houses mainly centred around The Common, along Ham Street and off Petersham Road.

Seeking work and advised by his cousin, Jesse Jnr now settles in Ham and later marries Beatrice Bliss from 20 Elm Grove, Kingston, after her period in-service at Petersham House* (now owned by the current owners of the trendy Petersham Nursery), marrying at St Lukes Church, Kingston in August 1894. **Researched by Gordon Elsden in a great read and book called 'People of the Latchmere'.* Moving into the recently constructed and one of the first major housing developments in Ham for sometime and 13 Evelyn Road, just off Ham Street, they had five children, Elizabeth (my Great Auntie Doll) b.1896, Gertrude Alberta b.1900 (my grandmother), Jesse b.1904. Siblings, Beatrice b.1899 and Edward b.1903 both die in their first year of life sadly, infant mortality was around 20% at the turn of the 20th Century, even worse in large cities and towns, average life expectancy for a man was 48 and women 52. The Census of 1901 shows a Charles Russell – a market gardener – also lodging in the same house, my great grandfather, whose occupation is now a builder's labourer. Jesse Jnr. and Grannie Beat (as I remember our family called her) moved to 1 Tollemache Almshouse in 1940, where he died in 1944 and she passed away in 1950, they are both buried in St Andrew's Church graveyard, their deaths are recorded, but unfortunately no record of their plots exist, the paperwork being destroyed by a flood in the crypt, I am told.

Interestingly Jesse, on the 3rd May 1915 at the age of 45, enlisted or was called up for WW1 with his experience, as his trade was noted as a Labourer. Drafted to the Labour Corp, as too old for active service, however the Corp were used to dig trenches and other manual duties, sometimes on the frontline, their cap badge denotes a gun crossed with a spade and in Latin "Work Conquers All". Not sure of the reason, if he did volunteer, perhaps he lost a friend or relative from the village or just wanted to simply serve his country out of patriotism, as many did in those early years of the conflict.

My father's mother Gertrude or Gertie as everybody called her, married in 1922 at St Andrews Church to a Harold G Clark, whose occupation noted as a railway bridge painter, living at 13 Church Rd Kingston and the son of a baker.

My father was born in November 1923, at Cedar Lodge, Ham Street, the building no longer exists but is shown I believe on a local Ordnance Map of 1910 and located opposite the Alley entrance to Petersham, with the old dog leg route of Ham Street shown, my grandmother would mention the famous village mulberry tree nearby, within the small walled garden or pig sty enclosure. As youngsters we all knew and climbed the wrought iron spiked rusty railings that encircled it and pick the fruit that would stain your fingers for days, in front of the entrance to the alley, we all knew as 'Cut Throat Alley'. I didn't find out till later, that the real name was 'Cut Through Alley', used as a short cut or thoroughfare for the Petersham agricultural labourers and its workers, gaining access to Ham Gardens and Lands and its market gardens and arable fields. It would allow them to walk through a purpose built high bricked walled path and land surrounding the rear of Ham House and its walled gardens, saving time rather than walking further along the river and around Ham House or Sandy Lane to Ham Street. The alley walls are carved with various implements from pocket knives, sharp instruments and coins from the nineteenth century onwards, locals have written initials, dates, love hearts, insults, names and other marks into the soft red bricks, going back over two hundred years. A walk through, reminds one of a series of hieroglyphics and the entrances to any Egyptian pyramids and tombs, I think mine are there somewhere from 'hanging about' one evening in the early 1960's and making sure nobody was looking.

My father, although Keith used George and nicknamed Nobby in the village, like many Clarks were at the time. Attending St Andrews School, leaving in 1937 aged 14 to become an apprentice baker's boy on Petersham Road. My father a keen sportsman, confirmed by a classmate of his Joe Poulter, before he sadly passed away aged 97 in 2020, told me he was a great all round sportsman and that with his skills, could have been a professional footballer, but for a bad knee injury, aged 17, Joe, actually went on to be a professional footballer with Arsenal. During the war years, while village men were away at war, it allowed the younger boys to make up first team places and develop their talents earlier. My father had also played for Ham & Petersham Cricket Club founded in 1815, Ham Rovers FC, both were played on Ham Common.

Amazingly and co-incidentally, Joe Poulter retired and later lived at 1 Tollemache Almshouse on Ham Street in the centre of the village, the same house as my great grandmother and father resided in the 1940s and 50s. My mother was also billeted and demobbed to the same address on marrying my father in 1946, my brother spent his first few months in the Almshouse as a newborn, sleeping in a drawer, before moving into their new council house in late 1947. My father, at the outbreak of World War 2 was just 15, soon to be 16 in the November after the declaration of war, the government decided to build a register of the population, on the 29th September 1939, 28 days after war was declared on Germany. Residents were told to record by household, current address, age and occupation. One can only assume the information would be used for conscription, reserved occupation, any skills, along with National Registration Identity Cards, which everyone had during wartime and had to carry them at all times – I still have my mothers. I also understand the aforementioned register would be used to compile a list, for the NHS and the National Insurance System and voting later, ready for 1948 and its commencement. The 1931 Census was unfortunately destroyed by fire in WW2 and with no Census taken in 1941 for obvious reasons, so it was a very useful piece of data from that time.

My father's occupation on that register was documented as a bakers boy and living with his grandparents, Jessie and Beatrice Slatter at No.13 Evelyn Road, along with Cyril Lever – the lodger and a Cowman at the dairy farm - later Hornby and Clarke - becoming my godfather in 1953, along with Francis (Pop) Whittaker. Cyril also drove a tractor and trailer around the village in the 1950s, moving milk churns, when the trailer was empty and as he passed my brother on the way home from Orchard, his schoolmates would jump on and take a ride, being dropped off to before he returned to the farmhouse, dairy barn and cowshed in Ham Street.

Another villager Gerald Stevens confirmed in his book 'Childhood Memories of Ham & Petersham' that my father worked at the bakers on the Petersham Road - now a residence called The Old Bakery - would pass the odd loaf, roll or bun out through the basement window to waiting local boys, not sure whether any money changed hands - but knowing my father - it probably did!

I am not sure why my father is not living with his mother or father at this time, however I know in 1947, my father's address was given as 48 Lock Road, his mother's and a 1930s council house. Another coincidence here, I purchased and lived in 4 Lock Road from 1983-88, my first house, after moving back from Richmond.

My grandmother Gert, was quite a character, from stories and knowing her when growing up. I understand she liked a drink and to have a good time, Ham was a rural village with just ale houses for entertainment or a visit to the working men's club called The Ham Institute in New Road, which was men only initially. This wasn't enough for her and even in the wartime years London was busy with nightlife and entertainment, the transit of Americans and Allied soldiers, just wanting a good time and to spend their money.

I was told she would often travel up to London during these war years for a night out, unfortunately the marriage to my grandfather eventually broke down and they divorced in the early 1950s, she then moved permanently to London and remarried in 1961. Rumours in our family, that during the war she made many contacts in the capital and worked the Black Market with alcohol, cigarettes and nylons, given, bought or traded from the visiting allied troops, which I think explains why my father was living with his grandparents during the early war years. Her husband, my grandfather is now living alone in Church Road, Kingston during the war, with whom sadly I never met, as he passed away in 1958.

Thinking about it and during the late 1950's and my early memories seemed to confirm these type of former Black Market activities. About once a month to try and bring some normality to our family, my mother would take my brother and I, via a bus ride to Richmond Station and board a train to London. Eyeing the Beechnut, Cadburys and Paynes Poppets dispensers with those pull drawers, we would travel on a steam engine that pulled racing green painted train carriages with British Railways gold signage and travel to a grimy London. When you are a five years old, that ride was fantastic, the noises of wheels over tracks, water dripping, a huffing and puffing engine, I can still smell that coal burning odour mixed with steam vapour in my head.

I didn't care if the seats were filthy, but if my mother was wearing a light coloured dress, suit or coat she would lay an unfolded handkerchief on it, to protect her clothing. Always telling us 'Don't put your heads out of the window, you will get coal grit in your eyes!'. On a Saturday, we would alight at Queenstown Road, it was the nearest station to her home on Battersea Rise, a Sunday timetable would take us to Clapham Junction and the sound of those slamming doors everywhere with its gargantuan twenty odd platforms at the time, that always seemed so busy with people rushing and running for trains, always looking for the right platform and carrying suitcases in the summer holidays. I loved the noise and watching the people in a hurry, with the Tannoy announcements, it was like a Pathe Newsreel film.

I was always intrigued watching people, arguing, smiling faces, happy families looking forward to a day out, dressed in their finery often. I was always amazed, it was like a giant train set with steam, smoke that pungent smell of burning coal, drifting down it seemed every flight of stairs, as we walked hurriedly or me being dragged to the main entrance.

My face would be filthy from touching everything and the soot in the air, looking at my grubby hands I always knew what was coming, my mother would take the same handkerchief she was sitting on in the train and tell me to lick it - if I wouldn't, she would - rubbing and wiping my face, I would wriggle and pullback embarrassed as people passed and smiling at my antics. A thing she did so often, especially, if we met after school to go out, at the bus stop - it was one those actions, that my mum did, like trying to give you a kiss when meeting you from school, it was so embarrassing!

When we got to the main entrance of the station, into a busy metropolis and knowing my grandmother liked a drink – half pints of Mackeson with a gin and a squirt from a soda siphon as a chaser - on a Sunday lunchtime, we would head to her local pub. A very large corner pub called The Beaufoy Arms on Lavender Hill, Battersea SW11, double fronted with three entrances, many doors and patrons, from Public to Saloon bars. A small Snug with older ladies in hats, sipping a glass of stout for hours, hoping someone would buy them another one, putting it down for medicinal purposes or to keep out of the cold in the winter months.

I was always taken initially to the Saloon Bar – my mother pushing the double swing inwards and being hit by that odour of beer soaked carpets, stale tobacco and even sawdust on any hard flooring to mop up spilled drinks, from the previous lively Saturday night – there, my nan would sit up at the bar on a high stool with her back to the wall at the end of the bar. A glass of the dark stuff and her chaser to hand, all I can say is she looked like she was holding court with groups of people, shouts of 'Wotcha Gert!', 'Same as usual?' or 'How about a drink, Gertie?', at just 4ft 11 it was a sight to beholden, her legs dangling from the high bar stool. I would be lifted up to give her a kiss, treated to a Smiths packet of crisps with salt in that blue wrapper, a bottle of Coke with a straw. My brother and I now being shown the door to go outside to sit on a big white marble step in front of the large door, so they could keep an eye on us or me, when he stopped coming, surrounded by an aroma of a busy London and dog ends!

So this is me, a small six year old bespectacled, curly headed little white boy from a rural village in Surrey, now sitting on the step of a very a busy London pub on a bustling thoroughfare, with red double decker buses belching out diesel fumes and other traffic, seeing legs walk passed quickly some slowly, taking everything in, I couldn't help thinking, it was such an exciting day out.

This is the late 1950's, migrants from the Caribbean Islands and the first Windrush sailings, living in SW, SE and W London postal districts and taking jobs with London Transport, British Rail, the NHS etc, they are finishing their shifts or have just been to church in their best finery. My first experiences of smiling black faces, dressed smartly in their uniforms or their Sunday best, all rubbing my head in that friendly way or pinching my pink cheeks, some saying 'You must be Gert's grandson, Boy!', in that Caribbean English lilt!?' I nod, out comes a big roar of laughter and the broadest bright white teeth smile I had ever seen, stepping over me to get into the bar, for a pint or a glass of rum, before closing time.

The public houses on a Sunday were opened from noon till 2.30pm, my Nan always got there early, as they served free bits of cheese and gherkins skewered by cocktail stick to pull the punters in early. At closing time, we would take the uphill long walk to her flat in the nearby street – Basnett Road, Battersea.

It was then, one of those typical London Streets, you would see on a post war black and white film or newsreels, sloping down with terraced and individual dwellings with lots of doors, not a blade of grass and lampposts looking like defoliated trees, pale children playing on the streets with smiling dirty faces due to the London grime and soot, or playing in a nearby bombsites scattered with rubble, a few pre-fabs had been erected, where bombed damaged ground had been cleared. I wasn't really used to this, as we had lots of greenery, open spaces, wildlife, the park and the river nearby and on our doorsteps, not cobbles, we suffered more with grass stains and dirty necks from the dust if dry and mud if wet. Our faces in the village were touched by the sun when it was shining giving us a healthy glow from being out in the open air and running about.

We would enter Gert's front door, we led immediately to flights of stairs, another green Yale locked door led into her living room and the aroma of a Sunday lunch, a large bedroom and a small galley kitchen, which overlooked buildings and rooftops as far as you could see. She was also in catering at the Grosvenor Hotel near Victoria Station, the smell of a slow roast beef and potatoes are waiting in the oven. She was always very generous to us and very kind to my mother, who she really liked.

It was missing a bathroom, quite a novelty for me, going to the toilet meant going down two flights of badly lit stairs, with a candle or torch to the backyard, a small wooden door with a six inch gap, both top and bottom, an outside toilet shared by three other families. On opening the door, it had a big brown wooden toilet seat sitting on a large porcelain toilet bowl, a wrought iron high cistern, a chain and a big wooden hand pull attached. A box packet of Izal toilet paper on the floor or some cut up newspaper held together with string, hanging on a spike, ready for use. In a warm summer there was quite a whiff, in the winter it was freezing or sometimes the bowl and cistern were frozen, a paraffin heater would be in there, especially in the winter months of 1962/63. It wasn't a surprise that my Nan kept a potty under the bed, for obvious reasons and if I stayed overnight, it was always fun using it!

There was always a few boxes scattered around her flat, filled with various products, packets of tea, sugar or other fast moving non-perishable goods. She often had boxes of Black Magic on her kitchen table, she would sometimes offer me one, always bloomed covered, because they were so old or cold – still had some though!

One of the big advantages for me and that my grandma lived near the magical Battersea Park Fun Fair, opened in 1951, for me a wonderland, it was a 200 acre site of wooden swings, roundabouts and other attractions, but the ride of rides was The Big Dipper, all this was opened to as part of The Festival Of Britain, as a treat my Nan would often take me there in the summer months. Living in Ham we only saw a fair generally around Bank Holidays at Old Deer Park Richmond or Hampton Court and this was permanent.

Battersea Fun Fair, could have turned into a main London attraction and venue, however in 1970 the Big Dipper caught fire, repaired and restored back into service. But unfortunately on the weekend Bank Holiday weekend of May 1972, one of its trains was hoisted up the first slope and the chain snapped hurtling its occupants backwards and smashing into the station, onto two other carriages. Sadly, five children were killed and thirteen others seriously injured. The ride was immediately closed and dismantled, with now and the loss of its main attraction, the attendance demised and the Fun Fair closed forever in 1974. Little remains of that funfair in Battersea Park, laid out and opened in 1858, still today its one of the best examples of a Victorian park. Incidentally on the 9 January 1864, it hosted the first football game played under the newly formed Football Association and its rules, the ground was home to Wanderers FC for training and the winners of the first FA Cup in 1872 at the Kennington Oval versus the Royal Engineers.

The other treat that my Nan used to take me to, was the big domed building on the corner of St John's Hill, the Arding and Hobbs department store, it seemed so much larger than my nearest stores of Goslings, Wrights of Richmond or Bentalls in Kingston. It had a lovely tea room, restaurant, ice cream parlour and a massive toy department.

After we had said our goodbye's to Gertie, - as she always wanted me to call her, she didn't like Nan, Nanny of Grandma - she would thrust perhaps half a crown or a florin into our hands. A ten bob note on a birthday, no card though, I don't remember her showing me any affection, a hug or a peck on the cheek. Because of the situation with her son - my Dad - and his failure to provide any dependable financial support at home. She would, from time to time give Mum an envelope with a few pound notes or some Provident Cheques, that could be exchanged or used in part payment on school uniforms or shoes etc.

Perhaps now thinking and given my Nan's interesting dubious past, I am not sure how she acquired those Provident Cheques or how she even got hold of them. Shops would display a sign in the window saying they would be accepted, you saved as you paid the collector and were then issued with cheques to spend at nominated shops.

It was always a dilemma for my mother to accept anything that was acquired illegally and as I was growing up, she had always drummed into us – 'always think of the consequences, of doing something wrong, or any feeling if it doesn't seem right!'. A phrase that served me very well, when a teenager and later when temptation knocked on my door of any kind of wrong doing!

As well as visiting a grandmother in London, about once or twice a year, we would make the long journey to Manchester to see my other grandmother. Again her house was like a scene from Coronation Street with cobble stones, we may stay there for one or two nights in a very cold and rundown house, that had a big chest in which had some props, that my grandfather used on stage. The best thing though was the fish and chip shop on a corner that sold not only those but other delicacies such as tripe and Baby's Head suet puddings with mushy peas, I must say this wasn't as much fun as going to London, but what was great was the four hour train ride to Manchester and having tea and toast in the restaurant car or a visit to Belle Vue which was nearby in Gorton, just like Battersea Park that opened in 1858, it had amusements, a zoo, a circus, an exhibition hall and speedway opening earlier in 1836 for a genteel audience, it closed down in 1977.

Chapter 3 – The Villages of Ham and Petersham

To say these villages and where I lived is just a nice place, is definitely an understatement, its unique, Ham or 'Hamme' and the name probably derives from Old English meaning 'a place in the bend of a river' was also recorded as Ham and Hatch. Nestled in a large bend in the river just south of Richmond, west of The Park and north of Kingston and a part of, in earlier times. Ham was much larger in land mass, than it is now and prior to 1640, the Common Land stretched to what is now the other side of Richmond Park to Kingston, back in the Middle Ages, the only buildings in the village, were probably centred near Ham Street and around The Common.

Originally a small rural settlement, the 17th and 18th Century saw construction of large houses around Ham Common, but the most famous is Ham House, built in 1610 for Thomas Vavasour, near the river - owned now by the National Trust since 1948 - it soon past into the ownership in the Earls of Dysart for nearly 300 years, being enlarged and remodelled in 1672. The Earl's daughter married twice, first to Sir Lionel Tollemache and then the Duke of Lauderdale – their names live on today in local streets and landmarks.

In 1637, following the trend for monarchs to enjoy their hunting, Charles 1st created Richmond Park, taking away agricultural land and Common land from Ham and Petersham, in exchange land was protected beyond the walls. Today Richmond Park is the largest open space in Greater London.

During the Restoration period of Charles II, Ham House was reputably a centre of political intrigue with its five members of Clifford, Ashley, Buckingham, Arlington and Lauderdale. If you take the first letter of each name it makes the acronym CABAL – today's use of this term usually carries negative connotations of political purpose, intrigue, conspiracy and secrecy. As I am writing these words, BREXIT talks were in a raised state of debate, with some similar feelings!

By the early 19th Century, the population of Ham is estimated at about 500 people, mostly tenant farmers and agricultural workers on farms covering nearly all the land in the village and owned by the Earl of Dysart. The village started to grow and by the mid 19th Century the population had grown to over 1,200 and 200 houses, with new houses being built along the Petersham Road and Ham Street.

Ham, didn't change much throughout the rest of the 19th Century, so there are less Victorian houses, like other growing Surrey villages, which got the opportunity and benefit of the expanding rail network. Some development occurred in the roads of Evelyn, Lock and New Roads at the very end of that century.

Lord Dysart offered to protect the view from Richmond Hill, reportedly one of the most painted scenes in the world, by donating large swathes of his land, alongside the river from the Petersham Meadows to Teddington Lock in perpetuity for open space and free from roads, structures and development.

A clever move on behalf of the Earl, in return he was allowed to end grazing rights on the common fields and diversify into extracting gravel alongside the river, which we knew as children in the 1950's and 60's, affectionately as 'The Pits'. The gravel extracted is supposed to be some of the finest in the UK and was used extensively in London and I believe the buildings and runways of the newly opened London Airport, from the mid-1940's onwards. Interestingly, the Heathrow airfield was owned originally by Fairey Aviation, then requisitioned under the Defence Of The Realm Act 1914, with a potential need for an international airport for and near London, replacing the first international flights from Croydon.

Ham was cut off from public transport until the 1970's, bypassed by the main road, our famous lifeline and familiar No 65 buses that ran along the A307 between Richmond and Kingston, before that horse drawn and motor bus services. No railway was ever planned, - didn't make financial sense and the topology made it difficult - nearest bridges across The Thames are Richmond and Kingston or between, a footbridge adjacent to Teddington Lock. Crossing the river to Twickenham was made convenient by two small ferries, one in front of Ham House to Marble Hill Park and one to the right of Eel Pie Island across to The Swan Pub. Always difficult to take in, that this tranquil and leafy village setting and the views up the river is just a dozen miles from The Houses of Parliament!

Ham and Petersham makes up part of The Arcadian Thames view between Hampton and Kew, this stretch of river provided the growing London from the riverside villages with goods. With the construction of Richmond and Hampton Court Palaces, aristocrats and associated royals wanted to move nearby, building houses, laid landscapes and hunting parks, with grand avenues of trees, behind the water meadows. A spectacular rural paradise was created by the mid eighteenth, to and from London along the Thames. A boat ride or walk along the banks of the river now, will give you extraordinary scenery and views towards Richmond Hill; ongoing work is still going on, to expose and show more of that landscape.

Chapter 4 – The Early Years, The 1950s

My brother Keith, helped and supported my mother from a very young age constantly in my early years, he loved having me around as that smaller brother. While at junior school, he took even more responsibility in my upbringing and would often take the bus from outside Orchard School to Richmond and pick me up at the Parkshot Nursery, - all to save our mother coming home and going out again, if her evening shift started at 5pm - he would jump on the bus at the station with me, jump off at Sandy Lane, walking or pushed me home, in near total darkness, there was no street lighting on winter evenings along the lane, which can be muddy and a little scary, especially in a full moon, fog or mist, its sounds of owls and other nocturnal creatures.

While I am writing about my earliest memories, research indicates that a young child between the ages of two and three years old, will start to form memory and may have the likelihood or ability to recall events later in life. But some earlier perceived memories can be imagined or recalled from photographs in albums or around the house or family members telling stories about your upbringing.

Trauma, in early years will have two effects, one the ability to block the incident or secondly, to remember an incident in detail and the lead up and its impact at the time. My earliest vivid memory is from January 1958, it's one of the coldest winters since 1947 with temperatures well below freezing, even during the day. Before he left home for school, a 10 year old Keith's chore would be to rake the fireplace out, remove the ashes, wrap in newspaper and deposit it in dustbin, laying the grate ready to be lit, with paper, kindling and a shovel full of coke on the top from the scuttle. Arriving home, he would give me tea, perhaps beans on toast or something that Mother would have prepared the night before or that morning. Washed or wiped my face with a flannel, cleaned my teeth and dressed me in my pyjamas, ready for bed.

At such a young age, it seems incredulous that such a small lad, would be able to manage such responsible and important tasks, let alone not complain. But, he just did and got on with it, helping our mother and for the love for his little brother, seems harsh, but what were the alternatives? If Mum couldn't have coped or was reported, the family would have been broken up and perhaps we boys at our age would be taken into care. We were already on the local authorities books because of our current circumstances.

My mother was raised in the back street slums of Moss Side, Manchester and very close to her older brother Fred, they looked after each, as their mother liked a drink, being left alone for hours and looking out for each other was a necessity. I am sure tenacity was Mum's middle name, somehow this compassion and caring must have transferred to my older brother as we grew up, assessing a situation, thinking about a solution and working with it.

The great thing about where we lived, our neighbours were like extended families, I believe there was still lots of wartime spirit still in reserve, they were a backup and our first line emergency cover, it there was a problem, we would just go to their back door, knock and let ourselves in and ask for assistance or advice.

Ready for bed, I am now fed, washed, wearing a grey woollen housecoat with maroon piping, extra socks and slippers, if you weren't directly in front of the fireplace. The rest of the house would be absolutely freezing, a lino flooring with a small half moon mat in front of the fireplace. Mum wouldn't be home until between 8.30 and 9pm. When the temperatures dropped in winter, we would move to the back room, as it was smaller – the fire warmed that up nicely.

My brother decides it's time for me to go to bed, from an early age we would always have a rough and tumble around the house, like a couple of puppies or bear cubs, we just played about. Upstairs was very cold, just lino and those rag rugs next to our beds. The lamp post outside shines through the inside glass of those Crittal frames, highlighting the fern like frozen shapes, breath appears from our mouths, the cotton bed sheets are like sheets of ice.

Our bedrooms are literally freezing, when the temperatures dropped dramatically our mum would let us sleep in her bed for warmth. My brother takes me to Mum's bedroom, it's a double bed, just the place to rough and tumble on the top of the bed. We are so cold, I assume Keith thoughts of me climbing into those freezing white cotton sheets will be horrendous, he suggests I put on my underpants and vest, under my pyjamas and two pairs of socks making it more bearable. We even lay our coats on the bed to trap any warmth in.

He has another idea, he wants to make me comfortable and sees a blue rubber hot water bottle and goes back downstairs to the kitchen. Filling the kettle from the tap, lights the gas ring and waits for it to boil, he manages to fill the bottle and replaces the screw stopper, he has seen my mother do this countless times. Turning the downstairs lights out and cuddles the hot bottle against his chest and climbs the stairs to the landing, I am sitting on the bed waiting.

He described what happened later in life – after laying the hot water bottle on the bed, he leaves the room. Like any small boy, I start to use my mother's bed as a trampoline, as he re-enters the room and watches me bounce up and coming down, as if in slow motion, landing on top of the hot rubber water bottle, on impact it explodes and bursts, spurting boiling hot water all over me at waist level, splashing over my thigh and around my back and my buttocks. To this day, I am so fortunate it did not scald me over my groin and genital area, the result of this I can remember vividly and the images that night, but strangely not the pain, perhaps that is blocked out, or was I just in shock?

I can only believe that my body temperature is so low with the cold, the burning must have been painful, like a cold lobster being plunged into a boiling pan of water, the scream I let out – he tells me - was piercing and heard by the our neighbours next door and across the road, my brother also lets out a scream and starts to sob.

Keith, also goes into shock, he is only young, his little brother, who was in his care and on who he dotes on, is seriously scolded and lying on the bed screaming.

Panicking, he scrambles downstairs and runs into the freezing night to our neighbours, Auntie Mary's who is in the kitchen, unable to talk, he takes her hand and leads her back to our house. I am also crying, the pain must have been excruciating soaking my towelling set of pyjamas, my underwear and thick socks, they are now sticking to my blistering skin, for a very small boy I have a large scold to my lower body.

Research on burns moved on in the 1960s and 70s, hospitals and treatments had advanced, the understanding of what happens when you are scalded or burned, treatment today is calculated scientifically, from surface area, to depth of burn, sterile airing of the burn area helps with healing, replacing fluids that blistering took away. But this is the 1950's, although a lot was learned about burns in world wars, the blitz in major towns and cities around the country, especially in the 1940's, death was common place with over 30% of body surface damage. Many casualties were just given morphine to ease pain and other effects on the body, mortality was high, in short they were left to see if their body could cope with the trauma or sadly left to die, as the burns were covered then, bacteria could thrive and sepsis may take hold leading to inevitable consequences.

That night, Auntie Mary, who had some wartime nursing skills, must have found someone with a phone, people in the late 1950's didn't use or need a phone at that time. We had a perfectly good kiosk down the road, phones in homes were rare, especially on a council estate, not even sure if the infrastructure was there in the ground.

I can remember the shadowy figure of an ambulance man coming towards me, crews in those days were just really 'casualty transport to the hospital', they may be able to do first aid at its bare minimum, but they didn't carry medicines like painkillers or fluids at all, any treatment was left until they got back to the hospital. Most ambulance crew members were perhaps ex-services, medics that used to put rough dressings on wounds or broken limbs, giving comfort and reassurance.

Not sure how long I would have been lying there, but still the pain must have been unbearable, the ambulance man initially tries to take my pyjamas bottoms off, but along with my underwear and cooling down period, they are stuck to my blistering skin, I am screaming and crying, my brother is uncontrollable. They decide to get me to hospital, wrapping me in blankets and carried downstairs in the uniformed man's arms and his silhouette, into the ambulance and taken to Richmond Royal Hospital just off Kew Road, I can still see that the cream interior and hearing the bell as we pull away.

In the 1950's burns units were rare, treatment of the wounds was in today's terms was crude. The pyjamas and underwear were removed using petroleum jelly and sterile water to soften the material and it was pulled away from the burns, peeling damaged layers of skin with it. I remained in hospital for over three months, with 20% of burns to my lower body, the healing eventually started, after they had initially dressed the wounds but air wasn't getting to the damage, it got to a point where they eventually tried a few skin grafts and one of those bed cages to lift sheets and covers off the burns and tried exposing them to the air. Wards, I can assume, were not as sterile as today, so infection could have set in.

I remember two events in that hospital, it was the days of young women from Caribbean Islands being interviewed, recruited and invited to train or take a position in the 'Mother Country' to fill vacant jobs in our growing public service or the NHS. I was lucky enough to be attended by a rather large jolly West Indian nurse, with a smile and laugh as big as the double doors on the entrance to that ward, being cuddled every day by that lovely nurse and brightening my day. Being taken to the day room, with a radio and Listen With Mother stories, it's one of my most vivid memories from that period in her care and my mother it seemed visiting me every day, before or after work, Keith wasn't allowed. Both my mother and brother must have felt so guilty about what happened that cold winter.

I was in the hospital for Easter that year and people who visited bought chocolate eggs to cheer me up. Apparently one afternoon, I fell asleep with an egg on my chest which melted over me and the bed clothes, bringing great mirth to a ward full of patients and the nursing staff.

Trauma does two things to a person's mind, drives you crazy by residing with you, giving you perhaps other types of issues or you can compartmentalise and block out - I have always tended to do the latter. This way of managing problems or stress, came in very handy for the next coming years of my life growing up. To this day, my brother cannot really talk about the night of that incident.

Mum, now changes her job and is offered a role as housekeeper and cook at No.3 Maids of Honour Row, one of a magnificent row of houses on Richmond Green. The house is owned by the eminent Professor John Butterfield and his American wife Isobel, who he coincidentally met in Richmond, Virginia. From 1958, he worked and taught at Guys Hospital London, where he was appointed Head of Experimental Medicine, throughout the 1960's, pioneering clinical research in diabetes, resulting in an automated process for continuous measurement of blood glucose, which is still in use today. His major breakthrough in research was watching the effect of diabetes in his own dog and its drinking habits. He went on to be Vice Chancellor of Nottingham University, then Regus Professor of Physics, Cambridge University. Knighted in 1978, he took on the Mastership of Downing College, Cambridge.

A busy household, with three young children and with their continuous entertaining, was better paid and more enjoyable. At last she would be at home at night – unless they had a dinner or supper party, he would always make sure my mother was safely home, either giving her a lift in his Bentley, or his wife's Fiat 600 – always interesting and curtains twitched in our council house street, when the Bentley purred along and pulled up outside or they organised a taxi, called from Richmond Station Taxi Rank.

If they had dinner parties, she would always bring food home, we tried many different dishes. That magnificent house has special memories to me, in the school holidays my mother would take me to work, the Professor was at home but Mrs Butterfield would return to The States with her children for the summer. Maids of Honour is a row of five grand houses, having four floors, all covered in wood and a basement, that I would tap dance on, a nursery on the top floor with a giant rocking horse that I would climb on nd put into motion, along with playing in the sunken walled garden. These houses are situated, just back from the river and south side of Richmond Green and were built on the ruins of Richmond Palace, built in 1724, originally to house the maids of honour to the Princess of Wales, Caroline of Ansbach. The Royals at this time were at Richmond Lodge in Old Deer Park.

Keith now eleven, enters Grey Court Secondary Modern School in the village, brand new and built in 1956, two years before. Mum manages to get me a place at the attached Grey Court School Nursery in the same grounds, for my last year at nursery, run by the tough and strict Mrs Peagram, located in Newman House, a Grade II listed, brown and grey brick three storey building, with a central porch built in the late 18th Century. The childhood home of Cardinal Newman, it was just a 15 minute walk from our house on the council estate. The good thing about this was that my brother, could now walk me to and from the nursery and just a short distance to his new senior school.

The nursery had noisy wooden floors and coloured pegs with named animal stickers, when arriving in the morning to hang our coats and belongings on. The big shady garden had a small round pond with raised walls and one day I was pushed in by one of the other boys, without pointing fingers - I think it was Aubrey Anderson or Latch as we called him later! - it was a thing that happened to a few of us. With soaking clothes, you would be taken in, the worst thing about this was, after peeling off your wet garb, we would be told to dry ourselves and shown a box of lost property in which to find some clothes, while yours would be drying on a radiator or hanging outside to dry in the sun.

The nursery had compulsory afternoon naps, we would be led upstairs to the top floor and a room that had some, I am sure some ex-army camp beds. All neatly lined up, some 15 to 20 toddlers lying down and told to go asleep for an hour, in preparation for the final session of the day. One of the nursery ladies would walk around, like a prison officer on patrol, between the beds, making sure we were settled and we had our eyes closed then eventually left the room. When she had gone, opening one eye slowly, to see who else is not tired, being careful to listen for noises on the wooden stairs outside the closed door. After a minute, a natural 'all clear' would be felt by the naughtiest toddlers, giggling, insulting each other and even sounds of the odd fart! This mayhem would go on most afternoons until we heard the footsteps of Mrs Peagram coming up the stairs and into the corridor outside, jumping back on our beds pretending to sleep!

You can imagine, by this time I was wearing NHS round brown spectacles, because of a stigmatism, with the obligatory flesh coloured sticking plaster blanking over one lens, interestingly on your strong eye, hoping to strengthen the weak eye, a gap in my front teeth. Mad wavy hair, small in stature and thin as a rake – I might as well have put a target on my back, I must have been like that undernourished antelope, trailing behind a herd on the

Serengeti, waiting to be pounced on or picked off, by a hyena or other form of predator.

Our village was renowned for its nicknames, any imperfection or personal flaw or taking your older sibling's made up name, would drive someone to give you a 'non de plume', little lads were now coming to that age, at this stage mine was 'Prof' or 'Goggles'. One example was the Catlin family – being called 'Dogger', another lad was 'Kipper' with his Spratley surname! In senior school, even the teachers used these nicknames, especially useful during any sporting activity on the playing fields.

In fact to this day, some people still use them and you have to ask, 'By the way, what is you Christian or proper name?'.

Chapter 5 – The Primary School Years, early 1960s

Most of us took it for granted that we would go to a local primary school, with village friends, which catered for the rapidly expanding families in both villages. At this time we now have local schools to accommodate the baby boom children of the post war years, of the 40s and early 50s, along with its growing housing, the plan worked.

St Andrews School opposite the pond, this school opened in 1890 replacing the existing a smaller Ham Village School, it accommodated 100 boys and 101 girls. Funding to build the school was raised by local charities, subscriptions and the National Society, a Church of England body for the promotion of church schools and Christian education. St Andrews Church, built in the 1830's is just opposite on what we called as youngsters, the second or wooded common. Being the main village school, which my father attended from 1929 to 1937, before the 1950's nearly all the children in Ham, attended this school, Catholic schools we located in Richmond or Kingston, which meant a long journey for some and not so much playtime after school.

St Andrews School - today St Thomas Aquinas, a Roman Catholic church - closed around 1966, many children moving to the new St Richards School on the newly built Wates Estate. Then as now and with the availability of green space in their new location, outdoor activities were part of the curriculum, especially football, not surprisingly the school team were called The Hammers and still are today, as I understand.

Next door to Orchard School was Petersham Russell Infants School opened in 1954, which replaced the original Russell School, paid for and opened by Sir John Russell b.1792 and built for the poor in 1851, originally just within the Petersham Gates of Richmond Park - Sir or Lord John was the prime minister of Great Britain twice, 1846-52, 1865-1866, a Whig until 1859 and Liberal, who resided in the nearby Pembroke Lodge, where he died in 1878 - today a magnificent Georgian Mansion set in 13 acres of landscaped gardens and the highest point in Richmond Park, with spectacular views to the west and the Thames Valley and to London City eastwards, you can sit on the terrace and look towards The Surrey Hills and enjoy lunch or a cream tea in its elegant rooms.

In 1980, both schools were amalgamated and used the original title of The Russell School going full circle and again, having educated the children of both Petersham and Ham and surrounding areas for over 170 years. In 2018, work began to construct a new school on the same site.

In September 1958, I enter Oakfield Primary School in Ham Street. Age 5, I seem to be able to recall most memories, the start of full time school, especially when I revisit the street where I grew up. A council estate held something special for making friends, many young families having multiple children, you played in back gardens and streets. Even at a young age, I was left alone in the house, Keith being older would be now out with his friends from senior school, especially in the school holidays. If it was a dry day, I would collect my marbles, the standard and the king size ones and the odd ball bearing that would have mysteriously made an escape and assisted by someone's older brother who worked at the local Hawkers Aircraft Factory on the Kingston side of Ham, that started life making Sopwith aeroplanes and in WW2 made Leyland Trucks and Tanks. Interestingly there were cobble stones at the front of the factory, put there to stop the tanks tracks from destroying the road surface as they swiftly turned up to Richmond Park for testing.

Starting school means mixing with other children, especially on a council estate, as I sat on the kerbside and played marbles with myself along the gutter, or kick a tennis or football in the street. Being up early, eventually the kids from the neighbouring houses would start to emerge with their own marbles, balls, cricket bats, Jacks Roller Skates etc. This is where I made my first real friends in the end of the our road, now slightly older, Paul Sossick, Robbie and Irene Good – known as 'the twins', Julie Smith, Auntie Mary's youngest daughter next door and sometimes Peter Bush, from down the road.

We five would be close friends for the next decade in that street, playing in each other's houses on rainy days, always outside when dry, getting in trouble, sharing birthday parties, occasional day outs, boat rides on the Thames, to the seaside or long walks, spending hours together. Especially in the long summer holidays over at Riverside Drive Rec', a green play space with swings, a roundabout and a very dangerous wild red and blue rocking horse that at least five or six children could mount on at any time, causing a few incidents! The horse would be rocked to the edge of its life, nearly taking off like as if jumping a Grand National fence, the mechanism now in full view under its body, until it bumped or was on its stops, causing panic and screaming and holding on for dear life, now wishing you could get off!

The spinning roundabout, where you would lie down on your tummy, feet towards the centre, head over the edge, someone would run around and get it up to speed and you would play pick up lolly sticks or marbles, grazing knuckles and perhaps the odd feeling of sickness or dizziness. Not forgetting swinging dangerously high, to what we called the 'bumps', where the swing seemed to hover in the air before the big drop, or the baby swings, where a bigger boy or girl would squeeze themselves into the seat and get trapped, making them now a target to be given the bumps! The Rec' was also a place to give a friend 'The Birthday Bumps', which would entail taking hold of their limbs and throwing up in the air for the number of birthday years and stopping just before the playground tarmac! This also could end in tears, the ground was hard!

Being born in the early 1950's means we are the first benefactors of the new National Health Service, treatment at point of delivery was promised, eradication of childhood diseases like typhoid, smallpox, polio and others, inoculations or sugar cubes available at school or the local clinic. I remember visiting London and also seeing two children in our village who wore leg braces after contracting polio and of course tuberculosis (TB) that was still around – of which my father suffered from mildly as a child. To back up this excellent service we had access to Doctor's Baggley and Woodhouse at our local surgery in Bench House, Ham Street, no appointment necessary you just arrived. You went through a wooden door in a perimeter wall, down steps and turned right into a small square waiting room, consisting of random dark wood dining chairs positioned around a low table, with well thumbed magazines and newspaper supplements strewn about. You would sit in complete silence with just the tick of a grandfather clock or people sniffing, stifling coughs and whispering. In winter, it could get busy, you then needed a 'sick note or sign off' for employers, but in summer it would be very quiet. Families then, I believe didn't want to disturb a professional like a doctor, unless really poorly or some other painful medical condition, in some cases treatment, or raising any health issues for many, came too late.

I do not remember if there was ever a receptionist, I am sure the Doctor would simply call "Next! or hit a buzzer or sounded a bell through the door, you knocked, went in and he asked 'what's your name, date of birth?', how 'he could help?' or 'what's the problem?'.

In one slick movement, while listening to your reply, he would spin in his brass wheeled chair to a large dark oak wooden filing cabinet with many drawers labelled A-D, E-G etc. lifting a well worn brown envelope, containing your records. Other medical help and advice, came from Back Lane and The Ham Clinic, a weather boarded black painted building next to the Boys Club, where also I attended Sunday School, sitting on an old carpet and listening to Bible Stories with other children, next to the boxing ring, where some successful local boys learnt to box.

The NHS was investing and starting to help rebuild a nation's health after the war. The clinic was an epicentre for a team of District Nurses, a Morris Minor for the senior one and others seen often cycling around the village visiting the elderly and infirm, pre and post natal help and still assisting with home births.

At this age we seemed to be always dropping in, holding my mother's hand to pick up mainly three things, a square bottle of the best orange juice you ever tasted, malt extract in a dark brown large screw top jar and cod liver oil. The daily ritual being before my mother went to work, she would call us down from our bedrooms, we would stand in the kitchen, a pudding spoon would be loaded with the extract, followed by the oil, smiling, she would say "Open up, it will make you big and strong!" and pushed the substances to the back of our throats!

As you walked through the door of that Clinic, you saw nurse's busy, pregnant mums noisily chatting and rocking pushchairs. An enormous set of scales with a large dial face, with a pointer that swung around indicating the baby's weight similar to the greengrocers, monitoring their growth and handwrite it on a folded card. Posters on every wall, with health warnings and what the new NHS Services are offering or dried milk adverts.

With my mother now working full time and my older brother walking me to school as a seven year old, of course he didn't want to play with me anymore. With his own mates, certainly didn't want me trailing in his wake or following on my trike.

We learned self sufficiency very quickly, getting ourselves up, a quick wipe of a damp flannel, brushed our teeth and dressed, Mum sometimes putting a couple of pennies under the soap, to check whether we had. Always a self service of breakfast, that consisted of perhaps Kelloggs Corn Flakes and cold milk in the spring and summer – I say cold milk loosely, no fridge in the late 1950's yet, a built in larder with a cool concrete shelf, a window with a grill to stop flies, an air brick that kept things slightly cooler, warm summers would see us filling a bucket up with cool water and placing the milk bottles in it to slow the process of the milk souring.

It wasn't until the 1960s, Mum had saved for an interesting wood effect finished Tricity fridge for our back room, because we had no space in the kitchen. I can still smell 'off' milk and rancid butter in my head in any hot weather, from those days before fridges.

Winter meant porridge, made with water and a pinch of salt, prepared on the stove and if lucky, sprinkled with demerara sugar and cream from the top of the milk, a special taste - before pasteurisation and homogenisation - made up the first two inches at the top of a bottle, where the fats had risen, it was like nectar to any young child if cold and fresh – unless your brother got there first! Cereal packets then, sometimes contained a free gift or toy – like a plastic submarine, which you added bicarbonate of soda to make it rise to the surface of your sink or cold bath - many a scuffle with my brother would break out in the kitchen, when a new box was opened or those Variety packets. Every time I would ask 'why do you also get them?' he would reply ' 'cos I'm older!' and twist my ear or dead arm me, while my mum's back was turned.

Laundry times were interesting, Mum filled a grey metal enamel receptacle and heated water to wash the clothes, clamping the mangle to the sink, turning the handle and squeezing the water out to hang on a clothes horse in front of the fire or if windy or dry on the washing line. She saved first, for a spin dryer that could rip you arm off if you put it in before the motion stopped, purchasing a Hoover twin tub in the late sixties, with its magical agitator movement and then lifting the wet clothes out with washing tongs to drop in the spinner.

That large sink in kitchen also served as my bath when very young, with Mr Wells waving at me through the window while digging the soil and vegetables up from his back garden in Russell Gardens before the Pope family moved in and later watching Kevin and Keith play in their garden.

Teatime after school was always interesting, Monday being the best, any cold meats leftovers from Sunday lunch and 'bubble and squeak' – made from chopped up cold vegetables and fried with onions, accompanied by mustard piccalilli or Branston - still one of my favourites today! The rest of the week was generally toast, with dripping or baked beans, poached eggs and toasted cheese or spam fritters in the cooler months. The warm summer months meant a green salad 1950's style, then seemed to be made of a wilted round lettuce, cucumber, bit of sliced tomato and onion, accompanied by a boiled egg, corned beef, haslett, tongue, spam, bit of grated cheese or if extravagant a little bit of sliced ham and of course lashings of Heinz salad cream.

As mother was the only main wage earner, the volume of food would get less as the week went on. My brother and I loved 'school dinners', our main meal of any weekday, meat and two vegetables staples, forms of various pie, from steak and kidney suet puddings to cottage or shepherd's pie and of course fried fish and chips on a Friday with peas. Mums interest in cooking was increasing, skills being improved with preparing dinner parties, we had even curries – savoury mince and rice, pasties, pies, homemade rissoles (what British hamburgers were called, before we used that American word) also watching and learning from chefs for a more continental feel, like ragu and spaghetti or French omelettes. Phillip Harben in that striped butchers style apron or Fanny Craddock, assisted by Johnny and just like Annie Walker's, Jack from Coronation Street, their henpecked husbands. Unforgettable puddings like Manchester or Coconut tart with custard or and rice or semolina puddings, with that blob of jam in the middle.

Saying this, food wasn't high on our list of needs, it was basic fuel, enough to keep you thinking and active, something to eat quickly and get back out in the playing field or playground, we seemed to be constantly on the move and running around. We were like walking washboards, our ribs even showed through our school shirts, t-shirts even with our vests underneath.

I think most of us dreaded that bell ringing after lunch, signalling lessons beginning for the afternoon, all red faced and hot after another game of tennis ball football, or Bung The Barrel with piled up bodies against a tree. It seems quite strange now, how short an hour for lunch and how long forty minutes was for a lesson. Those lessons you didn't like, a glance to the classroom clock, the big hand never seemed to move and that great sound of the bell to end a lesson.

As mother worked in Richmond she did some of her shopping in Victor Value and the new Sainsbury's supermarket in George Street, - previously a Joe Lyons & Co restaurant I believe - my first pot of strawberry yoghurt, in the early '60's, very runny but seemed very exotic at the time and a new snack called Chipsticks, a nice change from Smiths Crisps.

My life at Oakfield Primary School was now in full swing, from nursery life to timetabled lessons like Reading, Arithmetic, English, Art etc. Meeting other children from the village was enjoyable, making new friends, just doing what young children did in the late 1950's. We often used Ham Library opposite for story time, this was also held by a volunteer or librarian on a Saturday morning, for Story Time, memories of sitting on the parquet floor cross-legged and listening in silence looking at those stand alone index card sets of drawers.

I was an acutely shy child, strange with my mother being so outgoing and chatty. With my now National Health spectacles, adults and teachers asking me questions, I would just panic, forget words and get tongue tied with that reddening glow of embarrassment, I found it excruciatingly painful and debilitating. One day on my birthday, the classroom celebration was to stand you on a chair in the front of the children, who would joyfully sing 'Happy Birthday To You'. One child noticed, I was going red and shouted out, "Beetroot Miss!" just to make things worse! I still remember that occasion, I was wearing my new birthday shirt, with short sleeves and small coloured boxes with a letter of the alphabet on each one, I loved that shirt, I wore it till it fell apart.

I so envied the kids that would confidently be able to sing or play a recorder or some other instrument, put their hands up first to answer a question – even if they didn't know the answer – or volunteer to read out loud in class. Even more annoying when you knew the answer and you hadn't bothered to put your hand up. Would have loved to hear the teacher say to me 'Graham, let someone else answer for a change!'. Shyness was a trait, that would affect me, regrettably into well into my twenties and when you are younger it just seemed rude to others, with that lack of eye contact, not talking etc. Worse of all, it made me very quiet and embarrassed in front of young ladies in my teens and slow off the mark to engage in any conversation.

It's now the start of the 1960's, my brother Keith is now 13 and his final senior years at Grey Court, I am 7.

What I remember of home life at this stage is that my father would suddenly make an appearance from time to time, dropping into our family life. I am now at that age where any male adult comes into your life it will add importance, especially if it's your father, I was pleased to see him, it was 'My Dad' taking me for rides in any cars and for small treats, it all seemed so exciting, especially in his Thames Haulage tipper lorry.

Many of my street friends have their father's, who seemed to be constantly around, I would see them in the road or garden and taking the family out now and again at the weekend. Many of the occupations that men had in those times were manual, say a tradesman, working in the local factory, a cycle ride away or a short journey on the bus.

The man's role in the house was to do practical things when required, Mums if they worked were mostly part time, as I seem to remember, perhaps cleaning jobs, catering or working in retail, but still expected to 'raise the kids', 'put food on the table', 'clean the house', 'do the shopping' etc. Fulltime working or a professional career was very rare in my street or on the estates, although I did know one of my classmates mothers who worked in a bank! In our village and after a day's work, I saw these men go to the pub for the odd pint, their dinner would be in the oven ready for them on return, but always home at a reasonable time, unless doing overtime.

Fathers at weekends would help their children to fix bicycles, perhaps make a go-kart out of pram parts, play football in the road or on the Rec', cleaning or repairing their newly acquired second hand car or motorbike and sidecar. Digging the garden and best of all some playing together with their children and taking an interest in what their children were doing. Sitting on the kerb, I would look on with envy to me that state of affairs was idyllic, I was surrounded by seemingly happy families, two parents in each home. Unrealistic to think every household was like the Walton Family, we watched later in the early 1970s TV. At this stage, I don't even remember questioning anybody about my father's absence, outweighed by him not being around.

In March 1961, we heard some terrible news, Auntie Mary's husband Pip, was found collapsed over his steering wheel in a lay-by in Buckinghamshire and sadly passed away after a heart attack, only in his late 40s, it was a shock for our street and especially for the family. Brian at this age of 16, decides to join the Royal Navy and will never return really to Ham, only for family occasions. My mother and Mary became even closer as friends as for all intent and purposes, were both single parents, with our father away, they would have to financially support a household and two youngsters, Julie and myself nearly 8 years of age.

It's at this age, I start to get curious about my father, the infrequence that he was at home had started to get longer, on his return that initial feeling of adulation and excitement of seeing him. He may take me briefly out with my mother or kick a ball in the garden, but never spent much time with my brother or myself strangely. Over time, I felt a strange disconnect between us, he would come home from 'work', not really acknowledge me, climb the stairs to the bathroom, wash, shave and dab Old Spice from the bathroom cabinet, get changed and I might hear "Going to the pub, be back later!" between 6 and 7pm, then the front door closing. All before my mother could ask and even challenge where he was going.

He always seemed to be out for hours, sometimes I would hear his keys turning in the door late at night and hope he would pop his head around my bedroom door, perhaps to say 'Good night, son' or a hug, but I never remember this ever happening. Later hearing a muffled discussion or argument downstairs and behind closed bedroom doors, causing me to cover my ears, close my bedroom door and luckily just drift off to sleep after an active day.

I would sometimes ask Mum, 'Where's Dad?' after he failed to return home or was away for long periods, just to be told he was a 'Long distance driver and needed to be away', confirmed by my brother, which seemed very plausible at the time because he would often bring home a truck, a delivery van and later a huge shiny black, chromed trim, double headlamped Humber Super Snipe, a chauffeurs hat propped up on the dashboard.

At this time we had a television installed, early memories of Watch With Mother, The Woodentops, The Flower Pot Men, Muffin The Mule and others, I would prop my chin up with both elbows and be very close to that small 9" screen. Later with now more children's TV programmes and on rainy and winter afternoons settling down to Twizzle, Sara and Hoppity, Four Feather Falls, Popeye and Olive Oil, Yogi Bear, Huckleberry Hound, Champion The Wonder Horse, Zorro, The Lone Ranger, Last of the Mohicans, Lassie, The Flintstones, later Daktari, with Cheetah the monkey and Clarence the cross eyed lion and many, many more. Television became more addictive, especially in the winter.

When my father was around, which now didn't seem that often, we may have some 'family' time, the odd trip to the coast but he would always just remain in the car, or London to see his mother. Visiting Petticoat Lane on a very busy Sunday morning, like many areas where people gathered there was always a man in a trilby who would thrust a small monkey dressed in knitted woollen clothes and sucking on a Polo Mint, into your arms. A dodgy character with a Mackintosh raincoat would appear in front of you, camera in hand and detonate the flashbulb, alternatively a monkey curled around his fist, then deposited on your shoulder, before you could say anything, the man would then quickly take a snap and give you a ticket and told us to be back in our hour to view the photograph. A seaside trip would still see another monkey in a sailors suit or pirates outfit, or a parrot placed on your shoulder, as you strolled along Bognor Regis, Brighton, Newhaven or any other South Coast seafront.

When mother returned from work, she was always very attentive, asking me questions about school or what have I done today, sitting me on her lap for a cuddle, which I now think I am too big for! At weekends for long walks, to the river or the park, taking a picnic and Thermos flask, along with sandwiches of corn beef with Branston or egg chopped in salad cream, wrapped in folded greaseproof paper, sometimes sitting near the pond within Ham Gate. I did enjoy these times when just the two of us would be together as she was also very witty and with a great sense of humour. My favourite was the gardens of Ham House, many hours were spent sitting on a sunny day making daisy chains or a blade of thick grass between your thumbs to make a loud noise, dandelion heads that you blew through and counted the time.

My memories of sunny Sundays, my brother wouldn't be at home and Mum would ask me to help prepare lunch, she would give me a handful of pea pods, sit me on the back door step and shell into a well worn green enamel colander. Always complied as my brother did when young, sometimes we would hear the chimes of the ice cream van, always seemed to be 'Greensleeves', I wouldn't ask direct but I would look at her and she would look back at Keith and I, she would go to her purse and her coats and find exactly the right money, to buy a brick of ice cream, I would line up with the other kids in the street, the block would be wrapped in newspaper to stop it melting and put on the cooler larder shelf for pudding after lunch. She would be at the sink, peeling potatoes, carrots etc with the BBC Light Programme playing from our brown Bakelite radio sitting on the shelf in the kitchen with Two Way Family Favourites playing, she was always singing, Ella Fitzgerald, Billie Holiday, Perry Como, Frank Sinatra, Tony Bennett, Matt Monroe and many crooners of that time and the 'charts' then. I loved her singing and she loved to sing, I now believed it lifted her briefly from any issues, made her forget momentarily any other problems. The Sunday radio schedules also included The Clitheroe Kid, Around The Horn, The Billy Cotton Band Show, Educating Archie, unbelievably a ventriloquist show on the radio! She even encouraged me to learn a song on these walks, to this day, I can still remember the words, off by heart to – early Tommy Steeles's, Singing The Blues, Emile Ford's and his Checkmates 1959 hit "What Do You Want To Make Those Eyes At Me For?" and Elvis's 1962 hit "Return To Sender" from his film Girls! Girls! Girls!, or Tommy Edwards 'It's All In The Game' which later The Four Tops covered for a slow dance at the youth club, if there ever was ever a small gathering at our house, my Mum would encourage me to do my "Party Piece", alas too shy or mumbled into my Clarks sandals looking at the ground. Another very popular singer at the time was Lonnie Donegan, a Scots Londoner who spoke an sang with an American accent and deemed 'The King Of Skiffle' using basically homemade simple instruments, washboards and thimbles, t-chest bases, with a broomstick as a double base and banjo or guitars. I can still remember the words to 'My Old Man's a Dustmen' and 'Does Your Chewing Gum Lose Its Flavour..', he unbelievably had 31 UK top 30 records and two hits in the US. Very influential as an artist but literally disappeared overnight when The Beatles appeared and as tastes changed.

Meeting my Mum after school to be taken out was always very exciting, but I had to have that 'rub of shame' at the bus stop on Petersham Road, where she would tell me to or get her own handkerchief out lick it and wipe a school day dirt from my face, with me squirming away from her, don't forget this is after being tried and dodging that kiss at the school gates! A trip to the cinema, - my Mum called it the 'Flicks' after a much used word in the 1930s, when the film when projected seemed to flicker - the series of Elvis films like, It Happened At The World's Fair, Viva Las Vegas, Jailhouse Rock etc. Ben Hur and of course re-released Disney films like Bambi, Snow White, Dumbo etc, although I struggled watching Fantasia, these treats were all appreciated in these grand local 1930s built cinemas and picture house cathedrals, like the Odeon, Granada and ABC in Richmond or Kingston.

My mother always like a 'perm' and later had a 'contract' at Raymonds Teasy Weasy's in Hill Street Richmond next to the Gaumont cinema, which strangely had a fireplace in the foyer, as the building was originally a Georgian house. I would sit in the reception with that smell of peroxide or perm lotion lingering in the air, which I thought was horrid, watching the ladies with their heads in the driers looking like aliens and reading Women's Own!

If early for the start of a film, one of my Mum's favourite treats to herself, was a 'frothy coffee' and was sold from an Italian owned cafe or sandwich bar at the back of the Odeon Cinema near the bus station. I looked in amazement at that hissing, steaming machine called a Gaggia and the coffee being served in a wide clear glass cup and saucer. I loved the cold milk and a spoonful of milkshake powder or a treat of a chocolate covered KitKat, Penguin or Club biscuit. It seemed so nice to sit down and chat, her and me always avoiding any 'Dad' questions. Tom Thumb was one of my favourite children's films in the late 1950s, was it because he was small or that 'talented and dancing shoes' sequence?

My brother later, took me to war, cowboy and adventure films, at the local cinema's, even to our last film together in 1968, Bullitt, starring the really cool and THE best dressed actor Steve McQueen, not forgetting my crush on Jacqueline Bissett at the time and a film famous for that green modified Ford Mustang GT390 Fastback being pursued by a black Dodge Charger 440 Magnum, with a roaring V8 engine the car roared through the streets of San Francisco, regarded as the most influential car chase scene in movie history. They used two Mustangs in the film, one totally damaged and scrapped, the other one sold in 1974 stored in original condition and sold at auction in 2020 for £2.2 million. Excited by the car chase, we walked back to Keith's car, parked in the River Lane car park, as we opened the doors and sat in we imagined the streets of San Francisco, he looked at me and started the car, putting his foot down around Richmond Green, swinging it through the one way streets of Richmond. As we sped down Petersham Road and Star & Garter and it wallowed around Tommy Steele's Corner, we quickly note that his 1956 Morris Oxford Series II, just didn't have the same cornering dynamics of a '67 Mustang, as I slid across the bench seat!

In 1961, my school Oakfield Infants, was acquired by Grey Court School to be converted to The Art Block, where students painted, sculptured, made pottery on a wheel and sketched with two fulltime art teachers. A classroom was set up with technical drawing desks, some great facilities for those times and a lesson I loved later. I am sent to Orchard School in Petersham for my Primary years.

The gap in my front teeth - a diastema - is now very large, even to a point of being able to pass a thrupenny bit through it, which makes other kids laugh and being able to whistle loud without using your fingers, bought on mostly by the sucking of my thumb from an early age, a thumb that would be forever clean and white while playing and stand out from my dirty hands. My mother takes me to the dentist in Dukes Avenue, who seemed to like putting fillings in for any reason, but decides to remove some teeth saying it will close the gap. I always found the dentist a little scary, pretending that a silly bit of cotton wool was a rabbit on the drill mechanism and it was supposed to take our mind off any anxiety, but the smell of burning enamel changed that. Secondly, removal of teeth then was done by administering laughing gas or nitrous oxide, which believe me didn't make me smile, as the vile smell of that rubber mask being placed on your small face, just made me go into a state of hallucination. Hearing the tooth pliers and a graunching noise as he twisted it out, the sound of it dropping into the kidney bowl, while in a semi sleep, yes 1950s and 60s dentists wasn't a nice place to go then and bought trauma to many a child.

It's 1961 and following the success of Sputnik, the Russians now launched dogs into space and a manned rocket, in April we get news that Yuri Gagarin in Vostok 1, has had a 108 minute flight skimming the earth's atmosphere making him the First Man In Space. Although John F Kennedy congratulated the Russians and with The Cold War at its height, wondering does this give the Soviet Union the technology to launch intercontinental missiles? A great accomplishment for a country that just 16 years earlier was devastated by war and the loss of 25 million citizens, interestingly the Americans only thought they only had the capability to make tractors in post-war Russia!

The President declared to his country that the US was behind technically and that they had lost the first round of The Space Race. Just a month later JFK, challenged Congress and declared to the nation that they will put a Man on the Moon before the decade was over!

"We choose to go to the moon, this decade, ...not because they are easy, but because they are hard....that challenge is one we are willing to accept...unwilling to postpone....we intend to win!"

Besides an inspirational piece of oratory, it developed my interest in innovation and all things engineering and technical. The federal government allocated the Apollo Project some $25 billion dollars. $100B today.

About this time, I started to notice world leaders, JFK was one of the first that didn't look old, when you think that Russia's Nikita Khrushchev, France's Charles De Gaulle, Britain's Harold Macmillan, China's Chiang Kai-shek and even Dwight D. Eisenhower who Kennedy replaced at the age of 43, the second youngest President after Theodore Roosevelt, who toy bears took their name Teddy from. His wife Jacqueline, that had such an impact on beauty, styling, clothes and above all image from a First Lady, that still matters today.

Politics to me, was an event that came around and in the news every four years with elections, between this times, except for the odd scandal, it seemed to be off the front page of newspapers, radio and TV. Living on a council estate was also interesting as many working class voted Labour, although on the outskirts of a very Liberal Richmond town.

Canvassing time was always good fun for my brother and I. The political representative would knock on our front door, my mother would be polite and have some prepared questions depending on the Party, she would nod, kindly listening to any answers. The representative would feel confident now to ask that all important question 'Mrs Clark, can we depend on your Vote then?', replying quietly 'That's between Me and the Ballot Box!', to a bemused electioneerer standing on our doorstep, they had no idea how to reply.

Even when I asked her every election time, she would give that same answer. Although she was born in the early 1920's and around the time of The National Strike and The Great Depression days of the early 1930's, she believed that the unions had protected and stood up for the workers and their conditions, but had gone too far in some areas. So I believe, she voted a reddish Blue or Yellow.

My mother always believed that the modern world was a time that we could always take advantage and improve ourselves, her role and experiences working on Richmond Green saw people with good education, upbringing and wealth and hoped 'her boys', may one day take advantage of the new world of learning.

She introduced us to different experiences, especially me, listening to Children's Favourites every Saturday morning, presented by Uncle Mack, playing requests, one I particularly liked was Peter and The Wolf and some other classical pieces or covering Danny Kaye's, Tubby The Tuba. Mum seeing and hearing my interest, took me along to the Royal Albert Hall quarterly Junior Concerts on a Saturday morning or afternoon. Trips to the Science Museum where you could play with the exhibits, pulling levers and pushing buttons, Natural History and the V&A museums, for my interest in history etc., also to Richmond Theatre to see a play now and again. I think she was just trying to open my mind and encouraging me to try other things, educate myself and she did it very well, leaving me with an interest in many topics and areas.

Manners were a big thing with Mum, basics and how to lay cutlery, don't drop litter, what type of glasses to use, breaking up a bread roll, not cutting it when served with a meal. Holding doors for people, being respectful to the opposite sex, a 'Good Morning', 'Good Evening' and 'Hello', or acknowledging as you engage with people, day to day politeness, which was so difficult when very shy. The ability to small talk, be curious and be interested in people, my mother would speak to anybody at a bus stop, something strangely I would start to do and still do to this day. 'Manners, cost nothing she would say', doesn't matter where you live or come from.

It's now September 1961, after the closure of my Infant school, I enter Orchard Primary School, some go to Meadlands. Again I meet new children and make more friends as a slightly bigger school and cross the Sandy Lane border of Petersham. The last three years of my junior education before coming back to the same site and Grey Court senior years.

My first day and with my hand me down oversized uniform and NHS specs with a lump of plaster holding the arm on, I stand on my own briefly watching the boys play tennis ball footie in the playground. A lad comes over and says 'you new to Orchard?', I nod yes and he says 'My names Danny, what's yours?', 'Come and play!'. An unconditional relationship which lasted for 60 years, until he sadly passed away in 2021.

However the walk was a little longer, but more interesting, we could choose to meander along the roads, which seemed to us the longer way to school, or shorter through Cut Throat Alley and walk alongside the copse. Not that you realise at the time, but this way was an education in natural history, as we laughed, ran or walked our way to school, with our Duffell bags strapped diagonally over our back, which left both arms free. Whether we threw snowballs in the winter or peered through early morning thick eerie mist and fogs, viewed caterpillars and other insects crawling along twigs or across leaves, in the summer we chased butterflies and kicked autumn leaves at each other or stuffed then down someone's raincoat in freezing fog and watched frosts melting by the rays of a warming sun in the morning, Stag beetles squared up to each other, led by us. Collected conkers and chestnuts, being fascinated by those dew or frost covered hedgerows, which would show the detail of a cobweb and the spider in the middle with his cocooned prey, sometimes making a loop with a twig and scooping the web up to study more and scare the girls in the playground. A great start and part of any or normal school day to us, kicking a tennis ball or one of those gossamer weighted cheap plastic Frido footballs for about 2/6d with the pimples you got for birthday or Christmas, which were blown easily by the slightest breeze and would make a lovely red mark on your thigh, should someone kick it at you, shouting they were Danny Blanchflower or Jimmy Greaves, before they toe punted it, in your direction. These balls would easily puncture on thorn bushes, repairing them was easy, you held a knife over a gas ring heated the blade and smoothed the melted plastic over the hole, there was a more expensive heavier ball, but that was 10/6d.

My new school was aptly named, being constructed on an old apple orchard, that seemed to be planted in a rows, making a great scene from inside the classroom's large Crittal French style opening windows. I remember the fantastic blossom in the spring, come July we ate unripe small apples and of course early September windfalls were plentiful for any hungry growing lads or lasses for a playtime snack. The downside was the many wasps around and getting stung, an apple could look perfect lying on the ground, but pick it up without checking and you would feel something similar to an electric shock, shoot up your arm, a wasp had been feeding on the rotting apple! As you got older in the school, you would booby trap the young ones in setting up, literally a 'sting' for them! Hilarious tomfoolery and perhaps consequences from teachers or the dinner lady on patrol in the school grounds at playtime, one hundred lines were frequently dished out for playing field misdemeanours.

This school to me, seemed to have acres of green space, netball pitches painted onto the playground and football pitches on the fields in the winter and then magically transformed into a running track after the Easter holidays. Activity was a big thing to us villagers, the Sports Day was an event at every school, we all seemed to get very competitive and there would be inter-school athletic competitions. To get chosen for an individual race or gain a place on the relay team. The best honour was being able to safety pin that large capital 'O' for Orchard to your vest, when challenging another local school.

It's about this period that life changes for me, I would walk to and from Orchard different ways, often passing the bigger boys and girls from Grey Court the senior school. We often kicked footballs or tennis balls on our way home either by road or across the woods and through alleys and they would fall at the feet of the bigger lads and we hoped we got it back.

I started to get remarks about my father and his whereabouts which I found confusing as they were using phrases or slang that I did not recognise. I had assumed my father was a 'long distance driver' and although he changed job every year, to me he just worked away, when he returned from these 'travels' and any school holidays, on rare occasions he took me to work. Either in lorries or in vans, I distinctly remember that he worked for Reliance Nameplates in Twickenham that made the famous plastic oval blue Ford badges that were on the front grills. Delivering to Langley or a longer trip to Dagenham, with me sitting on the engine compartment of navy blue Ford 15 cwt van that just preceded the famous Transit of the 1960's.

We chatted but the conversation was only and always about where he would like to take me for treats and making lots of promises, however, these never seem to materialise. My friends in the street seemed to be with their fathers at the weekend doing something interesting, I looked on, a little resentful and wondering, why I had a different type of relationship.

However, my best ever treat, that did materialise, was in late August 1962 to see a Division 2 game, interestingly the season after that prolific goal scorer Jimmy Greaves was the youngest player to score 100 Division 1 goals, at the age of 20. Disillusioned with Chelsea and Mears in need of cash, sold him to AC Milan for £80,000, Greavesie is Chelsea's 7th top goal scorers of all time. My trip to Chelsea that day, saw them playing Scunthorpe United, Stamford Bridge, a massive oval with open terracing, that could hold some 82000 standing spectators, where besides football, it contained a dog track and speedway, which meant as a spectator you were separated by the width of the track, looking like a gladiatorial Roman amphitheatre. This layout lasted until a major development, leading to an all roofed and seating for 34000, that increased the crowd noise. Now for me this was a fantastic experience, I lived on boasting about that experience for ages, becoming a very keen Chelsea supporter, still to this day.

A trip to the coast may happen, but recall painfully the many promises that never materialised, unfortunately, my mother and brother suffered from the same promises. Even if we went to the seaside, my mother would take us to the beach, while he sat in the car, always a great time unless you got tar on your feet or towel, which could be removed when home with a bit of margarine. It takes a lot to break the trust of a child, but I am learning the hard way and sadly being constantly let down by my Dad, a person who shouldn't, I naturally thought. Did it affect our relationship going forward, I still looked up to him as a father, but quickly learned never to ask him to do things, if he took me to the pub at the last minute, I sat on the kerb with a Coke and a packet of Smith Crisps, at least it was something.

Strangely, he would disappear after a couple of months or so, without any goodbyes to me - I assumed to work away, but the mood in the house would always changed, strangely for the better, my mother would take me for long walks, we would chat, if I asked about my Dad, she would quickly change the subject.

When I played football for the cubs or school, mum would be there standing on the touchline with the other Dads, shouting me on, if she wasn't working.

My brother now 15, leaves school in July 1962, to become a apprentice painter and decorator at Clift & Sons in Twickenham, a funeral decorator and buildings maintenance business, interestingly who maintained The Castle Ballrooms. Also dabbling in plumbing and roofing which came in very handy, when our cold water tank, froze and came through the ceiling of his bedroom in that long winter of 62/63, he replaced it, which led to him being offered a job as a plumber on the local council.

About this time, Robbie, Paul, Danny and myself are allowed to go to Saturday Morning 'pictures', a cacophony of noise, excited boys and girls in a big group and watching films, from Daffy Duck to Road Runner, The Lone Ranger, British children's action films and a young Dennis Waterman in his first child acting roles. We preferred the ABC with its luminous badge to put on your raincoat, if it was your birthday you could go up on stage and get a very small gift – some bigger boys had two or three birthdays a year strangely. 'We are the boys and girls well known as...Minors of the ABC' we would sing! The Odeon also had a song and Children's Club. A trip on our own at seven and eight on the 65 bus, after a long walk to the bus stop, handing over your fair '3d half please' and waiting for the ticket to come out of that aluminium contraption at the turn of a handle!

This was the first time that we stole things from shops, not big time but the odd sweet! We would walk back to The Poppy Factory bus stop, on Hill Rise, there was a sweet shop run by an elderly couple, as Danny pointed up to the sweet jars on a high shelf and the owner turned his back to climb the ladder. Danny grabbed a handle of penny sweets from the counter, thrusting them in my hand and shouting at the same time 'Run!' and we did. Naughty I know but I think we got about tuppence worth! I think for three days I was waiting for the police to knock on the door!

That autumn and that awful return to school and lessons after the summer holidays and that smell of sawdust when the classroom floors had been cleaned and perhaps re-varnished along with sanding any desks and of course the removal of chewing gum from underneath, at that time we would look forward to conker and chestnut season and the impending 'Firework Night', as nippers we always had a little bonfire and fireworks in our garden, organised by my brother Keith, with no lawn because of constant flooding it was ideal. Jacket potatoes and Toffee Apples for mates in the street, along with sparklers and of course the odd burn, singing 'Light Up the Sky with Standard Fireworks', when Keith launched a rocket from a milk bottle or nailed a Catherine wheel to the shed door which would always scorch it! Don't know why, but our end of the village didn't really attend the Ham Common communal Bonfire event and I never remember ever going. Making a 'guy' with old clothes and stuffing it with newspaper, getting a mask and placing it in a pushchair was always good fun and two Saturdays before 'bonfire night' we would prop it up against the newsagent on Ham Parade or the betting shop, waiting for the Hawkers factory workers to come out, feeling good after their shift, they responded to our phrase of 'Mister, Penny for the Guy please?' Firework night and the run up was always full of risk, buying bangers to put in various objects to blow up and experiment, holding a 2d big banger between your fingers, when a bit older buying 2d rockets and launching them out of a half inch copper pipe to fire into a target with a hole in it, which we looked through, in Dave Brown's garden with Danny and Roger, not wise, stupid really, could have lost an eye!

Keats described autumn as being full off "mists and mellow fruitfulness", living by the river and the common and its pond, this ode always reminds me of those village days and the walks to and from school, with its transition between summer and winter.

That winter, known as The Big Freeze, one of the coldest winters on record in the UK, freezing temperatures and snow lay on the ground from December to March, light snow showers started in mid-December - so exciting for kids especially on the run up to Christmas, with more significant snow falling on Boxing Day until New Year. Strangely our village wasn't or didn't seem to get paralysed and most people still got around but post and milk deliveries were hampered by the frosts, milk bottles and the cream freezing and pushing through the foil tops, forming a milk lolly on many a morning. Riding a bike became nearly impossible in frozen ruts and roads. Many people walked everywhere, Mums wearing those low 1950s zip-up boots with some sort of faux fleece lining, large coats, headscarves and rabbit fur lined gloves or mittens, trying not to fall over on the snow and ice.

We sat in front of our fires in the small back room, pulling the sofa and chairs as close as possible, with wet gloves drying on the fireguard, we warmed the kitchen leaving the gas rings on, when Mum was out. However, going upstairs to bed, freezing cotton sheets, sharing a hot water bottle, first me, then Keith, then mother. Mum would pin me in those crisp white cold sheets, I could see those frost ferns again thick on the inside of those Crittal windows, lit up by the lamp post outside. I would then disappear beneath the sheets and with socks allowed, I would try and warm myself by curling up in a ball, breathing warm breath into my knees and searching for where the hot water bottle had been.

The BBC News showed pictures of trains trying to force their way through snow drifts and abandoned, along with buses and lorries. The South West of England was hit especially hard, the first time a Pools Panel was put to together, postponed matches would be adjudicated to provide a result. No horse racing during that period over one hundred meetings were cancelled that season, I took a particular interest in US boxing at time, as it was televised on Grandstand to fill the schedules.

Fresh vegetables in the fields are frozen in the ground, tins of peas, mixed vegetables, butterbeans, potatoes, carrots and dried peas etc. quickly disappeared from shop shelves.

Interestingly, I never remember our school being closed, we would see it as an adventure to get there, playing in the snow. Steaming woolly garments would sit on the radiators until break, ready to make that slide on the playground again or throw snowballs.

Along with parts of the Thames frozen along our stretch, Ham Pond was rock solid. An enormous slide was built across it, running down the bank, where we would launch ourselves onto the ice, hoping there wasn't a frozen stick or branch, to do you some damage as you uncontrollably slid and skittled people over.

That winter although very difficult for transportation and adults, we as village youngsters had some surprisingly interesting advantages. Spring tides had flooded what we call Ham Lands, that sits between the river and the village, this land had flood and when you have constant temperatures below freezing it forms a complete avenue of ice, allowing us to play and many of us had second hand ice skates, great fun we could skate from Ham Street river car park, right around to nearly to The Mariners basin. The walk to school was also good fun, throwing snowballs and sliding on ice, even the bottles of school milk were still delivered, sometimes frozen solid again pushing the foil top off!

Come the weekend, it was a winter sports bonanza. With lots of layers of clothing was the order of the day, second hand from your older brother meant you could put more layers on, the traditional vest being the first layer. Balaclavas, a scarf, strangely still wearing your shorts a pair of socks and some Wellington

Boots and of course those gloves held on with a length of elastic, wool or string that ran from one wrist up the sleeve across your shoulders and attached to the glove on the opposite hand.

Wellies are either too big or too small, if they were slightly too big, your socks would, what my mother called – 'go to sleep', which meant they slipped down right over your heel to the middle of your foot, when you are out and about in ice and snow, pulling them up became difficult. That winter, Paul, Robbie and myself, sometimes Irene and Julie, would often trek to Petersham Gate, dragging our homemade sledges as on an Antarctic expedition, to the slope below Pembroke Lodge we would be there for hours, tobogganing up and down, gathering at the bottom sometimes to pepper a bright red bus with snowballs as it stopped outside the gates. As twilight came, the long cold walk home and temperature dropping, ready for a hot bath or thaw in front of the fire.

Arriving home one afternoon to an empty house and keen to get warm, I lit the gas rings in the kitchen with a taper, however I left it smouldering onto my Mums new red laminated drop leaf table and it burnt and left a six inch long scar, right in the middle! I did warm up that night with some corporal punishment! Another time on my own, I put the pan full of fat on the stove, in the hope of making some chips, going out into the garden I got distracted and returned to see the flames, luckily I remembered that you put a damp tea towel over it before lifting it from Cubs cooking badge knowledge, I managed to wipe the ceiling marks and throw away the tea towel! I also set fire to my brother's hemp wrap he used in plumbing, hanging up in the shed with a lit taper again, looking for something in a dark corner! I saw the damage to that table for many years reminding me that you must make sure a taper is out fully, however that surface of that table was the best for the Gas or Electric meter reader and collector, who would deftly count the coins with their fingers so quickly as I watched them sitting on a kitchen stool! They often turned a blind eye to a washer or foreign coin in the cashbox if no parents at home.

Bizarrely, my brother took me to see Cliff Richard and The Shadows in Summer Holiday that was released in cinemas that February of 1963, the single got to number one.

The Big Freeze, ended its run in March – the coldest, since the winter of 1947/8 - and for the first time that year temperatures rose above freezing and in some parts of the country recorded a balmy 17C, bizarrely!

Unbeknown to me at this time, but best known to my brother and his mates, Richmond and its music clubs are becoming very popular, with the likes of Eel Pie Island and many clubs springing up, it attracts youngsters, up and coming bands or groups from South and West London areas and further afield, who travelled and tried to get residences or bookings throughout the town and nearby Twickenham. Eel Pie Island, became a major jazz and blues venue in the 1960s, the name coming from the food that was served by in the 19th Century Inn on the island. The Eel Pie Island Hotel, surrounded by gardens, hosted ballroom dancing in the 1920s and 30s, the late 50s saw jazz sessions held at the renovated hotel and in the early 60s saw it as a venue for Blues, R&B and rock. Famous names started their careers and developed a following namely Long John Baldry's Hoochie Coochie Men, joined by a young Rod Stewart after Baldry heard him busk on the railway platform with a harmonica at nearby Twickenham Station, inviting him to Eel Pie, the following week. The Rolling Stones, The Yardbirds, Pink Floyd, The Who, Screaming Lord Sutch. David Jones, later to change his name to David Bowie, after the success of Davey Jones of The Monkees found fame in 1966. The venue closed down in 1967, due to cost of repairs and briefly opened in 1969 as Colonel Barefoots Rock Garden that saw Black Sabbath, Genesis and Hawkwind plus many others perform. Shortly after was occupied and became the UKs largest hippie commune in 1970, the hotel was virtually destroyed, mysteriously catching fire in 1971. It is said that Phil Collins parents ran the club as stewards and some management, in the early 1960s, taking a young Philip to work with them, sitting him on the corner of the stage and picked up his interest in drumming from Keith Moon of The Who and his interest in Rhythm, Blues and Soul.

Picking up on the early local jazz and blues music scene and looking for profits, 1961, saw Harold Pendleton's first Richmond Jazz Festival, which took place at Richmond Athletic Ground. Along with local fans of folk, jazz, blues and a growing pop following it bought thousands to the town.

The Beatles on 5th October 1962 released their first single, Love Me Do, it peaks at number 17 in the UK charts and are proving that working class lads can make the big time and be popular across a large audience and of course, make money! Meanwhile, a central London jazz and blues club owner and promoter was looking for a venue outside of the capital after his own club closed down – an émigré named Giorgio Gomelsky fortunately knew the landlord of The Station Hotel, located in a very good position opposite the railway and underground stations. The club already had a very small jazz following, but with the youth of the day looking for something a little more exciting, as its attendances were dwindling.

That cold winter of 1962/3 caused lots of travel issues with freezing roads and rail, especially at night, some members of the house band failed to turn up, who occasionally used a 21 year old drummer called Charlie Watts and for a short time a 19 year old Ray Davies. That night an unknown band called The Rolling Stones stepped up, after playing their first gig earlier at The Marquee and Ealing Jazz Club. With Bill Wyman only joining the end of 1962 and Charlie Watts confirming his place in the line up in that January. However, due to the weather the attendance was very low, Gomelsky even offered two tickets for the price of one, to residents of The Station Hotel! The club's name - The Crawdaddy, after Bo Diddleys 1960 song 'Doing The Craw-Daddy'. The date February 1963 goes down in history as their first commercial gig, with its legendary line up and roots in Rhythm and Blues, the word was out, Gromelsky - now their manager - offers them a residency, their popularity grows, they then secure a weekly booking at Eel

Pie Island. Another member of the band keyboardist, Ian Stewart is dropped because he was a little older and it said didn't suit their image at the time!

The Beatles first visit to Teddington TV Studios was on Sunday February 17th 1963, the story goes while in the area they visited The Station Hotel to listen to this 'new' band and Paul McCartney gave them their own publicists name, in May Andrew Long Oldham becomes their contracted manager unlike Gomelsky who had no contract. Their success grew leading to the release of a Chuck Berry's 'Come On' in June '63 rising to number 21 in the UK Singles Chart. For Gomelsky, The Crawdaddy Club, engaged The Yardbirds, that featured Eric Clapton from nearby Kingston who took up residency, along with artists Long John Baldry, Elton John and Rod Stewart.

Saturday 23rd February 1964, The Beatles visited the TV Studios again, using a boat on the Thames, to record a sketch and set on Mike and Bernie Winters Big Night Out Show and broadcast the following Saturday. The word was out in Ham, crowds gathered on the banks and the footbridge. Unfortunately, I was only 10 years old, my mother said because it was too cold and bleak as well as dangerous, I couldn't go! The Fab Four visited Teddington many times to record and appear on TV programmes, such as Thank Your Lucky Stars (Summer Spin) and a live version on Saturday 11th July 1964

The Crawdaddy became so popular with the young mod set that it moved to premises on Richmond Athletic Ground, which I frequented around 1970/1, not live bands but DJs vinyl playing reggae and soul. Where I heard Witch Queen of New Orleans in the summer of 1971 for the first time, an interesting Native, Mexican American Funk Rock band Redbone (Cajun for mixed-race), which was very popular in the clubs.

Interestingly, The Stones second hit a 1 minute 43 seconds, 'I Wanna Be Your Man' was given and penned by Lennon and McCartney 'as they liked Bo Diddley stuff', reaching number 12 in the UK Charts and on 1st January 1964, their first ever song performed on the brand new BBC's Top Of The Pops, hosted by Jimmy Saville and broadcast from Manchester at the time. Their popularity increased, their next single 'Not Fade Away', exactly a year after their appearance in Richmond reached number 3 in the charts. What a music scene my brother and his friends were witnessing in our local town without the need to travel to London.

The Stones musical roots, especially Jagger, a fan of Muddy Waters and Richards, lay in The Blues and black American music genre and they covered many songs in their early years. Their manager believed that writing their own songs, would be more beneficial for bringing in money and having a hit record in The United States. In June 1964, their manager arranged a tour, looking for the same success as The Beatles earlier that year, with no hit record in the US, Wyman would later quote 'it was a disaster'.

On the same trip, they were also invited to appear on The TAMI Show as part of The British Invasion line up to follow on stage James Brown and his Fabulous Flames. Jagger watched from the wings, saw Brown strutting his stuff and his special moves, being influenced, Jagger tried to replicate his footwork from then on! The highlight of that tour for Jagger, was a visit to Chess Studios where they met Muddy Waters. For two days they booked a recording studio one session included listening to The Valentinos and a Bobby Womacks penned 'It's All Over Now' which they covered and would give them their first number one hit in the UK in July 1964. As they say the rest is history. In the 1960s the Stones had 15 top ten hits and 8 No 1s. The Beatles, 24 and 17 respectively.

The Station Hotel and The Crawdaddy still exists in the form of, in the 1970s called The Bull and Bush Pub and a place to meet and a Schooner and now One Kew Road, a restaurant and bar which sometimes feature Stones tribute bands and has also featured, an original R&B band from the 1960's, called The Outlaws. It's well worth a visit, combined with a trip on a 1960's Bus Tour to past music venues locally and of London and its scene at the time.

The Richmond Jazz Festival gained momentum and the organisers being aware of the growing popularity of R&B. And in the summer of 1963 the organisers invited Georgie Fame, Long John Baldry and a little known group called The Rolling Stones for a £30 appearance and before their first hit, a Chuck Berry song 'Come On' entered the charts. By the time the event happened, thousands more youngsters visited the festival site. The next year they were top of the bill and reputedly took 50% of the takings with an attendance of some 27,000.

The following year the event was renamed The National Jazz and Blues Festival, in 1965 it sold 33,000 tickets. The bill that year included from the world of modern jazz, Ronnie Scott, Chris Barber, Kenny Ball, from Ready, Steady, Go, Blues and Soul artists, The Yardbirds, The Who, The Moody Blues, Manfred Mann, Georgie Fame, The Animals, Spencer Davis, Jimmy James and the Vagabonds, then billed as a Jamaican R&B band. Long John Baldry who invited a 20 year old up on the stage called Rod Stewart – I wonder what happened to him. The festivals popularity, now a victim of itself and pressure from the local community, noise, vagrancy and reports of people camping in Richmond and Old Deer Parks convinced Richmond Athletic Ground management in 1966, that it was not going to happen again. The Festival moved to first Windsor Racecourse and then Kempton Park in 1969, in 1971 it settled in Reading and was part of the towns Festival Of Arts a weekend ticket to see Wishbone Ash, Genesis, Lindisfarne, Ralph McTell and Rory Gallagher would have cost you £1.50 or £2 (£20 today) if camping!

Chapter 6 – A White Lie Revealed.

Living in a small village, most people will probably know about your business, news and especially bad news travels fast. People then read local papers, The Richmond and Twickenham Times, The Richmond Herald and The Surrey Comet, local news is interesting and sales were very high. How else would you find out what's on at the cinema, events in the village or local town shops offers, buying a car, renting or sales of homes or look for recognisable names at your local Magistrates or County Courts.

My walks home from school start to become quite difficult, some of the bigger lads are saying things about my father and his whereabouts, phrases like 'doing time', 'doing porridge' and 'jailbird' are starting to reach my ears, which is a little confusing. My mother seems to be working more at this time, my brother is working and out a lot and I spend many hours on my own now, catering for myself and even putting myself to bed, not bad for a nine year old. I had many questions for Mum and my brother about these remarks, but because Mum is so busy and very tired, my offer of brewing a cup of tea for her is enough, I really didn't want to bother her.

When she is at home, its great we sit down to watch TV together many nights, letting me stay up sometimes, watching programmes like Dr Kildare, No Hiding Place, Bonanza, Rawhide,

Wagon Train, Branded, Lucille Ball Show, Car 54, Where Are You? Phil Silvers Sgt Bilko, a programme that would be replicated into a children's cartoon of Top Cat - later Boss Cat - a pastiche of Bilko and many more of the characters. Refreshments being a glass of cream soda and a bag of her favourite coconut mushroom sweets and her fifth cup of hot tea!

The same bigger lads are starting to say things and only being small and skinny, wearing NHS glasses and school blazer and shorts, I am probably not in a position to launch myself at them, or load a sling shot like David, this time there are two Goliaths. I just cross the road and ignore them, on instructions from Mum, not to give them any reason to keep saying things and hopefully they will get bored.

Shortly after, I was late walking home from school one day on my own, I had to walk down an alleyway with fences either side, as I am coming to the end of the alley, the two lads are in my way. One of them says "Oi speccy, how's your JAILBIRD Dad!?". In that childlike manner, my face screws up in denial and try to hold back the tears, I shout "What are you talking about, he works away from home!". "Just talk to your brother!" they say in a spiteful tone, I start to well up, push through the gap between the both of them and run home.

Again home to an empty house and wait for my brother to come in, always around 4 to 4.30pm – obviously, he did work for, now the council! As soon as Keith comes home, I tell him about the remarks by these two boys, he asks me who they were, I know their families and give names – he says "Don't worry about it, I will speak to Mum". I see these boys again the following week, they see me, my heart sinks, they suddenly cross the road, look away and hurry by. I found out later that Ham runs on a self policing rule, meaning anybody who is small, being bullied and has an older brother or mates is protected. These boys were 'dealt with or threatened' by his mates or my brother himself and 'warned off', to leave well alone. It seem to work.

In our house, being negative wasn't done, any bad news you generally kept it to yourself, mother always used the expression: "There is always someone worse off than you, so always look on the brightside and look forward". If ever I failed a test at school or lost a race on a school sports day, she would place her hands on both of my shoulders and ask "Did you try your best son?", replying "My hardest!" and she would say, "That's all you can do Graham, your best" which would leave you feeling a lot better. These things still resonate today for me and throughout my working life.

A couple of weeks later, on a rare occasion when Mum is home and we are sitting down, she switches the television off and invites me to sit close to her. "I need to tell you something", she says, my mind quickly races "what have I done wrong?" 'has she found my catapult, that cracked window, an ink mark on my bedroom bedspread, know that I found my brothers pellet gun and firing it?' She says "You will soon go to 'Big' school, in senior school for a time you will be the youngest and some child may say a horrible thing" after a pause....... "It's about your father". I still remember my Mothers face as it must have been very painful, she explains "Do you ever wonder, where your Dad goes from time to time?". I reply "He works away driving and abroad, doesn't he?". Mum used the term "a white lie", meaning a harmless or told to avoid hurting someone's feelings. "Well I have told you a Big White Lie, only to protect you..............until now and a little older", she proceeds to tell me that my father isn't a long distance lorry driver, but he does things wrong and as a consequence, the Police arrest and the courts put him in jail. To be honest, I do not know how I felt at that time, hurt, angry, disappointed?

Only a little later in life, I still can't imagine it must have been a form of embarrassment she felt at that time as she told me, it must have been heart wrenching. She was the most hard working, trusted and honest person you could wish to meet, so to live in a close neighbourhood community with this stigma of all this hanging over her for many years and one day that her 'youngest' would have to be told, it must have been similar for my brother.

Also my reaction must have been interesting at that young age, my father was never one to sit me on his knee and have a cuddle, in a fragmented way, things now start to make a little sense, but luckily Keith was always around and the male influence and very protective for me and the situation. It wasn't until a little later, that I was told by my brother, that he was a swindler, a serial fraudster, a confidence trickster, a con' man – not a big time gangster, but someone who repeatedly got caught, given an eighteen month to two years sentence, served a around a year or so and released for good conduct. Sadly this went on from 1948 until the late 1960's, my brother has no little memory of him being around when he was young, till nearly four years old, because he wasn't! But eventually he would come home, as if he had returned from hard day's work, when released from prison, he told and promised Mum, it wasn't going to happen ever again, for a short time there would have some kind of normality, acting as if had received some form of dispensation or forgiveness. I truly believe Mum, prayed and hoped it would be the last time and we would have a 'normal' family life, for me also it would seem that it was alright for a time, though only brief. However, after a very short while the atmosphere would decidedly change, arguments would become more frequent between my parents, generally about money and needing some help with paying bills.

Little did I know, I can only assume my mother knew that he was playing the 'Big Man' somewhere and pretending to have money by entertaining, buying drinks for others in bars, trying to impress. Sometimes he would target, perhaps vulnerable single, divorced or widowed women who had money, cars or property. He was an absolute charmer and quite a good looking chap, always well dressed and in his early years, the archetypal philanderer. Later I found out he led a double life for a while, with another woman, my brother tells me we have a half sister or perhaps two somewhere. The trouble was he would always eventually make a mistake, the indiscretions would be stupidly local, Twickenham, Kew, Richmond or Kingston, obviously people knew him and saw him in a bar or pub within the district, when it came later to any identification. Added to this, he might even use his own name when engaging with people he might later 'sting'!

After finding out about my father is a 'jailbird', I am confused, do my friends, classmates, the street, the village, my cub pack know or even been told not to mix with me, which I never felt at the time. Again when I am out playing on the street with mates, I push any 'father' thoughts to the back of my mind and wondered did they know?

I am now more aware with my growing age and brain about the situation, the cycle would now repeat, my father would return home, be alright for a time and then 'con' someone else. The first frightening experience I can recant is that one early morning at about 5.30am, the door knocker was repeatedly used, loud bangs on the front door and the shouts of "POLICE, OPEN UP!!", through the letterbox. My brother runs downstairs in his underpants and trying to pull his jeans up at the same time, followed by me, opening the door after seeing uniforms through the windows. They push and rush past us and up the stairs, finding my father is hiding in my brother's bedroom, as he is led down the stairs, the look on my mother's face is horrendous. I was told later, a warrant out for his arrest had been issued, a phrase that I would hear more than once in the coming years, related to my father. Strangely the CID detective from Richmond knew my father's form when it came to his 'cons' or fraud and his multiple convictions, knowing his 'modus operandi' and after investigations would just know it was him. "Alright Nobby, you're nicked – sadly again!", "You know the form" and read him his rights, they lead him away, the detective looks at my mother in that 'So sorry, Mrs Clark' way. My father is now taken away and put on remand, courts seemed to act quickly then and again he would be interned. You can only imagine the impact that incident had on our family, for me at this age, I was just struck dumb, neither crying nor speaking and take myself off to my bedroom, to the garden or a ride on my bike around the block. I assume it was a form of shock, keeping it all bottled up inside, always looking for something positive, like an up and coming game of football or a trip with the Cubs. From an early age I had learned how to compartmentalise, easily imagining boxes in my head with doors that I can lock or hold shut tight.

I still have my primary school report covering 1961-1964 at Orchard, subjects include English which was divided and marked in five areas, Written Composition, Written Language, Spelling, Reading, Speech and Drama, Mathematics in areas of Mechanical, Mental, Tables, Practical and Applied. Not forgetting, Religious Knowledge, Music, PE and Games, Science and Nature Study, my favourite subjects of History, Geography and Art are marked B- upwards. The class teacher Mrs J M Horsfield remarks that July 1962, "Good progress although rather slow. Graham would do well not to be so shy and then he would possibly get on a little quicker. However, he has done well this year, considering." Considering? – did the school know about my home life, or my naughty Dad? Signed by Mr K R McCall, Headmaster. School Report July 1963 "Graham has worked really hard and this term particularly has shown signs of good progress. He takes a lively interest in all subjects and is keen to find out facts for himself" "A very likeable boy". Class Teacher Mrs E F Sibert. Year 4, July 1964 final year in Orchard Primary. "A keen member of the class. Interested in all topics, works to *capacity*". – Signed Mrs D M Duff. The word capacity looked interesting!

I have always wondered about teachers and school reports, did they prioritise the bright ones and write remarks that aligned with that particular pupil and as they got to the 'not as bright', use the same remarks after the tiring effort of a terms end?

Overall, I enjoyed my junior school years and the experiences it gave, a few that come to mind are not the lessons but activities. My first call up for the school nativity, I am selected for a role as an Eskimo – luckily not a speaking part, too shy - who stood around the Crib along with the obligatory Three Kings, the usual shepherds, but that year we also had Cowboys, Indians, Egyptians, Africans and any other ethnic factions that would include some of the pupils with t-towels on their heads and bit of makeup, believe someone was a cosmonaut also! I rush home all excited and when my Mum comes home, explain my starring role, we have to make an outfit up. After some thought we decide on my anorak that I wear to Cubs and a little rabbit fur collar pinned around the hood, a pair of my brother long trousers tucked into my wellies with my brothers socks folded over the top, to give that fur boot look. Great for someone who is shy, just to stand on stage looking at Baby Jesus.

However, from this school period is an activity that strikes terror into to any little shy boy and that's the Country Dancing lesson that was always seemed part of the Music curriculum at junior and primary school in those days. A lady or teacher on the piano or a record player and those instructions from the teacher, like a English Ho-Down. The music played we took or given a selected partner, hopefully one of the nice girls, who you liked, not one that didn't like you, or who may come from an interesting family in the village, where hygiene was not high on their list of priorities and looks, it wouldn't be a good experience and something to avoid if you could. Couldn't wait for that lesson to end!

It's late 1963, returning from Cubs one night on a cold foggy frosty night, I let myself in the back door, entering the front room, mum is sitting quietly shaking her head, looking physically shocked, just staring at the TV, waiting for a news flash, "We are interrupting this programme again to bring you update on the latest news from Texas......the announcer says "Today, Friday 22nd November at 1230pm local time, the President of the United States, John Fitzgerald Kennedy was fatally shot while riding a motorcade in Dallas Texas, the President was pronounced dead at 1pm at the Parkland Memorial Hospital, more news to follow later". I just sat there also, dressed in my cubs uniform, I was only ten, but still remember the event vividly, a young President like our Queen and his attractive First Lady, a couple that promised so much change. Especially more for many African Americans and Hispanics, Kennedy's acknowledgement of 'civil rights had become everything' and had embraced the movement, he represented the hope for a new world free of racial discrimination and segregation, he became an icon, but was sadly cut down. My mother was physically shocked.

The following day the newspapers and TV news were full of the events of that fateful previous day, photos of her blood splattered white suit and the handsome good looking couple of the early 1960's, and their following of young Americans, JFK was a great orator and I remember his speech about putting a Man On The Moon by the end of the decade and space travel and of course Civil Rights. The following Saturday night at 5.15pm, we were to be introduced to an interesting space and time traveller, The Time Lord – Dr Who, the first Doctor being a 55 year old William Hartnell, a month later we were introduced to those famous aliens and for the next few years, kids would run about with a sink plunger held to their forehead, shouting 'I Am A Dalek!' in a strange voice, for a kids programme it was quite scary, many children watching through their hands or from the back of the couch and later the Cybermen. The following was phenomenal with Dr Who branded annuals, toys, even feature films being released. Although for the practically minded – how did those Daleks get up those stairs? Boys and girls pointed out every police box as The Tardis - Time And Relative Dimension In Space - and you always imagining how much bigger on the inside it was, that landing and take off noise! However, due to some power failures and the effect of the JFK assassination it drew minimal attention and was repeated the following week. It would come to draw an audience of over 12 million viewers, early on a Saturday evening. Introduced by the first electronic musical TV theme, created that year at the new BBC Radiophonic Workshop and sent children to hide behind the settee.

It's December 1963 and the run up to Christmas, Mum would usually go out of her way after a visit to my Grandmother to take me to see the 'Christmas Lights' in London, a magical experience walking from Piccadilly Circus up Regent Street, then Oxford

Circus and that length of Oxford Street adorned with seasonal twinkling lights and of course a visit to the Selfridges windows to press my nose to the shop windows to see the scenes inside, mixed with a smell of a Chestnut vendor and being treated to them roasted and making your fingers filthy, nothing better on the runup to Christmas. Like any 10 year old and many other children after making those paperchains in class to help decorate the room, the belief in Father Christmas is one of those things you must hold on too. Christmas Eve, I always read 'The Night Before Christmas' from the age of six and still believed I could hear sleigh bells, shutting my eyes tightly and wishing it would snow outside, pull the bed covers up and try and get some sleep, be it fitful because of excitement. Only to be alert and awake at 5.30am to check the end of the bed to see if a Santa had put a few things in my Christmas Sack. Because if you didn't believe or denied his existence that you may not get a delivery at all, our Mum was very good at letting me hold onto the belief to a good age. I look back on this period with great nostalgia, my birthday is in June, so lucky to have two annual occasions that were six months apart - always thought, having a birthday on or near 25th December, wouldn't be as fun, getting one gift would cover both events! - getting very excited about any presents and perhaps a few extra treats around the house. I am not sure how my mother budgeted, especially on her meagre wages and the burden of bills, after all it must have been just a living wage, with my father not contributing for most of the time, along with his absences, for the all the Christmas expenses to come, along with her skills in making a weekly food shop last, but she was a great saver when it came to treats. Even if we were on the edge of 'poor', we never felt or looked it, with my mother's management, she certainly provided special times and left great memories of the Yuletide.

To this day, I still love the run up to Christmas Eve, rather than the actual Christmas Day itself, which could seem anti-climatic, one of the reasons being that once you have opened any presents and after lunch, it was the longest time till that next magical time of the year.

Our Christmas season in our house started on the first day of December, this meant that a yearly visit to the loft, to get the tree lights out and any decorations left from the previous year. It was always my older brothers and myself role to decorate the front room, along with buying the tree from the local greengrocer. Because of the rush to get the tree down before Twelfth Night the year before, we didn't care how the tree lights went away. Regretting that decision, the next year when untangling those 1950's strings of screw-in bulbs and switching on to see if they all light up, or that tedious job of tightening up to see if one is loose or you need to replace. If a bulb had blown or needed replacing, it normally meant a trip to Woolies to try and find the right type of bulb, which was always confusing. While you were there it was worth trying to convince mum to upgrade at the same time as buying another packet of paper chains to drape across the ceiling, or a fold out crepe paper. It always gave me great pleasure to walk or a bike ride down our road to see Christmas Trees and lights through people's front room windows and the decorations, seeing families laughing and enjoying themselves. Woolies was always a great hunting ground for any young child, in search of everything, a place where you could disappear because you were smaller than those counter tops around the store, certainly the place any 1950s kid wore those reigns around their chest, to stop you slipping away in search of toys!

Mum, being a good cook would always make the Christmas Pud in advance, obviously with my help, we would get the ingredients out. Raisins, candied peel, other dried fruits, flour, a whole pack of butter or it could have been Stork Margarine, eggs, brown sugar, a little alcohol, usually brandy, a bottle that had been in our pretend 'drinks cabinet' for years, which was just a shelf in our sideboard. The ingredients, all tipped into one of those large Mason's cream mixing bowls that everybody seemed to have. I was good with a large wooden spoon and stirring with two hands, with Mum checking progress now and again, then placing in a sixpence folded in greaseproof paper. Who ever got the portion with the coin would have good fortune for the coming year and the cash – who wouldn't want that! The mix was then poured into one of those white pudding bowls and I think wrapped a muslin cloth and tied by string. It didn't seem to take long to make, but then it would go in a boiling pan and seem to bubble for hours and disappear in seconds in our house, with custard on Christmas day. Along with making the Christmas Cake, I helped with the icing and got out the old battered toffee tin with miniature chalk cake decorations of Trees, Santa on a sleigh and a few reindeers and the odd one legged Robin to decorate the top. My next cooking lesson a few days before Christmas was the homemade mince pies and sausage rolls. They were the best and a real treat, especially sausage rolls and a spoonful of mustard piccalilli on the side.

Our mother loved music, we would have the radio on in the kitchen, it always seemed to be playing Christmas songs or carols, a magical time in the house with just Mum and myself, my brother always seemed to be out or just going. With the Christmas tree lit and decorated and settling down to watch a Christmas special episode on the TV, munching a warm freshly baked sausage roll. Our family from Manchester would send a Postal Order or present down, parcelled in cheap wrapping paper, that I would try to look through to see what it said on the box lid. One main present seemed to be the thing from Mum, along with my birthday. Remembering some of my main presents for Xmas or birthday, a Give-A-Show Projector, beamed onto to the wall, with slides of Walt Disney stories, a William Tell crossbow, with a tin target to hang on the wall, later an Airfix motor racing set, Matchbox and Triang Spot-On cars or Matchbox in the early 1960s, a Zorro mask, cape and plastic sword with a piece of chalk in the tip, to write 'Z' on the walls in alleyways. When 13 a Moulton bike to share with mum which had carriers at front and rear, some early gifts of a drum and sticks, a plastic trumpet. A microscope and glass slides, for my scientific, which was given by the Professor and his wife because of my science book prize at school! A doctors coat, stethoscope and bag, because I loved Emergency Ward 10, a twice weekly and the first hospital drama that ran for ten years from 1957, which also featured an interracial relationship between a black female surgeon and a white doctor, interestingly she was posted to Africa shortly after and died from a snake bite! An obligatory windup monkey with symbols, a pirates dressing up outfit, second hand rusty trike and scooter, Beano, Dandy or Blue Peter annuals, yo-yo's that I didn't have the patience to be skilled at like some kids, who could show off 'walk the dog' move and many others and a set of Dabs. Sooty and Sweep hand puppets, an army uniform with helmet, water bottle and Tommy gun. A toy crane that I would dig up the garden with, uncovering the odd cartwheel penny or coin, many broken white clay pipe bowls and stems that we would pretend were cigarettes, all left from Ham's previous agricultural labouring days in the fields and farms. Never found one intact, assume they were discarded as soon as the they broke.

As 1963 comes to an end, some very important events happened that year, in politics the French and mainly Charles De Gaulle veto's our entry into the European Economic Community, that wouldn't happen until 1975. Harold Wilson becomes leader of the Labour Party, vying to campaign against the Conservatives who have been in power for some 12 years. The John Profumo scandal and Christine Keeler became a household name, Harold McMillan is replaced by Sir Douglas Hume.

In sport Manchester United win the FA Cup, their first major trophy since the Munich Air Disaster of 1958. In transport, Ford Motor Company announce the Ford Anglia, with the innovative sloping back window, in 1970 I own one from exactly that year. Dr Richard Beeching, commences to put a report together that will close some 2000 railway stations, scrap 8000 railway coaches and lose 68,000 jobs from nationalised British Railways. In March The Beatles release their debut album 'Please Please Me' after a 30 week spell at the top, it gets knocked off and you would believe, by their release of 'With The Beatles' and that brilliant album cover, which was photographed by graphic designer Robert Freeman at the Palace Court Hotel, Bournemouth while the group were playing at the local Gaumont Cinema, the image shows four left hand side shaded Fab Four heads on a black background, iconic.

My brother had this album, the tracks now included eight of their own compositions and showing the Liverpool groups love of black music, with six covers of R&B and early Motown written by Smokey Robinson, Berry Gordy, Holland and Dozier and also Chuck Berry. Many Motown sounds were covered by Mersey Beat groups at this time, it's understood that Liverpool was still a passenger route and shipping gateway to important US ports. Many merchant navy seaman being from the Liverpool and the north west of England, when on shore leave in the States they would take advantage of looking through record shops, bring them back to play themselves, being sold onto DJs, played in local clubs or share the sounds with friends. Many early Motown and later Northern Soul favourites found playing at that time in many clubs around the ports and many become rare grooves. R&B and Soul recordings that didn't chart originally or were minor hits in the US, sometimes sold off or abandoned, found their way back to Merseyside or other ports, groups covered these sounds in the early and middle 1960's and for some re-issued later by the original artist or groups. Some examples are Brian Poole and The Tremeloes Twist and Shout (UK hit 1963) and Do You Love Me (1963), hits for The Isley Brothers (US 1962) and Motown's The Contours (US 1962) respectively. Motown original recording dates are sometimes released three to four years earlier, before charting in the UK.

Best example of this was Motown's songwriter, record producer and singer Frank Wilson who in 1965 recorded 'Do I Love You (Indeed I Do)', only 250 demo 45's were pressed on their Soul label for promotional purposes only. Berry Gordy, had a thumbs up or down policy to releases and as Wilson decided he would rather focus on producing rather than singing, it was decided that the demo's would be destroyed. It is rumoured that only five original copies survived, in May 2009 one was sold for £29,000, in August 2020, a newspaper reported one had been sold for £100,000!

It was an interesting year for news, that summer The Great Train Robbery took place and a major news item, stopping a train and stealing £2.6 million in used notes, some £50 million today. I remember that day vividly, 8th August 1963, by coincidence my mother took me to the 'pictures' to see Jason and The Argonauts , the robbery was so important that they announced it over Tannoy at the intermission and a special 'stop press' edition of the Evening News, sold outside Richmond Station. In the following months they were captured and in January 1964 being committed for trial, which lasted until mid-April, after 51 days. The judge handed out sentences of 30 years, describing the case as 'a crime of sordid violence, inspired by vast greed' they paid dearly mainly because an iron bar was used, which the public and jury found abhorrent. I believe they may have taken on Robin Hood status, if it weren't for the use of violence and bodily harm. The names of Biggs, Edwards, Reynolds etc. are still familiar with many of us today.

After the excitement of that Christmas and the run up to it and mixing the winters bought on childhood illnesses, influenza scares, bad colds and coughs, contagious outbreaks like measles or chicken pox. Visiting a doctor wasn't the parent's initial act for a medicinal cure, not wanting to bother them, especially for a bad cold. Remedies like menthol crystals into a mixing bowl, dissolved by boiling hot water, a tea towel over your head, you breathed in deeply and the vapours hit your lungs or Vic rubbed into the chest and smothered on your pyjamas for a stuffed nose, but all helped for a better sleep. Earaches, dealt with by warmed olive oil – available in the chemist, mum holding me over the sink, bad ear up pouring it in using a piece of cotton wool as a plug, you could now hear and feel the warm oil gurgling in your head, a hacking cough dealt with spoonfuls of good and bad cough mixtures into your hesitant opening mouth, frightening croup for some toddlers, eased by a steamy bathroom or a boiling kettle nearby.

However, the promise of the magic elixir of Lucozade, with the orange cellophane wrapper from the chemist, would always put things right, the champagne of poorly kids! Mum convinced me all these were special remedies would work, I would feel fine very quickly and a form of faith healing. Being poorly in our house and staying at home to be looked after wasn't really an option, because mum had to work, to pay bills and put food on the table, not being able to afford any time off. When younger and you weren't feeling well in the morning, Mum would say "What I suggest is, you go to school and see how you feel at lunchtime and if still feeling poorly, tell the teacher, who will try and contact me to pick you up or go home, I will try and get there as soon as possible, OK?". Generally by the time you had walked to school, played at lunchtime, you felt better and would wait until end of school day and just go home as usual! It's a practice, I used throughout my working life. When older at Secondary school, it was alright to stay off and at home to look after myself, if you were really poorly - but before all day TV and entertainment, it was all so boring - and mother always insisted that when really poorly, you should stay off. Sleep all day, keep warm, drink lots of fluids and take some aspirin, listen to Home Service, hoping I might get a bottle of Lucozade bought in later.

About this time chores are part of our daily routine, as brothers were not perfect and argued regularly, whose turn it was to clean out the fire grate, fill the coal scuttle, wash up and vacuum, with those torpedo shaped Hoover cleaners, on gliders not wheels.

My brother Keith always helped me with the odd thruppence, tanner or bob for helping with his timesheets now he was working for Richmond Council. On a Friday afternoon, with his weekly time sheets, writing down the location of work, how much time to get there and the time the job took. He would dictate and I would write and add up making sure it totalled the correct hours, although it was a bit confusing, when he told me that twice as long as it really took, but he did work for the Council. Keith seemed to struggle with writing things down in order and the maths, it wasn't until he was in his early 60's that he was diagnosed as dyslectic. However, he is able to retain information by visual detail, where every major water pipe and their routing, instead of reading diagrams and schematics. After he retired, he was re-employed by Richmond

Upon Thames Council under a consultancy for emergency water issues and the pipeline infrastructure within the area, his skills in visual memory recall were invaluable if any floods or fractured water pipe incidents.

With Mum working 5 days and had weekends off, however having underlying health conditions, she would sometimes feint – describing it as a black blanket moment, due to a low blood pressure or getting over heated and when overtired. We kept smelling salts in the kitchen drawer in case she collapsed or felt feint, which was also used as a 'toy' if mates came around and you dared them to smell it, with great amusement! Sometimes on a Saturday she would take to her bed exhausted, my chores were then a list of shopping items and a folded note for the chemist in Back Lane, that was only to be opened by the lady behind the counter! I would hand over the note she would nod her head disappear around the back, without saying anything she would return with a package, roughly the size of a shoebox, wrapped in newspaper? I would clamp it to my bike rack, cycle straight home hand it to Mum – for some reason I did not ask what was in the package!

A few years later, after doing this many times, I stopped off at the local sweetshop, some older mates of mine snatched the wrapped package, ripping it open, a package of Kotex or Tampax Sanitary Towels dropped to the ground, one lad shouted 'err my sister has those, we call them Mouse Hammocks!', then tried to explain what they are for, which went straight over my head – thanks Mum, not a thing you want to be caught with on the rack of your bike when buying your Saturday comic and fruit salads and black jacks, four for a penny or a farthing each, with that robin on it! Another trip to the pharmacist would be for a diet product that came in a massive box, my mother was always concerned about her weight, she would send me to buy a slimming product called Energen Rolls! Now, these so called rolls were a little bigger than a golfball, a hard crust exterior with a polystyrene foam type interior and to be honest they tasted like it! If I was deliriously hungry during a school holidays and went to the larder to find the Jacobs Cream Crackers had been eaten, it would have been easier to bite on a block of Cookeen lard or drink Camp Coffee, than it was to eat those Energen rolls, but sometimes I did and of hunger! Another chore was to be given a green string bag, which had green plastic beads on the threaded on the strings. The greengrocer would weigh dried mud with the potatoes – I was told to ask the greengrocer to put the spuds in the string bag before weighing and the mud would fall through the gaps! Also better than a paper bag with string handles that would break in the rain and damp hanging from your handlebars.

One of my main chores when a little older was to count the amount of sacks of coke on delivery – would have been coal before 1956 and The Clean Air Act and to stop the lethal Pea Soupers and Smog – it was very important when tipped into the shed store. With a scary lump in my throat looking up to a massive coalman, with the whites of his eyes showing and even making his bad teeth look white, wearing a blackened leather jerkin, with a dirty cloth cap and coal dusted face and ask 'Could you please leave the empty sacks so I can count them for my mother please? Thank you', I would then pay the man with half crowns. It was said, if they delivered when you were out, they may short deliver by one sack, which no one could afford to have then.

You would often see me cycling up and down the road, to do the bread run etc, although your spring loaded bike rack, would do some damage to that squiggy soft white sliced loaf, that was so popular. At the same time trying to dodge Rebel the Alsation, owned by the big family down the road - that had sons amusingly called Tom, Dick and Harry - who could lock on to a spinning ankle as you peddled furiously passed, or an attack from another wandering dog, you learned this trick of shaking your foot, so they couldn't get a grip on your skinny ankle! If you didn't get to the parade of our 'New' shops in the village we were lucky enough to have three mobile greengrocers at one time. Paddy Conway, who lived in our road, a cart pulled by a horse called Kitty, Masons –

a converted pantechnicon (a furniture van) as my Mother called them, another word for a very large furniture van, converted with sloping sides to the roof in a A shape, with fruit and vegetables on display, serving the area around the northside of Lock Road to the river. Thirdly, Keith Fry, covering to the south of Lock Road including Lawrence, Lammas and Fanshaw Roads, Dukes and Dysart Avenues, several blocks of flats called Beaufort Court and Burnell Avenue with great riverside views over Ham Lands. Another horse and cart would be the Rag and Bone man, who called 'ragbone, rag.......bone' as he moved slowly up the road and paid you a few pennies sometimes for old pans etc, along with the 'scissor sharpening man', with his grinding wheel in a frame and would sharpen blades as he sat on the kerb.

It was at about this time I took an interest in cooking, if mum was making a Sunday lunch, a rotation of pork, beef or chicken, she would tell me to watch what she was doing as she prepared the meat, let me cut, chop and cook the vegetables, roast potatoes or make gravy or sauces. Often saying "You may meet the woman of your dreams one day, who may not be able to cook, always good to have some skills to be able to prepare meals when needed, remember cooking is always about prep' and timing".

As its now 1964, double figures in age, 10 which seems like you should start to grow up, especially as I will be leaving primary school soon and going to Big School!! Still can't believe I had those thoughts at that age of ten, going into my final stages of education.

⁂

The year is interesting, deep down inside Mum is desperate in the hope that our Dad might reform and see the light and perhaps 'go straight'. But I am also sure that she feels so pained in not being able to convince him, that the path he has chosen is not the right one with a family. Often my father's whereabouts are unknown, he would disappear for days, only the dread of him coming home and seeing my mother's face and a mood change, if I heard his 'key in the door', it would upset the equilibrium in the house. I became very anxious every time when I heard 'that key', feeling slightly sick to my stomach, my heart raced I felt it pumping in my head as I went seeking the silence of my small bedroom. I just knew the arguing would start and that a black cloud would accumulate over our house, yet again! I wrapped those pillows around my head so tight it hurt, in the hope that it would blank out the noise of those voices downstairs!

⁂

It's the summer term of 1964, Radio Caroline is broadcasting, introducing me to an alternative BBC Light music programme. A new young DJ called Tony Blackburn then 21 years old, was spinning American black music, especially Motown, the sound was slightly easier to listen to than Radio Luxembourg a station that faded in and especially out in the evening, when a good tune came on.

Top Of The Pops had first aired on New Year's Day of that year, music and listening was now in the air and on TV in a new format, it was the perfect distraction for me, especially any music I could get in my bedroom, now with a second hand small transistor radio and the time spent alone in an empty house. Ready, Steady, Go was first broadcast the year before, on Friday, 9th August 1963 airing on ITV or Channel 9 on the dial as we knew it, presented by a suited Keith Fordyce and an attractive looking '60's young lady called Cathy McGowan dressed in the Kings Road and Carnaby Street fashions of the day, instant crush for me, looking like some of my brothers mini-skirted girlfriends he had bought home. McGowan married actor Hywel Bennett in 1970 and later wed singer Michael Ball in 1992. With a strap line of the "The Weekend Starts Here" and theme tune of The Surfari's Wipe Out that got to number 5 in the UK charts in the summer of 1963, later Manfred Mann "5,4,3,2,1" that also got to number 5 in January 1964. A slightly different format with stage setups, very industrial look with scaffolding and interactive artists and audiences. Filmed initially at a small studio in Kingsway, London, its central location made it easier to attract groups and invite good dancers from London nightclubs. It never had the longevity of TOTP and was last broadcast in December 1966. Interestingly Dave Clark of the famous Five bought the rights in the 1980's. In April 1965, the fantastic Dusty Springfield introduced a Ready, Steady, Go – A Motown Special many of us being introduced to the sights, sounds and dancing of The Supremes, Stevie Wonder, The Miracles and Martha and The Vandellas. I still remember sitting with my brother watching this, he had the some of the singles and had recently seen the performers that March, The Tamla Motown Revue in the spring of 1965, starting at Finsbury Park Astoria, after they had toured the UK, covering 21 theatres in 24 days. Again Dusty was and part of championing the 'new sound of Young America' in Britain. Another reason for the tour was bought to the UK was to introduce and launch the Tamla Motown label in the UK, Motown and Tamla US labels previously used the Stateside label for distribution in the UK, The Supremes had the first Motown hit in 1964 with Where Did Our Love Go, getting to number 3, Baby Love and Motown's first ever UK chart number 1 in October that year, both on the Stateside label, along with Come See about Me, Stop In The Name of Love on the Tamla Motown label in early 1965 getting to number 7 in the charts.

What should have been a very successful tour of 20 cities and towns from Bournemouth to Glasgow, however the Mod scene was predominately in London and Liverpool and not perhaps Stockton On Tees or Ipswich. With only just one Top Ten 'Motown' hit in the UK with Mary Wells's My Guy when the tour was in its planning stages in May 1964, they over estimated the tickets sales and bolstered up attendance by adding Georgie Fame to the bill, a 22 year old lad from Lancashire inspired by R&B and Jazz, whose hit Yeh Yeh, got to number 1 in late 1964, except for two London sell out concerts. The Beatles were also fans and covered several Motown songs on their second album 'With The Beatles', in late 1963, Please Mr Postman, You Really Got a Hold on Me and Money, also The Stones's with Can I Get A Witness. In 1965, Motown had one more Top Ten hit, but by the end of 1966 they had eight – The

Motown Sound had truly established itself in the UK. The Revue visited The ABC in Kingston, Surrey on 26th March 1965, with poor sales, they sold tickets for half price and gave tickets away at music venues in Richmond. If they had left the tour until the following year, the ticket sales would have been so much stronger, Stevie Marriott said to Ronnie Wood at a London concert "Aren't we lucky to see this?".

The first UK Tamla Motown labelled number one hit was The Four Tops 'Reach Out (I'll Be There)', staying for three weeks in October 1966, two years after the Stateside labelled Baby Love both written by Holland-Dozier-Holland, spending two weeks at No1 in the UK charts in October 1964.

Dusty Springfield our own Blue Eyed Soul Queen, was a great performer and a regular on Saturday night TV with her own shows! Dusty ended up being one of our best singers of all time, that image of a peroxide blonded, bouffant hairstyled, very dark eyelinered, long eyelashes and makeup, the sensational Swinging Sixties dresses were replicated around the country and are forever in my mind when I hear any of her songs. She would cover many soul hits in the 1960s on her Saturday evening show called simply 'Dusty' in 1966 and the following year she invited Motown guests, but little did we know how troubled she was in her personal life.

Jane, a hairdresser, Brian Smith's twin had backcombed big hair but was a brunette, always looking very fashionable when she went out. The other thing I remember is a Triumph Thunderbird or Bonneville parked outside when she went out with Roy Farnden I believe, we young lads looked longingly at it, sitting at the kerb.

Music in our family is interesting, Mum was forever singing along with the Light programme, anybody who had an older sibling would know their record collection was growing, while mum was downstairs singing, I would be up in his my brothers bedroom, one eye to our front gate, playing his records and diligently reading record label details, EP and album sleeve notes. Realising not only the artist was good but the songwriters and producers were also interesting, especially on the Motown label, Holland Dozier

Holland always intrigued me, a little while later I would find out they were two brothers, with a Lamont in between!

I literally got lost in music, it became my safe place and church, I listened and it instantly took my head away from other issues, I would try to write down the lyrics by playing and starting tracks over and over again. When not playing records and Keith was in, I was constantly twiddling radio knobs looking for R&B, as black music was labelled then, even finding the American Forces Network (AFN) that played soul music for its black servicemen stationed in europe or Radio Luxembourg fading in and out, with Emperor Rosko.

In the UK that year, we went from two TV stations to the addition of a third, BBC Two. The first scheduled programme is Play School, a new type of format and so different to Listen or Watch With Mother in the late 1950's, Muffin the Mule, The Flower Pot Men, Andy Pandy, etc.

It was a tradition at Orchard School was that the leaver's year would put on an end of term concert. Of course, it's nearly the middle of the Swinging Sixties, popular music dominates, fashion, colour seems everywhere. Getting older is everything a youngster looks forward too, wishing their life away, on the way to being a teenager.

That Easter holiday we saw what the media labelled a 'Clash' of Mods and what we called 'Ton Up Boys' or Rockers at Clacton, again to happen on the May Bank Holiday and the infamous clashes in Brighton. Some say this was exaggerated and incited by the daily redtop newspapers that supposedly paid both sides to turn up and start trouble.

As my fellow classmates are now ten and eleven years old, we feel older and slightly more empowered and decide on the theme for the concert. We will try to mime to a pop group and song from the 1964 chart parade. Luckily someone had a toy set of drums, I had a old Spanish guitar that someone had given me, along with someone else and we will use a school desk as a Hammond Organ, wrapped in black paper from the craft cupboard, that will make a skirt around the legs. We were all probably influenced by music of our older siblings who played their Dansette record players in their bedrooms and visited local venues. We look at the charts and the groups of the day, The Beatles are prolific that year – I Wanna Hold Your Hand, Can't Buy Me Love, all the girls loved them so too obvious. An interesting bunch of Liverpudlians, baby faced nice Paul, the weird John and his remarks when interviewed, a quiet George the observer and thinker, daft and jokey Ringo, a personality to suit everyone. Seemed so different to The Searchers, The Bachelors or even Hermans Hermits.

The Stones, The Swinging Blue Jeans, Billy J Kramer and The Dakotas with Little Children – a maybe! We decide on The Dave Clark Five who had two hits in the first six months of 1964, Glad All Over, Bits and Pieces, we choose the latter. I always thought the Honeycombs female drummer and their million selling 'Have I The Right', should be a DC5 song.

The concert was a success and fun, leavers reading poems, playing recorders, the confident ones singing on stage. We play out the finale, I bring in the 45, owned by my brother and its get played on one of those school wooden brown boxed record players with a lid, with a label that said Surrey County Council. The good thing about Bits and Pieces is the foot stomping, "I'm in Pieces, Bits and Pieces......."

Summer term ends, I am now 11, I walk away from Orchard School that July of 1964 for the last time as a primary school pupil. I look forward to the 6 or 7 weeks off, wondering what we would get up to that summer, always a great feeling, we never thought September would arrive it was so far away.

Never really have been a book reader, except as part of the school curriculum, more of a fact and figures reader, loved my Guinness Book of Records, Times World Atlas and my encyclopaedias to read, pick a subject, especially on a rainy wet day. Strangely enough I even liked to flick through a daily newspaper replicating my mother, when she came home from work, with her feet up on the pouffe – sorry footstall, licking her finger and turning the pages that left ink on your hands. We used to take the Daily Mirror or the Daily Sketch. In July, The Beatles first film A Hard Day's Night goes on general release, as a treat Mum takes me as an end of term treat. As another treat my brother takes me to see Zulu.

Luckily I was a member of the Petersham & Ham Cub pack that was a thirty minute walk at the back of Douglas House, near the river and just beyond Ham Polo Club, I am excited by a few days camp in front of the huts in the adjacent field. Pitching tents, digging latrines in the woods with its stinging nettles and dock leaves, to soothe the itching if stung, trying to get a cooking badge (serving up sausages, boiled potato served with peas) and knot tying badges along the way, you wore them with pride down your sleeve. I am promoted to Seconder, never did make a Sixer, Thursday nights was Cub night, a good walk with flying May Bugs, Stag Hornies as we called them, midges and insects biting you in the summer months on the way through Ham Avenue and that dash through the frightening Cut Throat Alley on a spooky winters freezing foggy night, with the moon popping out from time to time, always made your heart race, often singing Beatles songs to take your mind of the spookiness of the ghost Lady Jane Grey, after looking through those iron gates at the back of Ham House.

Bob A Job Week always sticks in my mind, a little 10 year old knocking on strangers doors asking if they need any jobs done for a good cause for twelve pence, but we were safe in our village, we knew everyone. Sometimes just cleaning a couple of pairs of shoes, but when someone took you to their overgrown back garden and asked you to do the weeding, you couldn't even call for back up – all for that shilling (5p today). Filling out a card, with your total and putting a sticker on the door with a tick and 'Job Done', telling other Cubs not to knock. There was some unscrupulous kids that would pretend they are Cubs and Scouts, - cheeky devils!

Playing in the snow or running home if it was raining, seeing how drenched you could get, or standing by big puddles and the big splash, when a car or van went past. Blaming it on the naughty driver if your Mother told you off!

That September I will progress to the P&H Scouts, with a smart uniform, with Sea Scouts embroidered in white on the chest in an elliptic form, next to that was an gold embroidered Admiralty badge, the Group was recognised by the Royal Navy as one of the oldest scout troops founded in 1908/9, I felt really proud and smart in it, with of course my highly polished school shoes. The Scout movement was founded in 1907, after a group of 20 boys gathered on Brownsea Island, hoping to bridge gaps in society, learning new skills and bought together by Lieutenant General Robert Baden-Powell. His ideas and findings documented in his book, Scouting For Boys.

School summer holidays were always great fun, playing in the streets or over the Riverside recreation grounds nearby, until the sun dipped and Mum calling me across the rooftops to come home in after she returned from work. Cycling to Richmond Park, entering through Ham gate to play near the pond, swinging from trees. Returning home via Ham Common and see who's playing football on Ham Common, trying to catch tiddlers in a net to put into a jam jar or sail a model yacht, motorised boat if lucky enough, but that perhaps would encourage the odd big lad to throw stones at it!

Those summer school holidays always seemed to be so sunny and have a small heat wave for a time. A great treat would be to go to and for us in Ham was Teddington over the footbridge or Twickenham Outside Pools which involved catching the ferry near Ham car park ably rowed by a very freckled and red haired man called Ginger, assisted by his dog. I think the charge was a tuppence for kids.

The only memory of us friends playing indoors was the odd box game of Ludo or something similar or the assembly of Scalectrix or in our case the Airfix equivalent, if friends had the same set we would lay it out and make one massive track throughout the ground floor of a house and play it blind down the hallway, with someone shouting 'Lift the plunger, going to fast!'. I can still smell the hot plastic handset in the palm of my hand after an afternoon's play and an overheating transformer. We would play for hours, making hills and ramps under the track and of course a spare pair of brushes for repair of a not only my racing green Vanwall but a lovely silver Chevolet Corvette C2 model.

Mums would come home, checking how many biscuits eaten and pints of milk drunk, even illegally raiding cupboards for those stashed Christmas tins of Libby's fruit salad and those lovely small tins of tangerine segments and putting the empty tins in next doors dustbin to hide them. Being told to tidy up and the words 'Wait till your Father comes home, if not cleared away!'. I used to like their Dads returning, although perhaps tired from work, you could see the bond between fathers and son, I watched enviously at the interaction. Or their Mum's would be seen preparing an evening meal or tea, inviting me to stay, but I always felt that I was now overstaying my welcome and would say 'I have tea prepared at home, thank you' – which I hadn't sometimes. Slightly jealous of that family unit atmosphere, that I never had or really experienced, I would collect any belongings and return to an empty house, thinking, what it would be like for us to have a proper Dad..........? Little did I realise at that time, that my father only legacy would be to leave me with at least some guidance, always dress smartly, clean shaven and to smell good - the whiff of Old Spice or some other cologne, - I witnessed this many times as he walked out of the front door and not forgetting how to polish your shoes and of course supporting Chelsea Football Club and his interests in watching sport. Somehow, he never understood what Fatherhood was and what it should entail, sadly.

Lying in bed one night and reading a comic, I hear a car pull up outside our house. In a street when many families didn't have a car this was unusual, my box bedroom was well placed, over the front door and a street light with an old bike tyre caught over the ornate iron topped lamp post. It's a Jag shaped dark car, two men jump out open the rear door and drag something out and down our garden path, there's a loud bang on the door. They walk back to the car and speed off, luckily my brothers in, he opens the front door to see my father, who's been badly beaten, and lying over the front step, with bruising, cuts and blood to his face and hands, a ripped jacket and shirt. I peak between the banisters, my Mother shouts "Go back to bed now Graham!", I hear muffled conversations, my heart beating through my chest, wanting to know and strangely not know what's happened. That night, I hear Mum say something like, "Let him sleep in your room tonight, Keith, I've had enough" – luckily he had a larger bedroom with two single beds in – which would come in very handy for the years to come. It wasn't till later in life, that Keith explained what happened, my father was a very good 'confidence trickster', normally. He had the great skills of engagement in a pub or club or some social environment having the ability to speak to someone very quickly and find out their interests and determine what they might like on the cheap or 'off the back of a lorry' line thinking it may be a 'bargain', it might be a case of whisky, a nice watch, jewellery, tickets to the Cup Final, a record player, even a car etc.

What happened next was always very interesting, he would build empathy and out of that would come 'confidence' and that he could deliver most things at a 'good' price, his trick now was to ask for some money to 'get the ball rolling'. The 'deposit' was never a high amount but be worth the effort if he conned enough people. Sometimes people were embarrassed to report it or just put it down stupidity in the belief of getting something cheap or 'too good be true' and what's called now 'being scammed'. When it came to that beating, he certainly literally and stupidly punched above his weight this time. When he was in need of some money, desperation sets in and when I say money it wasn't to bring home or pay our bills or put food on the table. It was for setting the scene by buying new clothing, hiring a car to impress or spending it on a female for a meal out in London or buying a round of drinks in a bar or drinking club. His targets were now outside the village, where now his reputation now went before him.

What lead up to that beating, was a chance meeting in a large pub in Kingston, unbeknown to him he engaged in a conversation with two members of a Kingston Gang. As my father always stood at the bar, it was a prime position to watch how people paid for drinks and discussed matters, obviously my father gains their trust and a chat goes along the lines of what he can do. Kingston and most towns in the 1960's had gangs or a gang that had fingers and interests in many types of businesses, thankfully not as crazy as The Kray's from North and East London or South of the river gangs like the Richardson's at the time, but still people not to mix with or especially try to cross or 'con'. Realising there could be something in this for him, my father knows they are not actually law abiding. He makes up a story - he was a great story teller, - unfortunately never to my brother or me at bedtime! - about being able to get hold of reels of copper cable from the Power Station on the river, saying he had friends who work in the stores and it would be easy, as he was a driver, he could get hold of a van also. They get interested and he will say that he doesn't want any money yet, but says, he will need a little to pay upfront for the van, roughly £10? They ask to meet him the following night in another pub nearby, give my Dad some banknotes to get things going and a 48 hour timeframe. However, he takes the money and spends it on his next 'con', the money would never come home to help Mum with any bills! Needless to say, my father doesn't deliver, unluckily for him the word is out and they start looking for him, they visit three pubs in Ham, he gets innocently named by someone being helpful and it's dealt with as they say. There was always one flaw in my father's plan, he always introduced himself as Nobby or George Clark and they asked where he lived, saying Ham! It's not hard to go in a local pub in Ham, asking around and finding out where someone is, in the village.

My father was definitely not in any way a form of Robin Hood, like some gangs or local villains were and seemed to be with family and neighbours, he was a very selfish person, who was losing two sons and a good wife who had tried to do her best to make their marriage work. He could have had a great life, but he wasted it!

Mum, had cleverly warned against us doing anything illegal, we have both experienced the 'consequences' with our own father, which our 'straight and honest mother' had certainly re-enforced time and again, with the help of the Good and Bad Fairy on each shoulder!

Chapter 7 – The Secondary Schools Years and Youth Club

The last days of the Summer school holidays '64 are getting shorter, 9.30pm sunsets over Ham Fields are now 7.30pm, it's as if the sun knows we are going Back To School. Senior school or Big school as we called it are days away and waiting, my uniform is bought, some with Provident Cheques which my grandmother has given to Mum and spent at a shop in East Sheen. Navy blue blazer with stag image on the school badge, shirt, tie and trousers, all one size too big with Mum saying 'You'll grow into those!" ringing in my ears as I look in the mirror, hands covered by the jacket sleeves.

It seemed, (I know it's not an actual fact) but most summers in those 1960s were always sunny and warm, we were always outside playing, just having fun and mostly up to safe high jinks. One time we played 'Knock Down Ginger' to a grumpy man, who didn't give us back our ball after going in his garden. Taking my mother's, black reel of thread, we tied it to his door knocker, hiding in the bushes opposite, we pulled on the thread three times watching him, come to the door in frustration not knowing what's going on. As we snigger and crease up with laughter, we are unaware that the local Bobby, has parked his super quiet grey police Velocette and is standing behind us. The smiles now wiped from our faces, we are told to apologise to the man, as we are dismissed, the policeman says "I know where you all live and will be keeping an eye on you, from now on!"

⁂

Sadly that summer, our end of the village was extremely shocked and saddened by the news, that a very close neighbour, a 10 year old funny mischievous little red headed cheeky character, called Lawrence Fisher, drowned near the Mariners Basin lock on the Thames, where we all played and an area we were familiar with. The whole village and our hearts went out to the family and for many of us it highlighted the risks of being and playing near water with its dangers, he left a legacy and I am sure prevented more incidents for a long time, especially as many of us schooled with his sisters Angela and Maggie Fisher our school and playmates and knowing older siblings Les and Linda.

⁂

So there I stand, the first day of school September 1964, in the kitchen, mum inspecting me, ready to go to Grey Court Secondary Modern School. Luckily my street and play mate Paul Sossick, who lives opposite and went to St Andrews School is in the same year as me, Robbie and his sister Irene, will wait another year along with Danny Mahoney as just the wrong side of a September cut off date. It's about a 15 minute walk, we both feel a bit nervous, but we don't admit it, our new Duffel bags slung diagonally over our shoulders, we walk across the grass from Back Lane on our left is the newly build and still some being completed Ham Close flats, that replaced the 61 post war prefabs to accommodate displaced and re-homed families, newly married daughters and sons that returned from war duties and settled in Ham in the late 1940's.

We cross Ham Street and at the school gates, the returning pupils now in the third and fourth years are there preparing to welcome us first years, in that staring and slightly threatening way, we appear like fluffy vulnerable little ducklings, who have been separated from their mother, as we slowly waddle up the school drive. We were told short trousers in the first and second year are supposed to be compulsory, along with a school cap, however when arriving I saw many wearing long trousers and no cap!

The Secondary Modern was a post war system and catered for pupils between the age of 11-15, it offered an education and practical skills that prepared them, mainly for employment only up to the late 60's, all these children, who didn't pass the eleven plus, would leave school with no qualifications at all, except a cycling proficiently test, certificate and a little flag to put on your mudguard. Unlike the grammar school system, when passing the Eleven Plus, meant taking up education and going on to take GCE 'O' and sometimes 'A' level qualifications beyond the age of 15.

Before the baby boomer peaks, this Tri-Partite system – that also included Technical Schools - worked well for many Secondary Modern children. Made up mainly of the growing working class council house population, any bright ones that passed their Eleven Plus, introduced in 1944 would take them hopefully onto better things, given their more academic brains. Grammar school pupils, seemed to be mainly from blue collar and lower middle class and the 'brainier' ones from working class families, but as the birth-rate increased in the late 1940's and early 1950's, there were fewer places in grammar schools, helped by the growth in secondary modern schools, sometimes had an impact on academically strong pupils and constrained by the limitations of the teaching and lessons, sadly for some.

My mother asked me that because of additional places and availability in local grammar schools of Sheen and Kingston and if an opportunity arose, as I had just failed, would I have gone or liked to go? The choice for me, walk 15 minutes to school with others you have known since five or nursery, who you played with on the Rec', football and sports, cubs and clubs and who were neighbours. What should I do? Or, walk 30 mins to the main road, 30 mins on a bus and mix with nobody you knew and perhaps from a different social class? The choice was easy, Paul Sossick was very bright and should have gone to grammar school, given that and I was just above average at primary school, but I would go into the same class as him, was he disadvantaged or would I get the advantage of this education with brighter mates!

So here we are on the first day, at our last school we were considered big fish - well in my case a medium one in a small pond now starting school, where I am a tiddler in an ocean! As we walk gingerly up that school drive like ducklings and no reeds to hide in, also ready and waiting to be taken out by a sniper with a catapult. We are welcomed or more ambushed by a couple of fourth years, asking if we had sweets, tuck shop money or new fountain pens. We both shake our heads in that 'No' action and avoid eye contact and look down at our new shoes, as instructed by former first years, suddenly our brand new caps are ripped from our heads and thrown onto the adjacent bike sheds! A teacher shouts, 'Oi, you boys!' in a gesture to leave us alone, they say 'Yes, Sir' and have a complete change of attitude, look down and scurry off, the teacher shouts after them "I know who you are, I will take care of you later!". Immediately, I thought that teacher commanded authority, later on that day we found out his name was Mr Day, or nicknamed Wogger Day – why that name, don't think I ever found out at the time!

At the main door the new intake of pupils is around 100-120 of us are herded into the main hall for Assembly – a church based Christian session with prayer and a hymn followed by school notices, warning about good behaviour and the punishment for bad. The majority of the mature teachers had been in the armed forces or National Service and the school system for years, looking very experienced, so an air of discipline, taking appropriate action when required and always that threat of corporal punishment, hung in the air. We were lined up like a platoon and Mr Thomas the Headmaster walks up and down the ranks adjusting ties, blazers, checking for clean shoes, tidy hair and anything inappropriate gets a No!. One of the female teachers starts inspecting the length of skirts, well it was the start of The Swinging Sixties and lots of 11 year old girls skirts are getting shorter by the month, by rolling up their waistbands because of changing fashions and The Hit Parade! The Mini-Skirt had been born, reputably by Mary Quant and available at her Kings Road boutique called Bazaar and named after her favourite car, a Mini Cooper saying they were both 'optimistic, exuberant, young, flirty and complimented each other!'

Handing out the School Bibles, piles of blue or black bibles were on the stage, interspersed with the odd red covered versions. As we went to the steps we were asked our name and ticked off, I was given a bible. As I filed back I ask another pupil why have you a red covered one, they replied they are Roman Catholics or as we nicknamed them Rock Cakes (RC) from then on.

Our form teachers were ready to take us to our classroom. The headmaster said "Class 1D pupils, are as follows" our forms ranged from 1A to 1D or academic ability from teacher feedback from your former primary school. You can imagine in this case, D always meant Dunce to us smug ones, who were lucky enough to be called for 1A, but I certainly didn't expect it! We file off with Miss Cresswell, our designated form teacher, to be told about the school rules and what she is expecting from us in the coming year. We are all due to have the obligatory school photo that afternoon, a photo that came out badly for me, I wore glasses, - now a smaller gap in my two front teeth, that I could get a thruppenny bit - now a sixpence through as a class trick. Playing on the school field that lunchtime, getting hot in the late summer sun, I pose for the photo with my oversized jacket and hair all over the place and specs at an angle, my mother mentioned this constantly later and only bought one copy – which I still have to this day!

I get elected, well by the teacher to be a Milk Monitor, probably only because no one else wanted to do it, wasn't a popularity contest then! It also involved taking register back to the secretary's office, which meant missing ten minutes of any morning lesson and collecting those small third of a pint bottles in crates from the back of the school kitchen. Later being replaced by frozen Jubbly shaped type cartons, that we would stuff down the back of radiators to turn into cheese!

Timetables, Secondary schools especially at this time, as well as academic, had a good amount of sport and practical lessons from wood and metalwork for boys, domestic science (cooking, needlework) and typing later for girls, art and technical drawing.

As lads in Ham and Petersham, we are all just football crazy, Dads played, brothers played, cousins, uncles and even girls played. Many village surnames were synonymous with playing in one of the local teams, like Ham Rovers or Ham FC and later The Ham Venturers, matches were always well attended, the teams mustered at any of the local pubs before kickoff, like The Billet or The Tap, especially for a cup game.

We had acres of green space, recreation grounds, common land. Jumpers would be laid out everywhere as make-ship goalposts, playing football, practising dribbling, penalties, free kicks, nutmegging, slide tackling, we watched professional footballers every Saturday night on the newly introduced and initially aired on BBC2 the first being on August 22nd 1964, it was so popular it moved to BBC1 the following season, presented by Kenneth Wolstenholme, followed by David Coleman in 1967 and then Jimmy Hill in 1973 – Match Of The Day became a Saturday night favourite for many, on the return from the pub, despite the protestations of any females in the house, even later taking girlfriends home early on a night out, to watch with their fathers or brothers, to the dismay of any potential relationship.

Everybody owned a football whether a Frido, Wembley plastic one or an old leather one that was passed down, a soaking sodden ball when wet which would seem to double its weight, heading this especially with the laces making contact with your forehead, coming out of the sky at you like a brown meteorite, meant a quick decision, 'head or trap?', get knocked out or risk missing it completely? We learned to trap, especially in muddy conditions and during the winter, when football pitches turned from green to brown mud and puddles in the centre circle and the penalty area.

It was very common to see boys carrying a ball to school, even a tennis ball in their blazer pocket to practice their moves. These were the early times of football celebrities Danny Blanchflower, Jimmy Greaves and a very young good looking George Best, not then an obvious footballers physique or the skills that we were seeing on TV. The feints, the dribbling, riding tackles, running at opponents, along with his newsreels and perhaps his visits to a fashionable Kings Road, Chelsea and London Clubs. His good looks, hair, flash cars, pretty girls on his arms and clothes, the first real celebrity lifestyle we had witnessed from the world of football, so different to the sportsman like Denis Compton and Johnny Haynes who fashionably promoted Brylcreem!

The village had many proficient footballers, that in later modern times would have been scouted and perhaps moved on to a professional career via a club youth team or academy. I always thought there was a synergy and analogy between the white sand beaches of Brazil and learned talents and the acres of green grass space we had, the numerous games of football and practice, developed some great skills across all the local teams and as individuals.

Going to a Secondary Modern School in the 1950's and 60's, meant there was an emphasis on practical skills, for both girls and boys. We had excellent facilities and equipment – but football was the game, to get into your form year eleven was a great accolade and personal achievement, competition between the other 50-60 boys in your year was immense, you needed to be spotted by the games master or team captain and seen to be putting the effort in. Getting in the team was crucial to perhaps playing for a village team in the future and also to give you some standing around your mates and being picked first to make up a team, even if it was just for fun. And of course, young ladies watching from the touchline in our teens. The trouble for me was, I had a slight build and not very tall, a little comfort in that Best wasn't the biggest player, I watched him on television and he ran at people, during our football games periods, I found my number 7 position on the right wing, same as Bestie. I always sprinted, hopefully dribbling and keeping hold of the ball, before being hit or slide tackled by the opposing left half or left back, or successfully cross it into the penalty area, for our number 9 Dave Brown to head home.

The FA Cup in May of that year was won by West Ham, captained by a young Bobby Moore, little did we know what he would bring to English football two years later. We local lads were football mad and some liked the idea of a "Ham" being in the West Ham name, we even adopted their away strip of light blue, claret hoops around the chest with matching cuffs for a time, an interesting design of strip, well ahead of its time and appearance.

Strangely for a non-grammar school we also played a good standard of cricket and some school year teams excelled at rugby, and at a very good level. We played many grammar schools in the south west and west of London area – due mainly and thanks to Mr Hill at the time, a former Welsh International player, built like a coal bunker, with a booming voice. Again, I played on the right as a winger, hopefully using my speed, to avoid being heavily tackled by a bigger lad, when you have the build of Bambi, rugby is an interesting game, having strength, but being nimble is a must! I would either be grabbed and spun around by my oversized thick cotton shirt collar – by Tony Lloyd or Stuart Alexander - or on very wet days when hit, I would be sacked and embedded into the mud and leave the shape of my frame in the mud and puddles, just like a scene from a Tom and Jerry cartoon, when run over by a steamroller!

Not being that academic, I loved sport, especially football, but not that physically big or skilled, so for me it made sport and getting in teams difficult. I liked to think my enthusiasm and work rate rather than my skills got me chosen for both football and rugby teams, strangely something the same ethos I took into work and my corporate life that followed in later years, working with more academic and skilled colleagues. Someone said a few years ago to me at a school reunion, "Gubba, we also thought of you as a Super Sub or reserve, someone we could bring on in the second half, especially if we needed to get some energy in the game". It was always great to see one's own name on the team sheet pinned on the board outside the school gym, even if it was only as a reserve. I was always proud to go home tell my brother and wait for mother to get in.

The first year at senior school was very interesting, I am not the most academic, but tried hard to listen and absorb any interesting lessons, when not distracted. The curriculum was made up of forty minute lessons, sometimes doubled up for some and tripled up for a games period.

This is an example of a typical school week over your school years: worst day of the week, Monday - Music, French, 15 min Break, English, Maths, Lunch, Double Science, Break, Art/Craft. Moving classrooms between lessons and calls of, "Keep To The Left! Keep Quiet!" constantly shouted Mr Johnson, another sports teacher as the gym was at the end of the main corridor and a busy crossing point in the school. Tuesday - Maths, Gym, Break, Geography, English, Lunch, Double Science, Break, History.

Wednesday – Maths, English, Break, Double Technical Drawing, Lunch, French, Double Games, (whatever the seasonal sport was, football/rugby for the boys, girls hockey, netball in the autumn and winter terms. Summer would bring athletics for all, rounders for the girls and cricket for the boys).

Thursday - French, Geography, Break, Maths, RI – Religious Instruction! Lunch, English, French, Break, Science.

Friday – RI, English, Break, History, Lunch, Maths, Triple Woodwork or Metalwork. Typing, Domestic Science (Cooking and Needlework) for the girls, with the odd lad.

Sport became even more important to our wellbeing, the 1964 Olympics held for two weeks in October, heralded in many things. First Games in Asia, South Africa banned for anti-apartheid use in sports, after the IOC demanded a multi-racial team they refused and were banned from taking part. But for us viewing in the UK it was the first to be telecast internationally by satellite and some in colour and the last time cinder tracks would be used, the next Games an all weather track. GB came tenth with 4 golds, 12 silver and 2 bronze, the US and Soviet Union came top with about

30 medals in each. This made us even more interested in sports and encouraged many to take it up, starting at school.

The timetable takes me back, lessons you loved and lessons that you wanted to end from the start, certainly Religious Instruction was similar as going back to Sunday School, The Good Samaritan, The Prodigal Son, Kane and Abel, Exodus From Egypt - a great story when Moses was played by Charlton Heston, but when you had classroom load of council house kids to discuss the bible or read it out loud, it wasn't easy for Mrs Sterne. For all my years at Grey Court, my school report comments for RI would read "loses concentration far too early", "must learn to concentrate". I did ask a question once to Mrs Sterne, trying to get brownie points to avoid reading allowed "what's the difference between someone who is Church of England and a Roman Catholic, Miss?", she never answered directly, I think she thought I was being facetious!

"Easily distracted", would now in modern times be my Twitter hashtag! Most of us, who wore spectacles, were told to sit to the front and closer to the blackboard for reading – perhaps the teachers thought our spectacles didn't work! However, I was easily distracted because of various missiles that would be flicked to the front, when the teachers back were turned in the act of talking and chalking, chewed blotting and folded paper, pieces of rubbers (erasers), chewed Biro's and pencils, would fly to down with rubber bands and rulers used as launchers! Or I would often hear this 'PSSSST Gub!' and a passed piece of paper with a message about something, I would turn around just at the same time as the teacher did and when giggling started, of course I had to know what the joke was from the back of the class – got busted so many times!

If there had been a fall of snow, freezing conditions, frozen pitches or perhaps the playing fields were flooded. The games or PE master thought it was a good idea to organise a Cross-Country Run, this entailed a set route through local woods and perhaps into Richmond Park and back again, the run was anywhere between two and four miles, whether a single gym or double games lesson. It's interesting to note that some of our Physical Education teachers were ex-services - who made you feel that you were a newly recruited squaddie to Catterick, Lympstone or the Aldershot Camps just about to start National Service and were the masters of being very tough, when it came to instructions, whether you were vaulting over the horse or doing circuit training in the gym hanging from the wall bars by your arms, we were all shapes and sizes. The conditions could be awful, with sleet, snow, cold rain, thick mud and water filled trenches, just like an assault course. In our first years at school, the PE teacher initially showed us the route to take, forgetting that we were 11 year olds and soon the runners would string out. Luckily the return would follow adjacent paths through the woods, we quickly learned that if you were not into long distance running and that if you hung back, you could hide out in the woods and join the compliant and eager lads later on the way back, by cutting the route and we just joined them on the last half mile, splashing ourselves with mud and feigning breathlessness if needed!

Hanging about in the woods one day and sitting on a big log waiting for the group to run back, there was four of us, as we are crouching behind the brambles and undergrowth, we notice rolled up magazines in a rotting hollowed out tree trunk laying on the ground. As we pulled them out, we notice that copies of Parade, Reveille and lots of Health and Efficiency magazines, now all testosterone fuelled and rising, a bunch of 12 and 13 year olds, were normally out of reach on the top shelf of our local newsagent and now getting your hands on them induced such titillation, many will remember the pages could contain something of interest with that hormone process! We look at each other, wondering who is going to initiate the discovery and call the shots, we need someone to make a decision! Quickly, one H&E is quickly opened, black and white pictures of ladies, posing in an athletic naked stance, expletive depletives are muttered and we look around to see if anybody is watching us!

We can hear noises, what do we do?! Option 1, stuff back inside the log and risk them not being there next time? Option

2, relocate them to another log or hiding place? Option 3, take them back to school, great sniggering, perhaps a trading and selling opportunity or get found out and risk punishment with the cane! We can hear the first runner coming past, one of those well-behaved boys who never did anything naughty and a keen long distance runner, we panic a bit and stuff them back in the hollow log, making a mental note of where they were. We get back to school, pretending we were out of breadth and completed the whole run, we were more puffing with excitement, because who do we tell? We all keep quiet, waiting for next week, needless to say "the stash was gone" – we thought there was a mole in the group!

Swimming lessons were also on the curriculum in the winters, for me this was a horrid experience, I got very travel sick as a child, but the journey was horrendous. A late 1950's, noisy smelly forty seater coach would arrive, belching diesel fumes as it waited in the school drive outside the main doors or back gate. After rolling our swimming trunks in an old towel and stuffing it into our Duffel bags, we would jump on the coach, rush to get to the back seat for the thankfully short ride to Richmond. Forgetting sitting at the back allowed and always seemed to suck in the exhaust fumes through the bodywork, this awful feeling of sickness would wash over me, like a dog out of a car window, I would try to gulp in fresh air from one of the gaps in the windows.

Arriving at Parkshot Richmond Public Baths, we would file up the stairs to the entrance, I wore glasses, they steamed up as soon as the warm chlorinated air and that sickly smell hit my nostrils, compounded by the coach sickness. I just wanted to lie down, not to walk around to one of the poolside freezing changing rooms, with a six inch gap at the bottom. If you were in the pool and the edge you could see people in states of undress – which always caused a laugh between us boys! Again, it seemed ex-services personnel giving the swimming lessons, luckily their discipline got us all swimming unaided very quickly and ditching those blue floaties, with some of the naughty boys even being pushed in, to get them swimming. Getting dressed, you hoped you wouldn't drop any clothes, as you hopped about trying to put your socks on damp feet onto that soaking wet floor or through that wooden slatted floorboard in the cubicle, getting dressed quickly over a damp body, especially your vest and underpants, pulling socks over wet feet was never that easy, with some kids looking under the gap in the door laughing at you struggling!

Richmond Public Baths were built in 1882 and not really up to modern standards after 80 years, in 1938 plans to build an open air pool and sports pavilion for £35000 on land in Old Deer Park, but was postponed in 1939 – for obvious reasons. It wasn't until a young child got trapped in the grating at the bottom of the pool and unfortunately died, it closed immediately. Plans to build a complex named "Pools On The Park", consisting heated indoor and grass surrounds for sunbathing with an outdoor pool were soon in place and completed in 1966, where we would rush from the outside cold pool, through the glass sliding doors into the warm heated indoor pool, it was luxury. Now, interestingly a Grade II listed building.

In the summer holidays, much warmer days and living in Ham, we frequented the 1930s art deco Twickenham Outdoor Pools or Lido, travelling down Ham Street again using the ferry, with our bicycles and along the river. A lovely pool, big fountains at both ends, diving boards in the middle, concrete to sunbathe on, lockers and your key on a rubber band around your wrist or ankle. A cafe serving Bovril for cold days, or weak warm orange squash on hot days, along with a selections of Walls ices, Wagon Wheels, Kit Kats, Penguins, Potato Puffs and Mars Bars on the counter and early practice chatting up the girls. We also had access to two other Lidos of Teddington and Hampton.

After Gym, Games and or a Cross Country, showers were always compulsory. Now for boys in puberty and assume girls too, we are all in the various stages of sizes, shapes and physical development, for many this was an horrendous body image time. Larking about, changing room pastimes activity for the lads included nipple twisting, soap pushed in your mouth, grabbing the boobs of any chubbier lad, a flick of a wet towel, 'look at the size of that!' humiliating remarks about hair growth and physique, the hiding of clothes. The when lads remarked on my large burn scars on my thigh, I was generally was defended by mates and the antagonist was told to 'stop picking on him, leave him alone!'. It would get so noisy and raucous; the PE teacher would come in and tell everybody to get out of the communal showers. Now, this is a dodgy moment, because if you couldn't find, didn't have or forgot your towel for various reasons, you had one or two opportunities to explain why, the third time would involve punishment with a size nine gym slipper. Bending over in the nude and wacked, leaving an impression on your buttocks, literally for the rest of the day! Always thought, perhaps the teacher got some pleasure from this action, but you never forgot your towel ever again, unless you were stupid!

I really enjoyed Art and I took a GCE O Level in the fourth year, my interest in this subject was down to a Miss Patten (later Mrs Hamp), I think my first ever 'older woman' crush. Looking like a Ready Steady Go presenter, on the lines of Cathy McGowan, tall, attractive, that 60s Mod style bobbed hair, blouses and mini-skirts or a flowery Biba mod style dresses. When we painted still life, she would glide around the art room, sometimes standing behind me, I would catch a whiff of her perfume, shyly I would say "Miss, having trouble painting this apple, can't get the shape right, what should I do?", she would say "Ok, load the brush" and she would guide my hand to the paper and help me paint it, leaning over me! For any 13 year old boy with a crush – what more can I say, along with another 150 other boys, we were all in love with her. Mr Mapp also worked in the art department, he wore a trendy suit, shirt and always a bow tie, very arty looking, sometimes sandals, the sort of face you would see on one of those educational black and white schools programmes or late at night, smoking and having a debate, which you watched when nothing else was on the TV in those days.

I am pleased to say we had some really good teachers, Mr Harvey, our maths teacher, a young looking chap (compared to other masters who looked very old then!), tweed or checked jacket with leather elbow pads. It took a lot to get him annoyed, but noisy classes would see him throwing pieces of chalk to the offending boys or even girls across the room, even launching the odd chalk duster, when that didn't work. He sometimes struggled with his breathing, especially when trying to quieten down a class, to our shock, one day he collapsed in front of us all, the class went deathly silent very quickly, the form monitor ran to get help quickly from the next classroom. We never did know what happened, whether it was an asthma attack or something else. From that day on and that school year, we always were well behaved for him, it was if we knew that we should not get him anxious, for the rest of the school career when he was teaching Maths.

Mr Wittekinde, another good teacher, who took his English lessons mostly in the library in my time, also used as a form room, with desks sometimes going down into the book shelve aisles, which made some pupils hard to see. This teacher commanded the highest respect, his aura just told you to be quiet and listen, he would throw out questions and you got his reverence, if you were listening and answered them correctly, he had one of the quietest classrooms in the school, he was a lovely gentlemen. How did he do this, with some of the behaviour then, he had 'a system'. On a Monday morning, he would Sellotape his cane to the top of the desk, with three strips across the length of it, as the week went on and if pupils got noisy or disruptive, he would tell that particular boy or girl off - giving a firm warning to the rest of the class - and remove another strip of tape. On the third misdemeanour of the week, the offending pupil would get the cane or ruler across the palm of the hand, in front of the class, depending on whether you were a serial disrupter or first time offender. For the rest of the week, he would have the entire pupil's full attention! He did introduce me to Dickens, Great Expectations and a Tale Of Two Cities, which I enjoyed, because a film went with it!

Woodwork and Metalwork, was also a favourite subject of mine, I loved working with my hands and being practical, taking things apart and putting them together, so making something from scratch was ideal, whether in wood or metal. The workshops were adjacent to each other, Mr Day and a Mr Elliot ran these and taught you how to use chisels, saws, lathes, make joints, use a furnace and bellows to heat, bash and bend metal, with no real protective wear except a brown or white coat. We were all at risk from maiming ourselves, so the teachers were very strict in keeping us safe and well behaved and when they showed us how to bend a hot piece of metal or using a band saw, they wanted our complete attention and concentration. These afternoons or mornings could be over a hour and a half to two hours and all the boys from the same year and there could be over 40/50 boys across the two workshops sharing workbenches. The girls having domestic science at the time or cooking, we always asked and inspected the girls Tupperware of cake tins for any food going spare on the way home. All these skills allowed us to become Jack's and Jill's of all trades, never really masters of one, but served us well.

One day, we were being shown how to cut a dovetail joint, watching Mr Elliot, who was renowned for hitting you around the head with a bit of two by one inch piece of wood, for not watching or listening to his instructions, mostly to do with safety. A couple of the naughty lads from our year's lower forms, obviously not listening, one was in front of the teacher and one was behind. The lad in front, was being distracted by the lad behind who wasn't listening either. Mr Elliot was well aware of this, watching in the reflection of a window pane, in one motion as he pulled his arm back quickly in a sawing motion catching the boy right under the chin with his elbow, knocking him to the ground. We didn't know whether to stifle a snigger or laugh out loud, but the lad was a bit of a bully anyway! Needless to say the rest of us listened intently to his instructions for the rest of his lesson and our school years. I can still make a dovetail joint today, in fact I made a set of bookshelves in the fourth form that I used in my flat and first house until the 1980s.

Mr Day, taught us well, when it came to using a ruler, telling us constantly "Measure Twice, Cut Once" – every time I attempt DIY, I can still hear those words and see him standing there in his brown work coat looking on! Mr Day had a metallic blue three wheeler, called a Messerschmitt, it was like a Luftwaffe cockpit on wheels, it always bought some amusement, as us boys made RAF Spitfire machine gun noises as he drove up the school drive in the morning.

French was an interesting subject, I truly believe that we thought it was a good idea to learn another language, but unless you were one of the Ham middle classes who ventured to, what my mother called The Continent, 'What's the point!?'. To us, it was a place of naughty films, mime artists, frogs legs and snails, wine, garlic, strange looking cars (Citroen DSs, 2CVs, Renault 4s), stripy jumpers and berets, a man who sold onions from house to house on his bicycle, a place where British soldiers went to take part in two world wars and De Gaulle who seemed to be anti-Brit! Too many verbs and not easy to grasp for me, the wonderful thing about this lesson, is sometimes we would get a visiting, very attractive young French mademoiselle, who would be on an exchange programme or the early stages of teaching English. Now picture the scene, our frumpy British French teacher would introduce this seemingly very young chique, Parisienne mademoiselle, well dressed in the fashions of the times. Boys attention locked into this vision standing there and that sexy accent and scent, sweeping over us! Our teacher has now left the room, after telling us to behave as she would be back soon. Now, when you go to a state co-education school the classroom is a good mix, she starts talking, all the boys quickly have fallen in love and the girls generally taking a dislike, because she was so attractive. This one starts well and gains our attention – some in the past, have lost it already - she tells us to give ourselves a French Christian name from a list, copied on a Banda machine which had the odour of methylated spirit, the same smell and a reminder of exam papers – I choose Raoul, the idea was good every time she asked us a question, we would answer "Je m'appelle Roaul, et la reponse est...". Still the only bit of French, I took away from school!

However, as everybody knows when you stand in front of 30 state school council house kids, it takes about 30 seconds to lose control, many a trainee or young locum stand in teacher, broke down in tears or ran to get help in my day. The 30:30 rule, we called it!

This brings me to another occasion in class, it may have been the 3rd Form, at the age of about 14 going on 15. One of our 'cocky confident' boys, who really didn't get on with a new history teacher after a couple of run-ins, was asked to explain the "Corn Laws", after not listening, making some inane response, to do with Kelloggs. Obviously this didn't help the situation and the boy was sent to the back of the class to read up, after a while, we can all smell the citrus of an orange, it's the lad who was sent to the back, now with a big smile on his face, beckoning trouble. The teachers back turned, again chalking and talking, a buzz arises around the classroom, turning around and she knows who the culprit is. She asks him to hand the orange over, he denies having one, she goes toward him, instead he quickly passes it to the lad across the aisle, who then passes it on to the next pupil and so on. By this time the teacher is apoplectic, chasing this orange around the classroom, eventually she bursts into tears and shouts she is off to get the Headmaster. After a minute Mr Thomas crashes through the door, goes up to the boy, grabs his hair, blazer and an ear in one action and drags him off for "six of the best!". I always thought the good thing - if I can say that? - about corporal punishment is, it made you think about the consequences of disrupting class teaching and I think kept many a boy and girl on track, did me certainly!

Break times were always a welcome relief, especially after a double lesson of Maths or you were the next to read aloud in class. Pre-organised, tennis ball footie matches on the playground or a plastic football game bought in by a lad. Picking a team was always, great for good footballers and disappointing for the not so good players and down to the last comment "you can have him!" The game would regroup at all breaks throughout the day.

Other playground games would be based on a crazes like yo-yo's or sometimes get a little boisterous, British Bull Dog, played again on a set space in the playground. One or two players would be the bulldogs, the aim of the game is to get across the playground and not get tagged and if you were you became one. Until one person left, this was great practice for rugby, swerving, feigning a run etc., but could mean the ripping off of a blazer pocket. Another game was a group of boys would line up against a wall, someone who had a tennis ball, would throw it as hard as they could and try and hit you, which meant you were out. This happened until the last one standing, I have to say that this was usually organised by the 'bigger lads' who could throw hard at us 'smaller lads' against the wall!

Another game - Bung The Barrel, where a lad would put his back against a tree, we had enormous Oaks in our school fields, another lad would then bend over hold onto his waste, then a team of about six or more would form a line making a platform with their backs. When ready, another team with the same amount of players, would leapfrog onto their backs and shuffle up. This could and often and did end in tears with some painful injuries and even broken bones.

Lunch breaks or dinner hours as we called them, mainly because it was for some of us, the only hot meal of the day, a later meal or tea was usually taken around 4.30pm when returning home. The lunch breaks were great for me, because two of my friends group at school were sons of the cooks. At morning break, we would go around to the back of the kitchens and through the open windows with steam billowing out, especially on a cold day, Dave Brown or Danny Mahoney, would shout out, "What's the dinner today, Mum?", a head would poke out and say "Meat Pie, Mash and Peas or Liver and Bacon and for pudding a Manchester Tart or Rice Pudding with a blob of jam". Now, if you were second sitting, favourites would run out, because we knew literally 'people on the inside' they would hold back any requests and we would be in an ideal position to have "Seconds" – meaning another serving!

We were very lucky at our school that the food was always well prepared, I believe about 90% of pupils stayed for lunch then and on the whole mainly enjoyed it. Memories of school puds stand out in my mind, Coconut Jam Tart, Bakewell Tart, Crumbles of all descriptions, Apple Pie, Spotted Dick, Steam, Sponge and Treacle Puds, Cornflake Slices etc all served up with thick custard. All this for initially 2/6d per week! Friday was great, always Fish, Chips and Peas.

Sitting down in, with the posh name of a Refectory or Dining Room, meant in the earlier years, the older boys would have demanded your Manchester Tart from you, or steal a sausage from your plate, out of sight of the beady eyed Dinner Ladies. Blazers with stains of drying mash potato would abound, flicked from knives or you would sometimes find an upside down salt cellar, slightly unscrewed so that it would empty the contents into your blazer pocket to be found later during a lesson along with other cold food items.

1964 is a bit of emotional upheaval for me, having started a new school, realising its the last years of my education, home life for me is ok, especially when my father's not around – sadly to say, any son or daughter should see their father as a role model, I saw other fathers in our street doing 'Dad' things, coaching sporting and kicking football skills, fixing punctures, working in the garden on a Sunday, building sledges, trolleys using old pram wheels, taking the family picnics, holidays, on trips and days out. It just didn't seem fair at the time, that my brother, myself or together we never had those experiences. I became very angry at this time and had a few melt downs, generally on my own or fighting with my brother, controlling these was jumping on my bike and just peddling frantically looking for someone or something to distract me, especially if my father was at home. Because my brother, was a little older, I lived many years in that 'only child' syndrome, happy in the company of other kids, but at the same time happy in my own company and the hours I spent on my own.

My love of boxing from taking an interest from 'The Big Freeze' of 1962/63, in February 1964 it really gets a boost, a 22 year old 1960 Olympian gold medal boxer takes on the experienced heavyweight Sonny Liston in his mid 30s, beats him in a major upset to take the World Heavyweight Championship. Cassius Clay or The Louisville Lip, using expressions like 'Float like a butterfly, sting like a bee!', his mouth never stopped, but his skills and footwork were memorising, soon becoming The Peoples Champion.

A year later he changed his name to Muhammad Ali, famously he refused to be 'Drafted' into the Vietnam War, claiming that he should be exempt as a minister of the religion of Islam. It is reputed the Ali would rather go to jail than face reprisals from the Nation of Islam organisation where Elijah Muhammad declared that Vietnam was a 'White Man's War', even if he would accepted 'The Draft' he most certainly been offered a noncombat role as Elvis Presley in 1957 and Joe Louis performed in WW2. Sugar Ray Robinson stated that possibly he may have been assassinated like his friend Malcolm X who was killed by a member of The Nation Of Islam in reprisal for his criticism of the organisation. The deposed champion in June 1967 was convicted and sentenced to 5 years in jail and a $10,000 fine and stripped of his titles, but still kept his training up and kept healthy and in shape. That decision was overturned in 1971, he was an enormous inspiration for Black Americans and fought for Civil Rights. Famously known for historic fights, such as The Fight of the Century, - two undefeated heavyweights - against Joe Frazier, Smokin' Joe in March 1971, which Frazier won who seemed to represent pro-war feeling regarding Vietnam and Ali who was anti-war. The Rumble in the Jungle against undefeated George Foreman and reputedly watched by 1 billion TV viewers worldwide from Zaire in October 1974, Ali winning by a knockout. The Thrilla in Manilla and Joe Frazier again which Ali won in October 1975. Ali's boxing record, fought 61 and won 56, a great orator, spoken word artist, retiring from the ring in 1981, diagnosed with Parkinson's syndrome, he passed away in June 2016 aged 74, after making many public appearances. To our generation he will always be The Greatest. In the UK it inspired Johnny Wakeling to write and have a number 21 hit in the charts with 'In Zaire', produced by Robin Blanchflower who gave interestingly gave Carl Douglas a number 1 with Kung Fu Fighting.

Luckily, days out were a real treat for me with a capital T, Paul lived just across the road, like me his brother was a lot older, his father drove a really nice green Ford Consul Mark 1, the rounded shape of the 1950s, at least once, maybe twice a year during the summer holidays, they would invite me for a day at the seaside, sleeping over, to leave early, to miss the traffic of course. Generally, it would be to Bognor Regis or Littlehampton, two pebbly beach resorts with amusements, funfairs, fish and chips, sticks of rock, candy floss and sea food stalls. I always suffered from car sickness, but generally on the way down, the car games and excitement kept it at bay, with a constant supply of Barley Sugars. So we arrive and quickly set up camp on the beach, towel and woollen swimmers, ready for a fun day. Now the early sixties was not a time for protective sun creams – or in fact any form of defence from the rays, except a cap or legionnaires hat that also covered your neck or a knotted hanky for a bald headed man. Many hours playing in and on the edge of the sea, then the call came to get our rusty tin bucket and spades together and to make the trip home. Before we left we would visit a seafood stall and indulge in one of the little saucers of cockles, liberally sprinkled with pepper and a squirt of vinegar. At the same time in feeling the heat was rising on our burnt shoulders and backs.

The return journey and our pulsating, searing backs now red raw, we pull over and luckily Pauls mum always had a bottle of Calomine Lotion, a product that I always got confused with Windolene – you know that product you rubbed on your windows, not just to clean, but stopped people from looking through you windows when doing some decorating or blanking the larder windows to stop the sun turning your milk sour on the cold shelf, in a heat wave. Armed with cotton wool, she would now dab the forming blisters on the top of your shoulders and your back, we were told it would relieve the pain, along with this and now my travel sickness gaining pace in the darkening night skies as we drive home. Pauls dad would again, kindly stop in a lay-by, for me to be perhaps sick and regurgitate the cockles not to the sea, but to a grass verge on the A22. However, I always enjoyed the days, pack lunch or perhaps a bag of chips and the pleasure of his Dad's company, even if it wasn't mine and for that I will ever be grateful!

My father would just come and go, sometimes for days, to be honest when he wasn't there, I really enjoyed the time, spent with my mother, just the two of us. The evenings would be great, settling down to Dr Finlay's Casebook, Hancock's Half Hour, This Is Your Life, Sunday Night at the London Palladium, games shows like Double Your Money, The Wednesday Play, Armchair Theatre, Top Of The Form, Mr and Mrs, Take Your Pick, Perry Mason or Ironsid and perhaps a Friday night treat of some more coconut mushrooms, or a box of Milk Tray around Mum's birthday time from my brother, they were forever her favourite confectionary. Coronation Street was always a favourite as Weatherfield is supposed to be just outside Manchester central and the accents of the City were familiar, unusual on TV then. But I do remember discussing 'Corrie' with a fellow classmate one day and saying his Mum didn't watch 'foreign' language programmes! To add atmosphere to an entertainment programme or film we would turn the lights off watching the 'telly' pretending we were at the pictures.

My brother Keith, who was seven years older than me and now 18 years old, after work he just doesn't want to stay in watching the telly, especially with a little brother and his Mum.

My mother was always a very positive person, a happy disposition, a 'half full' person or the 'glass is just too big', with the ability to always see a silver lining and that glimpse of a blue sky, even on rainy days. Constantly hoping and reminding me that's everything is going to be OK and Dad 'may' change his ways one day, for the sake of his sons. As nearly a 12 year old, I seem to slowly realise she now could be holding on to a false hope and that he may never change and feel that in her own heart, being a tenacious person there was always optimism and real hope.

She is aware and doesn't forget that still in the 1960's, that divorce is not an easy thing and can be expensive in engaging any legal help. A women divorcing a man, had to prove or have evidence to use grounds of adultery, drunkenness or insanity, he did have affairs but they were generally for confidence trickster purposes.

I think she knew, deep down inside that it was never going to work out and that he was never going to leave our home, without a fight and she was caught in an emotional trap. Even, if my mother could file for legal separation through the court, which could still involve discussions of child custody and financial support. Unbelievably, it wasn't until 1969 that the Divorce Reform Act was passed, which allowed divorce after separation for two years, if both parties agreed or five years, if it was contested and only one person wanted a divorce. A term was introduced of 'irretrievably break down of marriage and mental cruelty', meaning no partner had to find or prove 'fault'.

Its early spring 1965 and as dawn breaks, again on an early morning theres a loud banging on the front door, in a strange half light in the sky that happens at that time of the year. My heart is thumping, not knowing what's going on, my brothers bedroom is next to mine and he runs downs. I can hear muffled sounds verifying who Keith is, I hear a voice say "I am a Detective Constable from Richmond CID, is your father home?" Keith must have nodded, they push the door open, I go to my bedroom door and see two burly policemen rushing up our stairs. They check mine, then my parent's room, my brothers room and he is there, lying in bed. They confirm his identity and say that famous phrase that we heard many times from Dixon of Dock Green, PC49, No Hiding Place, Z-Cars and many other TV shows of the time "Keith George Clark, your under arrest for..................." don't remember anything now, think I just got upset, it's not the first time that we have had a brush with the law and burly policeman and certainly when they come to your house unannounced, it's a shock for everybody. I saw the Police Force as protecting and an organisation that you respected, it seems so strange.

My mother was always concerned about me as the younger son and the consequences of our father's actions and their repercussions, literally bringing them home. My father is now put on remand, held in Wormwood Scrubs and Brixton, awaiting proceedings at Kingston Crown Court, my brother explains to me that it may be some time before he is free again. I am later told that he has received a two years prison sentence, I am also kept away from any local newspapers that would publish the court proceedings and any details.

I am upset, not for the absence of my father or myself, but I feel for my mother, a proud woman and any embarrassment within the village, her pain, and again the financial hardship and effort required to bring up two boys, throughout the 1950s but now in the early 1960s. Support or National Assistance as it was called only came in the form of free school meals for me, mainly because my brother was residing at home, working and his wage was included in any household income review.

Walking and going to school could have been a problem with people knowing, firstly no one has seen him and secondly he is in prison, ironically having not a time, considering its supposed to be a punishment, having three meals a day, his roll ups, a nice rest and in a cosy Open Prison with all the freedom that could bring and for him with no responsibilities, unlike my mother. I would say a comfortable life as he knows the system and would be a model prisoner and that would always help with any parole hearings.

His skills as a baker came in very useful, which means he normally got a job in the prison kitchen, while Mum was out of the house 10 hours a day, trying to put on a brave face in the presence of people she works with and around the village when shopping, never really having any social life. Our neighbours were great, especially Auntie Mary and Auntie Joan, trying to encourage her out to the cinema or around their houses for a cup of Maxwell House or a cup of tea and a rich tea biscuit for a chat.

Having a free lunch ticket was given for a few things, loss of spouse due to death, a father or mother who is chronically sick and cannot work, divorce or destitution ie there were still very poor families around in the village. A 'prison sentence' came under temporary loss of spouse's earnings – ironic, as we didn't get any money from him in the short time he was at home - and that's the only 'hand-out' or charitable payment, my mother would take, knowing that it would give us a hot meal during the week.

Every Monday morning register would be taken and after calling your name, you would go up to the teachers desk, hand over your 'Dinner Money' for the week of sixpence a day, for someone on free school meals, you didn't need to go to the front, one girl in our class had sadly lost her father due to an illness, it had been explained to us why, when she was absent, so we understood why she sat at her desk during registration. Given that divorce and separations are still quite rare in the early sixties – for good and bad reasons sometimes - there was still a stigma attached to divorce, but for a parent going to prison, would be a tremendous shock for any classmate and would involve me in handling lots of questions and to some point unbearable with lots of denials from me about my father and whereabouts.

However, the form teacher decided that I would walk to the front of the class and pretend to pay for my school meal ticket every Monday morning with cash, which kept any questioning at bay. Now getting used to my new big school with 350 pupils and its geography, finding my way to classrooms, science labs, workshops and art block. What you did learn very quickly was who the lads to avoid direct eye contact were, you know that angry boy look - sometimes labelled 'The Nutter' or the gang of Nutter's around the playground and strange how some could be just damn spiteful, dead arming or saying horrible things! And that lad, the repeat offender, weekly standing outside the headmaster's office, waiting to be caned, not bothered, thumbs up to everybody, claiming it was some Badge of Honour!

As everybody knows, crazies of Civil War cards with Confederates in various stages of mutilation and football cards with tasteless gum, yo-yo's, jacks etc they go around the different form years or perhaps the whole school.

Autumn Term bought 'The Conker Season', the only exciting thing the helped with that sick feeling of going back to school after summer, with that smell of sawdust, new varnish on school hall floor and sanded graffiti laden desktops. Living in Ham, we had endless Horse Chestnut trees, prime gathering spots for us living on the north side of the village was Riverside Drive Rec', with something like 5 or 6 magnificent aged trees. But it was all about timing, don't knock down too early, they were too small, don't leave it too late, they would fall to the ground and get picked up by everybody else, you would lose the ability to have the pick of the crop, harvested by cricket stump was preferable, but hopefully it doesn't get caught in the tree. Other good 'conkering' areas were Ham Avenue, Ham Common or the slopes of Richmond Park near The Dysart Arms and the pedestrian Petersham Gate entrance, although this was open season for day trippers, the kids from Richmond and around south west London.

Now what makes a Conquering Conker King? Depending on your experience, to play 'Conkers' do you use a fresh one, that's still relatively soft and can take punishment, or do you harden up in the airing cupboard or oven at home, before or after soaking in vinegar? The problem is with a dried hard one is, it can shatter on impact, leaving you with that embarrassing moment of holding up a length of sisal or string with a knot on the end – conker free, which would bring guffs of laughter! And the winner saying 'Who's next suckers?'.

Whichever strategy you adopted was risky. After preparing your conker, you would use a meat skewer to bore a hole through, carefully threading a bit of string or even a shoe lace. But do you adopt a long string or short method of attack. You hold the conker between your fore and middle finger, after measuring the swing arc. Now in theory the lad holding his conquer for the impending strike, must not move it out of the way when the strike is coming down, which could result in a foul, depending how big the lad was or a severe conker strike on a finger – and you do not want to do that. Hours of fun in and out of school, the school playground would have tens of dozens of squashed and smashed neglected conkers and now chestnuts, at home we roasted in the ashpan tray below the fire grate on cold winter nights.

With the Autumn half-term over, we return to school knowing in about six weeks time we will break up, after a rocky time with my Dad being arrested and a long time before he returns, somehow things become slightly little better at home and the tension calms, no muffled arguing from my parents and trapping my ears and head between a pillow, things are peaceful, even Mum seems happier. I can only assume she won't have to battle with my father's coming and goings for some time, however she must have been very sad about the situation for herself and what the future would bring.

At school, I enjoyed art, metal and wood work, science, geography and especially history. Struggled with English – all those adjective words – meaning 'a word whose main syntactic role is to modify a noun or noun phrase' What! - Living on a council estate, everybody calls you posh if you said a word with more than two syllables, we thought 'Awrightmate' had three! Mind you I always did get the homework in on time, even if it was written occasionally on the school playground, with the impression of tarmac on the page, like a brass church rubbing or someone's foot and with the help or copying Paul Sossick, Dave Brown or Stuart Alexander, the bright lads in the class! Stuart was a very clever lad, always first in class and a great sportsman out of the boys and had this knack of not looking as if he was attentive, just mucked about and distracted us, but he would do the tests and exams and always it seemed came top out of the boys. One year he broke his right arm and wrote left handed in his exams and still came top! It just wasn't fair!

Maths, well, initially for me was a subject enough to make anybody have a panic attack, especially when asked by the teacher to show the working out of the sum, let's take an Algebraic Equation of x little $5 - 3x + 1 = 0$, of course we all know that this is an algebraic equation with integer coefficients. I enjoyed my Log books and slide rule it made maths more tangible. French – assez parle, when to change the preposition and being careful not to confuse my Le and my La's with Au!! Verbs – Sacre Blue! The trouble is these are important subjects so I persevere, with my mother's words in my ear saying 'You can only try your best, son'.

I always thought, a bit like Liverpudlians, the Irish, East Enders, Geordies, etc and many not so well-off communities, that council house kids seem to have a survival mode built in, an innate sense of humour, many of us 50's born kids seemed to be very positive or optimistic about anything and everything, if anybody said anything negative they were labelled 'spoilsports' or 'partypoopers' and could risk losing their membership to a gang, by way of not being invited or included in any activities. When us boys or girls engaged in any conversations, it was just natural to broker humour around it, be witty, be funny, be entertaining, some were better than others, but it always raised your spirits, we were just 'haffin' a larf' or mucking around!'. It always gave me a bit of a lift watching and listening to groups of boys and girls engaging, I seemed to be more interested in listening, more than an interesting lad in a group, remembering Walt Disney's, Bambi film and the quote from Thumper (the rabbit) 'If you can't say anything useful, don't say anything at all!', however I think it was mostly down to shyness.

The downside to this, was our ability to concentrate in class, if someone replied to the teacher with a wrong answer, when asked, for a lot of us it would mean embarrassment and what we called 'a cherry up!' or to go bright red. Immediately certain people would start cracking jokes and inevitably would end up in me being distracted or starting to talk, reflected mainly and documented in our twice yearly school reports. Phrases like 'easily distracted', 'will talk instead of listening', 'could do better', 'lacks interest in subject', 'needs to concentrate', and 'attention wanders far too easily' – litter my report.

The great thing is, I am selected for the first year football and rugby teams, not a natural selection, but work effort in both PE and Games are thankfully noticed and it's easier than maths. I feel really proud of myself, we go from a team who swarm around the field unorganised, to a team where we play in position and pass the ball. Our rugby team is captained no less than by Stuart Alexander, not only academic but a very good all round sportsman except for football if I recall, helped by his athletic build for a 12 year old. Our football team was developed into a great squad, with Paul Sossick, Dave Brown, Paul Newitt, Kevin Blower, Billy Pritchard, Bob Murphy, Alan Tomkins and our very own centre half Bobby Moore aka Barry Catlin our team would consistently finish high or win the school leagues, from the middle sixties with the addition of the year below lads of Robbie Good, Danny Mahoney and Terry Richens, bolstering the team until the late sixties. Many of this squad would be the nucleus of the Ham Venturers youth club football team later.

I noticed that a couple of my team mates have the new latest three white stripes pair Adidas football boots at around £4 and available from Bob Simesters in Kingston, a revelation in the middle 1960's, moulded or with replaceable studs that had a spanner supplied, lightweight, low ankles, worn by the best English First Division football players, like Georgie Best in his 1963 debut for Manchester United, I was so envious of Dave Brown and Paul Sossick in my school team, they both had a pair! - Adidas was formed by Adolf Dassler after an argument with his brother Rudolf who went on to create Puma, another popular boot in the 60s. Still have the 1965 Second Year team photo showing them off and my 1950s styled boots. In the late 60s, we played a newly introduced and recently constructed floodlit five-a-side football grounds and league, surfaced with tarmac at Heatham House Twickenham, originally playing in perhaps 'tennis' Greenflash's or school plimsolls, we found Adidas and Puma trainers that were designed to play such a sport on hard surfaces and winter surfaces where traditional studs were not suitable, these trainers had a special toecap design, meaning they didn't fall apart. They were so popular and became part of our leisure and fashion footwear collection, throughout the 70s, model names like Rekord, Samba, Gazelle, Pele, Tahara, Tornado and many more will be familiar to you even today. Falling over or getting shoulder barged on these pitches gave you some serious grazes that seem to take a long time to heal, some even cinder surfaces, later being covered in Astro-Turf, now giving you friction burns!

Unfortunately, my football boots, were handed down, oversized ankle boots with big toe caps, capable of punting a ball, not like the modern football boot at this time, mine would not look out of place on Stanley Matthews feet, in a 1950's photo cigarette card image. With studs, when worn out - think made from cork, with nails at the base - that needed a set of pliers to remove and a hammer when replacing. They would absorb water and leak being used for both soccer and rugby games, what would help though, is a tin of dubbin from the cobblers in Ham Street, a day before each match you would rub it in when the surfaces were dry so they would hopefully become more supple and above all waterproofed, for a time.

Sport for me was a distraction and a focus, I keep trying my best academically, but finish a low 23rd place out of thirty that Christmas of 1964, my good results and position being Art 1st , Woodwork 3rd and worst RK 23rd , and History 28th in class and although I really liked the subject, just panicked during exams!

Music was always on in our house, BBC Light programme in the kitchen, mum singing away, things must have been hard, so I guess it helped her mood, something at this time I never remember her being in a bad mood, unless scolding me for something that was well deserved. I remember 1964 for two 45 records, one was a real favourite of my mother's that year one, Peter and Gordon's A World Without Love, it was actually the first record that we bought especially for Mum, money saved from chores, birthday and filling timesheets in for my older brother and cleaning his shoes. Interestingly, this song was written by Lennon and McCartney, luckily for Peter he was the brother of Jane Asher who went out with Paul McCartney from 1963 to 68, meeting a 17 year old Jane at a Beatles concert at The Albert Hall, it got to number one that year of 1964. I even believe that Jane Asher's father talked to McCartney about going solo and his financial affairs at that time, the Beatle lived in the Asher's house in Wimpole Street W1 and shared the top floor with her brother, many fans knew he lived there and McCartney sometimes climbed roofs and fire escapes, in and out to avoid them. I still have that 45 single.

Another song was My Boy Lollipop, a 17 year old Millie (Small), which literally bounced into the charts, she had won a talent contest in Jamaica, moved to Kingston town and was noticed by Chris Blackwell of Island Records, who took her to London as her manager in 1963, My Boy Lollipop the hit song was recorded in a bluebeat style, a music genre that preceded ska and reggae. It got to number two in the UK singles chart in March 1964 and sold some 600,000 singles. During this time, coincidentally she dated Peter Asher and appeared on a Beatles TV special, so these two songs are connected and my first taste of that reggae genre, there is also a musical rumour that Rod Stewart played the harmonica on the track. Millie appeared on Tops Of The Pops and ATV's Thank Your Lucky Stars, with Keith Fordyce and the famous Janice Nicholls who said "Oi'll give it foive" in a thick Midlands accent. In May 1964 Millie guests as a judge on the panel of Juke Box Jury with host David Coleman, with that famous klaxon that would indicate a "Miss", a bell for a "Hit". I will always remember faces of an bemused and embarrassed audience as the camera caught them, before the voting on the Pinky and Perky song of Eeny Meeny Miney Mo, as it played!! A programme we all settled down to, after the Saturday football results in the early 1960's. Early 1965 saw her host a Ready, Steady, Go! TV special called Millie in Jamaica, her guests included Jimmy Cliff, Prince Buster and Byron Lee!

In 1964 our own 'Millie' or blue eyed soul girl, Lulu recorded her version of Shout, an Isley Brothers composition and their US hit in 1959 not to be confused with their 1962 version of Twist and Shout, covered on the first Beatles album Please Please Me in 1963 and Brian Poole and the Tremeloes the same year. In

1967 Lulu, made her acting debut and sang To Sir, with Love, a film that dealt with social and racial issues in an inner London school, starring Sidney Poitier the first black male to win an Oscar in 1964. In 1969 Lulu married Maurice Gibb divorcing in 1973, in 1977 married celebrity hairdresser John Frieda, in 1991 they divorced.

In the early 1960's, Chubby Checker's 'Twistin' The Night Away', created a new UK dance craze, you could see smartly dressed and up and coming Mods dancing to, on many TV programmes, weddings and family gatherings saw people, trying to do The Twist, some Grandparents, lowering themselves with a big knee bend and the unable to get back up, inebriated Mums and Dads, Aunties and Uncles, splitting their trousers or breaking seems on skirts and frocks and Twistin' competitions at holiday camps up and down the land and around the coastlines.

My mother loved Nat King Cole – incidentally the first African American to host his own TV series, I can see and hear my mother now, singing and standing at the kitchen sink, crooning 'Unforgettable' from the 1950's. In late 1964, Nat was diagnosed with lung cancer and sadly passed away the following February aged just 45, leaving a daughter Natalie, who went on to have her own successful career, sadly she passed away in 2009 aged 65.

Up to this time the Teddy Boys, Bikers and Rock and Roll seemed to be the new teenager, followed by Beatniks who liked jazz, dressed French style in stripy tops and wore beret's but tended to be more middle class, well educated, being urban and generally well read intellectuals. However, in the early 1960s a new subculture called Modernists came on to the scene, mostly out of the love of jazz, blues, R&B, later soul music, a term that combined gospel, jazz, rhythm, blues but must be danceable, these 'Mods' predominately came from working class.

The Twist was covered by many singers, my mother also loved Sam Cooke - who went to the same school as Nat King Cole, a little later - at this time I remember his 'Chain Gang' and the dancer 'Twisting The Night Away', the emotional and stirring 'A

Change Is Gonna Come', aligned with its Civil Rights message, it's not till later and listening more closer, i would realise its cultural and historical meaning. Sam earned the title 'The King Of Soul' for his distinctive voice and the influence of Gospel and Soul in popular music. Sadly, news reaches us from The States that on December 11, 1964, that Sam Cooke at the age of 33, is shot dead by the female manager of a motel in Los Angeles. The Courts ruled that Cooke's death was justifiable homicide. Since that time, the circumstances have always been called into question by his family.

If you look into time leading up to this incident, Cooke is friends with Cassius Clay and Malcolm X, a keen supporter of Civil Rights, a business entrepreneur, who has his own record label, publishing company and is a prolific songwriter, a modern black performer who wants and did control his finances himself. Some say, he could have been another Berry Gordy within the music business.

In 1963, Cooke unfortunately took counsel from a new manager, Allen Klein - who initially he trusted, advising him to take shares instead of money for tax reasons. The relationship sowered, they fell out and Sam wanted to cancel the contract. The music business can be controlled by unscrupulous people, some say gangsters or even The Mafia and would want to silence people and the artists who wanted change.

The night he was shot, apparently he had invited a woman back to a motel, the woman said she had fled from the room, ran and made a call from a telephone booth to say, 'she had just escaped kidnap', Cooke went to look for her and walked to the Motel office to ask her whereabouts. The manager said, he turned violent, feared for her life and had to protect herself, fighting him off with a broom and five gun shots.

On December 18 1964, 200,000 people fans lined up to view his body, at the funeral home in Chicago. He is buried in Glendale, California. Discrepancies abound, although his was fatally shot, Cooke's injuries were more severe than being hit with a broom. To this day, there is no evidence of any criminal conspiracy, but many parties had motive to remove him from the music business. Cooke, the son of a Reverend moved his family to Chicago from a very segregated Mississippi for a new start, a neighbour was Lou Rawls from a rival gospel group. He joined The Soul Stirrers in 1950, Cooke had 30 top 40 hits in the US between 1957 and 64. In 1961, he launched his own record label, which signed The Valentino's, whose members were Bobby Womack, his brothers and Johnny Taylor of 'Whose Making Love' fame in 1968 and the 1976 club hit 'Disco Lady' fame.

One of Sam's hits in 1961 was 'Cupid', written by Cooke, the B side of Johnny Nash's 'Hold Me Tight' a great and early rocksteady, reggae hit for me from 1968 and again in 1969, flipping it to the A side! Getting to 5 and 6 respectively in the UK charts, Nash also covered Cooke's 'Wonderful World' in 1976.

⁂⁂⁂

I always enjoyed the Christmas run up, The Petersham and Ham Sea Scouts Xmas Bazaar and Jumble Sale, as Cubs and now Scouts, we would help decorate the hall at the nearby All Saints Church. A magnificent red brick and Italianate terracotta building, incidentally where my parents met, when dances were held there during the war, apparently an American soldier or some local lads was annoying my mother and my father stepped in. All Saints was also requisitioned during WW2 and used as a command post for the nearby anti-aircraft emplacements in Richmond Park. Strangely the church was never consecrated and built for the expected growth of Petersham that never happened. It's also been a music studio, where Pavrotti recorded an album in 1976, it continued to be used for weddings until 1981 but ceased to be used as a church in 1986, my friends Jill and Nigel married there in 1982. It's now a private residence, and next to Petersham Village Hall.

At the end of the Christmas term, the school church service would be held at St Andrews with carols, decorations up and looking forward to and the excitement of the festive season and all the treats it may bring, fingers crossed. Mum without fail and with a small amount of money would always make this time really special, for all of us.

Christmas morning and my sack at the end of the bed, as always from Santa (Mum, I know now!) with some presents, a Blue Peter annual or something similar, a lookalike Chelsea football shirt, well it was royal blue with white collars and cuffs, a selection of Cadburys chocolate on a card in the shape of a stocking covered by what liked like a fishing net. We didn't expect a lot and Mum would buy some not-so expensive things on a subject we liked (fishing was a big hobby as living by the Thames), even second hand items, like a pair shin-pads would go down well, but what we got we enjoyed especially with Dad not being around, Mum was enjoying her time with her two boys. With my father 'banged up' the house that Christmas seems like a cosy, safe harbour and a nice place to be.

Children's Christmas TV was always something to look forward to from Crackerjack and Eamonn Andrews to How? and Fred Dinenage, themed live programmes and cartoons that would feature snowy or Christmas stories, Mum always had The Radio Times and the TV Times just for Christmas, I would look through them, taking a pencil and circling the programme I must see. My favourite programme was Blue Peter, full of interesting facts, events from collecting silver milk bottle tops for charity or making Christmas decorations out of two metal coat hangers and wrapped in crepe paper, especially the multiple uses of an empty Fairy Liquid bottles. Fact is, that I had another older woman crush on Valerie Singleton, could never take Susan Shranks and Magpie, never had the same educational capacity for me, although it did have popular charting groups on, with bemused children looking on.

Like any good big brother, Keith would pass me 6d or sometimes a shilling for still filling out his time sheets, and an extra bonus that Mum, announces that she is going to give me pocket money on a Saturday morning, subject to a few more chores. Informing me now that Keith will relinquish some of his responsibilities because of his age around the house. The payment comes in a form of 9d, it will buy me a comic, my choice was The Hotspur and some sweets, Blackjacks or Fruit Salads. Because of the competition in the amount of comics in those days, they would often give free gifts, like Football League Ladders, with press out team names you slipped into a slot in League positions after the football results on a Saturday, 3D spectacles, jumping frogs, plastic pop guns, target tiddly winks, a flapping bat with tissues wings you swung around your head. My favourite a Thunder Bang, a triangular folded piece of cardboard, you flicked in the air and made a 'crack' noise – this one was very common, along with a balsa wood plane kit. Nearly all made from cardboard and brown paper and slipped between the pages of your favourite comic now and again to encourage sales and to try and get you to purchase or ask for a comic annual at Christmas, a Beano, Dandy, Dan Dare and many more.

At this age you are now becoming more aware of international affairs and its leaders, particularly the assassination of JFK in 1963 two years earlier. Imagining how things would have been, if he had not been shot that day, Kennedy had ideas around Civil Rights and talked to great black leaders and understood their direction, as a 46 year old, there was a synergy with young Americans no matter what colour and creed. The Vietnam War and how Lyndon Johnson handled it later in the 1960s – what might have been, what laws and changes there may have been, will always be asked. Conspiracy theories will always abound around JFK and the reasons behind his assassination.

Great leaders don't come along that often, being born just eight years after WW2 and its victory led by our Prime Minister Sir Winston Churchill is still recognised as our victorious wartime leader and widely considered to be one of the 20th century's greatest leading statesmen. A great orator and quotes, when taking office as Prime Minister the first time 'I have nothing to offer but blood, toil, tears and sweat'. On the evacuation of the

British Expeditionary Force of over 300,000 British, French and Belgium's from France in 1940, his speech of defiance 'We shall defend our island, whatever the cost may be, we shall fight on the beaches, we shall fight in the fields and in the streets, we shall fight in the hills; we shall never surrender'. Interestingly the original speech was never recorded in The Chamber, but heard on the evening BBC radio news, read by an impersonator and mimic Norman Shelley, an actor who did the voice of Larry The Lamb on Children's Hour. The Battle of Britain speech in August 1940, 'Never in the field of human conflict, was so much owed by so many to so few.....' mentioning the United States and freedom for Europe and the world, inciting defence of the British Isles against the Nazi's and Hitler. Long before the end of the war in 1942, 'Now this is not the end. It is not the beginning of the end. But perhaps, the end of the beginning!'

That image of Churchill in his hat and holding up his two fingers to signal victory, would inspire anybody to pick up arms and defend this Island. As did the defining image and poster of WW1 and Lord Kitchener's pointing finger and declaring 'Your Country Needs YOU'!

He had a second term as Prime Minister from 1951-55, I believe many of us didn't know that he was reportedly not a supporter of women's suffrage, he played a massive part in was responsible for tremendous losses at Gallipoli, bought the Black and Tans to Ireland to combat Irish revolutionaries. In 1921 negotiated with Sinn Fein, partitioned the six Protestant majority counties – known as Northern Ireland, and the rest of the country would make up The Irish Free State and a descent into a civil war. Tried to block West Indian immigration, in January 1955, telling the cabinet that the slogan 'Keep England White' was acceptable at the time.

In January 1965, Churchill now 90 years old and in failing health, we all knew his end was near, on the 24th day of that month, he passed away. For me it was the first time I had witnessed a State Funeral, unique as this was for a non-royal.

I remember that Saturday morning 30th January 1965, sitting in our front room, outside it was one of those gloomy, misty and one of those freezing fog days, with a hint of frost covering everything outside. After lying in State at Westminster Hall, where over 320,000 people filed passed, the procession and gun carriage draped with The Union Jack, 100,000's of people lined the streets to pay their respects, another 350 million people watched it on TV here and around the world. The funeral was held at St Paul's Cathedral attended by 3500, the largest gathering of world dignitaries for the next 50 years, including our Queen, one other queen, four kings, twenty two heads of state and ten former leaders. Notably absent was US President Lyndon Johnson, who it was said was ill at the time.

Churchillian is often used as a verb to describe people, certainly Churchill was seen as the wittiest, rudest, toughest politician ever to grace The House of Commons, thankfully for us in that time of the darkness in WW2. I love this quote from him, after being told that he might like to regulate his alcohol intake reputedly by Lady Astor, Winston replied 'I may be drunk, Miss, but in the morning, I will be sober and you will still be ugly'.

With working parents many of us that arrived home alone from school, were known as a 'Latch Key Kids' - the house key either being tied to a bit of string or sisal, to the knocker and pushed back through that spring loaded letterbox! – sometimes the front or back door key being hidden around various places in the garden - I don't really think security was a problem then, as valuables would be rare and the risk of break-ins was very low in the village. It was more about our ability to lose the key while playing at school or messing around on the way home. But it was always handy that you could open the small Crittal window by putting a spade under the frame at the corner and 'popping' it, as standby, I used to climb the drainpipe and was so small I could get in through the small toilet window!

Thoughts of, 'I'll do my homework later, it won't be a problem!', is you get to turn on the television, especially on winter nights, when playing outside wasn't really an option - you are in control of the tuner or the buttons on the TV panel and choose the programme, between 4.45pm and around 6pm you had TV viewing for the young on both channels, hence it was called 'Children's Hour'.

Puppeteering black and white programmes were on schedules, my early memories of seeing Muffin the Mule, Andy Pandy, The Woodentops, etc, on that small black and white screen, later cartoons like Popeye, Olive Oyl and Swee'Pea (whose child was that?), Wimpy – who liked hamburgers and Bluto or Brutus, did make me eat spinach though! Replaced later with The Double Deckers, HR Puff N'Stuff and many more are now in colour.

But a title that included the word 'Supermarionation', introduced us to some great early children's TV action, albeit that some of the scenes looking more like a giant model railway set. The puppets mouths moved in a different way, sometimes getting glimpses of metal wires, but what it offered was explosions around vehicles, hillsides, mountains and smoky dodgy water effects, but it was the late 50's and 60's, well before CGI, so it was quite impressive when young. The programmes were devised by Sylvia and Gerry Anderson, they had a tremendous run, starting with Twizzle in the late 50's, a boy doll that escapes from a toy shop with a black cat called Footso, they live in Stray Town a place that mistreated toys, his arms stretched out and made a ratchet noise. Torchy the Battery Boy, early '60's, another boy doll who lived in Topsy Turvy Land where toys and animals talked and cream buns grew on trees. A big favourite of mine – because I had a western cap gun in a plastic holster – very early 60's. Sheriff Tucker, his talking dog Dusty and Rocky the horse in Four Feather Falls, even think he had magic guns that fired by themselves when he was told to 'Put 'em up!', it foiled the baddies. Supercar and its test pilot Mike Mercury, who travelled the world in the air, on land and under the sea in search of adventures. Fireball XL5, a fleet of rockets, their Commander Steve Zodiac with Venus, Professor Matic and Robert The Robot. The middle 60's bought us Stingray, piloted by Troy Tempest of WASP and ably assisted by Phones and Marina. Led by Commander Shore and daughter Atlanta in a love triangle with Marina and Troy. Best thing though the haunting closing tune of Aqua Marina 'Marina, Aqua Marina, what are these strange enchantments that start whenever your near.....' with a nice latino beat behind it, what child didn't singalong with that!

1965 bought us Thunderbirds Are Go! Its 2065 and International Rescue are aiding humanity with the help of the Tracy family, Brains, Lady Penelope and Parker fighting evil forces. 1967 saw Captain Scarlet and The Mysterons, the evil Captain Black of SPECTRUM. Next was Joe 90, which lost my interest a bit, as now distracted by other things in life, but he did wear spectacles like me, similar to me, as adults said I looked like the reverse of The Milky Bar Kid, 'the Milky Bar Kid is tough and strong ....you finish it! The Andersons went onto make Space 1999, using real human characters, with some dodgy scenery! The yearly annuals sales of these were huge, there was even a glossy spin off comic called TV Century 21, published by the Andersons from 1965-71 and later called TV21, merging with other titles in the future.

Other earlier childhood programmes were Mr Pastry, a walrus moustachioed elderly man, dressed in a black suit and a bowler hat. He bumbled around, sometimes riding a wobbly bike and reminiscent of a variety hall slapstick comedians on stage. Oh, how we laughed at his antics in the and late 50's early 60's. Billy Bunter of Greyfriars School with Gerald Campion playing a 14 year old schoolboy at the age of 29 in that distinctive blazer! Another handled bar moustachioed, cane wielding headmaster Jimmy Edwards of Chisleberry School (using Great Fosters, Egham in the opening shots) in Whack-O! Some of you may also remember that it was a BBC Light Programme as a radio show, we would often see Jimmy Edwards as he often played at Ham Polo Club on a Sunday afternoon. Great fun running on that polo field and flattening the diverts between chukkas, other players who showed up were the Duke of Edinburgh and Prince Charles. Later on, comedians like

Dick Emery, 'ooh you are awful' and Harry Worth, who performed the optical illusion outside a John Collier shop I believe with lifting his arm and leg.

Captain Pugwash and his crew, one so called character called Master Bates and the associated urban legend that his name was something else? However, the somewhat dopey Master Bates had a tendency to mispronounce words – so read into that what you want. Warning, don't let the signature tune create an 'ear-worm' after reading this! Westerns, I think every lads escape with his toy gun and roll of caps, when fired gave off an aroma memory from my young days, who can forget Gunsmoke with Sheriff Mat Dillon, Wagon Train with Ward Bond, which ran from 1957-1965 with nearly 300 episodes. Rawhide with Rowdy Yates, played by a young actor called Clint Eastwood, who I believe went on to be very successful as an actor, film producer and director. Bonanza, High Chaparral and my last favourite western before going out, Alias Smith and Jones that ran in the early 1970s, two outlaw cousins trying to reform and earn an amnesty to go straight, starring Pete Dual as Hannibal Heyes and Ben Murphy as Kid Curry.

The Five O'Clock Club, with Muriel Young and Wally Whyton, featuring music of the day from charting artists, looking bemused at young children jumping and bouncing around to their music, with Ollie Beak and Fred Barker, this programme convinced me to try and learn to play my guitar, led by Bert Weedon and his guidance.

⁂

In hindsight and thinking 1965 is a watershed year for me, my second year at secondary school, now used to the school routine and mates, more importantly one year off teenagehood, being 13 years old was very much a milestone for any youngster growing up, similar to other milestones like 16 and having a job, 18 getting into places without false membership cards, youth hood finished at 21 years of age and then adulthood. Strange, how time drags during those school hours and flies when older!

Home life is good, Mum seems very happy mainly because my father is serving time again – I never want to know or even ask, mainly because his persistent crimes bought light sentences, normally having an easier time in an Open prison.

My school work improves during these times, because home life is more settled. Helped by mum, finding a great publication series by English University Press for Hodder and Stoughton in hardback, called Teach Yourself........, a distinction yellow and black dust jacket and a common design for each publication, a castle or building design on the front. First published in 1938, mainly for foreign languages, it was a series of books that was and especially throughout the war years to support studies, designed to help people that had time to read and to selfteach. The early war years saw schools destroyed by bombing and with daily teaching suspended, whether in the forces or perhaps even passing time in an air raid shelter, reading became an important part of life hoping to improve their grammar and of course listening to the radio. These books in the 1960's covered many areas from Air Navigation to Spanish. My own collection included French, Algebra, Mathematics, Science including Chemistry and Physics, the books stepped you through the learning stages and had little tests at the back to practice the skills learned and with helpful answers at the back.

Keith, always a keen angler, would often take me fishing on the banks of the nearby Thames, in the summer months, even night fishing which was a little spooky with all our nearby wildlife, but it was quite exciting to have a primus stove, for a cup of tea and take some sandwiches for a snack. Always interested in making up different types of bait and watching the maggots in the breathable container, sometimes left in the shed, when they turned into blowflies! Outside of the fishing season, he seemed to go out nearly seven nights a week and would meet young ladies, but I could and I would be a real pain when it came to him bringing them home 'for a coffee or drink'. If Mum worked late sometimes, catering for a dinner party, I was very much alone in the house generally watching TV in our front or 'sitting' room in the spring and summer months, great for entertaining, with a large comfy sofa, the ideal setting for a bit of romance, especially when you are eighteen or nineteen and with some wheels, as Keith was.

I could always tell when my brother was going to bring back a young lady, he would have a bath, shave and a change of clean underwear. I would smell the aroma of some deodorants and aftershave that would waft downstairs, dabbing on a bit of Old Spice, now upgraded to Brut, a cologne launched by Faberge in 1964 for a younger audience, advertised greatly with models dressed in mod clothing, sitting on scooters, in and on convertible cars. Later in 1973, saw the launch of a range called Brut 33, which had 33% of the original 'Essence of Man' in and reached a larger demographic. Many sports celebrities like Henry Cooper were used to advertise the brand and his famous strap line "Splash it all over!", - it should have come with a warning about splashing it near your private parts, - Barry Shene, David Hemery, and Harvey Smith were used in their marketing and TV adverts.

As Keith went out the front door on a 'hot date', I would shout 'goodbye then!' and ask what time will you be back? Rarely replying, but I knew when he was going to bring a young lady back, I would then set up camp, watching telly, lying on the main sofa, on his return with a very nice attractive young lady, I am prepared to do that cute little brother look, to the annoyance of my elder sibling.

On his return, Keith introduces me begrudgingly, him glaring at me with a 'get out now, leave us alone!' look, initially which I loved to ignore. He asks her if she wants a coffee or tea or even perhaps a Babycham or some other mid-60s refreshment, maybe even a 'Snowball' if near Christmas, not that there was a lot of choice, in our pseudo drinks cupboard. Again at the same time, Keith will now flick his head in that sort of 'Now get lost little bro!" or says 'I think Robbie Good and a couple of your mates are playing footie outside in the street, go and join them!'.

I sit tight as they head to the kitchen to make a drink, I may hear the girl say 'your little brother seems very cute?', the key words for me, now putting me in a bargaining position. They come back into the room, Keith's eyes rolling towards the door, he also now knows that it's down to some form of extortion from me, on the promise of money, sweets or perhaps a cinema trip, I will now leave the room or go out for a minimum payment, generally we agree on a shiny shilling or florin if it's a payday Friday! What a pain it must have been to have a younger sibling, a bit like a midge, wasp or mosquito that's annoying you!

⁂

At this time, music now starts to play a really big part in my life, a release, a distraction and therapy, now growing older, but aware that popular music TV programmes and radio are featuring new types of bands, The Beatles have now been around for a couple of years, The Stones are now also established, popular young music seems to be everywhere and featuring in the cinema regularly. The music scene is changing, my brother is lucky enough to see live bands – like The Stones, The Yardbirds, The Animals, Spencer Davis Group, around the Richmond club scene, most of the bands played at The Crawdaddy, Eel Pie Island, The Madingley Club, incidentally where The Beatles did one of their last photo shoots in April 1969, Richmond Jazz Festival having jazz and R&B roots, songs and sounds that start to dig into the black music genre, which I continue to get more interested in. The Castle Ballroom attracts the Mods in droves, Richmond is turning into the New West End of London an outerscene in music and venues, that summer of 1965 saw the opening of The Cathedral Of Clothing for the modernist scene, its collegiate clothing range and Ivy League look, 'The Ivy Shop' has opened.

Now because my father is not around and mother always seems to be doing more dinner parties, our house becomes a meeting place for my brother's mates, whether just before going 'up The Castle' or playing a game of Brag, bottles of Double Diamond, most of them would bring their newly acquired vinyl

45's and a copy of the New Musical Express, we had my brothers record player downstairs in the front room. This time I am definitely not going to leave the room, anyway his mates didn't mind me being around, their scooters, Mini's, a sporty Hillman Imp, a convertible MG, a new Triumph Herald and even a Lotus Cortina would sometimes be parked outside of our house. They would throw me a set of car keys and let me drive their car, (ie sit in the driver's seat, holding onto the steering wheel!), looking at the speedo to see what I thought was a cars maximum speed! But, when they bought their records around and stacked them on the Dansette, I stayed in the room.

Everybody had a nickname, Plum, Cookie, Cakehole, Golly, all a play on most of their surnames, as many were born in the late 1940s the tradition of having or sharing a nickname, with a 'Little' put in front of it, was handed down to us 1950s born. Living in a village, these boys and girls grew up together, the pits, the streets, the fishing, infant school, senior school, youth clubs, of course few stayed on in the Secondary Modern school system, especially if from a council house in Ham or Petersham, unless bright or went to grammar school, the majority all leaving at 15, some even working together in a career.

Luckily they did have access to metalwork and woodwork shops, giving the practical experiences and going into one of the trades, many never had any academic qualifications. Luckily the 1960s saw full employment, if you didn't like one job, sacked or a resignation, you could get another that afternoon or the next morning, until you found a job you liked or tolerated because you needed to earn. Mainly because your mother would make you pay your way for your keep and need 'some housekeeping', generally taking half, when starting out, if you were an apprenticed or just labouring, insisting on seeing that payslip or brown pay packet to confirm.

I felt very privileged sitting with these older lads, sounds of Bo Diddley, Chuck Berry, Sonny & Cher, Len Barry, early Stones and Beatles with US R&B covers, the new record label of Tamla Motown in 1965, Pye International, Stax, Atlantic and bringing great black music into the house. An unusual group name of The Skatalites with a song called Guns Of Navarone based on a 1961 film theme and although released later, entered the UK Top 50 in 1967, with the popularity of Ska growing, along with Dandy Livingstone's, Rudy, A Message To You, recorded at Maximum Sound Studios Old Kent Road – recorded later by The Specials in 1979 and the Ska Revival and Prince Busters Al Capone getting to 18 in UK charts, . Blue eyed soul singers like Long John Baldry, Len Barry, Chris Andrews, Andy Fairweather Low, Chris Farlow, Dusty Springfield, who that year along with Paul McCartney would endorse and support The Tamla Motown Revue to the UK and for television appearances, tunes of Barrett Strong, The Miracles, Little Stevie Wonder etc would be heard all around our house as my brothers collection grew. Whenever, I hear early Motown, I am transported back to those nostalgic days and that front room in our house.

So imagine the scene, here I am, a bespectacled, skinny, a wavy haired little lad, with a gap in my front teeth, squeezed against the arm of the couch, given the odd puff or drag of a fag and a sip of beer from one of the boys, obviously just for fun and to watch my reaction! Listening and looking up in attentive amazement, I just wanted and needed to grow older very quickly, perhaps releasing me from my angst and that 'key in the door'. For me, these are cool lads, one still wearing his Parka, a long leather coat, one a German Army sand jacket with four pockets, available from any army surplus stores and wearing desert boots, suede slip-ons, Chelsea Boots, turtle neck sweaters, buttoned cardigans, polo shirts and a new range of button down shirts from US brands and early Madras and check designs. But the favourites being Ben Shermans or Bennies, a company that was founded in 1963, by its owner Arthur Benjamin Sugarman, born in Brighton, observing the London Jazz & Blues scene and fashions, that fans liked to wear and were eagerly buying US made Oxford cotton shirts button downs, that visiting artists like Peterson, Gillespie and Miles Davis were wearing, mainly from Brookes Brothers, that also introduced Ivy League wear 1895 and imported Madras cloth from India in

1902, by the mid 1960s Mods had literally bought into this style of clothing. 'The Shirt', made in a short and long sleeve versions, in plain colours and lovely striped versions and made of high quality materials and stitching and with that distinctive pleat and hook on the back. Being twice or sometimes, three times more than an average cost of a casual shirt and of course available from The Ivy Shop Richmond, opened or should I say founded by John Simons. His experience in men's clothing goes back to the 1950s and a clothing entrepreneur since the age of 15, gaining experience in Cecil Gee, looking for a location he chooses Richmond, the music and club scene along with The Castle Ballrooms that attracted the Mods with their love for clothing, the location made sense.

Must say, I am slightly envious of that period and not being slightly older, still 'live' affordable music playing in pubs and clubs, DJs spinning the latest imported and R&B vinyl between the breaks. If you look at the best selling chart singles for 1965, the sounds change from a ballad period like Jim Reeves, Ken Dodd, and yodelling Frank Ifield, Elvis Presley, although he had two chart toppers that year, with a 1950s rock and roll sound. The new young sounds of The Walker and Righteous Brothers, a blue eyed soulful Tom Jones, very much influenced by black music in his early singing years in The Welsh Valleys in Working Men's Social and Miners Clubs. Again a lot of those R&B, Blues and Jazz records would come in with sailors through ports like Swansea, just like other docks in the UK.

The Beatles, still dominate, four No.1 hits that year, they back their popularity up with the film 'Help!', their second film and soundtrack album after the previous year's 'A Hard Day's Night'. Now familiar names of The Spencer Davis Group, Georgie Fame, The Animals, The Moody Blues, The Yardbirds, The Kinks, The Small Faces release their first single 'What You Gonna Do, About It', The Who's first release 'I Can't Explain' also that year see's the release of their iconic 'My Generation'. The Stones three number 1's that year includes a song written by Willie Dixon, a Chicago Blues artist and his Little Red Rooster cover, that year we would hear were the first penned hits of Jagger and Richards of 'The Last Time' and the wonderful '(I Can't Get No) Satisfaction', in which Richards guitar riff, was intended to be replaced by horns. Interestingly it was so soulful that Otis Redding paid homage to it and recorded his own version and made up some of the lyrics, mainly because Steve Cropper had tried to write down the lyrics from playing the 45 single time and time again, but couldn't understand or get them in time for going into the studio. Ironically, Redding's soul style production featured horns as the main riff as Richards had initially intended, at any Stones concert they interpreted Redding's version! That year saw Otis's 'My Girl' reach number 11 and stayed for four months in the UK charts.

From the US, Sonny and Cher, Shirley Ellis with 'The Clapping Song', The Byrds. Unit Four Plus Two a UK band, whose hit was produced with a latino vibe by Bob Crewe who also worked with The Four Seasons at the time.

1965 is seen as a great year of change in the 'Popular' music scene, from dominations by an older generation of singers and their buying demographic, the choice was a nice song with words that you could remember. To a younger set, with their new buying power and their need for entertainment and socialising, the words now were not as important as the music and the rhythm, backed by guitars and drums, especially if they had mundane jobs, they just lived for weekend and now many week nights!

⁂⁂⁂

1965, sees me get a job, well, just helping really, because I can't officially work as you need a permit from school. Along the road are The Cottee's, to me a large happy family that are just great to be around and never minded kids dropping into their house constantly.

They had four children at the time and to be honest I would have loved to be one of them, if it wasn't for the love of my mother and brother, I would have slept in their hall. Anne and Brian, must have been in their mid to late twenties when they moved into Stuart Road and didn't appear to look like any other parents at the time, younger, more energetic, dressed differently, this new family with initially four girls really lifted our street. They were to me, the role model of parenting and an open door policy for the neighbourhood, always busy, helping other people but always had time for you and to make anybody welcome. Anne would constantly be doing housework in her patterned pinnies, scrubbing doorsteps, hated any type of stain, even soaking the tea cups in diluted bleach to keep them spotless.

Brian, the father was my 'look up too', my advisor, my DIY instructor along with my brother, that role model male that every lad should and would have wanted. He was always improving his rented council house effectively to make more room, even knocking down walls to accommodate his growing family and their requirements, I am sure he wasn't allowed to do this under the council tenancy agreement, but he did!

In 1965 he worked for Lyons Bread in Chessington, the competitors at the time who sold that tasteless white sliced being Mothers Pride, Wonderloaf, Nevilles, the Co-Ops Wheatsheaf and Sunblest mainly, all tasting similar and made with the same formula, however it made great egg sandwiches and lasted for days, we loved it and convenient to wrap in greaseproof paper or Bacofoil, for a picnic in Richmond Park! The thick sliced made great toast especially with beef dripping and a sprinkling of salt! Proper made bread, was hard to cut when fresh and went firm and stale quickly, but made even better toast or Mum would make breadcrumbs for homemade fishcakes.

Brian invited me to help him and to earn a little pocket money, I think he was astute enough to realise I never really had any 'father' time, as he had the four daughters, Sharon, Debbie, Jane and Julie born in 1964, shortly after moving into the street! I jumped at the opportunity, 'Knock on my door at 5am tomorrow morning' he said, I duly arrived and we drove to a trading estate where the bakery was, in his navy blue Bedford Dormobile with sliding doors, one of the few 'people carriers' then, which I thought was so cool at the time! The bread had been preloaded into all the Commer vans with a large step up into the cab with big sliding doors, all lined up, like army trucks ready for action, bearing that famous Lyons branding, lettering and a dark blue livery, that we all would recognise to this day.

The bread and I mean only white it seemed, which came in thin and thick slices, identified by a waxy gingham patterned wrapper that was, I think blue for thin and red for thick. We delivered to large convenience stores and supermarkets around the Tolworth and Kingston areas. I think the only other product we delivered might have been doughnuts and a few other cakes like Swiss Rolls and perhaps those small Lyons Individual Fruit Pies that were about a 1/- as I believe they made these in the factory also and went great with custard warmed.

The bread was packed into trays that stacked on top of each other made from plastic with a metal bar at each end that made a handle. Now, when you are a small twelve year old and not a big lad, the width of these trays are about as far as you could stretch your arms, the handles had a problem of trapping your hands or fingers.

We would park up outside supermarkets and I particularly remember the then new Tolworth Tower on the A3, soaring into the sky and just recently opened in 1964, built on the site of a former Odeon cinema. It was outer London's tallest building at the time, of 22 floors that rose to a height of 265 feet, with the biggest supermarket that I had ever seen, Fine Fare on the ground floor and it's large car park. Because we did 'big drops' the round was quickly completed by noon or one o'clock. Driving around, easily parking outside supermarkets, stacking them on the shelves and pulling out the older unsold loaves, to take back – think they then had a process 'sale or return', however given tracking accuracy in those days, it was all a little hit and miss. There was no best before end or sell by marking or labels, people just squeezed the loaf, squiggy and its fresh, firmer and it could be older – simple!. Now anybody who worked on delivery vans and most places then would have perks, I should have taken these older loaves back to the van, taken a fresh tray of loaves and deliver the back to the store, but I repacked the older loaves, ready to be delivered to the next shop! As we jumped into the van and drove to the next shop or supermarket, on my first day I asked 'Brian, why are we going to deliver older loaves as fresh to the next shop?' He looks at me and touches the side of his nose in that 'You don't need to know, Boy!' way. I then realise this is a perk of the job, he would accumulate anything between 2 to 5 loaves a day to take home and to distribute, along with doughnuts and cakes, a large family then would get through then many loaves a week and use it for snacks, sandwiches or to fill up and accompany meals. He also had an extended family in the village, interestingly his Uncle Jack worked for Sunblest!

What a great experience that was, I also remember driving along, with the sliding doors open and your leg stretched out against the wheel arch, pushing you back in your seat as no seatbelts of course. A large transistor would be wedged between the dashboard and windscreen playing with the chart music of the day. One particular record I remember is the 'Boy from Pontypridd' and a new singer with a strong soulful voice, Tom Jones whose second release was picked up by the pirate radio stations particularly Radio Caroline and rocketed into the charts and reaching number one in early 1965. Meaning the BBC would now put it on their playlists, who initially didn't play it because of Jones's racy and sexy image at the time! That song was made for driving, with the powerful beat and introduction, the tune, the words being understandable, belting out the title 'It's Not Unusual!', the chorus and a slight word change 'It's not unusual to be loved by anyone, It's not unusual to have fun with anyone!' changing it to 'mad with everyone and sad with anyone!' in the last chorus. Really it didn't matter if you couldn't remember the words though as it was only two minutes long anyway! Brian would hold the steering wheel moving his shoulders in time to the music and sing his heart out, getting funny looks when we pulled up at traffic lights, junctions and shops. I would sit there laughing my head off and as a shy lad, embarrassingly joining in.

To this day every time that that record comes on the radio, I am taken back, to riding in that cab on those roads of Tolworth, in the mid 60s and just smile. Such great memories of Brian and Anne Cottee, and their daughters, in 1966 dad got his boy Brian jnr or 'Bronc'. Great days of fun, playing with the family and neighbours, in our streets and gardens.

Sadly, I wished Brian had been My Dad, someone who I could look up to and respect. Not like mine, as I got older I realise he was not just one of those fathers or perhaps he really didn't want to be one. The mention of him, would just make me shut down, not even wanting to talk about him. I ignore his requests to visit him in prison, I just didn't like the way he had treated my mother and brother. When my Mum or Keith would visit him, he asks after me and they take my school report for him to read and sign off. Sad really, he writes letters to me, saying he is going to change, he tells my mother he's going to change, I believed she truly loved that man, but obviously not his deeds and the hardship he bought to our family. It's about this age that I try to grow a tough protective shell around me, I just don't want to be hurt, I feel disappointed we don't have what I think is anywhere like a normal family life. I am so grateful for having a Mum, who was able to replace a lot of his short comings and Keith some of the rest in a male.

The Butterfields entertain regularly needing Mum, I know some people can't bear to be alone, being on your own can make you over think, resulting in negative thoughts. So I fill my quiet times with music, radio and TV, reading facts, taking things apart and putting them together again, model building, making things like bows and arrows with willow wood from near the river, experimenting with things like smoking and rolling up newspaper and lighting it up as a cigarette! I had a battalion of tanks, that you made from a cotton reel that you cut tracks in, a slice of wax candle, an elastic band and two matches, assembling and winding it up and letting it go across the kitchen floor. All these things help my mind by distracting my inner thoughts to something positive, which I believe post war children were very good at.

Assume today, I may have locked myself in my bedroom on my phone or laptop watching films or gaming, looking at social media looking at my friends enjoying themselves with other people and their families. I guess listening to music, but the physicalness of vinyl and reading labels really caught my interest.

The community was also very important to me, without anybody knowing it, I am very fortunate with our close neighbourhood, its schools and especially The People around me. There is an African proverb or saying that “IT TAKES A VILLAGE TO RAISE A CHILD” - to interact, experience and grow in a safe place and a healthy environment, even in busy London, local communities and streets acted as ‘villages’. And that was Ham village for me especially in the 1950s and 1960s, you would interact with people and respect your elders. In the early 1950’s, council house living and neighbourhoods were great for this, giving many of us somewhere to mix and congregate as youngsters. Youth Clubs, developed and promoted by the celebrities of the day – the entertainer Frankie Vaughan – of Give Me The Moonlight, Give Me The Girl......fame - was an ambassador for the National Association of Boys Clubs, working on many projects, he even donated his royalties from his hit ‘Seventeen’ to the cause. Local Authorities were given funds to develop community centres and clubs with facilities, which worked well for youngsters in many areas, keeping them from hanging about on the streets.

Around this time our village community is in a state of change with new housing and new people moving in, the original old village of Ham and Petersham growth and heritage was built upon mostly agricultural British and some Irish labour and service in the large houses and farms, made up mainly of people who have moved in from the counties to find work, especially the first forty years of the 20th Century.

Our own village of Ham, completely of white heritage in the mid 60s of what I can remember, areas of council estates and hundreds of houses, it was inevitable that vacancies became available. A family that had been living in cramped, substandard and expensive accommodation in the private sector were desperate to move away from those terrible conditions. The parents had struggled financially trying to raise their two children safely and healthily after five locations, trying to make them a home. Luckily, they were on the council's waiting list and in 1965 were offered a three bedroomed maisonette in Ham Street, just a short stroll from the river. To them it was home at last and with its spectacular views of the Star & Garter Hill, it was a beautiful one at that.

They were the first family of 'colour' to come to Ham, that I remember and aware of, as they were Anglo Indian. There was Mum, Dad and two children a girl aged 8 and a boy aged 12. The people who lived nearby were initially curious and came to stand outside the gate on the day that the "brown people" moved in. This could have been seen as a slightly menacing scene, but the Dad was an outgoing, friendly man who saw the small crowd as a welcoming committee and warmly invited everyone into the house shouting to his wife to "put the kettle on"! Everyone came in and were soon chatting away like old friends! This new family didn't see that they were different and after a very short while, neither did their visitors and the village.

Living just a hundred yards from Riverside Drive Rec' and its grassy area, their son David, discovered he was a gifted footballer. He integrated well with us local boys and soon became a loyal and fully accepted member of the local teams. Since the football team formed the heart of most entertainment in Ham, it was a perfect way to become familiar and solidify ties with the whole village.

Was there racism? David did suffer discrimination playing club football away from the village in the late 60s and the early 70s in West London leagues. In the village, both children were subjected to racist jibes on an almost daily basis, but they were mostly just childish name calling and were usually settled with a little scuffle! The daughter, Sharon famously threw one 11 year old boy over a low wall for his attempt to intimidate her. No harm came to him! I say "famously" because the local hard boy (not named!) was walking past and witnessed the whole thing with amusement saying "wow ... well now I know not to ever mess with you"! That comment earned Sharon life-long protection from him any further bullying in Ham or even in Richmond on a Saturday night in later years! Yes, there was racism but because of their reactions to it, neither Sharon nor David could actually say they were victims of it. I spoke to Sharon about any other prejudices and except for the odd remark about looking like a choc ice, she tells me people often called her a 'Paki' in the early 70s. On the first occasion, she ran home to her mother, who calmly explained in a cultured voice 'you must inform them, that Pakistan and India are two very different countries!' Well, Sharon didn't think her tormentors would be receptive to a geography lesson but that was Mum for you, she knew her facts! Institutional racism was a different matter and in the 70s it seemed to be acceptable for the park keepers to shout at David saying: "Oy darkie, get that ball off the grass. Go home to wherever you came from!". We can only hope that this is no longer the case.*

*Written with acknowledgements and help from Sharon Brizon nee Ireland.

For a relatively small village at in the 50s and early 60s, the original Venturers Club at Trefoil House on the Petersham Road and Ham Boys Club in Back Lane, which also had a boxing club within it. My generation couldn't wait to be older and attend these places and make use of the facilities.

With 1965 is coming to an end, that year we saw a massive change in musical tastes reflected in the UK national charts, at 13 years of age, my taste in music is definitely now centred on R&B and Soul.

Other events that year, we learn and hear about gangsters – The Kray Twins are arrested. Dr Richard Beeching and his famous report on the cuts in British Railways are talking effect. In sport, Sir Stanley Matthews hangs up his boots, Manchester United win the First Division Championship, Liverpool the FA Cup and West

Ham United, captained by Bobby Moore take the European Cup and the games rules, introduce substitutes for the first time.

A Great Train robber escapes from Wandsworth Prison, always wondered if my father met him? Ian Brady is arrested and opens up the search of the Yorkshire Moors, he is later to be charged along with Myra Hindley and become known as The Moors Murderers, their victims numbered five children buried on Saddleworth Moor, two of them were discovered more than twenty years later, sadly one was never found. An interesting one for us young lads, the word 'F*ck' was heard on British TV for the first time, by theatre critic Kenneth Tynan, on a live chat show. Does that mean that now 'We can all use it?'. I swore in front of my mother once when younger, she marched me to the sink, took a bar of carbolic from the soapdish, told me to open my mouth and bite, pulling it backwards scraping it on the back of my teeth, took ages to get rid of the taste! Strangely I never blasphemed again – well, not in front of Mum!

1965 saw Audi and Toyota start selling cars in the UK for the first time. Pizza Express opens its first restaurant in Wardour Street, London. Unbeknown to many of us, The Beatles perform their last live UK organised appearance in Wales outside of London. Fashion wise Mary Quant who introduced the miniskirt, available from her shop Bazaar in Kings Road, Chelsea and they are seen everywhere, especially by the older girls at my senior school. Biba co-founded by Barbara Hulanicki, offering a pink gingham dress to readers of the Daily Mirror, gaining orders of some 17,000 outfits she moves to bigger premises in Kensington Church Street later in 1973 moving to the previous Derry & Toms department store with seven floors with the backing of Dorothy Perkins, the famous store had an Art Deco interior and feel, but I remember it having a very dark interior.

As a lad and more significantly and what would was to have a great impression on me later, was the opening of The Post Office Tower, which then was the tallest building in Britain, 620ft and 200ft taller than any other building in the capital! Its design, basically a stick, would help with the growing need for more telephony and communications, more importantly our expanding television needs, for at least a generation. Telephone calls before the building of this leading edge construction, long distance (trunk calls), were completed over simply copper wires and routed with the help of operators. This new technology used microwaves that transmitted wide-band signals on wavelengths much smaller than even conventional television broadcasting and was capable of carrying 1800 telephone calls on a single carrier wave. For the ordinary person a technological miracle, Britain led the world in telephony at the time.

The reason for the height was that The Tower used microwave signals that needed to travel in straight lines clearing buildings and to connect a chain of towers by 1970. This communication technology will carry two way, city to city links for the new 625 line colour TV and well as telephony circuits, the eventual capacity of the system will be 150,000 simultaneous telephone conversations or 100 two-way television channels. To think at that time, only a third channel BBC2 had just been announced.

An obvious and built in attraction was the incredible panoramic views, it became a major attraction for the British public and tourists alike, a revolving restaurant and cocktail bar, seating 120 diners on the 34th floor and operated by Butlins, it made one revolution every 23 minutes and an observation floor were added. I was lucky enough to visit The GPO Tower, its official name, even to have a cup of tea and cake in the restaurant, having a 360 degree moving view of London and its surroundings, after a tour of its bristling technology, it was magic for a twelve year old boy, with a slight interest in electronics and future technology.

As my mother and I left the Tower that evening, I look back, it stands there, like a Dan Dare space rocket ready to be launched into the night sky, pointing to the stars, thinking of all those telephone calls happening all at once and how the hell does it all work? It makes me think and I want to enter that world of technology, it is the future?

Unfortunately, on 31 October 1971, a bomb exploded in the men's toilet on the restaurant floor, claimed to be put there by the Angry Brigade – a far left anarchist group. The Tower was then largely closed to the general public, the restaurant closed in 1980 for security reasons, 1981 sadly saw it closed to the public completely. Around that time it was superseded by The NatWest Tower in becoming the tallest building in London and the UK.

Yes, a classic year for me, for many things, school, music, friends and life. Today, I even have a 1965 Lambretta Li150 and a Fiat 500D, Transformabile with suicide doors from the same year as every lad will know, they have a 'C' registration suffix.

⁂

As I move into 1966 and mainly because my father was still absent, I really started to enjoy the school environment. I liked the walk to school, the interaction with other lads in the village, the chat on the playground, hearing the local gossip, talking about the latest episode of anything on TV and Match of The Day on a Monday morning.

My interest in art (5th in class that year), technical drawing (2nd), wood and metalwork (8th) history (9th), science (24th not sure what happened here again!). I was always trying to do my best, but academically and it was always a little difficult. Still envious about my other classmates, who joke and seem to play around all lesson, with me joining in, but they always came near to the top in tests and exams, it all seems to come to easy for them, even on the sports field, whether football, games or track.

Still struggling with shyness and confidence, I find it quite disabling, I should have asked more for help and been more involved in class discussions, but it's not easy for me. Now 13 years old and a 'teenager'! I really like sport, but physically not built for it, track and field sports really does need physicality, which would help with discus, javelin, hurdles, long jump, high jump, discus etc. I found a small niche in the 100 and the 220 yards, past that the 440 and longer around the track where my stride length let me down, I just could keep up, trying to finish head down and watching those lane markings on the last bend was always very tough and needed stamina!

All in all the start of those summer holidays and my birthday had fell on the 6/6/66 that year! Best of all we were all looking forward to The World Cup coming to England, lead by the World Cup Willie campaign, the first time that FIFA had agreed on a mascot for the competition! Even Lonnie Donegan recorded a single called 'World Cup Willie' along with adverts and marketing of Willie dressed in his football gear that appeared everywhere, from food to toys in the run up to the kick off game. Even petrol stations gave away World Cup Willie coins with a certain spend on fuel.

Looking forward to a week's Scout Camp at Longridge on the river at Marlow, just below the bridge, the year before we had stayed near Barmouth in the Snowdonia National Park in North Wales. In those times before motorways and good roads, a trip of over 200 miles is a very long journey, especially for a Scout Troop mode of transport of a 1950's furniture van! Sitting on the top of ex-army tents, it must or seemed to have taken us nearly 10 hours with stops on the road. To compound the situation, it was heavily raining when we started to pitch our tents and had to dig water runoff channels around the tents on the slight slope to the field.

That week in Wales, we never did really get dried out, although we had laughs along the way. I do remember people speaking Welsh when we went into any shops, quickly switching from English, they also looked at us suspiciously, thinking we were from Fagin's gang from foggy London, when we walked into premises to buy any provisions. One day while on an all day hike, as any Scouters know, you are given some map co-ordinates and told to get there and work your way back via another point. As 12 and 13 year olds, we unfortunately literally lost our bearings, coming upon a small village shop and Post Office, we ask for directions and the chap behind the counter just shrugged his shoulders and replied in a strong accent, indicating that he didn't understand what we were asking!

This year's summer camp was a lot better, not far from home and a nice dry sunny summer, easier journey, putting our thumbs up to passing motorists. By coincidence, we were away at camp that week of 1966, the England versus Portugal semi-final was played at Wembley, then England versus the magical Eusebio, a new star of that World Cup and was scoring many goals. There we were, that 26 July 7.30pm kickoff and the sun going down and meal eaten and washing up done. Sitting on the grass with our transistor radios that many lads had bought with them all tuned in, a surround sound experience, all very excited and of course football mad, that summer was the best for English football. It kicks off, we worry every time we hear that Eusebio has got the ball, being marked heavily by Nobby Stiles, but he manages to strike, it swerves Banks flies through the air to save, a roar from the crowd. Bobby Charlton, a 29 year old who looked 50, takes a rebound off the goalkeeper and slots the ball home, 1-0 England, we jump around like demented PG Tip monkeys!

Into the second half, Hurst squares a ball to Bobby Charlton, he strikes, he scores, again we go mad, running around the camp site and the pitched tents. For some reason, Bobby's brother Jackie handles the ball in the area, it's a penalty! Clenching our fists, Eusebio steps up and scores in the 82nd minute! Oh No!, we shout, our hearts pump! Luckily, England hold onto a 2-1 win, 'Eusebio has broken down in tears', the commentator declares. England are in The World Cup Final! Eusebio gets the consolation of the The Golden Boot with nine goals.

If anybody went to a Sea Scout camp in those days, it was quite strict and very much worked on naval service standards with kit inspection every day after breakfast, which each patrol took their part in making. A bugler would have played Reveille early morning as the Union Jack was raised up the flagpole. The disciplines not only helped to keep things tidy, but also kept us safe and looking out for each other.

But above all there was the use of the river and learning how to paddle, row, scull and sail. Rowing and being in a Gig was great fun, now when you are not very tall and sitting on a stretcher with a big oar sitting on the gunwhale in its rowlocks or rollocks – a name that always made us chuckle – catching a crab or smacking the oar into your chest or the lad in front, when the blade was at right angles in the water was common, you would feel battered, until you learned who to row properly and a great feeling of going through the water at speed!!

One morning I recall really well, we were going kayaking, all excited we ran as fast as we could down to the jetty, as we were running I felt a small push and at the same time tripped over the coir matting. Sending me head first into the shallow water and my head plummeting into the sticky mud, what felt like minutes and seeing my short life flashing before me as it went dark. I am literally pulled out by my legs, like a suction tipped arrow lifted from a pane of glass or a wellington from nine inches of mud, grasping for breath. After the initial shock and everybody looking at me, we all burst out laughing I looked like a chocolate dipped lolly.

Four days after the semi-final on the 30th July 1966, England are playing West Germany in The World Cup Final. We again set up the 'trannies' on the grass, it's a warm, sultry and cloudy summer afternoon, loaded with cans of Coke and a packets of Potato Puffs from the camp tuck shop, we again gather around the radio. For the BBC, Brian Moore - who soon after presented later, LWTs The Big Match - is one of the radio commentators.

It kicks off, the radio announcer says England are playing in red and the Germans in white! It kicks off, 12 minutes in, sadly West Germany score, 6 minutes later Geoff Hurst scores to level it with the help of our hero Bobby Moore, we breathe again! On the 78th minute Martin Peters makes it 2-1, we jump for joy, can we hold on? No! The Germans score in the 90th minute to draw level, the whistle goes, extra time! We all sink to our knees! Ten minutes into extra time Geoff Hurst takes a shot, it ricochets on the underside of the crossbar, the Germans appeal, the commentator says the referee is running to his linesman, the crowd goes silent. 'It's a goal!!' the commentator shouts, we all go crazy.

The Germans keep attacking, the clock ticks down, in the final minute the ball is cleared down the touchline. Geoff Hurst picks it up from Moore, the Germans tiring, he runs at the defence, he sees a gap, - the famous TV coverage words of Kenneth Wolstenholme will always come to mind, 'Some people are on the pitch. They think it's all over.....' Hurst shoots, it hits the back of the net 'It is now!!!'.

Alf Ramsey's three years tenure really paid off, he led with a fitness regime and tactics. Strangely the team had a celebration dinner that night in the Royal Garden Hotel, Kensington, without their wives, some players even went home on the bus that evening.

That's it, the last greatest moment in English football, when compiling this book. Early in September 1966, that event was and still is, so important that schools had outings to see the official FIFA film and cinema release of the '66 World Cup, simply called Goal!! Our school football teams saw it at The Globe Kinema in Putney High Street, we all cheered as the goals went in! Hero's every one of them and an event never to be forgotten for a 13 year old lad and many other football mad youngsters. A time and a place surely remembered by many.

That summer of '66, my school report is OK, finishing in the top ten in class in Geography, Maths, Science, Metalwork and Technical Drawing. Mr Harvey, a great teacher and our form teacher that year, mentions in my report that 'Graham has 'a cheerful, enthusiastic approach to everything and should do well next year in 3AC, a credit to the class'. I am feeling a little more confident with life, getting picked for schools teams in football, rugby and sprinting.

⁂

Suddenly a big black cloud bubbles up and is destined to stop over our house! Mum announces that Dad is being released from prison, I feel sick to my stomach, that horrid gut churning reaction that we have all had and have experienced at one time, when told something that you do not want to ever hear, an unexpected death of a relative or close friend, a fatal accident or terminal illness. My thoughts quickly go back to the periods of that key opening the front door, constant arguments, fingers in my ears anything to stop the sound reaching my brain, constantly repeating 'Why don't they stop, please, please, just stop!!'.

As always, Dad must has convinced Mum, that he needs an address to be released too, under the terms of his parole and that he has definitely changed his ways. Now a little older, I think and now it's obviously black and white to me, he is not a good man and to keep letting him into our lives, surely for Mum it must be painful. But in hindsight, she really still does love him and clings to 'the hope' that prison has reformed him - perhaps deep down inside I would like to think the same, but I really struggle to believe it.

The day comes, he knocks on the door, I run to my bedroom, closing the door. I hear the door open and a few minutes later, Mum shouts upstairs that 'your Dad wants to see you', I am overwhelmed with anxiety and huddle at the end of my bed, Mum shouts again. I go downstairs, head bowed, he greets me, but doesn't even attempt to hug or say anything - I think he knows how I feel - looking tanned and fit, after a 'holiday' in an open prison again, three meals a day, probably a job in the kitchen making bread or picking vegetables on a nearby farm for this he would have got paid, enough to buy tobacco. All this, while Mum has two jobs, working for hours to pay the rent and the odd treat for us. He promises me that he will take me out to various places and on day trips to the seaside and that he will even take me to see Chelsea again. Will he? Or as always are they empty promises?

Dad gets a job, easily then for an ex-convict, it's a time in the UK when it has the best employment rates since records began in the 1880's, in the low single percentage figures, in fact there are too many jobs and not enough people to fill them. He will always get a driving job, prison records were not really taken into account and no checks or references, strangely embezzlement or fraud is considered low risk when employing people in the 1960's.

* * *

Its September 1966, I go into Class 3AC, it's an academic class, where the curriculum is based upon a path to taking GCE 'O' Levels, if you are bright enough and stay on for another year (5th Form wasn't mandatory then).

Our form teacher is Miss Lewis, a no nonsense strict spinster, who always seemed to be picking on the attractive girls in the class and us boys were lucky enough to have many, Jean, Marilyn, Wendy, Toni, Rosemary, Annette, Anita, Anne, Laura, Sue and many more, unless they were very clever and interested in her own subject of Geography. She liked most of the boys, thankfully, especially the ones who took a keen interest in her subject. Our form that year was also the geography classroom, lots of information scattered around the room walls, about geological terrains and other interesting facts (for me anyway). I particularly remember that enormous map of the world made by Bartholomew from the late 50s, hanging from a thick cord, The British Empire countries printed in a bright pink. From Canada on the left down to New Zealand, to some pink spots in the Pacific Ocean on the right, as countries gained Independence from being Colonies in the early 60s, this would have changed if real time, but for now shows the breadth and coverage of The Empire. Miss Lewis had started to note the countries that had transitioned to become voluntary Members of the Commonwealth – the pink was eroding, changing times for an Empire and our economy. Schools from 1901 celebrated Empire Day, when countries were winning independence and it wasn't politically correct, in 1958 it was changed to The British Commonwealth Day and in 1966 just Commonwealth Day and sharing the day with the Queens official birthday and again in 1977 to the second Monday in March where the Queen now sends a special message to the youth of the Commonwealth.

At this time home life was just bearable, Mum and Dad on the surface were getting on, even being taken out for a few days out and a drink in a pub garden with him. Initially, Dad would hand over the housekeeping money, but as we ran down to Christmas, for some reason he was saying there was trouble with the company cash flow where he worked and they would get paid double the next week. I think Keith got on slightly better with our Dad, but for me when there was just the two of us together, there was a slight resistance to talk to each other and an atmosphere seem to prevail.

⁕⁕⁕

I really want to see Chelsea again, I engage with him one Sunday morning and tell him to come and watch me play football, he says 'I will Son, just a bit busy at the moment'. I mention Chelsea and Stamford Bridge, I ask if we can go again, he tells me to check the paper and see when the next home game is. I show him the date he says 'OK, OK then, let's go in two weeks time!'. Now for a thirteen year old this is a date for my mental diary, it brings on so much excitement. The second Saturday rolls around, on the morning I say 'You promised to take me to Chelsea today, it's a 3pm kickoff'. He replies 'Oh, did I?', I say 'You promised, Dad!'. He says 'Right be ready for 1230pm, I will be home before 1pm, I am working this morning.'

I am so excited, I am ready by noon, wearing my lookalike royal blue Chelsea shirt, anticipating the afternoon to come, I keep looking at my watch, it's now 1230pm, we had a large bay window where I could sit and watch the street to see any cars coming. I sit there on my Mums footstall or poufee as she liked to call it, hopefully waiting to see the Humber Super Snipe - then working as a chauffeur for Grovesnor Car Hire in Twickenham at the time. It's now 1245 then onto 1pm, I again look at our bakelite Smiths electric clock, with its grey face sitting on the mantelpiece of our tiled front room fireplace. Mum comes in, doesn't say anything and knowing that I will be let down – again, like she has over the years!

I sit there until 1.30pm and realise that even if he arrives now, by the time we get to Richmond Station jump on the District Line to Fulham Broadway, we will miss the 3pm kick-off. Now 1.45pm, I walk slowly away from the window, then run up to my bedroom, slam the door and put my face into my pillow, trying not to cry with disappointment. Yet again, I am let down by the one person that you should rely on in this world, my faith in trusting people and promises are wearing thin. Mum, knocks on the door and asks to come in, I shout "Go away, just leave me alone!" I want some comfort and Mum knows that, but my disappointment now turns to anger, punching my pillow.

I am very close to my Mum, only ever really known her love and my brother's, nothing from my father that I ever remember or felt. No sitting on his lap, no words of encouragement, no guidance, no saying well done after football matches or playing for school or any village team, even though he was a good footballer and cricketer when younger, he just wasn't interested in Keith and I and what we were trying to achieve in life. Never helped us with punctures on our bikes, no stories about when he was a child, the times that he was home between serving prison sentences, he always had driving jobs, I would ask if I could come with him in school holidays – never really got a yes or no!

What hurts Mum, hurts me, she will want to know why he didn't return home, the trouble with this and because he had something better to do or simply just forgot, to him it wasn't obvious or important. If Mum raises the subject with him it will just cause another argument and generally when he hadn't returned home at a particular time, it would be very late, I just hated that confrontation, yet again.

I dreaded his key in the door on his return and what it would bring, I am normally in bed and try and drowned out the noise with my pillows, going under the sheets or my transistor tuned into a fading in and out sounds of Radio Luxembourg. Concentrating on the music and the Horace Bachelor adverts on how to win money by predicting football results, spelling out the address on how to get more information, that's Keynsham, K-E-Y-N-S-H-A-M, Bristol, it still rings in my head every time I hear the word Luxembourg.

The mornings in our house after a big row is like walking on egg shells, long silences, my father pretending everything is back to normal and my mother fuming about his behaviour and not talking, but trying to act normal with me. I liked 'Bewitched' with Elizabeth Montgomery as Samantha – another older woman crush, I so wish I could twitch my nose to make everything right for Mum.

Again, although I love my mother, our home is not that cosy place or haven, when my father is around, when he is not it has normality. Keith is now 20, he knows and has experienced what I am now going through and that's why he stayed out a lot, I am sure.

⁂

Schooldays and being out of the house, is a world away from what goes on at home, when Dad is there, although I still have to concentrate and work hard with my homework. The need to be funny or get distracted is a must for me and I would like to think, to the outside world that I seemed pretty cheerful then and there wasn't all this 'stuff' going on at home. I never discussed my feelings with anyone, not even Mum or Keith, just tried to ignore any issues. However, home life could be upsetting, Mum again working hard at her job and trying to cover the rent, although I loved her dearly with my father around it was more like lodgings and somewhere to eat and sleep, it seemed to lose any comfort, love, energy and worse of all, any laughter.

Dad was again going into that phase where he would start to come home late again and not give any housekeeping. For my Mum, it must have been so stressful, for me I was sick and fed up with the constant state of affairs of trouble, uneasiness and her unhappiness.

Some school days I felt very down, getting up early, my paper round would keep my mind focussed, but sometimes I would get low. Conversations around the playground and classroom involved talking about Dads and what they had done that weekend ie built an Airfix model together, buy a new pair of football boots, repair a football, or talked about where they worked. I had nothing to contribute and certainly didn't want to be asked, 'What does your Dad do, Gub?'

Strangely and I don't know how, Miss Lewis my form teacher seemed to understood how I was feeling, I am never sure whether she ever found out about my home life, perhaps the authorities informed her or even my mother? I really liked her and the subject of geography, she took time out to try and talk to me, what I would like to do in life and my interests, ask me how things are, of course I kept positive and used the words 'I'm OK, Miss', even if I wasn't. It's not till later in life, I did think that she may have had a sixth sense or was trained in early pastoral care. Anyway, it worked there are few people in life that can guide and help you, I felt that Miss Lewis tried too. That year in 3AC in geography, I was 4th in class at Christmas and 5th in summer exams. Unfortunately, after leaving school, I never got to meet Miss Lewis again, before she passed away, it's one of my regrets in life and as Frank sang – 'Regrets, I Have a Few', sadly, I wish I had and should have made the effort!

As I have said, my father was a confidence trickster, the initial need to tell people to keep their money in their pocket was his first opening and approach, saying 'I will get the drinks', 'I will give you a lift', to potential targets - that's why, when he was trying to impress he didn't give Mum any housekeeping. Then later, go in for the sting, along with being a philanderer, my father would always be smartly dressed with new clothes and shoes. Mum worked late, he was often washed, cologned up and out again before she got home. He also was allowed to bring home the Humber which he chauffeured for early pickups the next day, literally a head turning vehicle, all black and chrome a car that would impress his victims of cons.

I believed now, at this time he will never change the pattern, it has started again and now I am now really aware of the damage his is causing. Like an alcoholic, 'only one last drink and then I can give it up or a druggie, one more fix, I don't need it'. It's an illness, only they can recognise or want to give up or change. I feel really sorry for my mother, she just wanted a close family life, but what can she do? In the past when I was a lot younger, the thought of losing her lovely council house and perhaps her boys going into care was too frightening, she certainly dug deep to establish a home for her sons, to this day I am not sure how she did it. Her options are limited, with the thoughts of the man she met and fell in love with, during wartime and a happy life that could have been, but never materialised.

⁂

School and sport, trying to retain my position in the football and rugby team was a driver for me. Handy being selected as you get afternoons off classes to play other schools, always good fun when you get a more modern small coach to travel, to far flung places like Ealing to play other teams and see other parts of West and South West London.

As I finish my school year in July 1967 and finishing 5th in class, my report comments says 'should do well next year, if he does not allow himself to be distracted from giving his very best', signed Miss E Lewis. This all despite my father disappearing for some time and seeing my mother struggle to pay the rent, Keith helps out by paying some of the bills and taking on the rental of the TV and the installation of our new phone, which cost £3 2s 0d (£40 today) per quarter, with local calls 2d (1 pence) for 6 minutes, 12 minutes off peak. An installation charge of £10 which doubled in 1968 to £20.

Spending so much time on my own and being a bit older I love US imported programmes like The Man From Uncle, Mission Impossible and its theme tune composed by the famous Lalo Schiffrin, who also did Dirty Harry and Bullitt, a composer who

I would listen to again in the 1970's, in a club. What I did enjoy was The Monkees, a bit like the 1990s Spice Girls a group that was put together in 1965 for a situation comedy TV series with the same name which aired from 1966-68. The band consisted of Micky Dolenz, Mike Nesmith, Peter Tork and strangely an English lad from Manchester called Davy Jones, a household name with the youngsters that would make a certain David Jones change his name to David Bowie! Very much controlled by record producer Don Kirshner, with the amount of filming that had to do, time was limited in recording studios, which for a band was frustrating, however in the 1967 UK Chart they had unbelievably six, yes six Top 30 hits, their first release 'I'm A Believer' reached number 1, Last Train To Clarksville (23), 'A Little Bit Me, A Little Bit You' (3), Alternate Title (2), Pleasant Valley Sunday (11), Daydream Believer (5) and a further four hits in 1968-9. The Monkees programmes were all a bit modern slapstick, but you would always remember and sing along to the songs, their double breasted shirts and 1960s clothes including Hippy styles and I would look forward to the opening credits and theme tune of 'Here We Come, Walking Down The Street.....Hey Hey We're The Monkees', strangely never released as a single.

Kirshner also developed a late night music programme called Don Kirshner's Rock Garden that ran from 1973 until 1981, that featured live bands, it is said that he tried to capitalise on the success of Soul Train, that first aired in 1971 and incredibly made over 1100 episodes. I do regret that Soul Train was never syndicated here in the 1970s, it would have been a great success with the Soul Frat!

So those light spring and summer nights, if nothing on the TV, I would again still sit in the garden rolling up newspaper pretending it was a 'fag', put it in my mouth and light it, being slightly hollow the burning paper would catch the back of my throat, after a few times I abandon that method and I will get hold of a proper cigarette one day. Keith owned a Mobylette Moped which he kept in the shed, at one time, in a fit of naughtiness and bravery, I took it and road it around our block a few times, hiding in the twilight, cycling like mad until it kicked into life, just getting it back in time, before Mum came home or a neighbour saw me, must say great fun though! I also liked to jump on my homemade 'Cow Horned' bike and just ride around in the fading light, now the good thing about living on a council estate and all the green space of a village, is the amount of children that can and will play outside, squeezing every moment of daylight, especially on school nights, children just didn't want to go in. Why would you, only three channels on telly, being sent to bed meant sleeping, on a school night most children were in bed by 9pm, your bedroom and if you were lucky enough your own was a haven or a place of solitary confinement. Not in a bad way, but because of our physical activity at school and running about, this obviously would include the girls who partake in games of football etc, as we did with rounders etc. We were tired and needed the sleep, perhaps after reading a comic or book, If you were unlucky enough to share a room with siblings, it would mean a small bundle or fight, chat or argument, then turn over and go to sleep.

With Mum working many nights on Richmond Green, as the Butterfields entertained often, my brother not at home and my father's absenteeism. I was at that age where I could look after myself until bedtime, often putting myself to bed at night, literally just jumping between the sheets just before Mum returned home, often getting caught out with washing my neck and teeth cleaning, if Mum had put a thruppence under the soap or toothpaste tube and it was still there! Strangely, again, my community became a very important part of my growing up, especially for me at this later stage, even though you can have a sad side to your home life. Playing on the street or a game of football or cricket and other games, playing by the river, riding bikes, sitting on a wall or tree with other children in the street, to me they were all as close as cousins by environment, their parents were surrogate Aunties and Uncles, that made me feel like everything was and would be OK. At Wimbledon time we would loan tennis rackets and balls found in the hedgerows and play sundowner games on the King

George playing fields tarmac courts. The humour of these kids was infectious, it wasn't just telling an odd joke, but observational humour just dominated every time you met up and I think as we all know now, that smiling and laughing is good for your soul and your health. Words and expressions were constantly made up and entered the local vernacular, even 'code talk', switching letters around and saying things in reverse which had the opposite meaning etc.

For me school now, was a means to an end of my education and childhood, but more importantly - not learning, coming up to fourteen years old and in just over a year I could have or get an adult job and get paid! We seem to grow up so very quickly in the 1960s, especially the kids from the 'estates', we weren't called Working Class for nothing, we entered it early! Many of us were ambitious, not academically or even career wise really, but for life and to get on with it, to experience different things, the bonus of earning a wage and having pennies in your pocket, buy some wheels and get out.

Although parents could support you, the aim of the majority of us was to grow up, get out there and be financially independent. As we are now a little older, many with a job, we were in a period of having customised bikes - who could afford a new one? - at this stage it was generally hand me downs from older brothers, or spare bits from mates. Even dredging, with a homemade hook and recycled rope, we cast it into The Pits or Ham Pond could reveal a bike! Once a year the River Thames would be reduced to a trickle held back at Teddington Lock, donning wellies we would turn into Mudlarks and scavenge for bikes, frames, cycle wheels or any other useful objects on the river bed. Some lads now had 'racing' cycles bought on by the emergence of a famous handsome Belgium called Eddy Merckx who would go on to celebrity status most successful track and road rider of all time. A bit like the Georgie Best of cycling, we would often cycle up to the Claude Butler shop in Kingston and check out the 'racers' in the shop window, with

Campagnolo gears of 10 speed – luxury, better than an old bike with Sturmey-Archer.

In the meantime we built our bikes – to the best of our ability, you may even have 24" or 26" diameter wheels on the same frame! Our testing ground was Ham Pits and its famous hill, we would prepare our bikes, a frame, wheels, tyres, a set of pedals and crank secured with a cotter pin, cow horn handlebars were the rage then, perhaps a fixed wheel, a broken chain may be given to you along with one of those chain repair kits that were slightly fiddly to put together, an old saddle, set of brakes taken from an old bike, with new brake blocks installed, hand painted with perhaps a bit of gloss found in the shed, you were good to go! Once, someone gave me a rattle can of black paint, spraying on a breezy day, it drifted across to my brothers off white Series 2 Lambretta Li150, he wasn't happy and my punishment was to polish out the black specks of paint with T-Cut!

As a quality checking process of durability, we would ride to The Pits, push our bikes up 'The Hill', poised like Olympic skiers at the starting gate, we would look down the descending track and launch ourselves. Always quite interesting sometimes you would make it to the bottom taking the quickest route and then suddenly lose traction and over the edge of the worn track, at this time you were trying to get the bike back in control, you do not want to come to a complete or sudden halt, because this would mean normally sliding you genitals forward along the crossbar and slamming then into the upright handlebar column, many a yelp was heard and the grabbing of a groin, as you laid on the floor holding on to them! Similar to missing a gear or a chain breaking and going forward, or worst of all, your front wheel exactly fitting down a kerbside drain lid, happened to me in Lock Road one night. As you were somersaulted over the handlebars, many a finger was trapped, broken, dislocated, scraped, sprained, worse a broken wrist (that bought a badge of courage!) when hitting the tarmac or the palm of your hands collecting grit as you protected your face from the road surfaces and what it could do to you. Throughout the summer holidays when young, we wore just shorts and t-shirts or short sleeved shirts, our exposed skin on arms and legs were like a scene from a minor injuries department in various states from new grazes to crusts of dried blood, the wound healing beneath. Ham Pits always beckoned, like The Wicked Forest – mother's fingers were wagged and pointed at you, we were told not to play there and warned of previous events. The words 'Why not?' would want to come out of our mouths and of course, it would make any adventure more appealing! Lifting corrugated sheeting and trying to catch mice scampering away, when the light hit them as well as the odd stick.

Stupidly building rafts to sail across the deep water from Stuart Road to Mariners Base, recklessly lashing old oil drums together with planks or wood and pushing off from the side, with bits of four by one as oars, or sticks in a Gondoliers action from the rear. We would play for hours and hours during the summer holidays when days were long, making our way across to the yacht basin and its lock and the river bank.

As we looked for things to do, we would generally end up by the river, especially on warm days as we made our way over in the river direction, where a big rope hung from the bough of a tree over the water, we would swing out after standing on another branch, doing an impression of Johnny Weissmuller's Tarzan as we swung, sometimes two or three of us hanging on for dear life. After playing there, we worked our way along the river path at the back of Ham Lands to Apple Island for lunch or snack. When I say lunch there was the remnants of old orchards from the farm period of The Dysart Estate, climbing on shoulders trying to get to the taller limbs to get the apples and load into our pockets and stretched jumpers, throwing some down to the other boys and sometimes girls who would come with us on our travels, picking up other kids on the way.

Interestingly this area of Ham was used for courting couples, generally same sex male couples who would pop their heads up above the grass and vegetation. This would frighten the life out of us, dropping everything we had collected and running back to our bikes, shouting insults as we went, not looking back! At this time we were confused by 'dirty old men' that waited around public toilets, offering you sweets and who may follow you in and what was going on in the grass. To be honest we didn't know the difference between perverts and homosexuals and at that time both were illegal, so in our naive minds, they were all criminals! This area picked up the horrid nickname of Bummers Island instead of Apple Island, there are stories of a local bobby encouraging the local lads to clear the area of these couples before 1967. Seems so strange and an attitude of a hundred years ago, must have been so difficult emotionally for many when homosexuality was illegal.

Making our way back to the river end of Ham Street where the car park is, which was always busy when Ham House was open, walk up past the Rifle Club entrance and King George V playing fields and turn right onto our end of the village's football pitches, further on Riverside Drive Rec', or The Rec' as we called it, always finding lads kicking a Frido plastic football around or a newly acquired leather ball with bladder that they had for a gift or saved for. Girls playing on the swings, which we are just starting to notice and as we launched our rockets on a journey towards Planet Puberty – a period at this age that you think pulling hair, pushing, calling them names and being stupid is just a good chat up line or action to make them like you - we are soon to learn the terms of engagement!

We would meet school and village mates like The Varney's and Poulter Boys, who all lived on Riverside Drive along with Danny at number 23, just a short walk from our houses. It would always be enough to start a game of football, two self elected captains, we all stand in a line and choose your players, this is where you find out where your skills with a ball are ranked in Ham. Danny, just three months younger and already a great footballer, however his rocket was already orbiting Planet Puberty, a cheeky likeable lad and very popular, especially when trying to impress the girls with the apparatus on the Rec'. One evening or afternoon, playing around, he dared us to load one side of the see-saw with three lads and he would sit alone on the other. As he shot up, holding onto the handlebar, we decide to dismount and he crashes down with an enormous thump, as he curses us, he holds his crutch and a trickle of blood runs down his leg, we take him home, he had managed to split his scrotum! Another legendary story with Danny, when climbing the famous Mulberry Tree close by, as he grabs the branch he slips, falling backwards onto two of the rusty spikes, on top of the surrounding circular metal railings. Panicking and holding his weight off the spikes and shouting for help, luckily and I think it was Andy Poulter, slightly older and taller manages to lift him off, he carried the puncture scars all of his life.

Those long summer evenings on the Rec', would see us playing until the failing daylight, along the horizon with the setting sun, the aircraft heading for London Airport were backlit, we were quite good at recognising these silhouettes – the first Comets, later VC10, Douglas DC8, a Boeing 707, 727 and later the giant 747 in 1969, Lockheed Tristar, BAC One-Eleven, Trident, Douglas DC8/9s, Russian Illyushin and the Tupolev's, earlier propeller planes like the Vickers Viscount, that were soon to be retired in the 1960's. As plane spotters we were good, knowing the difference between a Lancaster and a Wellington bomber, we imagined doing this in WW2 at the highest point of Richmond Park, looking out for the Luftwaffe!

Like many lads we were all interested in planes, making Airfix models and hanging them from bedroom ceilings on fishing line or catgut, leading us to one summer, planning an adventure to London Airport. This a tricky, even if they had spare cash, to get a bus or other transport, from our parents, it would bring a resounding 'NO!', 'to far', 'to dangerous' and that 'old chestnut' phrase, "Wait until you are older, then you can do anything you want too!", that normally bought an end to any negotiation stance. Anyway, the attraction of standing on the roof of 'The Queens Building', the famous building that Beatles fans welcomed their return from a very successful tour of America and its crowded viewing platform was too much for us, no money and little pocket money meant decisions, it led to a plan of "Let's ride our bikes over there!", after a look of 'are we men or mice', we decide to lay low, be good for a few days and plan.

So, a sunny day is chosen in the school holidays, parents are out to work early, Paul Sossick, Robbie Good and myself, check our bikes over, Paul is lucky his being relatively new. Rob's and my own, are pieced together and built by our own fair hands. We know there are signs to London Airport in Twickenham, so we make our way across using Ham Ferry run by a very freckled Ginger, our bikes aboard, we disembark and find the road signs making our way over in the direction of Hounslow, riding mainly on the pathways. We are a little nervous, but at the point of no return, we make it to the airport, the roar of engines and planes disappearing into the sky, that smell of Kerosene, it was so exciting, would you believe we just propped our bikes up on the side of the building, no security, just other kids with a set of binoculars and men in anoraks making notes of numbers in a little book. We enter and climb the steps to the roof and its viewing area, I will never forget that experience! We know we are doing something wrong, my bad fairy on my shoulder is having a field day, the good fairy never got a look in!

We made our way back, we were out for hours, light is now failing, secretly wondering what our parents might say. Pulling up outside our houses, as we cycled up our road tired and hungry – we never ate that day, Robbie's Mum asked us what we had been doing, obviously with the way we looked and red cheeks, Rob replied, "Oh, only in Richmond Park, been in there for ages, my chain broke and a puncture.", we never told his twin sister Irene or Julie Smith, under pressure it would get out and told on us! Bad Fairy 1 – Good Fairy 0.

Later in the sixties and early seventies, playing footie on The Rec' we frequently saw Concorde going into land, its powerful engines roaring and crackling as it lowered its undercarriage and nosecone, the supersonic shape dropped into the setting sun. We would always look at each other, holding onto the comment "Do you remember (chuckling or smiling), when we cycled to London Airport?" At the end of a summers night and the light failing on the Rec' and we could hardly see each other now playing a lot more football and the swings are now too young for us. When younger and returning home from work, my mother's voice could be heard shouting "Grrraaaa.....'AM!", her powerful voice slipping over the top of the tiled roofs of both Murray Road and Riverside Drive and landing on the Rec, I now know it's time to go home and so do the others. Or alternatively Rob's older brother's Kevin or Les, would be sent around to tell us to come home, sometimes we could delay going home, getting them to join in. Playing on that Rec' became a ritual, that we performed for years over and over in our youth, despite the midges biting, falling in or slide tackling in dog poo, or even worse broken glass, bottle tops or a squashed Coke can!

I always like to turn and read the newspaper, listen to the news and of course music. News from the US always interested me, as mum worked for an American lady on Richmond Green, her children would often be sent gifts from The States, because the children were away at boarding school, my mother would be given surplus toys and books. I was given microscopes, chemistry sets, Potty Putty, Play Dough, Stickle Bricks and many other US made toys, it was great, Mum got given a toasted sandwich maker that worked on the gas rings, my first 'cheese and onion toastie!'. As lads, I think The States was somewhere that we all would have liked to live or visit then, with lots more US TV programmes showing, the cars were larger, food portions looked enormous, hot dogs and hamburgers looked huge and more tasty, there never seemed any shortage of food (obviously not true as not so well off people there also).

However, at that time news from America was generally about Vietnam and the amount of soldiers being sent and up to 10% of the younger generation were now involved with the Draft process. Young people, students, some politicians were now seeing this war as a waste of time, money and especially life. But the public were very much divided, parents and an older generation mainly supported the engagement, after WW2 and Korea, initially sons wanted to fight for the US and return as hero's too.

Anti-war demonstrations became more frequent and a group of a younger generation from The West Coast, anti-war gatherings took place and in that hot summer of 1967, 100,000 people gathered in Haight-Ashbury in San Francisco, the majority wearing strange fashions and calling it 'The Summer Of Love' encapsulating hippiedom and psychedelic music, free love, a drug taking culture, pacifism and attempting to pressure a government to put an end to the Vietnam conflict and even segregation in The South. Another gathering of 30,000 Hippies at Golden Gate Park in what was called the Human-Bein where Timothy Leary addressed the crowd and coined the famous phrase of 'Turn On, Tune In, Drop Out' talked about the 'meaning of inner life', peace and the drug experience. Their actions and thoughts were generally fuelled by LSD which was legal in the US until October 1966, attending events and gatherings, being invited to take 'The Acid Test' a young psychedelic band called The Grateful Dead attracted and played at many. Peace and Love could be seen on t-shirts and graffiti, Flower Power ruled that summer and crossed the Atlantic, even our chart music was influenced and related to events in the US, and entering the charts, Scott McKenzie's, San Francisco ('Be sure to wear some flowers in your hair!'), The Flowerpot Men, Lets Go To San Francisco. Hippie-ism started to influence across America, now the UK and spreading to the rest of the world. British groups appeared in the UK charts, with a flower powered themed songs and clothing. The Beatles and All You Need Is Love, Lucy In The Sky With Diamonds (LSD?) The Moves, Flowers In The Rain, Pink Floyd and See Emily Play, a song about a sighting of an imaginary girl seen by Syd Barrett a band member, after taking drugs and hallucinating. Flowing Hippie clothes influenced groups like The Mama's and The Papa's, The Young Rascals, Traffic, The Herd, The Turtles and the memorable and favourite of mine 'A Whiter Shade of Pale' by Procol Harum, which was great to sing along too, but what the hell was it all about and a great favourite as the last dance at our youth clubs!

Watching Top Of The Pops on a Thursday night was difficult, fingers crossed I wanted to see live or on film, The Monkee's, The Foundations, Stevie Wonder, Diana Ross, The Supremes, Arthur Conley, Aretha Franklin, The Box Tops, The Who, The Four Tops, Gladys Knight and hoped that would appear that night on the chart countdown. This music was picked up by our older village teenagers and siblings and the Mod culture, my brother and his mates, the clothes and this being the music of Modernists.

Despite our village being influenced by the nearby Ivy Shop, The Castle Ballrooms and the mod scene, by older siblings and teenagers. Hippie-ism has entered even into our school culture, we junior mods and suedeheads, quickly named them 'Drongoes', this generation strangely and the majority, that followed this fashion, didn't seem to come in reality from our council estates, they were blue collar or lower middle class and living in private houses, that their parents owned most destined to stay on at school and take GCE O and A level's. Being invited to the odd party in the village, by any these classmates, meant listening to The Cream, Grateful Dead, Jefferson Airplane and other hairy bands, growing their hair and wearing strange clothing and smokey coloured round sunglasses, flowery shirts, Tie-Dye, military greatcoats and Kaftans, joss sticks and that sickly smell, which naively some of us thought was a drug! Us, young second generation Mods in waiting, looked at each other in a 'let's get out of here' way, we would collect any records we had taken and leave. It just wasn't our scene!

About this time and getting older 14 and 15 year olds, we started to hang out in the village, now more conscious of how we look, hopefully meeting with a few young ladies and girls we fancied from school and around. We usually congregate outside a local cafe called 'The Blue Peter' or having no money, sat on the library wall, opposite Westminster Wine, during the day, this was a typical cafe at the time, council workmen ordering copious amounts of tea, toast, sausage or bacon sandwiches on the only choice of what was white bread. Those Walls meat pies in a foil tray, sausage rolls, displayed in a warmer cabinet on glass shelves. A tray of stale doughnuts and those London Cheesecakes, with that sugar shredded coconut on the top, not a cheesecake we would know later in life. On a summers night the patronage would change, young boys and girls and older working siblings would hang around inside and outside. Cars that look great with modifications of a re-spray or larger wheels and wheel arches, scooters and motorbikes were all parked outside, Mods and Rockers in harmony and chatting. The pinball machine, inviting you to play, a themed glass lit panel on the back, flashing lights, with the players scores, the noise of those flippers, striking the ball bearing that hit the mushroom lit shaped obstacles, making a bell ring. It would then propel the ball anywhere, back to you and if your flipper control wasn't good, down the gully, the clonk and noise of this and the number scores clocking up, one of those sounds that never leaves you. Playing, you would be constantly nudging it with your hip. Sid, who ran the Blue Peter then and the most memorable, had no customer skills whatsoever, often swearing and shouting at us for pushing the machines, to a 'Tilt' or not buying enough drinks or food, we could make a can or bottle of Coke and a straw last for an hour. The popularity of the Juke Box, playing the tunes that we liked from the charts, young ladies sitting on tables across the cafe nudging each other about the lads entering and who fancies who. Us younger ones would ask the older boys and brothers or be given a sixpence or shilling to select a few records, every week, the chap who changed the records would come in, each record had a counter and if it was played a lot it stayed in the selection, anything that had few plays would be changed for the latest chart entry. The man, would often give away records that were taken out, Sid had to change the times of the Juke box engineer visit as we begged him to give us the 45 single, with its centre punched out! This was one of the earlier places to meet young ladies, although most of us were eventually banned from visiting The Blue Peter, for not spending money.

I can still hear The Supremes, The Happening and Reflections, The Small Faces, Itchycoo Park, Aretha's Respect, Eddie Floyds Knock On Wood, The Four Tops Reach Out... The Beach Boys, The Troggs, The Young Rascals, See Emily Play and many more, playing on that Juke Box. The Music, The Time and The Place will connect me always, as I was later to find out over the following years.

Another interesting band on the juke box then, was The Jimi Hendrix Experience's and Purple Haze, looking to me very much like a hippie with a big Afro, but he sure could play a guitar, even with his teeth and was very influential with his playing style. He began and took up the guitar late, at the age of 15, earning a place with The Isley Brothers in 1962, where a 10 year old and younger brother, Ernie Isley watched him and learned, but who initially took up the drums. As a 15 year old Ernie, got his first guitar, self taught and played bass on the very funky 'It's Your Thing' in 1969 and famously later the superb solo guitar work on 'Who's That Lady' in 1973. For me there seems a musical connection between Ernie and sadly Jimmi, had a short very successful career of only four years and was briefly the world's highest paid performer. After playing at Woodstock and the Isle of Wight Festival, he accidentally killed himself from a drugs overdose in a flat in Lansdowne Crescent, Notting Hill, London W11 on the 18th September 1970, aged just 27.

The 'Summer Of Love of 1967' was definitely the 'Summer Of Crushes' for me – young ladies that is! As that summer comes to an end, I head for Class 4AC at Grey Court, a semi-academic stream that now prepares pupils to take O Levels and the following year of the 5th Form. But for many of us, now the ability to countdown, leaving education and finally work and life beckons.

I also loved my time at Petersham & Ham Sea Scouts and initially the Cub Pack, learning to do things, especially knots and camping etc, but now it appears a bit nerdy, with the news of youth clubs opening up in the village for young teenagers with activities etc. Now the idea of wearing shorts, long socks and an itchy jumper, at the coming age of 15, with all lads, I am ashamed to say, doesn't have the same attraction, sorry My Bryant, but I do thank you for so many memories and the skills learned, suddenly now 'It's not very Cool' and there are no young girls hanging around. I break my spectacles yet again playing around and will be told by the optician, that I now can claim the record for replacements and repairs after ten years of wearing them. Mum, won't be happy at another trip to Batemans The Opticians in Hill Street opposite The Gaumont or The Flea Pit as we called it. She made me go on my own, to explain how I broke them again and now very embarrassing, eyes tested, I am told my weak eye has improved, I now make a personal executive decision 'NOT to wear specs ever again!' in my misunderstood and a delusional way, it might make me more confident and attractive to the opposite sex at last, I go home and say to Mum, my eyes are fixed!

That OPPOSITE SEX phrase. When you have an absent father or an older brother, who won't entertain The Birds and The Bees pitch to you, how do you find anything out? The school curriculum didn't even cover the subject if I remember, if it was covered, the giggling and chuckling made me forget that one lesson of Sex Education and preparing for life, us boys will in a couple of years, learn about sex crudely 'On The Job' and the experiences that will bring, not the best way to learn and would be consequences. A fantasy of an 'Older Woman' perhaps by 10 or 15 years my senior taking me 'in-hand' and showing me the ropes and passing on any experience may have been useful! As far as 'Getting Girls in Trouble', I was light years away from that issue, for many bringing any 'Trouble to The Door', wasn't an option and would touch on criminality in a way and be policed by Mothers and Fathers, my Good and Bad Fairy's will have some say and intervene for me. But other pubertal issues come into play, adolescence and early teen years for lads have consequences like 'nocturnal emissions' – I loved that phrase or 'Wet Dreams' to give it the street name, not to forget Master Bates in Captain Pugwash, I always laughed, but didn't know what lads were talking about initially! For me, obviously there must have been signs that my mother must have noticed and you lads will know what this is, don't think I have to list them, but you can remember distinctly and you know what I am talking about and the phrase, when Mum shouted to you up the stairs for a meal, 'Just cumin Mum, won't be a minute!', had a different meaning. But when you have your first experiences, thinking is this normal, what's going on, should it be happening, 'am I a pervert?' or 'even is it illegal?', to have any nightly thoughts about girls? If I can remember, many peers never mentioned it initially, similar to young girls, I assume talking about their first period, I believe going to a co-educational school gave us a lot more understanding of the opposite sex, just by piecing bits of life's sexual jigsaw together. To my surprise and great embarrassment, I arrive home yet again to an empty house, go upstairs to change and there is this government information blue printed covered pamphlet or booklet from The National Health – titled 'Puberty & Masturbation' - subtitled 'A Guide For Teenage Boys'! What the Hell!, I go crimson with the thought that my mother is aware of my body changing - but is this The Birds and The Bees Part 1 book? Always interested in facts and knowledge, at least to know that I am normal and these things happen.

Hanging around is OK, but we would like to perhaps be indoors as the nights get darker and news that the Blue Peter won't open on winter evening's anymore, but fortunately we have heard rumours that autumn and seen some construction of new youth clubs in Ham. The building that housed Ham Boys Club is now being demolished and the local authority will build a brand new clubhouse to replace it, activities like darts, table tennis, chess. They have combined The Venturers Club from Trefoil House on the Petersham Road with Ham Boys and calling it Ham Venturers Youth Club, we also hear it will welcome both girls and boys on the same night! After a proposal to the local council, asking for a purpose built youth club with facilities such as a kitchen, built on the dilapidating old boys club, the idea gained traction. Set up by the hardest working youth leader that you could come to know and respect, John Saville, who really cared about the local youngsters, activities and keeping mainly boys and girls off the streets, making the club mixed and being passionate about his football. For us boys, it was ideal, run like a proper football academy, with training twice a week on Ham Common, during the season and weekly during pre-season, he put so much of his personal time into the role.

The Club was open socially on Tuesday and Friday nights from 7 until 9pm, table tennis and darts were the main activities and the odd feature film in the club room, but generally it was chatting to the local boys and girls, perhaps even from other schools and local areas. This is a time and an age when clothing and music became a big part of our lives, literally 'sewing' the seeds of the clothes we liked and how we looked. John, was later assisted by another great man called Jim Lee, who was as a youngster a member of Ham Boys Club and who could box, another one who took football training very seriously and steered teams to cup and league trophies and committed so much time to the club in many other ways to drive funds to keep it going, like a fashion show one year to raise money, he really cared about the local youngsters being bought up in the village in the 1940s and 50s. Jim told me later in life, that his wife Nina threatened him more than once with the phrases 'I think you love Venturers, more than me!" and "Jim, make your mind up, me or The Venturers!". His discipline and approach to football developed some great skills and even made the local school Grey Court, a very strong team in school leagues, it even saw players getting regular spots in the Ham FC team when older and some thinking about football as a career. Another popular youth club was Ham and Petersham, also newly built, with a sports hall and rooms, just off Lock Road, at this age, the older lads, who had left school at 15 and now 16 had now had the ability to give a young lady a lift home, on a scooter, motorbike or even a Honda 50 or 90 was OK - looking pretty cool, drawing on a 'fag' - chatting to the girls, in front of the club. Girls of our own age, always looked up to and 'fancied' the older boys, it made sense to them, but some girls broke our hearts and told us, we were too young to walk them home! We younger ones just ran around in that mad way of kicking tennis and soft balls, tripping each other up, perhaps stupidly throwing darts the length of the room at a target, we had one lad that could catch them sideways and one who took it in the shoulder. Running around playing 'It' or 'Bulldog', where you were tapped to be out!

Over the following years, these Youth Clubs, were the place to go and be seen in the village, where we would serve our flirting apprenticeships - learn tricks of the trade - not in the work sense, but really in life or engaging mainly with the opposite sex. How to speak to a young lady - you certainly got feedback from some of them, if you got it wrong! - and not say the wrong thing, learning that first impressions that really counted, wearing the right clothes and shoes, differentiating yourself (smelling good, checking your armpits and wearing your brothers stolen aftershave?), music and the keeping up to date with best sounds of the day. Getting your name on a school football or rugby team sheet, really helped, asking girls to come and watch, being aware they might fancy your mate who was also playing, Danny in my case, we even swapped and stole each other's girlfriends at least four times. Dropping a hint to a girl, that you fancy her friend – a little risky if she liked you, although you could 'see' her or chat for a short while to get access to her friend, being passed a note from a friend of a girl that liked you. Looking across the club room at a young lady you may be attracted too, trying to catch her eye and then seeing if she glances back at you – later helped with a slow dance at the end of an evening, where you would test your thoughts and sometimes getting it completely wrong! Complementing a girl about her hair, makeup, dress or shoes or how easy she is to talk too, trying to be funny – watch this one, it was always a risky strategy and could backfire!

Little did I realise at this time that this is where I will serve my music apprenticeship as a soul boy cadet and everything that would surround it in the coming years. We are now spoilt for choice with gatherings in Ham Hall, Venturers, Ham and Petersham Youth Club (Thursday night) which we called Lock Road, we even crossed borders and we were invited to a Kingston or Barnfield Youth Club by some young girls, we had bumped into at Woolworth Kingston at the record counter to the displeasure of the local boys. It was in 1968, that I heard Pictures Of Matchstick Men by Status Quo, who the week before I saw on TOTP and thought were a Mod group after seeing Francis Rossi (a family member of the famous Rossi ice cream brand) looking so much like Stevie Marriot, little did we know they would don denim for the next fifty years and 'Going Down The Dustpipe' with their use of guitars and every chart entry sounding the same!

The new growing Wates Estate, another youth club at St Richards opens on Monday nights, this was more interesting as the girls, where their parents again 'actually owned' their new houses. A new social class in the village, many parents didn't like their daughters talking or mixing with the local state school and council house lads, let alone courting one. Now, you can understand what is going to happen now, exposure to all these young ladies, got to look good, hair combed and tidy, smell good, listen to the right radio stations and the right sounds. Youth Clubs at this time and our age were the places to go and be seen, St Richards Youth Club was where I met one of my first ever girlfriends called Lynne, which fizzled out after three weeks a pupil at Bonner Hill, an all girls school that got the not so nice nickname of Brothel Hill - I have no idea why, I think it just sounded funny.

At this age of 14 and 15 you are desperate to be another year or couple of years older, the bigger lads like Andy Poulter, Colin Burton, Alan Pope, Keith (Woofer) Barker, all worked, had a wages and money and it shows, they could also play football, did have the scooters, nice cars and unfortunately for us, we being slightly younger had no status. We were desperate to get older and find a job that paid.

Like many others I loved the youth clubs, to be honest what else was there to do at home in the 1960's, as allowed now to stay up a little later, something to look forward too during and every week, checking with perhaps the occasional young lady you might fancy or have a crush on and ask, if she is going this week, with the lads in the playground and a 'You going to Venturers, tonight?"

as we walked home from school and went in different directions. The trouble at this age is that crushes can happen with the bigger girls a year above at school, that 'older woman' syndrome kicks in again. Walking home from youth club at the same time as two attractive young ladies, a year older than me at school and living in Russell Gardens, close to my house. If I saw or heard them coming home from Lock Road club or Venturers, I would walk slower or faster depending on their position. If they spoke to me and they normally did, I went bright red or behaved like a little puppy – I suppose it would be called 'stalking' today, but I hope I wasn't! My Crushmeter needle swung to the right stop, not being very big, I was never a threatening figure picking up the label of 'safe', 'cute' or 'sweet', where my other friends attracted the girls and were a bit wild and naughty – it just wasn't and didn't seem fair.

During the autumn of 1967, a black cloud bubbles up yet again over our house, my father is released from prison and appears at our front door. My mother goes into a what seems like a melancholic phase, as always he starts, gets a job, tries to act as if everything is normal, she reminds him about where he is sleeping in Keith's room. As the weeks go by, my mother changes mentally and gets a little stronger, realising the relationship cannot go on for much longer. Right on cue, after a month or so the arguing starts again, about paying his way.

Yet again, those keys in the door late at night, would always wake me, making that unique noise, that sickens my stomach, my heart races but this time I am more prepared about the arguing and the fallout, shouts of 'where have you been?' or 'the rents due', 'where's the housekeeping', 'I can't do this all myself', 'this is not going to work!', then Mum disengages in continuing the argument. Shortly afterwards, I am at home with my mother watching the TV, my father still not home, I do not even ask my mother where he is. As bedtime comes, the nine o'clock news comes on, I offer to make Mum a cup of tea, generally at this time she asks me to go to bed, but she was so tired and emotionally down to tell me to go to bed, the words never came. As I make the tea, the dreaded noise of that key finding the lock and turning, makes my heart beat faster, it feels like its wants to burst out of my chest, my stomach churns with sickness. I so wished it was my brother returning home, but NO, it was my father! He walks down the hall and into the kitchen and talks to me as if he is the best dad in the world, 'Hi Son' he says, as if he is someone who cares. He walks past me smelling of tobacco and the pub, alcohol and strangely I notice a faint smell of perfume, which seems strange, rolls a cigarette and steps into the garden to smoke it and was probably quickly concocting a story about where he's been and who with. With the tea brewed, I put it on the kitchen table, Mum comes in looking very upset and angrily challenges his whereabouts the night before and tonight. Also mentions needing the housekeeping money because the rent and bills are due.

I am standing between Mum and the table and my father at the backdoor on the other side of the table. Mum asks 'Where have you been?', he tells a story and Mum interrupts saying 'No you haven't, someone saw you with a woman in Kew!', initially he denies it, but he has this innate skill of believing his own stories and can convince himself that it couldn't possibly be him!.

As Mum questions him more, I notice he starts to clench a fist in anger and with the other hand, he flips the table up, the hot tea, sprays both my mother and myself. He lunges forward towards Mum and for some reason, I step in between them, driven more by anger and emotion than bravery, I scream 'Dad! Dad! Please, please stop it, please stop it, stop, go away, get out, I hate you!!' I am bought to tears and sob holding Mum. This action causes him to stop and withdraw, his face shows shock, grabbing his car keys and storms out of the front door, slamming it as he leaves. We sit on the kitchen floor, me trying to comfort a teary eyed Mum, she in return trying to comfort me, if I didn't see my father ever again, I wouldn't care.

We wait for Keith to come home, we really need to help Mum to get through this. My brother returns, I tell him what's happened and gets very angry, jumping in his car and goes looking for him to give him a piece of mind, returning home, he tells me that this situation can't go on for Mum's sake and her sanity, it's gone on for 20 years.

That autumn of 1967 is not a good one in our household, very much reflected in my year ends school work, I drop from 5th to 15th place in class, teachers are taking me aside and ask about my concentration, not listening, disappointed about the terms classwork and homework not in on time. My end of year report states 'if Graham is to go into the 5th form, 'he needs to work harder and change his attitude, the lack of concentration will make it uphill between now and any 'O levels', along with comments of being quiet and withdrawn'. I don't share with anyone how I am feeling, not even Mum or my brother, as we are all trying to be strong and handle in our own ways. All these issues about home life are kept it inside my head, looking for corners and places to hide my thoughts and concerns, I just needed to lock them away.

Still seems a time when emotions should never show in the street, any negative feelings, we as a family never wore our hearts on our sleeves, show strength first and carry on second. If anybody asked me 'Are you alright, anything wrong?' I would just answer 'Yes, I am fine!'- that's what we were supposed to do and many of us did at that time, wasn't it? We eventually sit down together and discuss between the three of us 'That enough is enough!' with our father, Mum nods with acceptance and finally realises, even with all that hope, that her marriage is not going to work after two decades and that she must file for divorce, she is now 45 years old. We haven't seen him since that night, we change the locks and will endeavour to prevent him from coming in the house.

⁂

Getting lost in music is my therapy, it helps my well being, Keith buys me a brand new transistor radio of my own for Christmas, one of those with a plastic sleeve, perforated where the speaker is, a carry strap, and a little square piece of vinyl plastic with a press stud which held the earpiece. When in bed at night the earpiece in place I listen to 'Pirates' such as Radio's London and Caroline and of course the fading in and out sounds of Luxembourg all broadcast on medium wave, these blast out more R&B, Soul and Motown etc, with me listening under the bed covers, before feeling sleepy.

To combat the pirate stations and try and attract younger listeners, the BBC are about to rebrand old stations and launch new ones. On Saturday, 30th September 1967 at 7am, DJ Tony Blackburn was lured to the BBC after working on the Pirates, a DJ that promoted Tamla Motown and favoured black music, launches Radio 1, placing The Moves 'Flowers In The Rain' on the turntable for the first spin. The Move amusingly were consequently taken to court for using promotional material for the single, depicting a nude Harold Wilson – the PM won the libel action. Other BBC radio stations rebranded is the Light Programme calling it Radio 2, The Third Programme was renamed Radio 3 and the Home Service now called Radio 4. This change was not so well accepted as just over two decades earlier, The Home Service delivered The News and The Voice of Home throughout the War Years, relaying information to families, many missing the man of the house or sons, bought together by the sound of the BBC, in those very dark days, over six years. Soldiers and even prisoners in far flung distant places where conflict happened, the BBC delivered moral boosting news about how the war was going, best of all, it announced Victory in Europe and over Japan, along with speeches from The King and Churchill, change for some is difficult and brings emotions understandably.

Thankfully, this heralded the age of radio for the UK's younger listeners and music on the go in the later 1960's. 1967 saw the Marine Broadcasting Offences Act, that closed the loophole in international waters, I also believe in theory that it became illegal for any British subject to listen to Pirate Radio, Radio Caroline continued on until 1990 in various forms. Although 'pirate radio' would return again in the 1980's, from many tower blocks in

London promoting club and R&B non-radio and charting sounds, although some BBC DJ's tried to specialise in similar sounds, but it was difficult, adhering to the station controllers guidelines of popular music. I will always remember tuning into Radio Invicta from the 70s till 1984, using the slogan 'Soul Over London'.

⁂

However, as if by a miracle in this difficult time, the Gods shine on Mum, a wonderful piece of luck attached itself and fell through the letterbox for my mother - at last! She had always saved a little a week to buy one Premium Bond at a time, from the governments National Savings and Investments scheme, saving half a crown a week to buy a 'Bond' and knowing she could always cash them in if required. Launched by Harold Macmillan when Chancellor of the Exchequer in 1956 to control inflation and encourage people to put some money by and if very lucky to win some money. Interestingly, so different to other games of chance, like betting and football pools at the time in that with Bonds you did not lose your stake, it would be consistently entered into a monthly prize draw and randomly chosen by technology called ERNIE an acronym for Electronic Random Number Indicator Equipment and based on the Colossus system, the world's first digital computer and developed by the Post Office Research Station, being the size of a single decker bus, it could generate some 2,000 numbers an hour. Today, the fifth generation of ERNIE, which performs at speeds that can choose 3 million numbers in just 12 minutes each month, over 22 million of the UK population, hold Premium Bonds. Luckily for my mother and us, one of her numbers came in that year, in the form of winning the princely sum of £250, the equivalent today of some £3000! As always, Mum would think about her boys, finding a cancelled place on the school skiing trip to Austria that year, which many of my classmates and friends parents had saved a pricey £39 for (£450 today). She quickly put my name down and I was booked. That coming March 1968 there was also an organised educational cruise by Surrey schools, offering places to our school and a trip was again booked for me! And as a treat to herself, booking her own ticket as a group of about 60 adults was also catered for on the cruise! Keith was given a similar amount of money for a car.

Around this time we are told by a neighbour that my father, has been seen around and tried to get back into the house, thankfully unsuccessfully, now we have changed the locks, but he disappears again. Mum, shortly after gets a call from Richmond Police Station on our newly installed green GPO telephone that sits in the hall and is told that he has been arrested again and is held in cells, waiting for bail. Mum bravely says, 'We are separating and he doesn't live here anymore, sorry but it's not my problem, thank you!', putting down the receiver, so he is remanded, appears in court and will serve another short sentence, yet again for fraud as a result of another confidence trick.

It gives us a rest bite, Mum always made and created a great Christmas in difficult times, I was never really aware of how little money we had and thankfully us boys, never felt poor or neglected.

That New Year with the school skiing trip to the Austrian Tyrol, I had the feeling Mum would miss my company at home, especially settling down to watch TV at night. She helps me pack my suitcase, I put together clothes that will be hopefully be warm, my ageing Scouts anorak should be suffice, only the kids with parents that can afford it will have proper ski apparel. Now C&A in Kingston had started stocking clothing for this new growing sport, which had formerly been open only to the better off!

We embark on oily smelling tugboat style rusty British Rail ferry later to be Sea Link to Calais after a rough winters crossing and climb aboard a sleeper train overnight to Vorarlberg in Austria. With great excitement, we notice the carriages had drop down sleeping couchettes, six in each compartment, travelling through the night, don't think anybody slept because of the excitement of being away from home and the situation we find ourselves in. We will spend New Year's Eve there and welcome in 1968, for many it's our first time on foreign soil, some 800 miles away from home, we arrive at Bludenz railway station and walk around to our hotel, trudging through deep lying snow, through drifts and freezing air. Why would any hotel take a booking of some 30 state school pupils? I don't know, especially 14 and 15 year olds.

That UK winter of 1967/8, had bought a small flu epidemic, nowhere as contagious as the next winter's Hong Kong strain, that caused 30,000 UK deaths, but this year bad enough to spread around the pupils. Combine this with a snowfall that lasted for days with freezing temperatures, many never even got to see the slopes that trip, let alone learn to ski. Some that got to the slopes and had trouble even getting on to the button lifts, bodies would pile up on the slope and we just couldn't stop laughing. The lift attendants would shout at us 'Achtung, Achtung!' for us young boys that were born not long after the WW2 and watched war films – we shouted back 'Schnell, Schnell!' in return, a German word we caught from our comics, these were the days before good ski-wear, we were absolutely freezing in the driving winter blizzards in the Alps and not prepared at all, nothing like playing on the snowy slopes of Richmond Park.

Come New Years Eve, many girls and boys are feeling better and are determined to enjoy the occasion and see in 1968, we were nearly adults obviously! And let's face it, it's better than watching Andy Stewart's yet again and his New Years Eve (Hogmanay) Party an end of year White Heather Show, that ran from 1957-1968, being entertained by 'Donald Where's Your Troosers', was enough to make you have an early night on any 31st of December!

In the meantime many of the girl's now young ladies have made friends with the young male bar staff and have secured a channel to buy cigarettes, for those who wanted to try or already smoked and along with alcohol, mainly schnapps and small beers!! That evening was great fun, if I remember rightly there was an indoor skittles and a small bowling alley, with some slightly excited and inebriated teenagers becoming very competitive, after a few sips of alcohol.

I think the teachers were distracted with their own celebrations in the lounge, missing the goings on in the bar and restaurant area, there was another school party from the T'up North staying at the same time and we were all mixing. These lads had managed to get hold of bottles of beer, as well as chatting up and stealing New Year kisses from 'our' girls and collecting pen pal addresses, which was a popular pastime then. Some of the boys were having a little too much alcohol at the end of the night and approaching the girls and causing some issues. The teachers now alerted, took back control and ushered us upstairs and to our rooms, the hotel was quite small, with narrow corridors and many doors. I was sharing a room with mates, Dave Brown and Danny Mahoney. Danny was one of those lads who you could always dare to do things and would be up for it, easily convinced to smoke and drink alcohol that night, to be honest he didn't need much coaxing.

As the girls retired to their rooms, classmates Jean Enright and Wendy Campbell were just along the hall, we dared him to look through their keyhole, not thinking he would ever do it. Of course, we all were giggling and snorting with laughter in that slightly inebriated youngster way on very little alcohol, staggering and trying to manoeuvre into position to take a peek! Some of the other girls, Wendy Lewis and Sally Medland, heard the melee outside of their rooms and opened their doors, in a way that everyone was running up and door corridors and stairs, it was like a Brian Rix theatrical farce that you would see on the telly.

During this time, Danny was still taking swigs of Schnapps and beer, stashed in our room and becoming more and more, worse for wear but very funny – to be honest he didn't drink that much. But we were so inexperienced about the effects of drinking and skinny that the alcohol got quickly into our blood streams. After about 15 minutes, I think it was Mr Harvey, like a prison officer escorted us back to our rooms, with a warning to settle down, making sure our doors were closed. Still relentlessly snowing outside the bedroom window, from the inside looking very much like a Charles Dickens Christmas story, with heavy snow piled up against the freezing window panes. At this stage Danny goes from tipsy to feeling dizzy and sick, putting him on the bed, with an upward jolt he projectile vomits down his front and the full length of his body! Sobering up quickly, what do two 14 year old boys do? If we go for help and tell a teacher, Danny - who had a bit of a naughty reputation already – he would get punished, so might we! So we reluctantly decide to clean him up, the room has a small basin, not risking to take him to the bathroom along the corridor. So being good mates we decide to rinse his clothes in the washbasin, try and ring them out, but drying was a problem, while our drunken mate sings with a slur, it alerts Mr Harvey on patrol outside, who enters the room to see the carnage and the wet clothes. Looking to dry things with only a small radiator but piled with our wet ski wear, the teacher says 'let's put them outside!'. We force open the window, snow falls into the room, luckily it had a big window sill with some iron fixings, which we hung out all of his clothes and even his vest and underpants! Danny was now tucked up in bed, head spinning, oblivious to the goings on in the room and our hard work.

The morning comes and he is grateful we cleaned him up, but unaware that Mr Harvey saw it! That previous night it had got to about -10C and six inches of snow, we are unable to ski that day because of the volume of the fall. Some of the pupils are playing snowballs outside and look up and see Danny's clothes frozen solid, hanging outside. A pair of Y-Fronts and vest hanging from the windowsill - stiff as the proverbial board, with the girls looking up, pointing and laughing hysterically, one of the lads runs upstairs and knocks on our door, telling us to open the window. As he does the kids below start clapping as Danny holds up his frozen underwear, his trousers and shirt are stuck together and solid, Danny knocks on them and we all roll about in uncontrollable laughter. It wasn't the first and wouldn't be the last time that we helped Danny clean up after drinking and putting him to bed, over the next ten years or so, it happened a few times at home and abroad, he never could take his drink!

Nearly fifty years later, I look through some old paperwork, I find a letter dated and postmarked 1st January 1968, sent to the hotel, my mother a prolific letter writer has written to me, Dave and Danny at the hotel, dated 31/12/67, it reads: "Hello, Graham and Boys, Its very peaceful here, I am alone in the house and it's just struck midnight, hope you are somewhere having a good time at a New Year's Party. Hope you are enjoying Austria and the food, I would love to try some, can you bring home some recipes. Hope your colds are better, I am missing you, but glad you got away from the flu epidemic." Your Loving Mum xxx

She must have been very lonely with her thoughts and very sad at the time I didn't realise how much. Empathy is a slow developing trait at that age and as a youngster, if anything my emotions towards my father made me feel very angry and took any away. In one way she wishes my father was around and had obviously mended his ways, she would have been very happy. But that New Years Eve, with Keith out and me abroad, must have given her a glimpse of the future if she were to stay single and be alone, as my brother and I grew older and would eventually fly the nest.

We return to England, after great fun and memories were built, as boys learning a bit more about young ladies and how to treat them, probably drinking too much at that age. I still look at a bottle of Schnapps to this day and chuckle about that week in Austria, some understanding their limits and some not. One broken leg, - I think it was Phillip Wilson - a few sprains and bruises, secrets, pocket money spent on that fantastic tasty Milka chocolate for Mum and an inexpensive small cowbell with an Innsbruck sticker on it, which she kept for years on her kitchen shelf!

1967, the main events of that year, in sport Alf Ramsey receives his well deserved knighthood after England's fantastic World Cup victory, Booby Moore receives an OBE. Chelsea beat Spurs 2-1 in the FA Cup Final – hurrah! Donald Campbell is killed on Coniston Water ironically attempting to break his own record. In politics, the UK enters into negotiations to join the EEC and the PM applies for membership, again President Charles de Gaul said

'Non!' and vetoed our entry. The British National Front is founded. The first black officer is recruited by the Metropolitan Police Force, the decriminalisation of homosexuality between consulting adults and the Sexual Offences Act is passed. First voucher based Barclays ATM or cash dispenser appears. First scheduled colour TV broadcast of Wimbledon tennis, The Prisoner starring Patrick McGoohan or Number Six (formerly Danger Man) driving a Lotus 7 pursued by a large white ball, which turned into a cult tv series, always got confused with the name Patrick Macnee in The Avengers as John Steed and other older woman crushes for me with Honor Blackman as Cathy Gale and Diana Rigg as Emma Peel, we nicknamed Jean Enright 'Emma' our classmate for some reason, probably because she could look after herself!

The Beatles, Sgt Pepper's is released and they created the Apple Corps for tax and business reasons, the Apple label that featured Mary Hopkins of 'Those Were The Days' fame, sadly, their hugely successful manager Brian Epstein, dies of a drug overdose. The Stones, Mick and Keith receive prison sentences for possession of illegal drugs, later affecting their visa status and touring in The States, the sentences were later quashed on appeal. Harold Wilson, who had attempted to gain favour with a younger generation and put forward The Beatles for MBE's and famously puffed on a pipe wearing his Gannex raincoat, devaluing the pound hoping to tackle the economic situation.

Football is still a big thing for us, on the back of that World Cup win, hoping to make it to the school team, but with Venturers, it's getting tough to get into the squad. I tended to get relegated to a reserve and cut up the oranges, stand in linesman, many times but still fun, travelling about South and West London playing games with tough and interesting opposition, with Asian and Afro Caribbean players, seemingly taller and more muscular than us skinny village boys. We had some great players and won many cups, trophy's and league titles.

At thirteen I took a 'legal job', visiting the school secretary to apply for a work permit in the local newspaper shop – for me Lee

(Southern), the newsagent opposite our school, getting a job as a paper delivery boy wasn't easy, normally selected and given the nod by 'The Paper Marker Upperer' the El Cappo Da Newsagents, a job that carried status, being paid a little more and they didn't have to go out in all weathers, especially cold rain, snow and freezing fog and sub zero temperatures. Generally a lad who was brighter and slightly older and pencilled the paper with a house number and road and also took the paper money in the shop and warned people they hadn't paid that the delivery may stop if they came in, tracked with a large book with tear out small strips, that was your receipt for payment. The Marker always arrived slightly earlier than our start time of 6am onwards, to either catch the delivery or take the papers into the shop, sometimes he was even given the key to the shop if a manager didn't live above or could be late. He had power, if you needed more pocket money, you would be get paid extra for another delivery, should another paperboy not show, this could be lucrative. This role was a very popular first job – over 80% of households had theirs delivered in the 1960s - for many lads and some lasses, most wanted to be one, but you could get excluded, unless you knew someone, hardly ever saw the job advertised. Our Marker - Paul Sossick was our sponsor, street and classmate for both Dave Brown and I and we received the nod! I think Danny was offered one, but he was either let go for not being able to get up, or couldn't be bothered! Completing the round as quick as possible, getting back to the shop and seeing if any of the other lads had failed to get out of bed. I did seven days a week, believe we got paid 12/- for six days and Sunday was worth 5/-, extra rounds were 1/- or 2/- on top, which Paul gave me many. On a Saturday morning, you would return to the newsagent to pick up your pay, ready to buy your comics and/or sweets and those little A5 sized war publications that cost a shilling. Hubba Bubba chewing gum, or a frozen Jubbly or Jamboree Bag, I do remember at the time Civil War cards were very popular, a little folded packet with picture cards and scenes that were sometimes very gruesome, with cavalry guns exploding into a group Union soldiers, included was a cheap bit of gum in, that lost its flavour after two mastication's. Treating myself to the Eagle, a glossy, informative comic that was also educational and featured Dan Dare – Pilot of the Future and his struggles with the Mekon, I think it was based in Britain's 1990's, it also featured PC 49, who seemed like George Dixon's cousin.

Paper rounds were very interesting, up early in the fresh air, loved the spring and summer months, winter could be gruelling, in a time when clothing was not particularly waterproof or warm and with unreliable bicycles. An anorak was the jacket of choice, - that scouts one again! - frost and snow were manageable although with that bag of newspaper either balanced on you handlebars, around your shoulder or a bike rack, but when the slush or snow had frozen solid, bike tyres and a full bag of papers wasn't easy. My first round was Woodville Road from Back Lane onto the new Wates Estate and nearby roads, our council estate had deliveries of the Daily Sketch, Express, Mirror and even Horse Racing News, The Daily Worker and The Angling Times of course living next to the river, not forgetting Woman's Realm or Own and many other publications. The Sun was first published as a broadsheet in 1964 and was formerly The Daily Herald, all had not many pages but easy to fold and go through the front door letter boxes, making life quite easy for a quick delivery. The Wates or New Estate, had a slightly posher paper and mix The Guardian, The Times, The Telegraph, Daily Mail and even The Sun was later targeted at the 'new' Lower Middle Class with their own homes. Sadly I missed out on viewing Page 3 as a paperboy, when introduced in November 1970, but had a peak as an apprentice when at work, on a regular basis, Jilly Johnson, Sam Fox and Linda Lusardi names come to mind!

Earning money meant one big thing - your hair styling, after many years of sitting with a plank between a barbers chairarms, Mum watching over and at the mercy of Slasher Harris at the back of Vickerys Newsagent on The Common. It meant one thing, a short back and sides whatever you asked for, after pointing to a photograph of a 'Boston Hair Style' and him saying 'and how would you like your hair today, Son?' I now jump on a bus to Kingston and visit a hairdresser Beverleys near the station entrance and ask for Ugo, ignoring the sign 'No Boys On Saturday' and have a Mod cut with a Boston!

Collecting your Christmas Box was also a challenge, you would normally knock on the door on a Saturday morning or afternoon, obviously after their Friday payday. The Council Estate was great, they generally knew you and who the paperboy was and easier to collect your tip, pressing in your hand a 6d or 1/- , 2/-, some even preparing a cheap Christmas card, with a thank you and some money in the envelope. Now about this time, the scallies of the village would knock on random doors, claim they were the paperboy and naively the householder would believe them and hand over MY tip! For me knocking on the doors of the big houses, bought a look of amazement from the owners about why you would even ask, or it would be explained that they are already paying for delivery on top of the price of the paper, so why would I give you a tip or sent to the Tradesman entrance! Or sometimes they understood and appreciated what you did, offering something, but generally the council estate houses gave more. I was a paperboy for two years, getting to know the manager and relief manager was always worth doing, in an effort for him to have a 'perk' he would open a packet of cigarettes – normally Players No.6, launched in 1965, as a cool and trendy fliptop and advertising claiming it was 'Of The British Scene', strong and about 1/9d for a packet of 10, less expensive than other brands. For 6d he would sell one cigarette and a couple of Swan matches to strike on brickwork, making a lot profit from the paperboys! Everybody lad seemed to smoke or experimented, like a 'right of passage of manhood' similar to an Amazonian or African tribe boy and their adult initiation ceremony, mates had to watch you taking a drag and finishing it! So at 14, I approach the stand in manager and complete a little nod, the sign for a 'fag' purchase, offer my coins and the transaction is done, feeling like an undercover agent and trading a microfiche film on a handover. I now have a paper round in the posher part of Petersham, Bute Avenue and around Sudbrook Lane, River Lane, Petersham Road and Tommy Steele's big house on the bend. Less houses, but the launch of Sunday supplements in the late 1960's was a nightmare for any lightweight paperboy, especially with The Sunday Times Magazine colour supplements. Two options split the delivery ie half a round first or go back to shop collect other half and deliver them. Second option take all the papers, stacked on handle bars, the bike felt like it was going to tip forward. Now the trouble with Sunday broadsheets and supplements is they don't fold like a thin Daily Mirror and although these posher houses had slightly bigger letterboxes, trying to push through the door caused ripping on the front or rear pages, jammed papers as well as the householder pulling it from the other side, instigated a few complaints back to the shop. If you split the newspaper up, it fell apart on the other side of the door, if you left it on the step it got wet or would blow open and scatter, you couldn't win, it wasn't easy, especially if you wanted to get an extra round in. So, that morning prepared for my first smoke, it's a dark winters morning, I finish my paper round, prop my bicycle up, sit between two bushes, place the cigarette between my lips, strike a match and the head breaks off! Second match ignites, I bring the match to the end of the cigarette and take a drag, the cigarette is now glowing and alight, your head and mates have told you that smoking is cool and will make me feel older and hopefully taller! But no one really tells you about the taste, the cough as it hits the back of your throat as you inhale, are you supposed to enjoy this, like it or just get used to it, like bitter or mild beer later? It's still a time when you don't waste anything or throw it away, I sit, dragging and puffing like a complete amateur and practice holding the cigarette between my lips, trouble is, the smoke gets in your eyes. The holding of the cigarette and that classic secrecy hold, the cigarette between thumb and forefinger, the smoking tip pointing at you palm, just hiding it from view, with the filter tip just showing, the classic school bike shed or walk home pose, spitting or rudely 'gobbing' constantly! So many men had tobacco stained fingers from smoking without filters and their choice of Senior Service. As I am cycling back up Sandy Lane, dizzy and nauseous, I stop halfway at the 'Rec and vomit behind the rubbish bin! That's it, my view of cigarettes as a cool implement of fashion evaporates like the cigarette smoke I coughed out that morning, I never smoke again! A paperboy rarely had breakfast, truthfully most ablutions were done when you returned home, the ink from the papers stained your hands and of course any breakfast, eg cornflakes (summer) and porridge (winter) came just before leaving for school at around 8 or 8.15am. So, that smoking on an empty stomach didn't help that morning, strangely I don't find the smell of smoke disgusting, because everyone smoked then it seemed, I find it very nostalgic in a perverse way and it's a reminder of my childhood and especially my teenage years, standing with mates who were having a sneaky smoke, at school, outside the youth club and of course pubs (except the next day, when you realise your clothes were impregnated!).

In February, Mum's win on the Premium Bonds see us packing now for the school cruise, she is so excited and it's great to see. But before this we needed injections for the countries we are visiting, Smallpox being one, the only trouble is that, I react later badly finding out that my father had TB when he was younger, giving me reactions to many vaccines, raised wheals and a red rash all over my body. The smallpox vaccine or vaccinae (latin for cow) and is a mild form of cowpox, it was discovered in the late eighteenth century, after it was noticed that milkmaids were less likely to be infected with smallpox! Luckily it abated before the trip, a smallpox eradication programme from 1958 to 1977 by WHO, was one of the only human diseases to be eradicated, along with Polio around the same time, I went to school with two children who wore callipers to support their legs. Later on at school, I also reacted to BCG injections with the test and was never left with that famous upper arm mark that many had. These mass injections were always done at school organised by the school nurse, who a few years before would have called our classes for a medical, where embarrassingly you would strip down to your vest and Y-Fronts always on a cold day it seemed to check for any skin infections, nits, bruises or lesions, but what I remember is her asking you to cough, pulling out your pants quickly to see if your testicles had dropped! Well? I think I even remember the girls standing there in the same garb in those first years, but surely not!

The school cruise was on SS Nevasa owned by British India Steam Navigation Company along with a sister ship SS Uganda in the 1960s, now a retired and refitted troopship carrier used for Educational Cruises. That year it left Southampton and travelled through The Bay of Biscay and hit a terrible storm of winds and rain. It also had 127 cabins with 307 births available to teaching staff and the public of which my mother was one. A thousand schoolchildren were in fifty dormitories below decks, against the bulkheads and with the sound of the pulsating engines, you can imagine the seasickness and malaise for a couple of days before we arrive in Gibraltar. Seventeen classrooms and a 450 seat assembly hall and cinema, cafeterias, recreation rooms, deck games space and a swimming pool. It was like a giant youth club and the good thing for us boys, there were 500 girls!

The ship sails onto Malta, Piraeus and a coach to Athens and a trip to the Acropolis overlooking the city that looked fantastic, onto Mycenae. These excursions meant lots of coach journeys and meeting other schoolchildren, I would get brave and engage with the young ladies, if it all went wrong I thought I wouldn't see them again anyway, however every time we went sightseeing and I talked to these girls, I would hear my mother shout 'Coo-eey Graham!' as she seemed always on the same trip with the other adults, they would ask who was that mad waving woman was and I would reply 'No idea, who she is!', I was so embarrassed!

We also travelled through the Corinth Canal, a sight to be seen with its steep sides and the narrow passage. After visiting Delphi, we sail up The Adriatic to that wonderful city of Venice and all its attractions, where we disembarked. The trip lasted some ten days, I cannot recall how we got back to the UK.

To this day, I still have a piece of art book paper signed by other pupils in our dormitory and ship, mainly girls from local schools, with names addresses, telephone numbers, memories and the odd kiss, well I am nearly 15! But most of all, I will always be thankful to my mother for spending £70 on me, the equivalent today of nearly £800, so many parents must have used life savings to send us on that trip of a lifetime! And thanks to ERNIE for picking mothers Bond numbers, she talked about that cruise and sightseeing for the rest of her life.

That spring of 1968 in Class 4AC is an interesting one, for me the school work becomes slightly harder, other excited lads in the fourth year are talking and thinking about leaving school and earning money. The more academic pupils in my class will definitely stay on and take their GCE's in the 5th form starting September. In the meantime another friend, Roger Squires, just slightly older and currently in the 5th Form and also played for Ham Venturers recommends me for the errand boy job at Elson's the Greengrocers in Ham Street, a shop that in the past and future that would employ many a village boy and girl. Roger takes another job with a travelling greengrocer around the village but I still kept my paper round hoping to juggle both as different times of the day, it pays a bit more because of the hours and more importantly the possibility of tips. An extra bonus and if Mrs Elson likes you, using the free film passes, as they have an Odeon and ABC advertising on their side fencing. (Regret, that I didn't keep the film posters, although they were offered!), I worked Tuesday and Thursday nights after school and then Friday nights filling empty banana, apple, pear and Jaffa Orange boxes and tomato trays with weekend orders for delivery on the Saturday. Mr and Mrs Elson had interesting personalities, she was a somewhat large lady, my thoughts is that she is similar to a Giles cartoon character of the grandma dressed in black with the hat and who carried an umbrella, a formidable lady. School girl friends of mine, Wendy and Sally also worked serving in the shop, she would always keep her overseer beady eyes on them, while serving. Embarrassingly, checking the change every time given to customers from one of those old giant cash tills with the drawer that shoots out with a 'ching', learning how to push down the enamel topped keys was an art! Even on a quiet end of day, she would keep both the girls them till the clock hands hit closing time, the sign changed to 'Closed', which meant tidying up and sweeping time, for this they earned a princely sum of half a crown (2/6d or 25p) and a special treat of an apple, handed over ceremoniously as though it was an expensive jewel, into the palm of their hands. Every time she asked you to do something, just her glare caused a jolt in your body to tidy up grab the broom to look busy.

I can still feel how cold it was in that shop on a winter's day, with the front and the back doors open, inviting an easterly wind in to take any warm air away from any paraffin heater! Mr Elson or Bill when 'She, who should be obeyed', wasn't within earshot, was a very kindly man, slightly overweight, a big pair of grey or brown trousers and big brown brogues, a wide belt holding them up as well as braces, a cardigan and old battered leather jerkin with one shoulder slightly worn where he carried bags of spuds and vegetables. Driving a big early 1960s Austin A40 Somerset green van, with W. Elson Greengrocer, We Deliver (that was my job!) sign written on the side panel, in pale yellow. Bill wore this big flat cap perched on his head all the year round, slightly cocked to one side, don't think I ever saw him without it – except the occasions where Mrs Elson scolded him, the one thing with Mrs Elson, if she caught you out with a lie, it could be fatal, Bill had learned this over their many years together! If he had failed to deliver an order, not take the money to the bank, remove wilting leaves from the lettuces, he would be honest and say 'No Dear, I haven't' looking down at his feet in that sorry dog pose. She would strut across to him, remove his cap, grabbing the peak and whack him with it, in a swishing movement, to the amazement of myself or any others in the shop at the time, we would look down, stretching our eyes open in that disbelieving way and make out we were busy again.

Rides in his delivery van were interesting, he lacked spatial awareness going down our narrow village roads, the big Austin would wallow around corners, he drove with his cap tilted up on his head, rubbing his balding head from time to time. We would chat about football, life etc, he was completely different to when his "Mrs" was around, he seemed very relaxed, I was the one tensing and grabbing the car seat, as he just missed another parked vehicle. I really warmed to that big portly and gentle man.

Working in that shop was quite demanding as the errand boy, I would boil the beetroot in the back yard, trim cabbage, lettuces, the spring greens and steep them in two old enamel baths trying to extend their freshness, all in freezing water. Mr Elson always picked up Mrs Elson at the end of the day as they lived very nearby in Lock Road I believe, I would be left in charge, for those few minutes. If someone came in I served them, it made me feel so mature and responsible. Spinning those brown paper bags after placing half a pound of 'toms' on those big scales, taking the money and 'ringing' up as the cash drawer flew open towards my mid-drift. On return Mrs Elson would come back to cash up the days takings, don't think she trusted Bill - sorry, Mr Elson to do it. That Delivery Bike! As you are now well aware, I am a slightly built lad I have tried to correct this by drinking loads of milk, a bit more circuit training at school and football practice, even thought of sending away for a Charles Atlas course, or saving for a Bullworker – which I bought later, you know that contraption that you compressed and pulled apart like an archers bow, you saw it advertised in comics and newspapers at the time, with advertising strap lines that announced, "Now you too, can laugh at skinny weaklings!" but to no avail, should have asked for my money back. I used to hold my arm up in that strength pose to show my bicep, my brother and mother always joked "I have seen a bigger knot on a piece of string!". That cycle was one of those familiar 'trade bikes' big, black, rusty and with that built in tubular cage/basket over the front wheel, under which it had a stand, which you kicked down and in one go you pulled the bike backward. My legs were just long enough, to stretch my toes similar to a ballet dancer position, 'on points', to hold it up straight at road junctions. Stopping would mean dismounting by hopping off the large saddle, being careful not to catch my testicles on the broken seat or crossbar, which also had a rod going across it to the back brakes, that were operated by the massive levers below the handlebar grips, my hand span was just enough to pull them up. Although I would do midweek deliveries, with smaller tomato trays loaded with top ups of vegetables and fruit, Friday and Saturdays were the busiest, perhaps ten drops on a Friday night and twenty on a Saturday, this was a problem for me, now I would miss out on afternoon football, but Sunday was still OK as they could be scheduled over both and two different leagues. I have to be honest although I loved my football, but earning and saving money became a little more important and sadly I wasn't as skilled as some of the boys in the team.

Going to Venturers Youth Club on a Friday night became mine and our 'main event' weekly, as now it played records and became a dance night, after the Thursday 'Record Room' night at Lock Road Youth Club, these became a ritual and our local social scene. Girls, records, wearing the right clothes along with buying Potato Puffs, Wagon Wheels and a bottle of Coke, but you need money to fund these items! At this time and I believe for the majority of us council house kids, money may only come at birthdays or Christmas, generally from an Auntie or Uncle in the form of a postal order form or a brown crisp '10 Bob Note', in a card! There was no expectation of being given any, especially when we had a part time job, if any pocket money was earned for chores, it stopped instantaneously, but the chores didn't! Elsons, also used to sell eggs from a local farm, I even approached the local farmer to buy trays of eggs weekly, that I would sell door to door in my street and around the block, to earn extra money. Many of us boys and girls had multiple part time jobs, I even helped with The Evening Standard and Evening News papers on a Saturday night, with the football results and reports, if someone was unavailable or subcontracted by Andy Poulter or Colin Burton.

In no particular priority at this time, you started to think what's important to oneself? Namely, music and records to take to the youth clubs, clothes - trousers, that looked like Sta-Prests, jeans that look like Levi's, a button down shirt (sometimes a real Ben Sherman that was lifted from my brothers cupboard, although too big, it was the business), wheels (a racing bike at this stage, or a self assembled fixed wheel with Cow Horn handlebars, with a Lambretta scooter on your wish list, roll on 16, please!), shoes - monkey boots or moccasins, that hopefully looked like Ivy Shop loafers. I will be so pleased when I am sixteen, bigger and taller, at work and adult clothes that will hopefully fit me!

At school and at youth club, some young ladies are now catching my eye, the trouble is, I don't catch theirs! Sadly, I am not one of those boys that most girls 'fancy', - a great term and well used at the time! – Strangely they seem to like the naughty, roguish ones, that wasn't me, out of respect for my mother and my good fairy on my right shoulder, working overtime. I am not tall for my age, short in stature, gap now coming together in front teeth, hair goes wavy when hot, it won't do what I want it too, some lads seem to come out of the showers at school towel their hair and it's in place, so annoying! I now want sideburns and even let my hair grow in front of my ears and Sellotape them down at night, hoping they could and will even attract the girls. Heard a girl say one night, I am in the 'cute and nice' category, as they were ranking boys – that's certainly not going to attract the girls! I used to take my older brothers - without asking of course! – vinyl records and some of mine to the youth clubs, making sure my name was written on them. Loaned to the DJ, the lad spinning the records that night, in the hope that some young lady with whom I have a crush on and would notice I have the sounds in my possession. Thinking it would be so cool to spin some records and give the DJ thing a go, alas I never did step forward and my confidence lets me down again and John Medland, a school friend from Orchard gets the 'residency', John a very confident lad and an early entrepreneur, went onto to run his own very successful business and married a very pretty girl, that we all fancied.

I so wish, I could have sent a message to my younger self then, 'that it's better to give something a go and perhaps fail, rather than not try it at all and fail to never know!'. It's something that I really only found out about in later life, if you give things a go, it increases your chance of success and builds confidence, a great lesson in life.

Again back to my mother's advice of 'You can only try your best!'. I was really too shy and lacked self confidence.

I now have a good collection of records, because my mother's family were from Manchester they have now stopped sending Postal Orders instead on my request now they send me record tokens, for birthdays and Christmas, mainly from Auntie Margaret and Uncle Fred, who looked so much like Fred Flintstone and was really a long distance lorry driver for British Road Services and when he had a London trip, he would occasionally stay overnight, must have taken ages then on the A6 and 'A' roads, he always bought some mirth to the house with his antics and strong Mancunian accent and this massive truck sat outside our house!

Those EMI record tokens, which could be exchanged only for 45's and LP's at designated records shops, Boots, Woollies, Potters and Richmond Records in town with listening booths, some book shops, electrical shops and I even believe Timothy Whites (bought by Boots in 1968) had a record counter in the 1960's, there you could hang around and listen to the latest sounds, pretending you were older. Thinking about those final years in education and school, seems to be a very social time for me, as my peers are looking forward to adulthood. Living in a quiet empty house, means I wanted to be out, jumping on my push bike and riding to Riverside or Sandy Lane 'Recs and also down to the river or Ham Common to see if anybody was having a 'kick-a-bout', or groups boys and girls gathering. School now became a thing I just wanted to get done and over with, you became aware of the older teenagers in the village, who now are looking very cool and smart, have scooters or even cars, all this was because they now worked and could afford them. In the run up to the end of my fourth year in Grey Court, do I leave school in that summer of 1968, aged just 15 years and one month?

Pleasure times, besides my interest in football, now take on a 'going out' look to them, as a group of youngsters we are so lucky to have Richmond Ice Rink just over the Bridge in Twickeham, the site was a former roller-skating rink and abandoned pre WW1. In

1914 it was bought by a French industrialist, Charles Pelabon for use as a munitions factory and who developed the original site. During WW1, when Europe was being invaded by the Germans, around 6000 Belgium's refugee's and injured soldiers settled in Richmond and Twickenham, many of them hearing about the war work in the factory. Eventually, the site was sold in 1924 and the big red brick building we all could see from the other bank of The Thames was converted to a major London Ice Rink by 1928, as skating clubs from Hammersmith and Earls Court moved in to the 'biggest ice rink in the world' at that time, before the Arosa Rink subdivided it. During WW2 the American Embassy persuaded the Government to keep it open for North American servicemen who played ice hockey back in their leisure time back in the US and Canada. It was later a home base for several ice major league hockey teams including Richmond Flyers who which we used to watch. Although we went when younger, but now on Saturday nights we would go to 'en masse' from the village, meeting at the bus stop. That weekend night you were allowed to wear your 'hockey' skates, thicker bladed and a lot easier to skate on than 'figure' skates, mine we given to me by my brothers mate Derek Harding. It was a great night, they would have sessions of pop and chart music playing, us lads skating around to and talking to the young ladies from other parts of south and west London and not from our village, hanging onto the side and falling over, asking them if they needed help. It also had speed skating sessions, we watched in amazement at the rate of travel and the length of their blades and how they leant forward just lightly putting their hand down as they turned in the corners.

At the end of the night and one of our first introductions to 'fast food' and a great treat, walking back over to Richmond via the bridge onto Hill Street and the corner of Palm Court with our skates slung over our shoulders. We queue orderly at The Wimpy Bar for a cheeseburger or chips or both and of course a squirt of sauce from a plastic tomato. All ordered through a sliding window and a server, armed with a paint scraper on a smooth faced griddle, flipping burgers and frying onions, it was so American and so exciting, except when the bigger lads took a few chips! We would then walk down to the Poppy Factory bus stop and our trip back to Ham on a noisy bus with everybody chatting. Hopefully avoiding paying the fare of a 'thruppeny half', sometimes we knew the driver, again Derek Harding - who lived in the village and instructed the conductor not to ask for our fares!

⁂⁂⁂

That spring at school and down towards May, we complete our mock exams for experience in preparation for pupils, wanting to stay on and going to the fifth form to take GCE's. I must admit I was struggling to keep up, hearing that my father is released yet again from prison to our home address, after pleading to Mum, by the Probation Services, yet again unbelievably gaining parole for good behaviour and promising he will mend his ways.

Mum has now filed for separation, I believe after enjoying herself on the school cruise, her confidence is now growing, knowing she can cope on be on her own and has now bravely considered the situation with my father. Living with him must have been unbearably emotional, although she wasn't around because of those many working hours, but I never felt like she didn't have time for me and we were always very close and we enjoyed each other's company. Driven by staying together for 'her boys' and keeping a roof over our heads – it could and should have been so different, if she didn't have that inner strength and tenacity.

My father at this time was unaware that the 'notice of separation' papers that will be served soon, the decision must be now slightly easier, with my brother and I now supporting her plight to end this relationship. I will shortly be in a position leave school and have the ability to support Mum financially, like my brother who is now 21 years old and will no doubt be leaving home in the not too distant future.

As always, when he returns and knocks on the door, it's as if he has been just away on a business trip, trying to be 'a pal', over friendly, promising to take me to Chelsea in the hope it's going to make me bond with him - for me, it's the reverse, quickly reliving an image of sitting in our bay window, waiting for him to return and being let down, yet again! Worst of all, he sits my brother Keith and I down, all smiles telling us that 'He has finally learned his lesson, once and for all, he will get a job, look after Mum, settle down, won't get in trouble again - backing it up with - 'I promise on my mother's life!'. Keith and I look at each other, with the look of.....'We will see?'. Personally, any trust has gone and disappeared, I have learned to harden my emotions, distract myself with positive things that make me feel good, music, football, clothes, youth clubs and outside activity. In fact if he is going to be home, I will be out, I don't want to be near him. Sad, that you can reject your father, your own flesh and blood, the person who was responsible for giving you life and bringing you into this world, but so far, making it a difficult one for everyone over the last twenty years.

That evening Mum surprises him, by calmly saying that she has filed for separation, basically 'enough's enough' and from now on you will be again sleeping in Keith's room, as for separation you can live under the same roof but no 'cohabitation'. Trying to be calm, but this time he doesn't react, shout or get angry, expecting him to plead again that he will change. Now, I notice a different type of confidence and strength in my Mum.

He says he has nowhere to go at the moment, Mum gives him a front door key, as he could make life difficult with court proceedings and his probation officer, if he disappears. This way is better, he gets a job, trying to make it up with Mum, he pays housekeeping on time, perhaps an invite to the pub or cinema, bringing home the odd gift to Mum or myself like a pair of shin pads and for a couple of months it is tolerable, as if he is trying. For him, I personally hope it is 'Too much, too little, but far too late!' Mum is now in control of the situation.

Revising for me for the mocks is difficult, still using my 'Teach Yourself' books in Maths and French with exercises or old exam papers. Another method of revising was to write things down and learn things 'Parrot Fashion', go through your books, highlight areas of learning and put on paper. Very time consuming, but it always helps me, if a question came up I pictured the words and expanded on them. Now this is alright, if the 1800 Corn Laws came up, but with maths, how do you revise or English – those please discuss questions? I am not an avid reader, I prefer, short stories, ghost tales and publications on How Things Work, The Guinness Book Of Records, Edgar Allen Poe and his short stories and books showing a cross section of an aircraft carrier, got to assume it's my attention span. Although, I did enjoy our course books like Shane, To Kill A Mockingbird, the weird Animal Farm, Lord Of The Flies and many others. But a book, that made me think about how cruel human beings could be to each other was The Diary of Anne Frank, incredulous reading and a story set only twenty years earlier in my life.

Trying to focus on my schoolwork is difficult, feeling overwhelmed with the amount of concentration needed, in an effort to help me after seeing my revision notes and trying to ingratiate himself to me, my father get holds of and makes a big deal of getting me a small reel to reel tape recorder with a microphone. Although I am thankful, I wonder where he got it from, however, I don't ask, I just use it for my revision, I dictate into it and listen back, it helps a lot.

My father now and like an alcoholic or junkie, can't be cured, he needs to realise and help himself, he is gradually slipping back to his old ways and habits, coming home late, not paying housekeeping, forever making excuses, breaking promises, would he ever learn? I am now very much aware of my mother's feelings and the pain and anguish she must have carried over the last twenty years trying to keep a family together and her own guilt, that it had failed. My father had now spent a large proportion of his son's and married life in prison, perhaps my father's relationship with his mother hadn't helped him growing up, not living with her a lot of the time, as I think she was involved with situations that weren't exactly legal and entailed delving into some forms of confidence tricking also. My grandmother moved to London during the war and it was rumoured she operated in black market circles. However, in my mother, my father was lucky enough to meet a woman that truly loved him, a strong person, a fantastic grafter and mother, it could have been so different for him, instead now the writing is on the wall, it's gone far enough with his behaviour and his attitude to his family, she is now finding the strength to end relationship forever.

At least our mother broke that cycle of any wrong doing with us, his sons, raising us to think before we acted and to realise the consequences of doing wrong, she really kept us on the straight and narrow, not being attracted to a pathway of perhaps any criminal behaviour. And for that my brother and I are eternally grateful.

As we run up to the summer of 1968, I am in a dilemma, most of my peers at youth clubs, footie and school are going to leave school, many of us being together throughout our education and even nursery years, only a decade but literally a lifetime for any young teenager. Many influence each other with decisions of not staying on and starting work, a camaraderie and a village 'band of brothers', some now think of staying together working in the same organisation, some even thinking of joining the services, emigrating or starting a new life and career by moving away. Popular careers at the time were with North Thames Gas as an apprentice gas fitter, Manor Road Gasworks depot nearby or the 'Leccy Board' to train as a 'sparkie', others to the Motor Trades and garages as mechanics or fitters. Some off into the building trade, joinery, bricklaying, plastering, plumbing and roofing, Royal Mail postman or The Post Office and if you want to work inside some of the time – an apprentice carpenter, very few lads chose an administrative or clerical roles. I even considered taking up hair dressing Jeff Cottee who was Brian's brother and worked at Gillons in Richmond, I would see him in the village looking like Stevie Marriot with a roll neck sweater looking really cool and a small cravat tied around his neck, however when asking him one day about an apprenticeship he replied 'Don't bother, there's no money in it, young Gooba, you don't want to sweep hair up for the next two years!' That was enough to put me off! Then thought about being a GPO Telegram Boy or Messenger on a push bike and then they trained you to pass your test on a small motorbike!

Advice from most parents at the time was to go somewhere and get a 'forever job' and 'preferably a trade', which would allow you to earn extra money doing 'PJ's' – or Private Jobs, where you can do work on the side using your firms tools and join the 'CIA' – 'Cash In 'And' brigade. In one way you didn't think of a career, but what it pays long term, the plan to have money in your pocket and a bit extra that would allow you to save up – even opening up a Post Office Savings Account or a Building Society with your own paying in book! Most parents were very supportive of you going to work, a skill via an apprenticeship, that would be better paid than a labourer after 'serving your time'. A long term career in the same organisation that pays a nice pension when you retire, Hawkers factory down the road or Watneys Brewery in Mortlake and Isleworth and some other local factories and companies. However, I think in few cases, parents were more interested in you just 'getting a job', not wanting to see you as an idle or an out of work 'village layabout'.

Not forgetting at that time you could leave school at 15 before Easter, if you were in the Secondary State school system, literally walking out of school with no qualifications, tempted many a lad and lass.

Three of my classmates and best friends at school with me from primary school were really bright, but left school to go into apprenticeships, or they just wanted to earn, I don't know. They would and could have easily passed GCE 'O' Levels if they had stayed on, but for us kids on the estates, that what's seemed to happen and I think having a job and earning money outweighed any further education thoughts, especially if you struggled or not academic, we were working class and lived council homes, that's what we thought we should do, not a bad thing, it was a work ethos.

I have seen some Grey Court Secondary school archived documents that list the name of the pupil, when they left and the company, organisation or apprenticeship that was taken up. It makes interesting reading, even the least academic secured a job. The post-war period and the 1960s saw some of the lowest unemployment rates, this was helped by an economic boom and a commitment to full employment. The 1960s was a great decade to leave school and the amount of opportunity along with the growth in technology.

⁂

My father, since release he is sleeping in my brothers room, I have this strange relationship with him and I don't feel home is an easy place to be with him around, the one thing in his favour is that I was never physically beaten by him, it was more of a mental cruelty, always worried about that 'key in the door' and that arguing would start. Even thinking it would be nice to get a job, earn money and leave home, leave a village and live in a busy London – I think most teenagers in those days had a goal to do this especially around the age of eighteen, when you could vote, drink alcohol and go to night clubs – you were 'Of An Age!', you were an adult! Some even left home to squat, but that wasn't for me.

We are at end of term June 1968, just before the yearend exams, I have applied for a couple of vacancies through the school's career master both in clerical roles in the Civil Service in London, mainly because of a potential career opportunity and pay levels. Extolling the pay rises in future years and of course there would be a good government pension at the end. This news gets back to Miss Lewis, who was my form teacher in Class 3AC, asking to see me after school for a quick chat, I meet with her and she enquires why I am thinking of leaving without giving it any serious thoughts of staying on. Showing a lot of empathy, she explains that she is aware how difficult my home life may been over the years and that it couldn't have been easy, but I should at least consider my next steps carefully, perhaps to look for some jobs that would take in my real interests in life, instead of an administrative role.

Encouraging me to try my best in the up and coming mocks, advising me that in the meantime why don't I go back to the careers master and talk about looking into another job, taking in my real interests if I was to choose a career. I sit down, tell him I did have an interest in telecommunications after visiting The Post Office Tower, he makes enquiries into the then government department of the General Post Office (GPO) Telephones who ran the national phone service at the time, later in 1969 it became a public corporation under The Post Office Act. I ask about applying, but the downside is, that it's an advanced engineering apprenticeship of three years but needs at least 3 GCE's in Maths, Science and English, for obvious reasons of reading drawings, fault diagnosis and writing reports. Luckily for me the careers teachers manages to get hold of a recruitment officer from the GPO, to come to the school and interview, he also explains what qualifications I need, otherwise I could consider and start a four year apprenticeship scheme working externally with them.

It would all now depend on exams and my results. I go home thinking about another year at school, downside being not working, more exams which I am not comfortable with – I tend to panic, getting a feeling in the pit of my stomach that aches, my brain races and struggle to focus on any questions – I just want to get it over or rightly or wrongly, not bother putting myself under that sort of pressure. But of course earning some money now is very important.

I talk to my mother, with all of her own problems and now with some ill health, bought on by stress and trying to be strong, feinting and blackouts that she suffered genealogical problems from my birth, all those years ago. She offers advice of 'You can only try your best and it is important to do something you like, don't forget you will work for a long time. I know you have it in you'. There is no real pressure from her, but she raises my spirits and I get the feeling that's its worth stretching myself and tells me that even the best sportsman sometimes doubt themselves, many more will come second, third, fourth than win races, you learn from any experience, not everyone's a champion, but to give it a go!

I give it great thought, taking in advice from my mother and Miss Lewis and decide to stay on for the 5th Form, ignoring peers, who asked 'staying on?, is for swats and twats!'. I never thought I would, as most of my friends are leaving to get a job and above all to earn money! With football, youth clubs, ice skating, cinema trips with mates, money is still needed and going to work will accommodate that.

Working at Elsons for over a year, was very enjoyable alongside Bill, a lovely gentleman and soul. Mrs Elson who could be quite brusque, but compliments me on my politeness to customers and their feedback (I have learned very quickly, smiling, being willing and helpful – costs me nothing and gets you a thruppence or tanner tip, most times!) supplemented with a work ethic, picked up from Mum and Keith! In a strange way it teaches you to know how to treat people generally, an investment in time and energy that is worth doing and helped to build my confidence a little. They would regularly offer me the free cinema passes for the ABC and Odeon in Richmond. Having these was great and led to an interest at the time of going weekly to the 'pictures' on a weekend on a Sunday afternoon regularly, even for dodgy films with Dave and Danny, with others joining us, like Paul. The cinema was another place where you might start cheekily chatting to young girls sitting nearby, during the intermission after your ice cream, Kiora or Mivvi from the usherette with the trayholder and a small light over those intermission treats.

The late 1960s produced some great movies, but I liked Pathe News and Look At Life and their interesting subjects, a double bill with two films. Classics like Bullitt, Bonnie and Clyde, Easy Rider, Where Eagles Dare, Witchfinder General and many Hammer films, The Graduate, You Only Live Twice, Planet of the Apes. The masterpiece of 2001: A Space Oddysey a computer called HAL (An acronym, one back from IBM!), written by Arthur C Clarke, who also worked on the Eagle comic as a young science fiction writer and its use of Artificial Intelligence (AI), Yellow Submarine which I didn't really enjoy, although regarded as a landmark of animation! The great Georgie Fame and his 'The Ballad of Bonnie and Clyde' number one hit in 1968, recorded by Fame after seeing the controversial film in 1967, written in a 1920s, 30s style and the piano introduction picked up from Fats Domino's 'Blue Monday'.

One band, The Small Faces and after their hit from 1965, of Sha La La La Lee, incidentally written by an entertainer and one of the first black artists to appear on British TV screens and his 1962 hit of Up On The Roof – one Mr Kenny Lynch. All or Nothing, Itchychoo Park and many more, as we know then the Sabbath afternoons could be very quiet, a cycle out, a walk up the park, no retail opening and sometimes very boring, with school homework or work the next day, the release of their Lazy Sunday shortly after Tin Soldier, a sound of that spring and summer sung in a Cockney accent and slightly even in a music hall style, inspired by arguments and discussions with his East End neighbours but reverting back to his normal singing voice and fading to the sound of birdsong and church bells, classic, clever and sublime. John Lydon of the Sex Pistols, said later that his vocals and delivery were influenced by Stevie Marriot on their first release from the Ogdens' Nut Gone Flake album in May 1968, against the groups wishes apparently!

Now in the 5th Form, I give my notice at Elsons and get another job -again on a recommendation from Roger Squires, who starts 'a real job' and a career at Brentford Market - with Keith Fry, a travelling greengrocer, running a converted 1950's furniture van, sloping sides to stack all the produce, covering the streets and roads, south of Lock Road, north was the territory of Mason's and Paddy Conway's with his horse and cart. Great thing it is twice the pay and more responsibility, I now also resign also from my paper round – the new job means wearing a money apron and I would serve people directly and would cross and upsell other items! So much fun, the van crept up a road stopping twice, at similar times every week, jumping out of the cab I would knock on doors of our regulars, touting for business, like a mobile market stall, giving me a list and or a string bag at the door or coming out to the van for a chat and checking the produce. Quickly fulfilling their orders, I would it deliver back and ask for payment, often they would say 'Keep the change Boy or Gub!', as they got more familiar, as Roger's were big shoes to fill coming from a well known family of nine on the corner of Craig and Lock Roads in the village.

Over the course of a Friday night or Saturday full day, our money aprons would be heaving with coins and I had wads of pound notes in the zip pocket. That Christmas of 1968, we took so much money and the orders were so big, with extras like Xmas crackers, nuts to those boxes of Eat Me dates. Yet again, I would carry and deliver a 56lb bags of potatoes to the larger Irish families (and the best tippers!). Lifting them from the vehicle and down garden paths or even to a door at the top of Beaufort Court - a four storey block of flats with no lift! Keith Fry, blonde, full of chat, good looking cheeking chap and a lot younger than Bill Elson, was always joking, especially when it came to the younger Mums and the odd innuendo. He would sometimes set me up, telling them to be slightly flirty with me, knowing I would go a vivid crimson – like one of his ripe tomatoes - when embarrassed, especially after they had asked me to take the greengrocery into their house, shutting the door behind me, hastily I would put down the goods and make my retreat to the front door! Keith would look at me from the cab of the lorry, then burst into fits of laughter at my brush with a 'flirty' older woman, although I wouldn't have known what to do if they really meant it, as would have thought of any consequences! Could have been a film there, 'Carry On Mobile Greengrocer', for the antics we got up to!

The lorry had no heating, again it was freezing, it also had this enormous steering wheel to lever the steering box, starting it would be always tentative and a crash gearbox, this large blue lorry crawled its way up the road in a whining low gear, it was the only way we could get some speed up, crunching the big gear stick into second and perhaps third. On a Saturday, we would bring our Tupperware box of sandwiches and a flask of tea. Don't think

Mum paid for any vegetables of fruit that year with me working on that round. The lorry was kept in a lock up yard on Park Road Kingston, behind Porters greengrocers' shop, where I would chat to the owner's son Tommy, a lot in common as the same age. That Christmas period we prepared lots of box orders, working very late into the night, this was recognised in my wages and Christmas Box from Keith, dipping into his money belt and peeling off pounds notes from a large roll of money!

For a young lad, I now had a few not only pennies in my pocket and would be able to now afford more clothes and records. An interesting time for us youngsters, Ivy League shirts, smarter Levi Sta-Prests or cords that replaced my 501's, Harrington Jackets and shoes, but now a growing interest in a form of wearing certain clothes and a natural one on for us junior Mods, especially at this time with music and more hearing more Reggae spins in the youth club and even now on radio. The close influence of London, we had already picked up the subculture of Suedeheads or Skins and an early visit from saving to buy just one Ben Sherman from The Ivy Shop, I did have a cheaper Brutus shirt, never a Jaytex, but definitely not the real deal. I believe and think they were around £3 19s 6d, with the lookalikes about a pound less at the time. The Levi's, cords and Sta-Prests in various colours from Jack Brendons opposite the cinema, near Kingston Station, I just managed to fit into a pair, as I think then that 501's started at 26" waist, with the use of a tight belt and that the advice of sitting in a cold bath would shrink them to fit, or stupidly bleaching a pair once after which they fell apart!

Just the feeling of me wearing these two garments made me four inches taller, walking into both Lock Road and Venturers Youth Clubs wearing that twin set of brands, more like a fluffy chick than a Cock, but hey, I had them! Especially when some of the other lads were still at school and still hadn't saved or earned enough money to wear them yet. The older lads would nod, in which seemed like approval and a mental thumbs up. Of course the footwear from 'The Ivy' – weren't purchased yet, a look-a-like pair of loafers, brogues or another design from Freeman, Hardy and Willis, Saxone or of course your pre Dr Marten's, - still a large investment - a cheaper pair of monkey boots from Kingston Market or Harry Harrisons in the village.

Youth Clubs for me, were the highlight of the week and of course I was out of the house, I just longed for Tuesday's hanging around with the other boys and girls, chatting, laughing, full of energy, playing darts, table tennis, even board games, a can or a bottle of coke, from the serving hatch run by Danny, Dave's or Mum as volunteers at the same time keeping their eyes on us. But as the week ran down, Thursday and Friday were the music nights! The records, both dancers and slow ones, trying to pluck up enough courage to ask a girl for a dance, wondering if I had a chance, hopefully if they fancied me, especially with testosterone rising as every week passed by.

Like most lads, now being a 15 year old boy and a late starter, Mum still leaving me NHS pamphlets about birth control and other subjects on or under my pillow! Any lad would give anything to get a glimpse of a breast or even the top of a stocking, flicking through Freemans or some other catalogue in the lingerie pages at the time when around a mates house during the school holidays or calling for him, it was the closest we got to porn! As paperboys we would looked for Parade, Reveille, Health and Efficiency and any other publication that would show a glimpse of the woman's form and breasts. You even noticed when the young girls in your class got there first bra's and not wearing their vests now, but that distinctive back white or black strap through their school blouse, the odd boy even pinged their bra straps and made a small comment, in return receiving a slap across the face and a form of humiliation, where made them think twice next time. I remember Jean, knocking a lad down one day, with a slap or punch after such an incident, strangely he didn't bother her or others again. Not me, too small and too damned scared!

Those 'educational' lad discussions that you regularly had, they boasted and talked, as if they have had sex every night with a different girl and other tales of new experiences, like undoing a bra strap with one hand – many of us we were the original TVs 'Inbetweeners', all words, no action and making up stories. I think at this time, a bit of swearing was the vernacular as it seemed a little cool, but hard to do in case a club leader was listening or worse another parent or neighbour heard you hanging about outside the shops, the mental taste of carbolic soap still in my mouth as a before thought.

In search of such titillation and with discussions, we decide to look what's on at the cinema, seeing that the film Blow Up is X-rated and is showing at a real fleapit of a cinema - hoping for easy access - The Kingston Kinema just opposite Station Hotel and next to the bus garage. The film was released the previous year but the Kinema tended to show films again that had earned some revenue. Coming with a very provocative poster, based in a Mod Swinging '60's London, about a photographer, played by David Hemmings and also featuring Sara Miles and Jane Birkin both with what we believe had reputations, that year also Marianne Faithful is the Girl On A Motorcycle also. All right up a young 15 year olds street and we are told a few glimpses of female nudity. With military precision we plan, we choose a matinee, reasoning it will be quiet and no queue at the box-office. Arriving at the box office, with a very deep voice practised, the oldest of us says "One adult please!", now it's my turn, smallest, shortest and youngest running about in my head, already rehearsed "What year you born?" in case the lady behind the glass fronted ticket booth asked the question! I have '1950, 1950, 1950!!' going around my brain, blurting out "One adult please?" in the deepest juvenile voice I can muster, for a second she pauses, I think 'why did I ask it, like a question?'. The adult ticket appears from that shiny brass slot above the cash drawer, "Two Shillings please" she says while chewing gum, I look down and say "Thank You" in what comes out in a falsetto mumble, hand over my money and quickly take the ticket. "Were in!", to be honest to pay the staff and to keep the cinema running, I think they would have let in nine year olds in! As we shuffle into the dimly lit auditorium and step through the brass handled double swing doors, to our surprise there are about three or four men sitting spaced out, two are in those proverbial raincoats the other two wearing trilby's and smoke rises from the cigarettes in their mouths as smoking was preferred on the right of the auditorium then or a little later. We look at each other and go right down to the front, pull down the red velvet, ripped stained seats, giggling, just as we did at in The ABC or Odeon, at Saturday morning pictures. We also saw other films, an interesting war film that had an X rating called Beach Red, which for us was pretty gruesome, a story of an US Marine unit storming a Japanese held island and all the horrors that went with it. And of course Barbarella with the Orgasmatron and of course The Graduate and the seduction by an older woman and a very young Dustin Hoffman, who I would have loved to, swap roles with! As we sat watching these X films underage, it didn't stop us thinking that a policeman may put a hand on our shoulders and be taken away!!

About this time and subject to earnings and affordability, going to the pictures on a Sunday afternoon became a regular thing and would inject a bit of fun on that boring period before the start of a school week – afternoon football matches were still mandatory, but were generally a morning kick-offs. I always thought it was strange coming out of a picture house in a late warm summer's afternoon with the sun shining into squinting eyes. This was also popular when going out with a young lady for something to do in early courting days, it still left time to go out with mates at night, because you didn't want to miss out – it's all about the planning you know!

I loved this period of exploration, money in pocket, falling in love and crushes nearly every week at youth club, entertainment to hand, keeping occupied, head not worried about my home life or school – I felt very grown up. Going home or being indoors was still a real dilemma for me, if Mum was at home in the evening it would be OK, we would chat watched TV together and relaxed with a giant packet of Opal Fruits, Merrymaids, Frutellas or large bar of Cadbury's Fruit and Nut from the fridge, as home should be.

But when my father around, it was very painful and uncomfortable experience, anticipating that key in the door sound, still really haunting me. He was now in a desperate situation when at home, sleeping in my brother's room and officially not co-habiting. With Mum enforcing the terms of the separation order, I couldn't and wouldn't engage with him, I was still very angry and upset with the memories and the attempt to attack her in the kitchen that night, but the arguing seems to have abated, Mum has stopped worrying. Engaging with him in any conversation was a waste of time, what he did and how he has treated my mother over those years, broke any bond we could have ever had or even repair.

When alone in the house or out on my bike, sometimes I found myself again being invited into the lovely family home of Anne and Brian Cottee, a few doors away, a safe and welcome harbour for me, away from any storm that might blow up at home, five children laughing and playing, being offered copious cups of tea, both parents engaged jovially, me thinking and observing what the ideal family unit should be and act like. Brian came from a big established Ham family and was well known, he was more than well aware what my father got up to over the years and if he was in the local pub, he always politely spoke to him, but knew not to be drawn into any 'cons', goods he could get hold of like a TV and definitely not give or loan him any money! Anne was a really kind person, she would ask me about my relationship with my father, I would open up just a little and she would use phrases like 'He's still your father and bloods thicker than water' I can assume, only trying to help, but I had this anger about the situation and just wanted him to disappear or me to get away from home, needing to escape from any potential confrontation. About this time, my father was now getting very desperate, knowing that the writing was on the wall with his relationship with Mum and long term what it will mean to him, perhaps thoughts he should have had, two decades earlier.

Frantically trying to get some money together he engages with the janitor at the new school of St Richards on the Wates

Estate new pub, The Water Gypsies. My father buying the drinks and chatted, making up a story of needing urgently to visit his sick mother, now in Wandsworth, but getting to London would be a problem that evening. My father asked "Would you possibly, loan me your car for a few hours so I can get to hospital, hour to get back, be back by 11pm promise?" After being convinced, he hands over the keys and Sandy never saw his car for weeks, until it was recovered! My father had sold it, without any documentation. Embarrassingly for the janitor, he reported it to the police and my father was again wanted for questioning, nobody ever felt sorry for the janitor because he was always so miserable and grumpy, in fact the story was repeated many times in the village over a pint and bought howls of laughter to people over the years, about how Sandy was amusingly conned by Nobby Clark!

Most of my youth club and schoolmate peers have now started work or taken up an apprenticeship. It's September 1968 and I have now continued my education into the 5th Form, not sure if its voluntary or I feel like an absconder from a working world. I felt a little out of place, many other pupils are brighter than me and appear most seem to come from a settled home life, some are destined to perhaps get very good jobs or go onto further education. Lessons are ramped up, French oral, English Literature and maths is slightly harder and lots of self study in the common room, shared with the few Sixth Formers we had at the time, who are taking A Levels and perhaps going on to even thinking about something called a university – which at the time, I only thought there was only two, - Oxford and Cambridge - and that was because of The Boat Race, televised between the local Putney Bridge and Barnes! Furthermore, English Literature and Shakespeare, reading these plays in class that seemed to make no sense and I would get so embarrassed and change seats often to avoid that 'Graham could you read....?, along with French oral of course.

Now that my Mod and Suedehead influenced mates have left school, I would sometimes sit fidgeting in the Common Room listening to what we called Drongoe or Hairy Hippie music by Cream, Canned Heat, Humble Pie, Fleetwood Mac, Jethro Tull, The Herd and also folk music! For me, our own youth clubs sounds were far better, not only was Motown or Tamla as we used to say with that distinctive black label and branding, now racking up the hits and re-releasing mid 60s tracks and back in the charts, but Stax, Atlantic, all danceable and obviously collectable. Although we were interested in new releases, these sometimes older recordings were also very popular as long as we had records on the turntable we didn't mind.

We see the first London based multi-racial groups and a term used of British Soul appearing on Top Of The Pops and called interestingly The Foundations, their follow up to Baby Now That I Have Found You chart topper from a year earlier and Build Me Up Buttercup that got to No.2, the band collectively ran The Butterfly Club in Bayswater in the mid 60s. Also The Equals with Baby Come Back that got to No.1, with another socially messaged release in 1970 called Black Skinned Blue Eyed Boys, Eddy Grant a co-founder went onto to have hits in the 1980s and became a famous producer. Brenton Wood's Gimme Little Sign, Johnny Johnson and The Bandwagon's Breakin' Down the Walls of Heartache, O C Smith's, Son Of Hickory Holler's Tramp, one of my real favourites from that year, The Showstoppers from Philly and 'Ain't Nothing But A House Party' on Beacon Records released again in 1971 another funky sound for the time and who can forget Otis's 'Sitting On The Dock Of The Bay'.... Blue eyed R&B and soul in the form of The Love Affair, Union Gap, Joe Cocker, Tommy James, Bruce Channel, Cupids Inspiration and excitingly now a new danceable sound in our youth clubs nights after us kids bought in their older siblings or pocket money records, we listen to Johnny Nash, Desmond Dekkers – 007, Dandy Livingstones, Rudy, A Message To You, Tony Tribes, Red Red Wine as we go into 1969.

⁂

The 5th Form was interesting, surprisingly I get nominated to be a prefect. But, I think by a studious and clever Head Boy or Girl, because I knew the 4th Years mostly from the local council estates and youth clubs - who had a bit of a reputation for rowdiness and on bad weather days I would sit in their classes trying to keep order - to no avail obviously, especially Class 4A with Danny and Ray Holmes there, I think, I was the sacrificial prefect that year! My other duties included standing at the gates or main front door of the school, now in theory, you are supposed to note any late names for assembly and they would receive a bad mark or called into the headmaster's office if more than twice. Strangely, the lateness book list got smaller and smaller from the boys in the 4th Form, as I was taking bribes with sticks of Wrigleys or Hubba Bubba gum that would be palmed into my hand and their names were never noted and I would let them into the side door so they could join at the back, which was quite easy because we stood up at the time for assembly. I was praised by the teachers for my control of the 4th year's attendance rate, I also allowed the boys to use their bicycles and put them in the rack even if they lived around the corner, the school rule being you could only use a bike if you lived more than two miles away. I was very corrupt as a prefect – did I feel guilty, not one iota!

School and concentration is becoming difficult, pressure to do well for O Levels, my chances of passing are becoming less, on the run up to the 'mocks' and practice papers, that Easter of 1969. I start revising in earnest, as my interest and heart is focussed on that GPO apprenticeship.

I will use the tape recorder that my father has got me and try to learn 'parrot fashion' and put hours into reading and listening back. However, one afternoon I get home from school ready to revise again, to an empty house, going to my bedroom, books in hand and I see there is a space where the tape recorder was on a shelf in my room. Thinking Keith might have borrowed it, I look in his room, not there, at the same time my brother arrives home, comes upstairs asks me what I am I looking for?

His face changes, we both look at each other and we know our Dad has taken it, obviously to sell on, as now desperate for any money, quickly recognising what has happened. I sadly go back to my room, thinking how can he do that? Give something, steal and take it back and sell it to buy a couple of drinks desperately trying to impress someone so he can trick them out of some money or something else. What sort of father would do that, especially as he knows I have important exams coming up, I am sick to my stomach, any relationship with my father that was hanging by a thread, has crashed to the ground. I want nothing whatsoever to do with him, I am so disappointed, but I won't allow it or him to bring me down. I know, if challenged he will try and convince himself that he didn't take it, what he should do is think to himself that he will never have any sort of relationship with me!

He doesn't come home that night, is he ashamed or living with someone or dossing in some place trying to avoid us. Keith told me later in life, that sometime in the early 1960s that he had found out we had a half sister and could be leading a double life in Kew.

Around the house we were now being careful to hide any money that we had saved and not wanting cash in the house, we both opened Post Office Savings accounts and hide our passbooks in various places, under mattresses or carpets. One day, Keith unusually came home for lunch, as he walks through the door and sees the hallway is littered with things from under the stairs, looking in the gloom he sees both the meters boxes have been broken into and all the coins have gone. First of all, he thought it was a break in, running quickly upstairs, heart racing and very angry, looking for our savings books that we had hidden under a rug in his room - they have both gone! Sitting briefly on the bed and thinking what to do, he rushes out, along to the local village Post Office where he knows the Postmaster, he's on holiday and there's a stand-in working behind the counter. As always he has been very clever and convinced the woman that his sons have given permission to draw nearly all the money out to take our mother on holiday after an illness, even showing a signed letter (forged obviously!) and birth certificates as backup. He had withdrawn very cleverly, not all of it, £30 pounds from Keith's out of £49 15s and £7 out of £11 from mine, hoping to return the passports to our hiding places, before we got home and that will buy him some time. My brother was saving for a car and I was saving for a Lambretta for my upcoming 16th birthday and next stage of my life of having wheels! Keith returns home, I then come in from school, he is fuming, wondering what to do get a few of his mates and start looking for my father, recover any money, tell him to never come home again or call the police, report the crime and hopefully put a warrant out for his arrest? My choice is the latter, I feel no compassion, the detachment is complete, Keith feels very angry, but a little hesitant, thoughts of 'grassing on your family is a no, no and a betrayal!' come into his mind. But he goes to the hall and dials the local Richmond Police Station, unbeknown to us he is already 'Out on bail' and has just signed in at the police station, they think they know where he is. A detective who knows my father well, from previous charges and assigned to his case tells my brother, who literally wants to murder him or at least do him some damage, to make a statement at the Station. On arrival, Keith is then asked to accompany the detective to a flat in Kew, terms of bail means you must give an address, they arrive. Knock on the door, as the door opens Keith pushes in front and through, grabs my father by the collar and tries to land him one! The detective steps in and reads my father his rights "Keith George Clark, you are under arrest for fraud and embezzlement and stealing from Keith and Graham Clark....". As always he pleads his innocence and is taken off, back to the police station cells and later transferred to Wandsworth or Wormwood Scrubs Prison on remand, because of breaking bail conditions and awaiting another magistrates hearing at the Inner London Sessions!

Mum is devastated and heartbroken yet again, this desperate and heinous action of stealing from your own sons, wife and what her life should have been, now just hoping now she can just end this period of life and will concede to a failed marriage and end twenty years of what was heartache. Once hoping she would start a happy period of her life in the south after the war, a million miles away from the back streets and slums of Moss Side in Manchester, to all intent and purposes wanted to run away from her own home, the blitz and a bleak future and near to squalor. I guess from her point of view and it seems easy for me to say now, why didn't she just walk out of the marital home, it was for all intent and purpose today would be domestic and financial abuse. But thinking, back then, were there any women refuge's, or we may have gone into the care? However I could not see her giving into that, with her strength and resilience. The only upside was with him serving prison sentences, she did have rest bite and roof over her son's heads and with my mother's ability to just get on with it and to look forward, saved us all. How she did it, I do not know.

She had worked so hard to try and get my father back on the straight and narrow and to act as a father to their two sons. Not only has he continued to philander, cheat and commit fraud to people who trusted him, handing over their money for him to spend and move on to his next victim. What makes and why do people do these things? When it would have been just as easy for him to get a job, support his wife and family, is beyond belief and someone who was a trained and skilled baker at a very young age. He even had the chance to take over a family bakery business in Canbury Park Road, Kingston near where his father lived, my mother would have certainly been a great business woman and partner. But NO, he wanted and what he believed and that his way was an easier option.

The reality is, to steal from your children and money that they have worked for, is indeed an action of the lowest of the low! To be honest and not a nice thing to say, that if he had been killed in an accident or died young in his fifties from some illness and always been on the straight and narrow – we would have had a better life, I am sure!

Keith and I were very much aware how hard Mum worked, to keep us together over the last twenty years of him letting her down, every time him saying it's the last time, yet within a short time he was up to his old tricks, he just couldn't stop. Even when he was absent and even around briefly, we can't remember if he ever hugged us, kissed us or ever said 'Love you, Son', gave us any support, verbal or watched us playing a game of football or cricket, he promised us things but never delivered, time and time again. Keith vows that he will never, cross our threshold again, we know because of his constant re-offending he will 'go down' yet again!

Although Mum is on the way to be legally separated and to eventually getting her divorce, it could take five years, but there is news that the divorce laws are changing and she would see her solicitor again. We will prepare ourselves and we know that his name and now ours as the 'victims' will appear again in the local newspapers, like The Surrey Comet, Richmond and Twickenham Times or Herald, because he's a Ham man and it makes good news in The Court Proceedings column, local 'rags' were a form of 1960s Social Media. Again, we will have to go through the shaming and everybody knowing in what's a small village. However, as always she tells us we have got this far and we have kept together and we are both old enough to now hold our heads up high, you boys have never been in real trouble with the police or ever bought them to the door.

Our neighbours knew Mum was as 'Straight as a Die', even the local lads knew that, she always engaged with them walking down the road or Sandy Lane or at the bus stop, they always respected her, she always had time for them. Even knowing who she was married too and that you didn't ever trust Nobby Clark with or for anything. One night after leaving work in Richmond, she bought a rowdy crew of Ham village boys to silence as she climbed up to the top deck of a 65 Bus when they saw it was Mrs Clark, after the conductor had failed!

As always she hugs us and says "Believe me, there is always someone worse off!" which still resonates and "Graham, you are starting work this year and it's a new start all round - it will be alright!", meaning I think, she will end the relationship and we are older enough to handle any consequences from now on. Emotionally we are of course affected, for me, it's very hard to trust anyone, trying not to become to close to people, that might let you down, if you get let down to be very careful, I got angry and annoyed with people who moan about life and the little things.

More importantly, we as a small family unit of three, we can't, won't and dwell, we have to move on, try to forget and think about the positive things in life and what it could bring, working hard, keeping mentally occupied is cathartic. We have also learned about behaviour and what it does to members of your family, friends and neighbours, if you do something wrong, eventually you will and get found out and there are there are always - and that word again - 'consequences' for any type of behaviour.

The following Monday, I am called into the staff room by my form teacher, Mrs Carroll, Miss Lewis is also there, my form teacher from the third year and had talked to me about staying on. Somehow she has found out about my current home life and my father's current situation, now in prison again. My mocks have been very disappointing, falling into the bottom percentile of places in a relatively now small class, based on self study for many lessons.

The Secondary school system at this level in the 5th Form, catered for bright pupils who would go on take their GCE O Levels and even perhaps A Levels, myself, never pretending to be academic, I found it difficult. Looking on the brightside though, was that all the best school footballers had left that summer and I would be regularly picked to play in the school's First XI, rugby and cricket, mainly because I was one of the few in the Fifth form who played any these sports.

I am sat down with Miss Lewis, she asks me how I am and as always 'I am fine Miss, thanks'. In a nice way, she explains that me taking GCE's may result in some very low marks and she understands why that may be, with my home life and father's impending court case and divorce proceedings. And that it may result, in me perhaps even failing with U Grades, which would be a complete waste, especially as we know you are capable of these things in normal circumstances.

I feel like this is another blow and my stomach churns as she explains, I don't like to admit defeat in anything I do, even if not confident, because now I was so looking forward to a technical engineering apprenticeship. My first thoughts were that they are going to ask me to leave school immediately, however she explains there are some other options, of a new type of exam has been introduced and they are the equivalent of O Levels to some degree, and that the GPO will accept them. The Certificate of Secondary Education or CSE's, were introduced in the late 1960s, where going to a state school meant you could leave at 15, but if you wanted too, gave you the opportunity to stay on and get some form of qualification. These exams are introduced, coinciding with the raising of the school leaving age to 16 in state schools, later in 1972.

This new exam introduced innovative ways of marking exams and competence. A Grade 1 CSE meant that the candidate 'might reasonably have secured a pass at (GCE) Ordinary level', Grades 2 & 3 are given in approximately equal numbers to all candidates between Grades 1 & 4. Grade 4 describes a standard of performance for expected from an average student at 16 years of age. Grade 5 a standard within the scope of the CSE examinations, below that of Grade 4 and are not recorded on certificates. The important thing is that the majority of pupils left school with something to put on any job application. It's discussed and I am convinced - because of Miss Lewis's advice of someone who I trusted – and one of the few at that time who practised pastoral care and her approach as a teacher-mentor and empathy that she showed me at a difficult time, I felt she had faith in me and my future, I feel truly grateful to her to this day.

I arrive home from school, my brother says he has some good news for me, its May 1969, I am still 15, as an early 16th birthday present in June, he says he will take me to The Castle Ballroom the following Sunday night, an equivalent of that coming of age act and a tribal ceremony! Now this venue is a really cool place, with the influence of the now famous Mod scene, that had started a few years before and The Ivy Shop, the youngsters from Richmond and surrounding suburbs are some of the best dressed and trendiest outside of the Central London music scene and apparel, since the mid-60s and earlier, it was The New West End, with music and entertainment in the suburbs. The Castle Ballroom Sunday Club is members only and open from 7pm to 10.45pm, I am so excited, however I have the build of a twelve year old, small in stature and what the hell do I wear!

At this stage I have my Ben Sherman and a pair of navy Levi Sta-Prests, my school shoes polished to death with some sort of shine. I have my brother's old wallet and aluminium metal comb that we all carried as you need to be smart if you want to get into the ranks of a second generation Mods as we called ourselves or Suedeheads. The planning of what you will wear and the coordination of clothes is still and was a major part of the subculture.

I jump into my brothers, newly acquired second hand white, 1962 Triumph Spitfire to Richmond, my brother dressed accordingly and his long leather coat, that are becoming very popular with the older lads, if you can afford one. He inspects my clothing and says 'don't say anything until we get inside'. We meet some other village lads outside – Andy Richens, Keith 'Woofa' Barker and Andy Poulter to name a few, all suitably dressed from 'The Ivy', my brother, now 21 and these lads just a little younger. As I walk up the flight of steps to The Castle entrance, I can hear the music, trying to make myself bigger, a bouncer steps forward, a hand the size of a golden eagles wingspan goes across my little chest, I think "Oh No!, I am rumbled, but I must get in, it's like pilgrimage for me!". My brother calls out 'Its OK Phil, that's my little bro', he's with me, alright?' with a slight nod of the head and a wink in that 'OK way' I am allowed through, his hand swoops away, like a bird changing direction and he says 'have a nice time little Gooba!' and I walk forward to pay, the woman in the booth just waves me through! Keith knows her too! I still remember that night, like a baptism into much more than an adult youth club, this is a 'proper club'. I stand on the corner of the upper level bar, just observing and taking it all in, listening to the music, looking at the good looking and well dressed youngsters below. I make half a pint of Double Diamond at 11d, lasts me all night, I was introduced to many of brothers mates, accompanied by an annoying ruffle of my hair – "So your little Gooba eh?". Gooba was my brother's nickname, given to him by Alfie 'Cakehole' Blake after mispronouncing a comment about his big teeth.

I also notice some village girls, 'dressed up to the nines' (meaning perfection, perhaps a military term and uniform with nine brass buttons), with makeup and looking like they were in their late teens, some younger than me, 14 year old fourth former girls from my school and I am their class prefect!

What a great first night at The Castle, one little scuffle that night, I was told there were often fights against other towns like Hounslow, Putney, Acton or Chiswick's – The Devonshire Road Gang! What a story I had for school the following Monday and the next youth club night, I like to think I had arrived and along with leaving school soon – I am hooked and I will be back! Another Rite of Passage passed and I am now club bloodied.

⁂

Back to reality, from prison our father writes, a sealed letter with an HMP stamp on it, meaning it has been read and cleared, sending a visiting order and warrant, we decide not to reply or attend, we know he will go to court soon, trying to bridge build beforehand. Mum is really coming to terms with the inevitable and is being very stoic, although there were some nights that I am sure I heard sobbing from her bedroom. I think there is some relief that she won't have to engage with my father again, in asking for housekeeping or other arguments. Certainly from my perspective,

I certainly won't miss and dread that 'key in the door' and what that bought!

We start to buy The Richmond and Twickenham Times, Richmond Herald and Surrey Comet looking for any news of my father. It's there, we are shocked, normally a case like this would command one or two column inches of print, this time its interested the court reporter and it's some sixteen inches! Bearing the headline, '*Jail For Man Who Forged His Mother's Cheques!*'. Not only has he 'admitted' to stealing our savings books and asked for them to be taken into consideration and one other to be added. It mentions all ten previous convictions and times in prison. The list is shocking, larceny, false pretences, stealing as a servant, embezzlement and receiving going back to ironically 1953, the year of my birth, although it did start in 1948! This time forging cheques for £85 and £36, (equivalent of £2200 today!) from his 70 year old mother and his son's total of £37 (£700 today).

Sadly, a small paragraph saying 'His wife is earning £12 and he lived with her and their two sons', those fourteen words had such a backstory. He received a 30 month jail sentence and we then vowed he would never cross our threshold again! As far as we were concerned, he had lost the right to be our father and a husband not only to our mother, but also my brother and I would collectively divorce him from our lives, Mum this time, will not be 'conned', to let him back in our lives.

Personally and I don't like to use this term, but 'he is now dead to me', but relieved and at the same time angry, about the outcome. Luckily, guidelines and reasons to divorce were re-written in 1969, making it easier for the many women to have a case, my mother had re-filed now for 'Mental Cruelty and Irrevocable Breakdown of Marriage' and waited for proceedings to be scheduled at The London Divorce Courts in The Strand.

Chapter 8 – A New Beginning

1969 sees an enormous transition for me, not only will I be sixteen, but I can get my provisional driving licence for 'two wheels' and a scooter, I will take exams, finish school and hopefully get an apprenticeship and a wage. My sprouting love life may see an occasional relationship, lasting more than a week or a walk home to their house, clothes, youth clubs and music make an impression and I get my timing exactly right, joining a new subculture from the within the working class. At home, I see my mother more confident and hopefully looking forward to a life, she certainly deserves it.

I take my CSE exams in late May and early June of 1969. After the last exam you were allowed to and literally end your schooldays! Even your results were posted to you. No celebration, no school dance night or a prom, no thanking teachers, no goodbyes to other pupils (as most, lived in my village anyway!) and you would see them at football, on the rec' or the youth club. After 11 years at school, that's it, I have served my time in education, didn't even need parole!

That last exam, I just push my chair under the table in the exam room, pick up my ruler, pens and pencils, give in my paper and head for the door, out of the main entrance, walk down the drive with a smile and not even ask anybody, 'how did yours go?'

or 'how did you answer question 1?', I just did my best and thought that's it, no school, no exams ever again, without even looking back! One thing in my head, still slightly niggled me, will the grades be enough to start an apprenticeship in September? But I am not going to worry, I am now old enough to get a job and earn money, whatever happens. It's the late 1960's, with nearly full employment in the south east, even more jobs than an available than workforce, obviously Labour Exchanges were full of requests for more workers. Job vacancies in local papers just seemed to fill the columns, If I didn't get the grades at least I could still get a job.

However, after enjoying our youth club nights, one 'pupil power' victory that term was for the seniors, we Fifth Formers, lobbied the teachers to have a 'Record Club' in the school hall, where we bought in 45s on a Friday lunchtime. As a prefect I was the smallest bouncer ever, trying to stop the fourth years from closing the curtains and switching the lights off, to have a slow dance! Was the School Disco invented at Grey Court!

June the 6th and my 16th birthday, a pivotal age in my youthhood, although not age 18, you could slip into night spots with faked ID, when I say a fake, it just means applying and getting a paper membership card and putting your birth date down to reflect you were over 18, if you could grow sideburns, even easier! It always seemed so easy for girls to get in to any venue and at a very young age, with a little bit of makeup.

More importantly and gratefully, I now have my provisional driving licence and purchased from a family man in the village, a four year old Lambretta Li150, for £38 which I saved up from working over the last 2 years, despite my father stealing £11! Keith Fry – the mobile greengrocer, gave me a £5 birthday gift that June to help. A set of wheels and a licence to drive and go places, what else would a 16 year old lad want!

A couple of the other lads already had theirs, Paul Sossick, a former classmate, had left a year earlier and now worked, he had a gleaming red and white Vespa SS 180cc, a lovely scooter and fast! There were some expensive scooters around the village,

Alan Pope, Colin Burton (a Vespa SS200 Hurricane, I believe), Andy Poulter and Keith 'Woofa' Barker to mention a few, they also shopped at The Ivy Shop and wore The Shoes and frequented The Castle Ballroom a few nights a week – which all of us lads were inspired to be and would do very soon, we hoped! Interestingly at this time and reflected in later films, the majority of lads didn't adorn their scooters with lots of mirrors and lights and heaps of chrome. Most just couldn't afford those sort of accessories as apprentices on lower pay. Popular accessories were, a trumpet exhaust, backrest, for carrying someone who had passed their test or for giving young ladies a lift home, a rear rack to strap on a sports bag of some description, a whippy aerial with small flag or a tiger tail – an Esso fuel promotion at the time of, 'Put a tiger in your tank!'. Chromed crash bars (expensive!), spotlights were far too hard to wire in, especially, if you didn't have the skills, most of these accessories were picked up second hand or found down the pub – if you know what I mean?

Helmets, not compulsory then and Parkas were only worn in the cold, cool or wet weather and only to and from work or college normally. We also must not forget you could not make you scooter really secure, steering locks could be snapped, any ignitions, if you had one were jump wired, scooters would just disappear overnight and change identity and broken down for spares, chains were used and padlocked around drainpipes in your back garden. We took standard scooters, bought tins of paint spray rattle tins and tried to change them, adding stripes to mudguards and side panels, sometimes with bad results and of course stick on number plates and gold letters to denote, Li, GT, TV, SX or GS if you had an unmentionable Vespa!

I was lucky to start riding my Lammie at the start of that summer of June 1969, nothing better than riding a 'scoot' on a warm day with just light clothing or a Harrington and of course, no helmet. One of the few problems with summer would be insects, from breathing in a swarm of midges, to a wasp or bee hitting you at 30 miles an hour or a small insect or grit going in your eye. One warm evening a Stag Beetle hit me right between the eyes – I thought I had been shot! Clothes were always in danger, in over eighteen months of owning and riding a scooter, my protective clothing amounted to a pair of Levi's, jeans or cords, a pair of Ivy Shop Royals, a Fred Perry shirt with sleeveless jumper and cardigan over the top. Luckily I only came off once, a newly resurfaced and on top of the tarmac was finished with grit. I leant into the corner and my scooter started to slide away from me, I remembered what my brother always warned me about, after riding a scooter five years earlier, DO NOT put your feet on the ground to try and correct the slide like a speedway rider, otherwise your ankle could get caught between the running board and the road surface and could cause a more serious lower leg injury. The thing is as you lose the scooter to a slide is to keep your feet on the running boards and hold on, protecting your legs. Well I went with mine and picked grit out of my elbow, arms and palms, I was lucky! Many of my mates had more accidents but nothing that was life changing, only the experience and damage to clothing generally. Many ex-Mods ended up with limps and repairs to broken arms and legs or even in some cases they sadly lost a foot or worse a leg, with a side on impact.

That sunny summer of July 1969, a few lads and Danny – who had a scooter but wasn't old enough, I had a proper provisional licence but I think a couple of others were illegal, ie no licence and no insurance, which, was in hindsight was so wrong, but common then to take such risks. Think we followed The Tams 1968 hit of 'Be Young, Be Foolish but Be Happy'. But the police at that time, would only stop the majority of us for bad driving in any form, speeding wasn't much of an offence then as scooters top speed on a standard scooter like a Vespa or a Lambretta 150cc wasn't high! If you were unlucky to get stopped it was normally for a warning and you would have to take paperwork to your nearest Police Station along with the famous 'Pink Producer' issued by the Bobbies, within the next two weeks. So your pre-requisite to this, if you didn't have the right documents, is to give someone else's name and address, like an older brothers or a friends older brother, especially if you were a pillion on an 'L' plate ride, who had a full licence and insurance already, easy - pop along to Richmond Police, show your documents and as they say 'Bob's your Uncle!', no photo ID's then!.

When you got your scooter, you just wanted to and had to be out on it, constantly riding around, subject to having enough money for petrol, although there was a hose and siphoning trick you could use to supplement! It was that first motorised driving experience, pull clutch in engage first gear, twist the throttle, let the clutch out, feeling the acceleration, along with the smell of two-stroke, nothing more exhilarating! You were always thinking about a long ride out, we decide and because of our Mod influences, on a ride out to Carnaby Street, it would be a pilgrimage of sorts. Meeting up at The Blue Peter Cafe, to plan the route and a can of Coke from the cafe, who's got the tin opener? As I am legal, ie L plates and a provisional licence, third party insurance, I lead the ride, at the back was another lad with documents, in between Danny and any illegal's. We have planned to go up and over Richmond Hill, (always a real struggle with a 150cc engine and just over 6 brake horse power and a badly tuned Li150) along Upper Richmond Road, Rocks Lane, Hammersmith Bridge, the hideously busy Broadway roundabout system, even with the flyover that was constructed in the early 1960s, onto Kensington High Street and The Gore, looking back all the time to see if we have lost anybody. Glancing around we have lost a scoot', we see crowds coming along Exhibition Road and into Hyde Park and then the noise of drums and guitars, drifts over from the Park.

Pulling over and stop outside The Royal Albert Hall, we see lots of Hippies and Drongoes, pulling our scoots onto their stands, we decide to investigate. We asked 'What's going on?' and a long haired lad in a tie-dyed t-shirt and loons says 'Haven't you heard Man?', 'It's The Rolling Stones free concert in Hyde Park today!', we enter the gates to the park, walk to The Serpentine Lake and see Hippies spread in front of a stage, sunbathing and some paddling in the water, swaying their arms in a state of drug induced behaviour and that awful smell of joss sticks and pot. Strangely we ended up not far from the stage, we did like The Stones, but they were a bit off key that day of July 5th 1969! Not surprising really, Brian Jones who in 1962 was a one of co-founders of the band, had just two days earlier, been found dead at the bottom of his swimming pool aged just 27.

The smell of marijuana hung in the air, called more common then, 'Pot' as the shortened term of Potacion De Guaya - wine or brandy was used originally in which marijuana buds had been steeped and infused. Its literal translation meant 'the drink of grief' – says it all really for some lads who took up the habit long term and for its consequences. It was awfully humid and hot that day and we weren't keen to stay, our perception of hippies as middle class layabouts, who listened to dodgy music, not like us council house working kids, who listened to great music and of course wore smarter clothes, was confirmed that day!

The other problem bubbling up that day, was that lots of bikers or greasers were around and took it on themselves to self-police the event, looking very menacing around the stage and perimeter, we feared for our scooters across the road being kicked over and set fire as they did to Mods many a time in earlier years. When we arrived there must have been a few thousand in the crowd, its understood by the evening and the word getting out, at least half a million ended up in Hyde Park – although I would have disputed that. We continue our journey to The West End and Carnaby Street, exhausted from the tension and the stress of riding in London with the traffic, along with rider's cramp and that ache of the wrists from changing gears and throttle control. One good thing though – no one broke down or will have to produce their documents at a local police station.

Festivals were becoming more commonplace especially with rock bands and counterculture audiences, the famous one that year in the following month where the crowd gathered to some 450,000 at its peak, only expecting 50,000 originally billed as 'An Aquarian Exposition: 3 Days of Music & Peace but otherwise known as Woodstock held in Bethel, New York. Creedance Clearwater Revival were the first band to sign up, followed by many like Santana, Sly and the Family Stone, Joe Cocker 'With a Little Help From My Friends' fame and many more heavy music bands. Jimi Hendrix was due to close it, but due to the rain, his performance didn't take place till the Monday morning at 8.30am, when only 30,000 were still in attendance. Some bands that appeared at Woodstock also appeared at The Isle of Wight Festival that had taken place the year before for the first time, it attracted some 150,000 people. The Who included a set including their rock opera Tommy from that year after returning from a US tour and performing at Woodstock.

Interestingly another event took place over six summer weekends that year in Harlem at the Mount Morris Park, after the riots of 1968, New York's major gave permission for an event that was attended by some 300,000. The Harlem Cultural Festival or 'The Black Woodstock' celebrated African American music and also to encourage Black Pride. Promoted and hosted by Tony Lawrence and sponsored by Maxwell House Coffee. Notably Nina Simone, who had a hit in the UK getting to number 2 in 1968 of 'Ain't Got No, I Got Life' writing the song 'Young Gifted and Black', after a small theatre play in New York, which we all know that Bob and Marcia had a hit with in early 1970 and reached number 5. Top R&B bands of the day headlined including Stevie Wonder, David Ruffin, The Staple Singers, Gladys Knight and her Pips, Ray Barreto, Herbie Man, Mongo Santamaria, BB King, Chuck Jackson, The Fifth Dimension, The Edwin Hawkins Singers and the fantastic voice of Mahalia Jackson, who my mother liked. As the NYPD refused to police the Sly and the Family Stone concert, members of The Black Panthers took the role.

The whole event was cinema graphically filmed, sadly the directors and producers failed to find funding and channels to show the film to the rest of the US and the world, which we can all draw our own conclusions from. The tapes remained in a basement for fifty years until discovered by Ahmir 'Quest' Thompson, releasing the film 'Summer Of Soul (...Or, When The Revolution Could Not Be Televised)' in the summer 2021 and worth a watch, for its historic relevance at the time and now.

At home, Mum now seems to be much happier and seems more relaxed, with the divorce slowly going through, me with exams done and looking forward to work – subject to results. Our neighbours were very supportive towards Mum, but there were a few who gossiped – that didn't personally know and of her, who thought she may received some of my father's ill-gotten gains, or been given some stolen goods, he was definitely no Robin Hood, believe me! As she always kept reminding us, 'We have nothing to be ashamed of!'. About this time the family she worked for on Richmond Green are sadly moving, their children are now growing up and are attending boarding schools and universities, Professor Butterfield takes a Deanship at Cambridge University. Lady Butterfield was always very empathetic to my mother's situation, keeping in regular contact, by phone, letter and often sending photographs of the growing family and visits of the Queen and Prince Charles at Cambridge. Over the next 40 years, sending £50 every Christmas to treat herself to 'something special', until she sadly passed in 2010.

Mum, now being a bit more confident, interviews for a few jobs finally accepting one at the Littlewoods Store in Kingston as a Book Keeper. Trying to be a little more social and to get out, takes a part time job two nights a week in Twickenham at a local pub called The Crown. Travelling by two buses, the ferry or a lift from Keith on the way out home or a lift back as he is mostly out in Richmond at around closing time.

I get some very good news, subject to exam results my new job will start in September, so it would be nice to earn some money before then, as the travelling greengrocers role was not fulltime. Mum asks around the pub she works in for any temporary work for me and a fellow called George - who has taken a liking to my

Mum, says that he has a job on the back of a contract. Owning a light engineering firm opposite, tells Mum to ask me to report for work at 8am the following Monday, even without an interview. My mother tells me the 'good news' and I ask what will I be doing and how much does it pay? 'Find out, Monday' she says! If I didn't have my Lammie - it might have not been as tempting to get there, as it's a nice ride and saves two bus rides.

The following Monday morning, I kick-start my scoot', fingers crossed, it fires up, steer it up the side alley of the house, with that lovely smell of two-stroke and the trumpet exhaust popping and echoing. I accelerate off, it's a lovely summer's morning, no helmet and the wind hitting my face. I arrive at the building and I shyly introduce myself to the men and a couple of apprentices, George the owner, a stocky man and dressed in a smart grey suit and shaved head, looking more like an ex-boxer or gangster, introduces himself and he says my Mum 'has told me all about you'. Without any small talk he asks, "Used a metal stand drill before, Son?", "Yes, at school in metalwork", "Great" he says and beckons over the foreman, "Charlie, show him the ropes!" – thinking I must have got the job then! I am led away, "Your job", he says with a cigarette, just hanging on in the corner of his mouth and the smoke listlessly rising upwards, 'is to drill holes in these metal plates, placed in that jig, all day long for eight hours, it's boring, very uninteresting and it's called piecework!'. My face shows a query – 'the more you do, the more you earn, if you break a drill bit - it's deducted from your wages, right?!" "Any other questions?", he mumbles as he goes back to work on his lathe. I am shown how it works, by an apprentice and making sure that the soluble oil is always running over the drill bit and the metal to be worked, he points to a very large pile of cut plates, about four feet long and four inches wide. I wonder what they are coming into my thoughts. I am given a brown work coat, thinking, just being fresh out of school, I quite like metalwork.

The first day finishes, normal ribbing by the other workers about being young and 'it's not like my day, you youngsters have it so easy!' and of course making copious cups of tea and being sent out to buy 'A Sky Hook' that afternoon from the local ironmongers, the guy behind the counter in his brown overall says, 'Oh, your first day at Crown Engineering?' I nod, he says, 'Think about it son?', and walks away. In the days of many apprenticeships, the older staff liked to play tricks on the youngsters joining their trade, by giving instructions to go out and buy objects that didn't exist! Oh what a laugh it was! NOT! But we all did it, when we were qualified, they also suffered initiation ceremonies, when completing their apprenticeships.

My first week complete and if anybody has ever worked in an engineering shop, the atmosphere and smell of that soluble oil penetrates you head and your clothes. Before real protective clothing, the soluble would soak your dirty work coat and seeps through the rest of your clothing, you would take that odour home with you. The other thing was swarf, the bi-product of the a drilled holes in metals, it was lethal, it would coil and launch itself the sharp edges catching your clothes, small cuts over hands, which you were aware of, when that white soluble touched it, or your nails filthy from handling the metal, luckily there was the biggest tin of Swarfega, I had ever seen!

Its Friday, I am really looking forward to the weekend, the wages was delivered of course at lunchtime, weekly in cash from the bank or by an old armoured van - no wonder that there were so many 'wage snatches' in those days before monthly bank payments were to change this way of paying wages and now calling it a salary. At lunchtime we queue up at the bosses' office in the yard, I am playfully pushed to the back of the line. Last one in, George stands up, closes the office door and asks if I am OK. "I'm fine thanks Mr...." interrupting he says "Just call me George". He hands over a brown envelope, expecting to have a few pound notes and coins jangling in it. But there is a folded note looking like a 'tenner' which I can see through the perforations, I open it and see two crisp tenners, my mouth drops looking at £20!, I think it's a mistake, but it's written on the outside, it's now worth the cut fingers and that smell of soluble oil! He says, you worked well, but 'how many drill bits broken this week?', 'Three' I say, he says OK, no deductions this week, he winks. 'You could earn more if work faster!' he says, I ask what am I drilling, he explains they make up a frame, support a plastic lit up box, and will end up as Shell or BP garage signs. I ride my scooter home, with £20 in my pocket (around £200 today), I am very lucky!

I two-stroke it across the Richmond Bridge straight to Hill Rise and park outside The Ivy Shop and procure my first pair of Ivy Royals for around £6 guineas, I believe was the price at the time?

Seems strange today, but having an annual summer holiday wasn't the normal for many of us lads at this stage, due to perhaps affordability, bothering to organise it, even thinking about it - many families had a day outs, many on public transport, before car ownership, a train or organised 'charabanc' outings. I don't know why, but I didn't take any time off between leaving school and starting any work. Thinking about it and living on a council house estate, all families were financially similar, working Mums probably made a little difference, any spare money was spent on white goods, the odd treat or paying hire purchase agreements or weekly catalogue payments. There may be some exceptions with a professional status, but the majority of females still worked in some form of service, ie housekeeping, hairdressing, cleaning, retail, clerical or catering professions, many on minimum pay. While the husband was still seen as the main breadwinner and taking any time off, could result in lost wages and any overtime.

Many companies still didn't have holiday pay and other benefits didn't really exist, that lovely 1950's image of a housewife in an apron, serving her husband and one daughter and son, sitting at a table, with cereals and a jug of milk, a teapot, boiled eggs, him smoking a pipe and reading the newspaper before he leaves for work and catches the 7.48am train, waiting for his kippers, boiled egg and toast and a fresh pot of tea, were more Ladybird Book images, than 1950s and 60s council estate scenes!

However, some families still got away for generally no more than a week, although foreign holidays were on the increase many people still didn't bother or couldn't afford to go to The Continent. In those early days citing things like 'the food is not the same as being at home!', 'got funny money!', 'it's too hot!', 'I get burnt too easily, sun doesn't agree with me!', 'I hate flying and it's dangerous!', 'Can't watch the telly, it's all in a foreign language!', 'So hot at night, can't sleep!', on the positive side, 'the weather is great and the beer is cheap!' and of course a little bit of one-upmanship in the street when you returned with a tan, wearing a sombrero, carrying a donkey and carrying bottle of Sangria. Some people took the risk and drove to France and even as far as Italy, unbelievably. Also getting a suntan in that time was seen as now very cool, it showed that you had a few pennies in your pocket and that you had travelled and reflect prosperity perhaps, you looked good and healthy and hung about on The French Riviera – where ever that was! – hoping to see Bridget Bardot!

Though, if you didn't have the skin that took the sun and then sun protection lotions weren't the normal, you could end up with really bad burns or worse sunstroke with shivers and headaches, as I think we all suffered at least once, trying to get a tan after falling asleep, with one too many drinks at lunchtime! Getting sun burnt was the norm in the UK, when the weather was hot and sunny, somebody told us to get burnt first, peel and that would help to get a deeper tan! Treatment was an afterthought and we dabbed on the calamine lotion with cotton wool balls, when red and blistered.

People, still generally holidayed in the UK, where the issue with food and a good pint was fixed by going to a B&B, caravan and/or camping site on for many families in the area on the South Coast, teenagers in groups headed for holidays camps and its entertainment potential. Transport was a train ride, coach or car or in some circumstances a loaned one, travelling the A3, A35, A30, A303, A22, A23, A2 or any other road that headed to the South and South West and East coasts, Dorset, Devon but Cornwall was more like going abroad with the travel time and the distance involved and of course a reliable car. Traffic jams were common and the sight of steaming, overheated cars in lay-bys, letting them cool down before adding more water to a leaking radiator. Sitting on grass verges and in lay-by's were a common site along busy trunk roads and summer weekends and couples and families setting up a primus stove for a cuppa and homemade sandwiches. Thanks goodness for the introduction and the sight of a Little Chef, introduced in 1958 and its expansion in the middle sixties, its Olympic breakfast, by 1976 there were nearly 200 roadside outlets.

Strange, these self catered UK holidays, couldn't have been much of a break for 'The Mr's.', the wife still had to cook and do all the family chores, along with the shopping even though she was on holiday, although Mum might partake and relax with a gin and orange or a port and lemon! Camping was also a favourite, cooking outside, sleeping under canvas and the stars, skills from the Cubs and Scouts or even National Service would help erect a tent, but always hoping it wouldn't rain, storm or blow a gale! Caravans, some then looked like they were constructed out of cardboard boxes, more solid mobile home ones started to appear. However, if it rained the sound of the rain and seagull's tap dancing on the top, would wake you up at 5.30am on a rainy summer's morning. Holiday camps, brands like Warners, Pontins and Butlins - who I believe had a 'showroom' in Oxford Street to promote their package, were all still very popular, with meal options and child, teenage and adult entertainment.

In the early 1960s, my mother's employee on Richmond Green, Mrs Butterfield, guessing and knowing of her home life, luckily for us paid two or three times, for us to go to Warners at Puckpool and their Chalet St Clair holiday camps on The Isle of Wight. I still remember the excitement of getting the train, which I think the tracks went right to the quayside at Portsmouth Harbour and then a ferry trip across The Solent to Ryde. The train waiting at the platform on the other side and ranks of charabancs and buses, with excited children and those brown rectangular suitcases, loaded onboard. Everybody seemed to have their best clothes on for travelling to the various resorts on the island. I have a photo of me, on stage with a magician holding a giant Magic Wand over a giant Top Hat and the three of us at a meal time and one on a horse. These holiday camps had entertainment full on, meals were served at a particular time and in sittings depending on your block and room number in great large noisy factory like canteen rooms. Waitresses running around, dressed like Lyons 'Nippies', with plate racks stacked six deep of meals, which you had chosen sometime the day before by writing on a card.

Beauty pageants, painting, glamorous granny, knobbly knee contests and sack races, egg and spoon races, swimming galas and many more activities. If the weather was good, by this I mean not raining, it would be a bonus. Mum loved her dancing at night and being asked and was very good at it, after securing a little round table, I would perch on her toes being taken around the dance floor, to various groups playing and big band sounds and shows by The Bluecoats. My first sight of One-Arm Bandits, six pennies piled in your hand, ready to put in the coin slot and pull that big handle, looking out for the winning symbols to appear in the front, plums, cherries, bars etc. Children's clubs, I was in The Wagtail Club one year, the badge pinned on your t-shirt, to indentify you, when earning points to get the team's prizes at the end of the week. Mother was so relaxed on these holidays, she loved mixing and talking to people and the activities, especially the ballroom dancing evenings. A week away, went so quickly, relishing the times where you would enter a sandcastle building or a fancy dress competition, it would give you something to talk about when returning to school and the run up to autumn days and the last of the summer sun. Those chalets, with basic furniture and ex-barrack room beds it seemed, a small wash basin with walls as thin as an ice cream wafer. Sharing a shower and toilet block nearby.

To try and capitalise on going abroad, Pontins opened, what they called Pontinental – which I thought was a great name, but it was still a holiday camp, but with guaranteed sun, on the continent and local entertainment! Catering tried to create British food like a Sunday roasts or fish and chips - which sometimes didn't come up to the mark, swimming in oil. Butlins, that first opened in Skegness in 1936 I understand, stays were the equivalent of a week's pay, I even understand it had one in The Bahamas in the 1950s. The 1970s saw the demise of holiday camps, with the attraction of The Continent and its weather.

⁂

That summer of 1969 bought us The Moon Landing, American astronauts were aboard Apollo 11, with Michael Collins piloted the command module, Neil Armstrong, followed by Buzz Aldrin stepped onto the moon. We watched on our mainly black and white televisions with our jaws dropped, mouths opened watching these World Heroes. They made the impossible, possible and followed out Kennedy's famous Congress speech of 1961 "I believe this nation should commit itself to achieving the goal, before this decade is out, of landing a man on the moon and returning him safely to Earth." This was all at the time the US were trailing the Soviets in space race and its developments, it was the Cold War era. Driven by NASA, in 1966, saw the launch of the first unmanned Apollo Mission to test the systems and hardware, but along the way, sadly three astronauts were killed in a fire at Cape Canaveral, during a manned launch pad simulation. Stages of testing later completed leading to the launch of Apollo and we watched that historic launch from the pad on July 16th, that would travel some 240,000 miles in 72 hours, before Neil Armstrong stepped on to the moon on July 20th and spoke to an estimated 600 million TV viewers said 'That's one small step for (a) man, one giant leap for mankind', NASA reported that static eradicated the 'a'. A couple of very worrying times when the module went behind the moon and causing a communications blackout and the relief to us all, when the same thing happened on re-entry. All covered so well by the Tomorrows World presenter on the BBC, James Burke, the technology correspondent, a programme I watched every week without fail, so informative as How? or Blue Peter was to us children. Will never forget that image of Earth, the blue seas and outline of the continents from their module. The project and with a workforce of some 400,000 cost $450M ($5.2B today) it was questioned at the time, that this would have funded many projects and jobs for many unfortunate families, especially in the black and Hispanic communities.

That year of 1969 saw a few village parties in homes, their coming of age of sixteen and leaving school, a Party Seven (whose got a tin opener!?), illegally procured from the pub off licence, by an older lad hanging around for us or a few cans or bottles of beer would certainly get you through the door. Along with having a few records under your arm, especially British Motown Chartbusters although released in 1967, it was still very popular, or volume 2, definitely Trojan's Tighten Up Volume 2, a bargain at 19/6d, Atlantic's This Is Soul, all very danceable and those classic Motown tracks that never aged, singles and albums were like a VIP pass to any gathering. The other trick of entry was to get in was to get your timing right, as soon as the front door opened, the biggest lad, would shout across our heads and acknowledge some fictitious person at the back of the hallway, in one mass you would all go forward holding the beer up, as if you had been invited.

The best or worst parties were when the parents were away, serious stuff if fridge and cupboards had food stocked up, the lads would attack them like locusts on a field of crops! These parties would normally end suddenly by the arrival back of the parents, aunties or uncles keeping an eye on the situation, or the local Panda car arriving, after complaints by the neighbours about noise. A fight could also kick-off and sixteen year olds, so drunk on little alcohol, the young girls on cider, that they fell asleep in the front room or worse a garden bush and needed to be taken home. We have all experienced taking a mate home to disgruntled parents, knocking on the front door propping them up and them being dragged in!

Chapter 9 – And So To Work!

Its early September 1969, after the good news is that GPO Telephones had accepted my exam results, an offer letter explains that I attend their regional South West region headquarters, opposite the Ely's Department Store in Worple Road Wimbledon for an induction day. Where we would be briefed on what would happen over the next three years. We are a group of about thirty, 16 and 17 year old lads, an interesting collection of current subcultures of skinheads, suedeheads, hippies, drongoes, what I would call prefect or headboy material (swats, brainboxes, you know the ones who always did their homework and highest mark in tests and exams!), dressed in their finest Sunday Best suits from Dunn & Co or Burtons or even a blazer, with shirt and tie.

Our training is broken into various areas of engineering learning, firstly practical experience of working in the open, known as external maintenance ie up telegraph poles, down manholes, running cables around buildings, through windows sills and walls, both commercial and residential. Driving around in dark green vans, a colour called for some reason called 'Mid Bronze Green'. In October that year the name 'Post Office Telephones and GPO Telephones and PO Telephones branding ceased to be used, on junction boxes, equipment etc, as it now broken away from The Civil Service and as a Government Department, the infamous John Stonehouse, the disappearing and faked own death was Post Master General and then Minister of Posts and Telecommunications when I joined. This new business division within The Post Office Corporation became known as 'Post Office Telecommunications' coinciding with the change in the colour of the vans to a more safety conscious colour of that golden yellow branding and change of image heading into the 1970's and a separate part of The Post Office and Royal Mail.

Secondly, training on telephone installation which was very common at this time as the growth in telephony was phenomenal households went from using a telephone box a short 10 minute walk away to actually having one in their house. As a toddler, a trip to a red glass panelled telephone box was a treat, being placed and sat on top of those lift and unfold telephone directories, later standing and asking if I could push Button A when the person at the other end answered, also Button B to get your four pennies back when no one answered! Full instructions were on the back wall.

Unbelievably you could now have a telephone in your home, but it took some time for many, not only the cost but because of the lack of cables from the exchange and to residential roads, some households would wait months or even years for a phone, until more cables were placed in the roadway and exchange infrastructure in place or telegraph poles erected, don't think we ever realised the growth at the time. Initially many people had to have a 'Party Line', where you shared a pair of copper wires between two houses, pressing the button on the top of the phone that gave you a dial tone for access to the exchange, unfortunately, if the other party was using it, you would have to wait! If the young lady next door had a boyfriend, you could be really wicked and listen in, but soon got rumbled, hearing the click on the line and being told "Hang up that bloody phone you little devil, or I will tell your Mum!"

Telephone Boxes, when embarking on those early relationships days and didn't want to use the phone at home or didn't have one, brings back memories of which some were good, some were bad – calling your first girlfriends at a designated time and for me being excruciatingly shy, fingers crossed that her Mum or Dad didn't answer. Hoping you held your courage, then to let yourself down, by you speaking in a high pitched voice and saying "Could I speak to Sue please?", a reply came back "You mean Suzanne!?", squeaking a reply of 'sorry, yes I do...mean' gulp, panic, panic! "Who or whom, shall I say is calling?", "Graham" I'd say. Now this is crunch time, will Mum or Dad shout "Suzanne, there's a Graham on the phone, shall I tell him you are in or out?", trying to listen closely to the reply and hoping she came to the phone, or you didn't hear 'Tell him, I am out!'. And those times where someone is in the phone box for a long time and you are ten minutes late to make that call, oh, the anguish of it all!

Those public phone boxes could be a hideous sensory experience, someone may have relieved themselves after the pub and associated odours and there was an ashtray or cigarette holder and that mouthpiece impregnated with spit and stale smoke. Early vandalism of the handset chord would see you picking it up and not attached to the mechanism, directories ripped up and out or set fire too, cigarette ends on floor, chewing gum stuck everywhere, earpieces with Brylcreem or other substances. The door with those leather hinges that could decapitate a small dog, a child or a finger if slammed hard or if the door mechanism failed. The smell of those kiosks – it's still in my nostrils memory to this day!

It was great when we got our 'phone on the back of Keith paying for it, our mum taught me the etiquette of answering the telephone, - in a clear posh voice like Annie Walker of The Rovers Return, "Richmond 9133, who's calling please?" As an apprentice, I enjoyed working with the residential installation engineers, I believe the best job, people got used to waiting ages to get their first home phone and were pleased to see them, biscuits and tea was offered and served constantly. As you are aware, most of our households had them installed in probably in the easiest and coldest place in the house, the hallway. A new telephone seat would look lovely, with a shelf to put the local directory, having an extension upstairs was real luxury, generally installed in the parents' bedroom and really handy for making a call to a boyfriend or girlfriend, lying on the bed, where no one could hear you especially an older sibling as they would when it was in the hall.

When working with the external maintenance engineers we used to spend, what seemed like hours in a cafe on Sheen Lane, every morning, eating thick buttered toast and drinking tea. GPO vans parked everywhere and anywhere – they seemed to be exempt from any parking restrictions. I would look at my watch and get a clip around the ear for caring how long we were in there.

I often earned extra money by installing extensions for my neighbours as a 'PJ', or Private Job. Somehow extra phones were available for a small drink, under the counter from the GPO stores. Ordering an extension with an installation was very expensive because you only ever rented the line and the phone at that time. The other role was exchange maintenance and our training included being told about the current technology and the forthcoming rollout of electronic exchanges mainly manufactured and installed by Plessey – with no moving parts and silent running and free of maintenance. We also sign The Official Secrets Act on a bright yellow form, this would cover listening into phone calls at junction boxes and telephone exchanges when fault finding and anything we may hear and not to repeat to anyone. There was a downside to any apprenticeship training, on our induction a representative from Wimbledon Technical College came in. I must have been quite naive, because I thought when you left school, you worked and further education wasn't really involved, but block release for three months September to December for the next three years! The room mood changed a little, looking at each other in disbelief, especially the Skins and Suedeheads, realising that we were starting very soon. The only saving grace being is that I can ride my scooter everyday to Wimbledon from Ham. We also have a practical induction course at Charles House the Post Office Engineering School in Kensington. This course would show us how to use safety equipment when going down a junction box in the road, how to climb a telegraph pole and exchange Strowger switching equipment. Arriving early, I peer through the window of The Bristol Car Company showroom directly across the road from the school, on the corner of the High Street and Holland/Warwick Roads, which is still there.

Entering the school, it's the same group of lads, we sign in and are told to go to the stores. We are handed what I would describe as a doctors bag, full of interesting tools, from simple pliers to soldering tools and an amp meter. It was really interesting, telegraph poles in outside classrooms on the roof, taught how to lash a ladder to a pole, safety harness practice leaning back, in that rock climbing stance. Racks of telephone equipment, to practice fault finding and learning cabling colour codes, which you will never forget, for the rest of your life.

Heading to the store, we were issued with a navy blue donkey jackets, a brown overalls like what the owner of an ironmongers would wear both with GPO embroidered on the collar, two pairs of bib and brace overalls for outside and safety boots. My first day of technical college comes, the night before, I check my scooter, tyres, oil and fuel are all topped up.

Try starting it a few times, anybody who owned a Lammie would know that feeling, if it didn't spring into life on the first or second kick. After a time you will learn a little method of choke out, with the help of a clothes peg, twist the throttle, build up a bit of compression on the kick start and keeping your fingers crossed and kick it over! Bringing to life a cold scooter was always interesting and often, if you were with a group of lads sitting, chatting and someone says 'Let's go for a ride!', the worse thing was to be, the last one away – just like the Le Mans start, kicking over the scooter, if it didn't start at least you could 'bump start,' running alongside it up the road, clutch in, second gear and that interesting noise of releasing the clutch, the piston sucking in fuel and air, running along and hoping it would burst into life!! Pure joy if it did! Sometimes this method had some dire consequences, throttle fully open, clutch out and escaping from you and slipping on your leather soled shoes, loafers or brogues on a smooth tarmac surface.

Ongoing repairs were always interesting, many lads in groups had pulling tools which you could, as long as my started I was OK. But one day, I found I lost power and the fault was diagnosed as a broken piston ring. Using a Haynes manual, I managed to replace both of them, taking the head off etc. However too late to get a gasket from Blays of Twickenham on a Sunday, I traced the shape onto a empty Kelloggs Cornflake packet to make one and it lasted!

Using a London A-Z – the road bible of the time, Gladstone Road SW19, a round trip of some miles 16 miles. Now being a suedehead, we did not wear helmets or protective clothing! A Perry, Bennie, cardigan or Harrington, if lucky a warm American ex-forces Parka or Bomber Jacket as outerwear, you couldn't be seen in anything else, unless approved by Suedehead Central and of course your mates! Having an accident was what happened to other lads, coming off you scooter was a possibility, but as long as you are road aware in the wet or icy conditions, especially in rush hour, you knew the brakes were rubbish, avoiding potholes and sunken manhole covers, that treacherous glazed black ice on a winters morning, became very obvious after having a few near misses you gained knowledge and experience. We had a lad in the village, who damaged his ankle, coming off his scooter, trapping it under the running board, although it was painful he never went to A&E and thought it would be alright and correct itself, the bones set at an angle, I saw him a few years later and it had disabled him.

Our class of about 30 TTA's (Telecom' Technician Apprentice's) start their education towards a City and Guilds Certificate in Telecoms' Engineering. Many of us are Suedeheads, DM's, Monkey Boots loafers, brogues, Puma, Adidas, Bumperboots or AllStars, Harrington's*, Levi's galore etc. Yet again our Hippy or Drongoe classmates were wearing those ex-military Great Coats in services colours of khaki, airforce blue, or navy and it seems, greasy long hair and strange footwear. The block release is hard going, the benefit is that I will get paid £7 guineas a week (£7 7s 7d) wages, plus fares, lunch subsistence and a payment for working away from your workplace – mine was Richmond Telephone Exchange (940/948 dial code), which meant I grossed about £9 a week. But lessons in Engineering Science and Physics, designing circuits, theoretical fault finding for seven hours a day for me was hard going, yet I enjoyed the practical playing with Avometers, fault finding and soldering irons etc. Again not being that confident didn't help me, because I still struggled with to say 'I don't understand that, could you explain it again, please?'. There was always this overriding feeling that I would sound stupid for asking an easy question for some, that everybody knew and would then 'cherry up' when all eyes would be on me!

The majority of the class were from very similar backgrounds, many Chelsea, Fulham or Wimbledon supporters, Sun readers, reggae and soul fans except for the Drongoes. We always finished at lunchtime on a Friday, which was also payday, being paid by Giro Bank Cheques we all walked to the main Post Office in Wimbledon, queued up and got the cash and return to the college for fish and chips in the refectory. Some of the lads were good card players and set up a poker school, inviting other students to play, it became a bit interesting sometimes with cash in our pockets. If I didn't have a strong hand I always folded immediately.

Regularly, we would jump in someone's car and go to a big pub in Tooting High Street, needless to say it was tremendously busy and an eye opener for me, because it was Topless Dancing, girls in brass bird cages! I started to develop a new set of work mates, which was a bonus as going out more to different areas of South West London. Now working with a couple of the lads are from Fulham and invited me to Stamford Bridge to see the Blues for home matches and the odd away matches in and around London. 1969, was a shameful time in football history, with hooliganism growing along with the rivalry of teams and a faction of supporters and many attending Skinheads, with a mix of some serious 'Nutters', with little intention of watching or supporting the team or game, they were just there to cause 'Aggro!', a word that would enter the dictionary. As always, it's always a small minority of mindless yobs that spoil the enjoyment and atmosphere for the majority, they would goad any opposition supporters, chanting or pointing, challenging and picking up on any players, diverse it was not. Initially, I was warned not to look at anybody in the eye directly, these lads knew the local 'nutters', named for obvious reasons is and duly pointed out by the lads and the ones to avoid. It would not matter even if you were a Chelsea supporter, on match day these lads worked themselves up into a complete tribal frenzy, fuelled by beer and the odd pill or poppers, making sure that no opposition supporter would get into the pub - The Rising Sun - opposite the main gates, there was a trend to have a Chelsea Lion tattooed on the top of their shaved heads or forearms. Strangely, some of these lads had a normal job during the week, never thinking or looking like they were the type to ever 'Kick Off!' on a match day. Standing in 'The Shed' before seating and safety were considered, wasn't always a pleasant experience most of the time, any excitement that I had was a affected by anxiousness as the terracing was made up of concrete steps, any pushing of the crowd could result in falling over or being squeezed against a standrail, which people would even stand on. Because of the amount of pints people consumed before the match, they would urinate into a condom and throw it into the opposition crowd or down to the pitch side, alternatively just pull down their fly zip and let it flow down the terracing. You listened very carefully for lads in the crowd shouting 'F**k it, I need a piss, watch out!'.

You would always feel the tension rising within the crowd, especially if Chelsea were drawing, losing and against the top rivals of Leeds, the Manchester teams and heightened with local rivals like Arsenal, Spurs and at that time very scary Hammers supporters. If they weren't going to win on the pitch, they would try and beat them in the street, literally. Visiting teams like Liverpool and Everton seemed calmer and friendlier than I always thought they would be. Although I had followed Chelsea since 1962 as it was my first ever top flight visit, then just dropping into the English League Division 2 for one season, just a District Line ride away from Richmond, 1969 was a great period to start following them. Owned by Brian Mears and the owner of a Ford Dealership in next to The Bull in East Sheen called Mears Motors. It was Chelsea's club top scorer (with 202 career goals) Bobby Tambling last season, managed by Dave Sexton, they won the FA Cup for the first time and that famous replay win over Leeds! Coming third in the League, scuppered only by Leeds and Everton for the title. Peter Osgood was top league goal scorer with 31 that year, over 30% of his Chelsea career of 103, scoring in every round of the FA Cup that year, spending 10 years at the club from 1964. It was also the years of the "H's", it was nearly possible to send out a team beginning with the letter H, Tommy Hughes (GK), Ron 'Chopper' Harris, Marvin Hinton, Stewart Houston, Alan Hudson, John Hollins, Peter Houseman, Ian Hutchinson, etc.

Beginning the season with no new signings until October, buying only defender Paddy Mulligan for £17,500 (£200,000 today)! What a year, those rounds and leagues games with the grounds getting waterlogged, deep mud and piles of snow on the touchline as the pitches disintegrated over the winter, especially the new year and Cup matches. To be honest and I am not a big lad and I did do a lot of running, with a crowd of skinheads from Upton Park bearing down on you or the police with Alsatians or Mounted Police, wielding truncheons with horses rearing, the odd flash of a toy or real gun in someone's jeans waist, a Stanley knife or flick-knife. Personally I do not remember anybody getting stabbed, but the threat was enough to get you on your toes, got caught up a couple of times in scuffles, which generally meant lads steamed in and kicked out at you, the worst thing being a ripped shirt or pulling your and always seemed to be a new jumper by the neck. Although taking a couple of punches or kicks, I was mostly an observer, never 'wading in', a lot of running and generally being separated from anybody you went with, when it kicked off. After the match, I just wanted to get home and of course 'Get Ready' for a night out - well, it was Saturday! Picking up an Evening News Results edition outside Richmond Station and waiting to get a 65 bus home or scooter in station car park, it's been a busy day so far, overtime on a Saturday morning, watching a Division One game and the night to come – result!

Chapter 10 – Surburban Soul Boy – and Reggae Too!

That Summer of 1969 was a pivotal year for me socially, becoming 16, a few pennies in my pocket from initially a part time job and the a real job, leaving school and of course socially. Venturers Youth Club music nights are ramped up, come Friday the whole clubhouse is turned into a Record Room and a dance night, we are hooked and understand the common bond is music, clothes and meeting others. The previous night we would have been at the Ham & Petersham Youth Club, where they had set aside another room to dance and play music. Hanging out with likeminded village youngsters, most of us boys the now attracted not only to the music, but the young ladies who attended and bantered comments around, like 'She fancies you' or 'You fancy her?' and then a punch in the arm and 'No, I don't!'. The dance records were all good fun, the confident ones, dancing and making their moves on the floor, us shy ones, wanting to dance, but standing or leaning against the wall, watching and taking in the moves to practice in our bedrooms, ready for the next weeks attempt of boldness and to Get Down on the floor!

Then the DJ plays a slowie, maybe, Still Waters Run Deep, My Cherie Amour, Tracks Of My Tears, I'm Gonna Make You Love Me, What Becomes Of The Broken Hearted and even Procol Harem's

A Whiter Shade and many more, this for me was always a make or break moment, should would or could pluck up the courage to ask a young lady to dance, or hold back thinking she may say "No thanks", oh the dilemma! Dreading that rejection that would knock any bravery out of you, I so much envied the lads, that would get the girls, some even wouldn't care if they said 'No' and just ask another girl, straight away or as soon as the next 'slow one' came on.

Most of the 15 year olds, definitely the 16 year olds have money in their pockets now after leaving school and starting a job. What becomes important now is how you spend and save it, still very much a cash society at our age and paid weekly, with any Mum's housekeeping deducted, then dividing the days with what's remaining, come Thursday night anything left, would be used going out or may end up in your Post Office Savings Bank paying in book, for your next important purchase. Generally for me and later that year, as an apprentice it meant I bought home around £8 after stoppages, that's £3 10s to Mum, budgeting for the week, perhaps buying two singles at 6/8d each, two gallons of fuel for scooter at 13/-. Looking in the shop window or a visit to The Ivy Shop, to check the prices, now wanting some Bass Weejuns or another different colour Harrington or Ben Sherman and how would you would save. Adding more clothes to your wardrobe and a trip into Kingston to buy some Levi Corduroys and Sta-Prests, never got a white pair (too loud), navy or beige/khaki from Jack Brendans, or another cardigan or sleeveless jumper.

We are now at that stage, where we still go to our local youth clubs or play football, but with our 'Youth Degree' and Graduation phase to music clubs further afield beckoning on a weekend night, but still Friday nights and Venturers Youth Club was the best local, social and soul music scene for many of us. As a 16 year old it meant three places for us in 1969, firstly following the pattern of our older siblings or word of mouth of The Castle Ballroom, every Sunday night was a definite and in our social diaries every week, it became THE meeting place.

Obviously you had to be 18 to gain admission to many clubs selling alcohol, all generally relatively easy to get into, just a bouncer asking "What year were you born, Son?", in my mind now, it had to be 1951, which you would repeat over and over again in your head, carrying your forged membership card that matched. However these words were always a bit scary from a 6ft 5in and 4ft across heavily built bouncer in a Crombie, who was trying to catch you out!

Secondly to Kingston Station Hotel, a Motown and Reggae club opposite the railway station on a Saturday night. A group of us would go from Ham, we wouldn't ride our scooters, because they may disappear and change identity, the safest way was not to take it on a night out, unless locally where other lads knew your scooter and hopefully they liked you and it was left alone. However, I do remember seeing a row of scooters outside The Castle, that summer all looking very cool. A bus or 'shanks's pony' if you missed the last one, but not our preference especially with new shoes.

The other Soul, Motown, Reggae and Ska club we went to was The Bull Hotel in East Sheen another great place for sounds and an atmosphere on a Friday night. Standard dress for those nights, were a Harrington, cardigans, short sleeve jumpers over a Ben Sherman for £3/19/6d or Fred Perry, Sta-Prests and now slightly smarter and affordable, a pair of Prince of Wales check and now a blue/green, brown/gold tonic mohair trousers, which you could upgrade to a suit, choosing a jacket with 4" or 6" vent and a ticket and pocket flaps, finished off with a pair of highly polished Royals, Weejuns, Tassles and now Gibsons or Smooths, that ranged from about £5 to 6 Guineas from THE shop in Richmond. On colder nights, a much warmer Crombie coat and fake card hanky in top pocket and tie-pin, which was also transferable to the suit. Needless to say leaving a Harrington or Crombie in a club or it being stolen was commonplace after a few drinks with some of the lads.

Strangely, we all looked very similar, but we never felt it, changes in shirt pattern, trouser colour or shoes, gave us all, what we thought was a slightly different look. Although some kids cropped their hair or had a neat haircut, we used the term Suedeheads or Smooths to describe ourselves. We rejected being Skinhead, Skins or Peanut Heads - although people cropped their hair, if it stood up in that flat-top way, mine didn't unfortunately and I went college boy style – The Skins were now a recognised subculture, constantly gathering bad press column inches for racism, fighting, Boot Boys and Aggro. Disruption at football matches and hooliganism were escalating making it worse, families groups were now worried about attending matches and getting caught up in any melee. Growing our hair slightly longer with a side parting at first, which replicated 'The Ivy League or College Boy Look' that Steve McQueen, Paul Newman had and Rodney Harrington, whose name is synonymous and that wearing of the British clothing company's Baracuta golf jacket model G9 made in Lancashire, he featured in Peyton Place that ran on our TV screens from 1964-69. A name coined by John Simons on a tag hanging from a zip in the front widow of The Ivy Shop, initially selling the 'Sky Jump' brand. This look influenced us, in the clothing from 1960s Ivy League America and along with the Rude Boy scene.

It is said that Eric Clapton felt that The Yardbirds were getting a bit scruffy in hair and clothing and when he visited Germany in 1964 he had seen and noticed that US Servicemen off duty, were wearing the college look of rolled up Levi's, loafers and a classic Baracuta, which Clapton wore on TV before leaving the band in the same year and reputedly a key moment in subcultural style.

Hairstyle's – in the mid 60s, Mods had a shorter neater style, differentiating themselves from Teddy Boys, Bikers and Rock & Roll, with that look of a swept back DA or 'Ducks Arse' to the back of the head and neck, heavily Brylcreemed in place of course. In the later 60s, we second generation Mods tried to get away from Hippie hair look that was everywhere. A college boy look again with a side parting, tidied continually by a aluminium metal comb that you carried and part of your kit. Unfortunately, if at football or in the street, if you were 'stopped and searched' this along with any small pen knife that we carried as Scouts were confiscated as weapons.

If still at school at 15 in the late 60s, except for 5th and 6th Formers, your hair still had to be tidy or off your collar, policed by teachers, some ex-military and very fierce, would order you to "Get your hair cut, Boy!" or "Do your tie up now! Properly!" or there may be some corporal punishment handed out on a refusal or the following week, which was still carried out very often in state schools. This form of disciplining was dealt a blow by the European Court of Human Rights in 1982, after a case brought by two Scottish mothers and their punished sons, although it wasn't passed in law until 1986 in the UK.

Going to these early music venues Richmond was always a safe place for us local lads, for us to go to Kingston and Sheen we had to be wary, we were always very careful in entering, splitting into small groups of two and three being advisable, as lads from Ham or living in 'Am, you had to be 'Ard (hard), having a reputation of being able to handle yourself - except me of course! – we were often challenged by other towns and groups. Once any gang found you were from a rival areas such as Putney, Chiswick, Acton, Hounslow, Kingston it could cause an atmosphere, especially now that crowds of youngsters – were starting to attend some of the best clubs in West and South London. One of those was our club The Castle Ballroom on a Sunday night – later Cheekee Pete's in 72/73, wasn't really a soul venue, perhaps initially more 'middle of the road' and a bit Chirpy, Chirpy, Cheep, Cheep at that time, that just played good tunes.

On the whole, most youngsters were brought together by the enjoyment of the music, we loved black music and racism didn't seem to exist or not obvious to us in our world or just wasn't and didn't seem to be any issue. Ham and nearby Richmond was very much a white enclave at the time and we just mixed dancing and listening to the sounds with other youngsters just like ourselves, it was more about what area were you from, not what colour you are or were. We were all simply blended into this multicultural, multiracial experience and environment – that followed the sounds and the social excitement of going to different places and those nights out. The most annoying thing was, you wished you could dance and be that good looking lad in the middle of the dance floor who all the girls fancied.

However, just like football, there was still a small faction in these venues that turned their attention to cause trouble, which would always spoil the vibe. A few times it would just kick-off big time with furniture and other things being thrown across the room and the dance floor, innocent people getting caught or beaten up, being scarred or maimed by flying glass and bottles. In The Castle Ballroom one night, I witnessed heavy chairs, tables and a person being thrown over the balcony, into the crowd below from about 15 feet, it was like a fight in a Wild West Saloon, I believe a lad drowned in the river trying to escape a beating in the mid 60's. If a small group of Skinheads would try claim the dance floor, generally one of them, a Big Palooka of a lad, who would have been coerced to place an upturned pint mug in the middle of the dance floor (the sign!), shouting "Come on then, take me!". Generally, some bigger lads - not me again, obviously! - who were there just to have a good night out, would side with the bouncers, manhandle the offender and literally throw him out, but sometimes fighting did break out. We witnessed troublemakers being pinned and lifted up against a wall, nutted, punched, dragged to the exit, threatened then thrown out and told they were barred for life! The worst thing was the evening ending early because of a fight, what always amused me, is that these troublesome lads, would be cut, bleeding, bruised, blood stained wearing now ripped expensive clothing, one shoe missing and saw it as a badge of honour, shouting as they limped away – "You wait, we'll be back........!", or while being thrown into a Black Maria. The father of local lads Andy and Terry, Alf Richens a Special Constable, would stand outside The Castle on the corner, quickly herding and telling us to get the bus home and out of harm's way, should fighting spill out onto Whittaker Avenue, or if it was brewing.

One bad experience we had as a group of lads was that August Bank Holiday of 1969, we normally went to the Fun Fair at Old Deer Park, Richmond, we saw this as a no trouble place really as on home turf knowing many other people who attended and lots of reggae and soul being played, turned up loud to drown out the noise of the generators around The Waltzers, Dodgems and other rides, along with the smell of candy floss, burgers and hot dogs. That August we decided to go to Hampton Court Fair, a much larger location and bigger crowds. We are a group of ten suedeheads from Ham, all dressed in our best refinery, unbeknown to us, a group of and what we called now, Greasers, but in this case denim vested over leather jacketed Hells Angels, (I think, spurred on by the filming and their policing of Woodstock and other outdoor events at the time!) and who didn't like our types and a growing reputation of Skinheads, who rode 'hairdryers' (scooters) spotted us and formed a pincer movement, like a well drilled Panzer unit in WW2. As they approached from both sides, we were totally outnumbered, a lot bigger and dirtier, they rushed us and started kicking out, getting a metal toed boot up your bum and shins is very painful. So like a herd of sheep we scatter and run in all directions, I unfortunately slip on the damp grass and receive a metal bootcap to the face, breaking my nose and damaging the cartilage, that's still visible to this day. Splitting up, we start to run, towards Bushy Park gates, regrouping at the bus stops in the direction of Kingston, all thinking we were very lucky to get away with a few mud and grass stains and no real injuries.

Another run in with the Kingston Greasers also that year, we lads – Danny, Paul Sossick, Paul Ryan, Paul Young, Gerald Poulter, Ray Holmes, sometimes gathered for a little ride-out to Richmond or Kingston on our scooters, choosing the latter on a warm night, which had a great one way system at the time, you would ride along Wood Street, our trumpet exhausts as you lent into corners, sounding great as it bounced off the shop fronts in the high street. The noise of our scooters attracted the attention of some bikers parked up in a side road, as we rode around again, we sense motorbikes either side like outriders, revving their 500cc plus engines, now this is scary, large capacity motorbikes alongside two-stroke, smoke emitting 150cc scooters with little acceleration! Like a scene from the famous Ben Hur chariot race scene, the riders and pillions start kicking our side panels, now to a young Suedehead, your side panels are sacrosanct, many of us screwing or securing them as they were frequently stolen and generally the best painted part of any scooter. One of the lads panels were kicked off and was flattened ironically by a following number 65 bus, much to the amusement of the bikers. As we go around the town again trying to stay upright, the road forks to the riverside or back around again, we split up and go different ways. To be honest, when I think about what damage or injuries we could have had with no protective clothing compare to them in their leather jackets. I believe Ray came off his scooter that night, sliding into the fence near the railway station, a night where when 'no mate is left' seem to pass us by.

The soundtrack and tunes from this era will always take me right back and align with any fleeting 'Young Girl' (Gary Puckett & the Union Gap!) relationships at the time. They never seem to last for many reasons, besides getting 'The Elbow' from a young lady, going to a club with a girl wasn't the same experience as a lads night outs, trying to meet girls not take them, it may spoil an evening's entertainment! My first real girlfriend away from the village - well at least two weeks going out! - meeting at The Bull Hotel in East Sheen, a lovely girl and a great dresser, I am smitten, with key-hole mohair dresses and suits, white tights and loafers, her name was Gaye, she lived just off Putney Common, every time I hear Desmond Dekkers 'The Israelites', 'It Miek' or especially, Marv Johnsons 'I'll Pick A Rose for My Rose', Marvin Gaye's 'Grapevine and Too Busy Thinking About My Baby', it reminds me of that club and that young lady. At the Kingston Hotel, a Suedehead girl called Marilyn with cropped blonde hair and two tone tonic mohair suits and the first time I heard Jackson 5's I Want You Back, followed by ABC, The Temps, I Can't Get Next To You. I was stood up by Marilyn outside Kingston Railway Station after two weeks sadly, wondering what I did wrong! I wonder where those ladies are now? The club slowies at the time, Eddie Holman's Hey There Lonely Girl, which became another hit in 1974. With Trojan now doing well on releases, you realise the how many covers they made, by just keeping an eye on US and UK charts, Johnny Nash's Cupid, Take a Letter Maria, by Dandy on Trojan and R B Greaves on Atco and Horace Faiths Black Pearl, a cover of The Checkmates Ltd on A&M being just a couple, in clubs at this time.

But Sunday nights are now the most exciting, although it would be work or college the next day, moving from those boring Sunday pre-work school nights and listening to Sing Something Simple on the Light Programme at 7pm and making sure your homework was complete and your school shoes cleaned, along unpleasant memories of my father disappearing to the pub! My new routine and sometimes back from 'Afternoon Pictures' or a footie match at 5.30pm, going for a bath and trying to shave those sprouting whiskers, obviously avoiding the odd developing zit or stupidly squeezing it and making it worse. Record player on and getting dressed and wondering what the night would bring, trying to remember what you were wearing last week from your limited wardrobe and to make a clothes choice, we looked after them diligently, they cost a lot of money!

The excitement of jumping on a bus with mates and queuing to get in the Castle Ballroom, meeting up with others rounded off the weekend nicely, to think when I first started going regularly they weren't late nights. The Castle opened at 6.45pm and because of draconian licensing laws at the time, it closed at 10.45pm! Although it featured soul sounds, made up mostly of charted Motown hits over the last year, a sprinkle of Stax and Atlantic, just a few reggae Trojan sounds starting to climb the Top 40, The Israelites, It Miek, Return of the Django, artists like Jimmy Cliff and a Chelsea fan and that suedehead's anthem of course The Liquidator and Steam's Na Na Hey Hey Kiss Him Goodbye. These reggae records became such a sound to us, I think at the time we didn't know that they came from an island in The West Indies called Jamaica, or even where it was on the map, but we soon learned!

Big sounds that year were Stevie's, My Cherie Amour, For Once In My Life, Yester-me Yester-you Yesterday, Smokey's, Tracks of my Tears, Martha's, Dancing In The Streets, Junior Walker's Roadrunner, The Isley's, Behind a Painted Smile, a 1967 release put out as a Motown spoiler after the groups departure in 1968 and their funkiest ever hit of 'It's Your Thing' on their own T-Neck label and Major Minor here, their classic This Old Heart Of Mine, was more popular here in the UK than the US.

The Castle needed to attract a good teenage crowd on a Sunday night the music choice was quite broad, the DJs relying on chart hits and popular plays, having probably just listened to the chart countdown with Alan 'Fluff' Freeman's Pick Of The Pops that evening on Radio 1. The Castle Ballrooms playlists would included The Archies, Sugar Sugar, The Stones of course, with Honky Tonk Women, The Beatles with Billy Preston and Get Back, Creedance Clear Waters, Bad Moon Rising and Proud Mary, Tommy Roe's Dizzy even Clodagh Rodgers and still some Blue-Eyed Soul, Mod sounds from the likes of Amen Corner, The Foundations, along with popular R&B hits. The Castle became our first main nights out as a big venue, it could hold over a thousand youngsters at a time, travelling miles to get there, so lucky to be just on our doorstep. You had to look good and dress well, knowing the sounds and knowing how to dance, just having a great time overall. As it closed at 1045pm, there might still be time to get a Wimpy and chips before they closed and catching the bus home outside the Police Station, with big crowds of youngsters, trying to board the last buses to pass our village and onto Kingston. Taking a risk at the next request stop of The Poppy Factory, hoping it just didn't sail by, full up! On the way home the bus would always be noisy with boys talking about girls and girls talking about boys they had met that night or nudging each other and looking across at a group of girls! Unless you met someone, you could be tucked up in bed by midnight, on your own of course! Later, another club at that time and now open was The Crawdaddy which had moved from The Station Hotel to Richmond Athletic Ground on a Friday night, the venue was the rugby clubhouse bar and room with a DJ into Soul and Reggae set up at one end, a more exciting playlist and new import sounds, we saw it as a luxury youth club with a bar and ages of youngsters to match. We have nearly graduated from our own youth club now, within a short time it just doesn't feel as exciting. It was the first time I heard the great sounds of Bob & Earls, 'Harlem Shuffle', Red Bones 'Witch Queen of New Orleans', our anthem You Got Soul by Johnny Nash, Aretha Franklins Think and later Spanish Harlem was very popular, The Liquidator by Harry J, Max Romeo's Wet Dream, the wonderful Sly and The Family Stone and a young Larry Graham and that slap base style (later Graham Central Station) and that new funky sound with a great title of Thank You (Falletinme Be Mice Elf Agin), a music critic once wrote 'There's two types of black music, before Sly Stone and after Sly Stone'.

These sounds were the ones I would try and buy in ordinary or chain record shops the following Saturday, if I didn't get picked for the local football team or go to a Chelsea game, going to Richmond or Kingston, perhaps window shopping and looking for clothes of course, but buying records and hanging about looking through albums and checking the listed charts on the wall, regularly late Saturday afternoon after work and perhaps Woolworths Kingston, where my mate Danny and I chatted with girls while listening to records. One a Saturday, I went in search of a Wet Dream by Max Romeo, One Stop Records in Richmond that I know stocked a small choice of reggae, mainly because of the demographics of the town, unaware if we just rode our scooters to Shepherds Bush we could have got hold of anything easily.

Imagine, I am a very shy lad and will go bright red, even crimson if embarrassed, similar to and if I were to ever ask for a packet of Durex in my village chemist - which I never did of course - or the first time you bought condoms over the counter, on a hope of perhaps having sex! I hang about outside, hoping the shop will empty, trying to remember the artist to lead with that and practice in my head, 'have you got a record by Max Romeo please?'. The shop goes quiet, I stroll in heading for the lad behind the counter, who says to the young lady, 'I am just going on my break, OK', Debbie will serve you!'. That's it, the trigger; I can already feel my face going red, she says 'Hi. How are you?', I realise it's a girl I spoke to at The Castle, my mind goes blank, 'Hi, I am after a reggae record and I have forgotten the artist', but I can remember the title, obviously didn't want to ask for 'Wet Dream' and I quickly look at the Top 60 singles list on the wall, to see if it's there. She asks me if I know the lyrics, all I can remember is and I say with a cringe 'Lie down girl......', she looks quizzically, 'Anymore?' she says. Embarrassed, now to a bright crimson, I mumble and look at the floor, she says boldly and loudly with a group of people in the store 'Oh, you mean Wet Dream!?'. I nod a yes, get a pound note out and get my change from and disappear quickly from the shop. The next Sunday in The Castle, I see her pointing in my direction and giggling with her girl friends. Interestingly, Wet Dream by Max Romeo peaked at No 10 in the UK Charts and spent 20 weeks in the Top 40, despite being banned by any BBC for overtly sexual lyrics, although the singer claimed it was about a leaking roof – really Max?

These were great times, as a group of lads we would travel to other venues. Not to the West End just yet, but to other places we heard about from going to other clubs and speaking to young ladies. We would meet up, just young adults enjoying life. Other venues, later visiting The Oldfield Tavern in Greenford or The Iron Bridge pub, The Winning Post, Chertsey Lock and the Galleon, The Drift Bridge Hotel, Silvermere Golf Club and many more, it was a time when youngsters just wanted to get out and experience the gatherings and especially the music and it was growing rapidly.

Another location we found and were lucky enough to have nearby, even playing imported soul music and a good place to meet others and especially young ladies from outside your local circle was now the The Birds Nest in Twickenham, opening its doors in February 1968. This location was the first and launched by the chat show star Simon Dee, who had started to host a twice weekly BBC's *Dee Time!* a year earlier and quickly became the face of the new young TV viewer and had also replaced Juke Box Jury's David Jacobs on TOTP. Dee was an ex-Radio Caroline and Luxembourg DJ, who on the closing credits of his new TV programme, jumped into a white Jaguar E-Type and drove away with some fashionable young lady, it attracted some 18 million viewers on a Saturday evening. What better person than to launch this first venue, a completely different concept owned by Watney's, its idea was to attract the 18-25 singles demographic especially young ladies (then described by the unacceptable phrase as Dolly Birds!), hence a 'Nest', which in turn would attract higher spending young men with a DJ (Alan Hardy in my time), themed decor and innovative system of having phones in booths and on tables. I am sure you could dial a table to speak to someone you may 'fancy' across the metal dance floor and raised cages with go-go dancers, a DJ request or order food. The Birds Nest brand grew rapidly taking over large pub venues, the second one to open was The Six Bells on Kings Road Chelsea, which we frequented a little later on late Saturday afternoons, not far from The Markham Arms and the Drugstore, the other popular venues. The Birds Nest brand caught the attention of us youngsters, with venues in North Kensington, Harrow, Muswell Hill, Waterloo, around London and South East, even down to Basingstoke, they were like beacons. The brand attracted many young DJs and especially soul music scene and plays, making it the perfect place for meeting and a pre-drink before clubbing, in 1975 it even had its own Birds Nest record label. Watney's had also opened a chain of restaurants called Schooner Inns in 1965, the first one being The Crooked Billet in Staines, another new concept of dining, with bright printed limited menus and prompt service. A little like the earlier Bernie Inns, but a Schooner was slightly livelier and aimed at a younger demographic. Inviting a young lady 'out for a meal', was then seemed to be an affordable option, a Wimpy and Chips didn't really impress a 16 or 17 young lady now.

But a Schooner Inn or Bernie restaurant with its prawn cocktail, steak and chips, black forest gateau offering, along with a warm glass of wine from a brightly lit, supposedly chilled optics cabinet, that offered Liebfraumilch, Riesling, Hock, Blue Nun, Mateus Rose and many other sweet tastes, or perhaps finishing off with an Irish Coffee? Fine dining indeed in the early 70s, for a date at The Bull and Bush or Brown Bear in Richmond, it was one of the first times that you ate in front of a young lady for the first time, hoping you understood the dining etiquette and got it right.

All in all, 1969 was a great year and my plunge into adulthood, I felt that I had become of age, which we all strived to earn good money and be financially independent - money in my wallet, learning how to budget, a scooter and being able to buy, especially clothes, records and the music scene. Pay mum her housekeeping and perhaps an extra pound from overtime, getting into clubs (underage!), talking to young ladies from different areas and backgrounds and a bit of 'courting'.

So for me a great year socially, rounding off 'The Swingin' Sixties', the end of 1969, means and a must have, is getting tickets for Christmas Eve and New Years Eve at The Castle Ballrooms, because of licensing laws it still closed at midnight or just after with a temporary extension. Missing the last bus and a walk of a few miles home in your new Ivy Shop wing tips or loafers were a killer, the blisters from rubbing on your heels, especially if raining or even snowing, as it did one year.

An eventful year musically the summer of '69, bought us youngsters, many in the suburbs, the new reggae sounds like, Desmond Dekker, The Upsetters, The Pioneers, Jimmy Cliff and Harry J, that orange and white recognisable Trojan label in your collection. All picked up by a new young demographic, by the end of the year riding high in the UK Top 50 charts we have seen, totalling some 50 weeks on the charts, Return of the Django, Wonderful World Beautiful People, Liquidator, Long Shot Kick de Bucket and more Motown re-releases and hits, mixing it with the likes of Clodagh Rodgers, Sandie Shaw, Lulu, Mary Hopkin, Des O'Connor,

Dean Martin, Donald Peers, Rolf Harris, Frank Sinatra, Englebert and Elvis for sales and chart positions. My favourite reggae single from that period and an all time contender, a single on the Gas label that I had on repeat – being only just over two minutes long - with the arm off on the record player is Pat Kelly's double A side of Try To Remember and How Long Will It Take. Superb for dancing with a young lady or on your own, a slightly different production, but what a voice!

Trojan, that was based at 326 Kensal Road and a warehouse nearby in London's W10, the label was launched and founded by Lee Gopthal and a partnership with Chris Blackwell of Island Records in the summer of 1968 and named after a record producer of ska, rocksteady and reggae called Arthur Duke Reid from Kingston, Jamaica, 'The Trojan' happened to be his nickname, who coincidentally launched his own career in the year of my birth year of 1953, running a sound system, promoter and DJ. Reid (Treasure Isle Records, named after his family liquor store business) along with Harry Johnson (Harry J Records) and Leslie Kong (Beverley's Label) provided the licences for Trojan Records in the UK. The distinctive orange and white label became a catalyst, distributor and channel for labels from Jamaica, it gathered momentum attracting a new subculture that embraced ska, rocksteady and reggae, really taking off in 1969. Introducing a budget priced collection at 19/6d of Tighten Up, Club Reggae and later Reggae Chartbusters, all available from Woolworths Record counter, which was clever marketing!

Still over fifty years later, these sounds like a librarians's book date stamp, resonating deeply with me and many others, taking me back to my youth and the scene at the time, looking forward to many nights out and life in general, the sound was so different and fresh, always wondering what was going to be the next release. Obvious therapy for me and overriding any negative thoughts for me at the time and what was going on in my home life.

Another musical milestone and unbeknown to many people, was while The Beatles were filming a documentary prior to another tour, in that January 1969, and little did we know that we would witness their final live performance on a very cold roof of the Apple Corp. Headquarters in Soho, struggling now to get on musically and drifting apart after the release of Let It Be and John Lennon recent close relationship with Yoko Ono having a big impact, The Beatles change to individual management. A new musical phenomenon that we had grown up and lived with for the best part of a decade, we often sang She Loves You and I Wanna Hold Your Hand, coming home from school and scary dark foggy nights from Cub Pack meetings. A new exciting sound, influenced by US vinyl and music bought in through Liverpool Docks by merchant seaman and played in local clubs, covers of R&B, Blues, Soul, Rock and Roll, many Liverpool Sounds and Blue Eyed soul hits ensued in those early 1960s - labelled The Mersey Sound! The Beatles early albums, credit Goffin, King, Bacharach, Chuck Berry and early Motown covers and their writers on albums, before Lennon-McCartney appeared under many song titles as with later albums, Motown artists later paid back the compliment by covering their songs on an album entitled Motown Sings The Beatles.

So here we all are, 16 and 17 year olds, starting out in life, not too many worries and the main things was that you hoped and that you didn't get any angry spots on your chin before the weekend, not cutting yourself shaving, your hair went right, the scooter would start, you had bought the right clobber and shoes, that 45 you went to buy was available in the record shop and that girl you saw last week hopefully at The Castle is there again the coming week.

Interestingly The Beatles Apple Corps (pun on core) company replaced The Beatles Limited and Co, was founded to save paying around £2 million pounds in taxes and spawned many Apple brands ie Apple Retail and many others, Apple Records famous for releasing Mary Hopkins hits , Apple Films and Yellow Submarine. In 1978 Apple Records filed a suit against Apple Computers founded in 1976 (Apple Inc.), paying The Beatles $80000 dollars and promising to keep out of the music business, they were successfully sued again over the ability to play/broadcast music via computing, paying $26.5M to The Beatles. Eventually in 2003, The Fab Four lost a case in litigation with iTunes Music Store and its ability to play music. Interestingly The Beatles back catalogue wasn't available on iTunes until 2010, after working out their differences.

We were enjoying ourselves immensely, all lads still at home being fed and laundry done, a world away from some other similar aged boys and girls, we were able to go out socially, mix with others, listen to music and dance, although scuffles and fights broke out they were normally quelled and peace was restored.

But on the TV and the press that year other youngsters of our age having a very different life, we saw The Derry Riots and 'The Troubles' start to escalate with British Troops being sent in to reinforce the Royal Ulster Constabulary, The Battle of the Bogside and sectarian rioting in Northern Ireland.

In the US, we witnessed NASA incredibly and miraculously, land a man on the moon that cost billions of dollars, while back on earth the number of GI's in Vietnam peaks at 550,000 personnel, demonstrations and public unrest increased about the draft and the amount of deaths, 17000 in 1968 and 12000 in 1969, that was 50% of the whole war and its fatalities in just two years. Kennedy had sent some 9000 troops in 1962, after advisors in 1961. In total, some 3,000,000 troops were sent to Vietnam, which would result in nearly 60,000 deaths. Most US soldiers drafted were made up from poor (25%), working class (55%) and 20% middle class and High School dropouts. Many escaped the draft, if you were from a privileged well off family, had connections and a guaranteed place at college, in university learning or could build a case not to be called up and never be drafted. 'Draft dodging' in the white middle class community increased as the war and need for troops escalated, having well off parents meant there was a good chance you could avoid being called up. It became a war of attrition, a large Western power that couldn't in theory lose a war, using leading edge military technology against an underestimated enemy, who would and will fight till the end. It drove the Presidents and politicians in all different directions and would only end on the fall of Saigon and the US withdrawing support completely in April 1975. I remember the images on TV, the News crews would film unedited frontline action that could be beamed back nearly instantly and it was the first war to have real time access. The images were in vivid colour and showed the horrors of war without being censored, along with the coffins arriving back in The States.

For us lads it was a million miles away and never really touched us and lucky in the fact that we wouldn't get called up at 18, even for National Service that finished only just six years earlier.

Vietnam, was a completely different war, initially youngsters from poor backgrounds and blue collar families wanted to emulate their fathers and heroism bestowed on them after WW2. Enlisting and then deployed meant only about 20% would ever see action, not forgetting there was no real frontline or ground to be taken like the two previous world wars. Helicopters took a major role in dropping GI's and Marines into positions, live battles and skirmishes many being ambushed and shot down, of the 12000 'copters deployed in all areas, 6000 were lost in an incredible 36 million sorties flown, the greatest benefit was that wounded soldiers could be airlifted, attended or operated on in Field hospitals within one hour, along with newsreel films which opened our eyes to the reality of this type of war, the use of Napalm and Agent Orange. A GI, would have a maximum of a thirteen month deployment in Vietnam, the fighting, the terrain, the weather, the relentless confrontation with fighters that could get so close during engagements, many with no uniforms and trying to recognise who was the enemy, was nearly impossible as they approached villages. One minute lying on your camp bed, and within a few minutes being dropped into a warzone, watching your buddies, getting shot or die beside you in some foxhole, if you were pinned down and under fire.

Compounded by anti-war feelings at home, it drove many to drugs, to take their minds off these constant unknowns, when under fire and in a combat zone. Amphetamines were already being used to keep people awake when dropped into an area when holding a position, especially overnight, nicknamed Purples Hearts just like the medal awarded for a wound. Marijuana was smuggled in initially by arriving soldiers and later grown by local farmers in the ideal conditions to earn them money. From combat to boredom it was used to just escape for that short time, along with R&R, which was 5 days leave, Bangkok being popular with single males and what was on offer and Hawaii for young married couples, before returning to the jungle to fight an unknown enemy, for many 'War is and was Hell!'. For the US Military Police the 'weed or pot' was easier to smell, track and control, so many turned to heroin, but not injected for obvious reasons, as nearly 3 million US personnel and civilians served in Vietnam, its estimated that 50% took part in drug taking. The impact on the returning veterans, reputably causing addiction and the need for substances to be used when in civvy street, forged a drug culture, not only to returnee's and their generation but the next, sadly.

The 'Stop The War' and 'Get Out Of Vietnam' campaigns and the public's view of a war that could never be won, along with Civil Rights, changed the US forever, no one would ever trust a politician again, 'Patriotism' took a real blow! In 1968, an anti-Vietnam rally gathered in Trafalgar Square, London with an estimated 25000 demonstrators marched onto Grovesnor Square outside the American Embassy, erupting into violence and protected by a 1000 policeman.

In the UK the voting age was lowered from 21 to 18 years old. I remember a discussion with mates on the US Draft system, reaching 18 you were registered, if you were selected by a local draft board as to suitability and availability to serve, for a war that no one really wanted. We youngsters at the time were looking forward to reaching that target of 18 and going legally into a night club, how lucky were we in not going to war instead. As non-skilled working class lads, we would certainly have been included in any draft system, interestingly of the US young male population, blacks made up some 11% of the country, the draft numbered nearly 15%. Because of their lack of skills they were generally drafted into the army infantry and combat units, early in the war, blacks made up over 20% of the killed and injured. Whites made up 96% of the Officers, Blacks 1.8%, others the difference. In comparison, the Latino population at the height of the war was 10% in the US and a later study revealed that they made up 20% of all troops killed.

Closer to home, we also had our own TV images of Northern Ireland and the violence and bombings. Here in London while we were we going for a night out on the town, for the next decade we would also experience the death and devastation of bombings, now on mainland UK. The first time that an Irish Republican bomb impacted London was on December 1867, the group, 'The Fenians' detonated a bomb up against the wall of Clerkenwell Prison in an attempt to release comrades. Unfortunately, the bomb damaged nearby housing, killing 12 people and causing 120 injuries. We at that time, were so lucky, a generation with no wars, the most discipline being school or in the Cubs or Scouts or a clip around the ear from a Mum or Dad and of course the policeman 'on the beat' or at a football match. My Mums phrase of 'Someone's always worse off than you' really couldn't be any nearer the truth.

On a brighter side a new car from Ford was announced – The Ford Capri! – to us youngsters who had seen the brilliant Bullitt the year before, it was our version of a UK soul boys Ford Mustang, over the next decade it was the motor to have and luckily the young ladies loved them! But at nearly £900 in 1969 (£11000 today) we would sadly have to wait, to buy one second hand. For any youngster The Raleigh Chopper was announced at nearly £37 (£400), with an innovative seat and gear lever change, the equivalent of a new £120 (£1400 today) 1969 Lambretta SX200 for us lads, sold to so many young children who wanted an early cool ride!

When we weren't going out, due to lack of cash or a girlfriend, TV was our other entertainment, I used to enjoy and sit down with Mum. 1969 saw the first episodes of Monty Python Flying Circus, Dads Army, The Clangers, Pot Black, The Benny Hill Show, Opportunity Knocks, Take Your Pick, Holiday, The Liver Birds, On The Buses, Paul Temple, Randle and Hopkirk, Softly Softly, a spinoff of Z-Cars and two great interesting series for me, Civilisation and The World At War. My favourite at that time was a new US sci-fi series, Star Trek made its debut on BBC1 with an episode called 'Where No Man Has Gone Before'. And for Mum her favourite Mancunian fictitious Weatherfield programme 'Coronation Street' is now filmed and broadcast in colour. From the US and often repeated late at night those classic US TV programmes of Dragnet, The Untouchables and Robert Stack as Eliot Ness, along with the weird One Step Beyond and later The Twilight Zone aired later at night.

In music The Beatles release their last album collectively as a band – Abbey Road. I now started to purchase the New Musical Express to keep an eye on the charts, R&B listings and reviews from Charles Shaar Murray later. And of course 1969 gave us the classic Marvin Gaye's "I Heard It Through The Grapevine", the last chance dance at any Youth Club evening or music venue and perhaps a walk home and a stolen snog outside her house – obviously out of sight of her father of course! Walking a lovely young lady home called Wendy, one foggy night from Venturers Youth Club, out of the gloom came her angry father, ranting about how she should have been home by 9.30pm because of school the next day, as he marched her away, I shouted 'See you then!', gathering pace to run away in the opposite direction into the dense misty night, not wanting the wrath of her father, it was enough to spoil any future romance and anyway she fancied my mate Danny.

It wouldn't be the last time that a father or a mother caught or surprised me when in the company of their daughter!

Chapter 11 – A New Decade - 70's Soulboy

Many books have been written about music and clubbing of the seventies decade, so labelling myself as a soulboy in lower case seems more apt, this section covers my own story and recollections of the time, going out and my personal experiences. Having friends from the village and meeting new ones, working and socialising with them, going out regularly, but lots of lads fell out of the circle for many reasons. Did we go to all the clubs on the circuit, definitely not, word of mouth directed us to many after chatting to likeminded in bars and clubs, uncovering and venues, which bought new adventures.

Is my memory and knowledge about these times accurate about these clubs, the scene and what music was played, probably not? Most music recalls the popular sounds and where you were, many records we heard were weeks before entering the UK charts because of popularity and the amount of youngsters clubbing at the time, some then becoming commercial and perhaps overplayed in a soul boys or girls opinion, but still standing the test of time from when they dropped and hit the dance floor.

Your memories may contradict mine and you may be spot on, that's OK, a lot went on and it's a stage of my life that I hope I will never forget, anticipating that the horrible disease of dementia doesn't take them away. The great thing is, I still have a 60 year old,

600 plus single and album vinyl collection and associated memories – so glad they printed a release year on record labels! Some reminiscences and memorabilia from that period, a pile of Blues & Soul to backup, covering the years 1972-77, it's a shame I mislaid some issues up to 1979. I loved and still do, the music and the scene of that decade, flicking through my relatively small record collection compared to many, mine are from the late 1960s the majority being purchased in the middle of the 70s and involved that great Summer of '76, which to me is when I became of ardent Jazz Funk fan, having heard some of the greatest singles and albums of that decade in my humble opinion.

Some say the popularity of 'Disco' and the use of the word, renaming places and the release of Saturday Night Fever in 1977 softened the edges of the music and clubs we gathered at in the early '70s, the rawness of Funk and its development, as the decade finished. Never did get into, understand or want too Punk music and it's scene, after smooth soul sounds of great writers of lyrics and the music that went before it.

I was never one of 'The Faces', The Best Dressed, The Greatest Dancer, or 'The Always Invited to Everything Guy', although it would have been nice, but my perspective comes from being a follower of the music and fashion, that I and many others loved, always a lad that observed and took it all in and was more 'Interested' than a lad that was 'Interesting'. Just an average lad in the crowd, probably wanting to be that dancer who created a space and took the floor, I enjoyed my dancing, especially the moves and those great sounds of our younger days and its influences.

I try to be as accurate as I can with clubs, locations and events, being reminded by the sounds and the year they were first played and reached my ears. It was also a time when some people still didn't have telephone at home, especially in the early 1970s, when we called for people at their houses or met on a street corner or the local youth clubs. I have a collection of letters and notes from young ladies, even lads on their first holidays abroad, because that's how we communicated at that time, seems strange now, but that's the way it was. Most lads were apprentices in their late teens, I think then if you were over that age, you were considered quite old as the average age for getting married then was just 25 for a man and for women around 22, add this to courtship of two or three years, your 'going out years', clubbing could be quite narrow.

As far as we were concerned at this time, our lives were about working and earning a crust, to pay for those things we liked to do, owning a motor, records, clothes, chatting and engaging with young ladies, but mainly going out, the music and a glass of beer occasionally. A cycle of work, nights out and short sleeps, most days of the week, interjected with football, window shopping for clothes and of course again back to payday and starting the socialising again, an enjoyable treadmill for many of us, the energy came from the music. Where I haven't been able to seek out people and get their permission, I have changed the name to protect any identities. If I have mentioned your name, I hope you won't mind me using it.

⁕⁕⁕

So here we are, at the end of 'The Swingin' 60s', we celebrate the coming of a new decade The 1970's, again at The Castle Ballrooms (later Cheekee Pete's), Christmas and New Years Eve's, did we ever think and did we ever wonder, what a new year and decade would bring?

New Year Resolutions? I don't think or recall that the phrase was even invented or used, the majority of us, especially us lads never really planned long term, thought, or would seldom picked up the phone to even talk to a mate (something that seemed a bit weird in doing that, we initially thought), plans were just drawn up by saying 'see you at football', 'I will give you a knock', 'shall I pick you up', or 'you going to pick me up?', 'see you there!', 'are you going to...?', 'meet you at the bus stop or pub' and of course with our final days of attending youth clubs, coming to an end and meeting up as a group locally. The Castle or some other club were the places to meet, meeting at a Sandy Lane bus stop on the Petersham Road, where we gathered at a particular time, jumping onto the bus as it arrived, being careful not to slip on our leather soled shoes. Living in a village under two miles away from Richmond meant another bus might not come along for 45 minutes, it may be too late to go out, so disappointing, especially on a Sunday night, but there was always, the option to walk. Many of our village mates will soon drop out of the 'going out circle', be with girlfriends or by now 'going steady' or just as we joked, when they wouldn't come out, because they were now 'under her thumb', we would wind up them up with.

Looking back, in those early years I really struggled with relationships, mainly down to a big blanket of shyness, especially young ladies, too slow to engage, tongue tied and embarrassed, or the difficulty of just forming any type of relationship and showing any empathy. Some of the letters that I receive from a young ladies, reflect this, 'I really don't know where I stand with you?' or 'can you let me know if we are going out with each other or what!?', 'it would nice if you just spoke to me', perhaps I just didn't have 'the bottle' or honesty to tell them, I didn't want to go out with them, because it may bring on some form of confrontation, which I was very uncomfortable with, perhaps going back to the quarrels my parents had! The distraction of my home life is more about the music, my form of therapy, knowing the latest club sounds and how would I get hold of them.

Don't get me wrong, I did enjoy and like chatting to young ladies and going out with them as friends and at most clubs you had a big circle of acquaintances. It seemed so easy then just to walk in to a venue or pub on your own and just meeting friends or even join a group of young ladies, you knew from school. When you 'fancied' or met a girl in those early days it wasn't easy, if you liked them it could be a week hoping they would go back to the same venue. Then the use of the phone was not common, you would never spend hours on the phone, Mums even put finger locks on the dial as so expensive to make calls! They were 'Only used for emergencies, distant relatives or someone might be trying to get hold of us!' or your Mum saying 'Don't be on the phone long, I am waiting for a call!' – the phone hardly ever rang! Little did we know how the telephone and communicating would become and so important in our life, for consumers and business as the 70s went forward. We all seemed to go from no telephone to everybody having one in such a short time, that decade, making it easier to get hold of people.

Working on Post Office Telephones was very interesting; we would be allotted a 'home base' telephone exchange. Very much run by the unions, a forty hour work week, you had two 30 minute breaks, morning and afternoon and an exactly an hour for lunch. My role moved from Richmond in Paradise Road to Mortlake telephone exchange (876/878) on the Upper Richmond Road, there were apprentices like me in their first to third years of training, young qualified engineers to senior engineers about to retire. I must say, it wasn't a demanding job on exchange maintenance, mainly cleaning banks of equipment that we called switches, with a trannie earphone hidden under your growing hair.

The boredom would encourage people to read books and magazines, repairing radios, hairdryers, irons and even TV's and the great pastime of listening to people telephone calls, illegally of course, encouraged by other apprentices, using a rubber handset or 'Butt' with a plug or crocodile clips and a dial embedded in it. Us apprentices at lunchtime would listen into calls, working out that young people used phones at lunchtime for free from their offices, talking to their mates about their relationships, adults having affairs. You would see us all connected into one call when if it was interesting, the best ones being 'loved up' young couples. One of us would drop in an "I Love You" or another phrase, this would really confuse them! We would just literally roll around the floor laughing, we were young, stupid and silly and as we were still under the Government Official Secrets Act and we could have been sacked on the spot!

Some of our other duties were to assist the police in identifying and call tracing, which sometimes was very exciting, thinking we might be involved with an espionage ring, the Secret Service, the Police or tracking down a major criminal. At speed running around the exchange, we could hold open a line and trace back to the caller, we then via our Cardex filing system in the exchange, having every subscriber on that exchange recorded and the address of who made the call and then to inform the authorities. The other thing that Post Office had control over was listening into calls, which was a special division (we thought Home Office or even MI5 and Secret Service, to make it more exciting) that would tap into a subscribers number for purposes of recording calls, hence the word 'wire tap'. At Mortlake, there was also one big advantage, we had switchboard operators, about probably 40-50 ladies and young girls. This was great to chat-up a young lady or look across the tables in the canteen. Given that I am 17 and these married ladies are in their thirties it could be an interesting time with the 'Older Women Syndrome', kicked in a few times, some flirted on a bet from the others and lead us young lads on. The older Mums would also use it as a dating service, asking you if you had a girlfriend, age, and then introduce their daughter into the conversation. The more cheeky mature operators were the worse, they would get problems with their positions and chords, that they plugged in, they would say 'Graham, I think I have a problem, can you have a look, please?'. Now, given you had to go under the desk, bending over as you went to check, they never moved out of the way and you would brush their legs. Being so very shy, this is where I went crimson or 'did a cherry' again, as I asked them to tug the chord, replying 'Tug your what, Graham!?' or they would tap my bum or give it a slight squeeze, all in good fun of course. Then you heard muffled laughter from the other operators and the supervisor coming over to see what the commotion was, sometimes me getting told off for distracting the ladies and the shift! The Exchange Supervisor was similar to a Matron in a hospital, these girls were run with armed services type discipline, if they wanted a comfort break, they either raise their hand or stand up a notice above their position. Because of the amount of call intervention needed then, with operator and emergency calls, it was only one at a time and they had to wait to be told, it's OK to go.

This was another group of lads that I would meet for a night out in Richmond, I remember, boss Clive Houghton, Jim Spencer, car mad Rod, Malcolm, Les Kenning, Simon Foster and a good mate at the time, an interesting lad called Big John (Sells?), who looked like the character from Scooby Doo, the tall one with long blonde hair, tank top, big collared shirts, bits of a beard and Desert Boots, his party trick was to eat a whole white onion for a laugh at lunchtime – Why? – got no idea, but it was always hilarious and in 1972 a young lad from Barnes called Howard Ambrose, who became a good mate, we hung about with and frequented The Castle and a few other clubs around Richmond area. The work was too easy, time to do any scheduled rack maintenance and cleaning, lots of overtime to do even more, fault finding was more interesting. All duties were very much controlled by the Post Office Engineering Union POEU, you had to be a member. At that time over 60% of all the UK workforce were in some union, compared with 20% today.

My Mum, who came from working class and a Labour voter initially, had explained to me that unions were needed to protect the rights of workers, their conditions and pay. But the late 60s and early 70s saw the growing dominance of the unions in the workplace and industrial inefficiencies. Like TV's The Rag Trade 'One Out, All Out' shouts, strikes raged throughout industry, car manufacturing, coal, steel, railways, Royal Mail, the print and many more. Under a Labour Government, they were taking more and more control and so many hours were being lost in manufacturing and the infrastructure of the country. The earlier 'I'm Backing Britain' patriotic campaign of working an extra half-hour unpaid and set up by five secretaries from a factory in Surbiton, initially gained pace throughout the UK and reaped benefits, but the unions scuppered the idea, who couldn't have employees working for no wage!

My mother who had at one time had multiple jobs, worked hard and not in the best of conditions, started to think about her vote and lost faith in the Labour Party and Unions and the amount of days now being lost to strikes and it seemed their work ethos and now the power of certain unions to bring the country down.

Every other week and during the season I was still going to Chelsea home games, I never really travelled to away games, - unless London – because I wanted to get home and go out on a Saturday night, some fan eh? Football violence was getting worse, where as fighting before was generally just 'handbags at dawn' and pushing each other, football fans or should I call them 'Extremes and Nutters', were now carrying weapons, sawn off scaffolding poles, hammers, ice picks, knuckledusters, leather coshes and when challenging opposition supporters, throwing bricks, milk bottles and any other street furniture. Concentrating on watching a match in The Shed, became more of 'Watching Your Back' in case you were hit over the head with a blunt instrument' thrown from the opposition. Some football hooligans, just didn't care what happened to them, even being coshed by a policeman, or manhandled struggling and thrown into and into the back of a Police Ford Transit, Black Maria or Meat Wagon as we still called them, with blood running down their heads, it was seen again as some form of a badge of honour and would increase their standing in the eyes of similar so-called fans. The fun and interest of going was slowly dissipating for me and it seemed to every game now was threatening to 'kick off'. Controlling a crowd of a thousand Skinhead Shed Boot or Bovver Boys was stretching police, frightening people and families who were there just for that football experience. The great thing that year of 1970 is that Chelsea won the FA Cup and the first replay in history, the following week at Old Trafford and to beat the time of Norman Hunter and Billy Bremner and the battling Leeds United, was a great victory with the winning goal from Dave Webb, I believe that the new method of the 'long throw' from Hutchinson, which seemed to be more of a 'free kick' with the distance into the penalty area for a header. It was time now to review going to football, what started off as a good experience is now becoming difficult with every visiting team ready to challenge the 'Shed End'.

The other thing that I was reviewing that year, was my mode of transport, in the run up to my seventeenth birthday, I must think about the advantages and getting a car. Travelling to work on a scooter was OK if dry, cold or sunny, but in the rain, cold wet or sleet and even snow, was not comfortable or a pleasant experience. The other thing is obviously the compelling reason to say to a young lady you may meet using that golden phrase of 'Would you like a lift home?' getting the keys out of your pocket and saying 'My car's outside' smugly – I couldn't wait! And of course, travelling with mates and not missing that last bus home or getting wet clothes and ruining your expensive footwear.

We could go out at least 3 to 5 nights a week, depending on how much of your apprentices wage was left, hearing about new clubs opening locally. 1970 was another one of those years of discovery, from going out to asking girls out for a drink or meeting them on a Sunday afternoon for a walk along the river or to the cinema. All a bit of a rush and secondly the big dilemma of being with a nice girl, walking or taking her home late afternoon or saying 'Did I tell you that I was meeting the lads later at The Castle for a night out?', which wasn't their expectation for a Sunday evening.

You are probably wondering why I haven't mentioned the word 'SEX' as part of that growing up stage. Just a couple of years earlier, my mother was always hinting to me gently, not preaching or wagging her finger at me, but just planting seeds – thankfully, instead of me planting them - in my brain about and her favourite phrase of "There is always a consequence to any action, Graham!". 'The Good Fairy' and 'The Bad Fairy' on each shoulder treatment, certainly worked, meaning - before you do anything, don't rush at it without thinking about any re-percussions, ie, is it a good thing or a bad thing, you are about to do? This worked very well with me now and as a contraception method, because if I was in a situation to possibly have sex, an empty house with no parents around, baby sitting invite and after a nice amorous lingering snog and any attempted foreplay, goaded on by that Bad Fairy, now Bad Boy on my left shoulder. The Good Fairy would be tapping me on the right shoulder asking, 'Think Graham, if this young lady became pregnant, what would be the impact be, in a few months, your youth or even the rest of your life, just think about it?' Taking this in and running through my mind, I would be saying to myself, even in the heat of the moment - 'I like going out, buying clothes and records, the freedom of no responsibilities and being selfish etc'. Thanks Mum! It worked well, a couple of lads that I knew, didn't think, for one it worked out long term, but for the others it all ended in tears, getting a girl pregnant and not being able to pursue a career up North and one joining the RAF.

Now, as most of you know if you have been out with someone new, your peers need to be 'debriefed' about your performance, like a Spitfire pilot returning to base after a sortee! Lads would be a lot cruder and we called it 'The Bases', base one a kiss, two – a hand under bra, three foreplay and four or home base was penetrative sex. With or without a condom, the withdrawal method or as many called it 'The Catholic Way!'. Base four, would scare me rotten or would literally end prematurely, so as to say! Now being a very shy lad, I would refuse the interrogation or nod after someone saying 'You got to Base 4, didn't you?', I said nothing and walked away or changed the subject. The strange thing was that they would assume, because of my silence I got to all the bases, which was a bit of a result for my ego, so I just smiled and let them believe! Birth control at that time was a bit haphazard buying condoms was so embarrassing, especially if you went into Boots The Chemist with complete confidence and then you knew the young lady that was serving on a Saturday afternoon, I just couldn't do it! And I certainly wouldn't have gone to the village chemist.

Another opening gambit from the lads was 'Is she on the Pill?'. Introduced in the early 1960's, initially it was only available to married women, it wasn't until 1967 that single, unmarried females could even enquire at their Doctors surgery. Unbelievably, it wasn't until 1969/70 that GPs – the majority male at the time - were formally trained and were in a position to give family planning advice irrespective of marital status. Which meant, depending on age and going to see your family doctor - who knew your parents well in some circumstances and that would create issues in confidentiality! - asking for a prescription and the discipline of taking it every day, I assume would have been difficult.

It was all so complicated, strangely listening to my mates, who talked constantly about having sex and sexual activity, or "going bareback" bemused me and thoughts of 'did you really?'. I always liked the idea of being a boy that 'put it around', but the reality frightened me because of potential consequences. Anyway I am nearly 17, I am sure and thought I was only Village Virgin over 16! The lads that did have unprotected sex and took risks, sometimes lived on this monthly knife edge, if they were going out with a girl and had unprotected sex. Hoping that they never heard the words 'I am three weeks late with my period and I think, I am pregnant' something at this time, thankfully I didn't have to worry about, fills me with dread even now about the thought of telling my mother if ever I had got a girl pregnant at such a young age.

'Living for the weekend' is still on the agenda, going out to Richmond a couple of times a week, the odd visit to the youth club and its football training still has its draw, great times banter with the boys, everybody enjoying their youth. My local football team Ham Venturers, win the two weekend league titles and shield trophies, I think it was about five honours that year and an article in the local newspaper. I think I ran the line a lot and cut up the oranges, being bought on as reserve or now substitute status that season.

In the late 1960s and 70s, my village had access to about seven pubs, it was quite easy to spend all your money standing at the bar and drinking too much, so it really didn't matter to have transport to get into either Richmond or Kingston, but there was the bus and its restrictions. Our village life and previous generations, mostly socialised around the pubs, like many communities, we were historically an agricultural village with no trappings of a small town, ie cinema's and other entertaining spaces. Not being a big lad or a big drinker and having a driving licence at 16, I wasn't able to keep up with the volume of drinking, strangely when you stay sober it's very easy to see the effects of alcohol when you go out in a group, from being over confident and getting 'lairy', to starting a fight or a punch in the face, after approaching someone else's girlfriend. I was being told to, 'get a few pints down you, enjoy yourself!' 'a drink will take any shyness away', sadly, some of the other quiet lads drank too much regularly and some spiralled into alcohol or drug problems later, trying to make themselves happier, unfortunately when you wake up in the morning, it's not so pleasant and you need another to perk you up.

One night when the local youth club first opened and it was music night, Danny and myself decided that we (mainly me!) needed get some 'Dutch Courage' to talk to the girls. Searching for his Dads secret stash of Irish Whiskey, we found it at the back of a wardrode. Opening a half bottle of Jameson's, we knocked it back quickly half each with screwed up faces and burning throats and stomachs, waiting for a happy feeling, as we walked over to the club, the alcohol hit us, laughing first but with heads spinning and becoming legless we fell into a hedgerow, while trying to dispose of the bottle and the evidence, now unable to stand and feeling rough – while a group of the good looking girls passed, looking at us with distain and all our credibility gone and a lost night too boot! We vowed never to drink whisky again, Dan's tipple became a 'Lager Top', mine a Claushaler when driving, which was 'supposed to be' the world's first, great tasting non-alcoholic beer, which was disputable in the early 1970s! Mainly driven and to try and find a low alcohol drink for motorists and blood alcohol concentration with the introduction of the new laws and roadside breathalyser. Publicans throughout the country protested about the change, saying it would make them bankrupt, I seem to remember so many people spending hours in the pub and going back to a crowded car park and driving home in the 1960s, even with their partner and children holding on to the steering wheel, on the drivers laps in the car.

There's a slight change in the music I am listening too on the radio and in the clubs. I will always be a Motown fan, but the winds of change are moving through the company. The youthful, Jackson 5 with that distinctive voice of young Michael, hits of I Want You Back, ABC, The Love You Save. The Temptations, Ball of Confusion, reflecting social and political change, Psychedelic Shack and psychedelic soul following on from Cloud Nine (about the struggles of the poor and social statements) in 1969, along with Edwin Starr's War and Stop The War Now and comments on the US's involvement in Vietnam, a complete change from 'relationship' songs of previous releases. The Supremes and I think some of their best sounds from this time, Love Child, Living in Shame, Some Day We'll Be Together, and after Diana Ross left to go solo, Up The Ladder To The Roof, Nathan Jones, Stoned Love, Floy Joy, Bad Weather.

However the sound of James Brown, from his 1965 hit of Papa's Got A Brand New Bag, I Got You. 1967's Cold Sweat – surely my first shot of funk, before I knew what that infectious beat was called and even had a name? 1968s Say It Loud and There Was A Time and 1969s Ain't It Funky Now and the use of that F word! This year, see's the release of great Sex Machine and Super Bad, James Brown over his career released over 140 singles and around 120 albums! No wonder he was called The Godfather of Soul !

The anticipation of going for a night out was nearly all consuming for a youth club graduate soul boy or girl and that next step of adulthood and hitting a club where the music was spot-on. What will always be a great memory and will fill you with nostalgia, the thought of walking through the doors of a club in a group, hearing the right sounds and seeing your mates and knowing it will be a good night. Priceless memories eh?

I loved Ham as a youngster and growing up, but it is a village and London with its bright lights and thoughts of sharing a flat with mates and perhaps moving into London certainly crossed my mind, but that may take years, who knows what would happen in that time. My brother is now 23 and thinking about leaving home,

I really couldn't think about abandoning Mum just yet and easy to get on with and what she has done for both of us, especially me as I believe my brother had it tougher, helping to raise me. My father is still serving his time under Her Majesties Pleasure and not knowing any release or parole action, we never asked, but he has had a clear message never to return to our house, ever again!

Spring passes and early summer is here, the year before I didn't take a summer holiday, but someone suggests we take a 'boys' holiday, 'on our own!', an unbelievable idea seemingly at the time for me. We all book off the last week in August, covering the Bank Holiday to save using up all our vacation days. The four of us, Dave Brown, luckily an apprentice car mechanic at HA Fox in Richmond, very useful for any breakdowns, took his Triumph Herald. Roger Squires, worked at his Dads greengrocers and took the delivery Ford Anglia 5 cwt green van, with a mattress in the back. Danny, always great for a laugh, very affable and could be little interesting after a lager top, was an apprentice gas fitter on North Thames Gas. We were one of the first group of lads amongst our peers, to have such a 'lads' holiday.

We planned to go to the Isle of Wight after they had been there the year before on a youth club trip, it involved a ferry crossing, seeming as good as going abroad at the time and we had heard that the bright lights of Sandown, Ryde and Shanklin that had pubs and clubs we were told after making enquiries with the older lads.

With the football season on the horizon pre season training was also happening and friendly football games were organised, led by the manager Jim Lee. Jim was one of those 'good blokes' who got very much involved with the youth club and just helped all us boys and girls. He did become for many of us with a few issues, a surrogate Uncle or Dad, with his advice. A good football manager he made you work for your place in the team, just because you were good at football, it didn't mean your place was automatic, he wanted you to take part in training and dropped if you didn't conform. The hours he put into to raising money and coaching football were immense, he must have invested three or four nights a week in the youth club, without the games on a Saturday and Sunday. A couple of seasons earlier Jim had a big yellow and white Vauxhall Cresta, having a transport issue one Saturday, he got a whole football team in of twelve youngsters and a couple in the boot, for the short ride to Kingston to play on Fairfield.

The weekend before we went away, we either had training or a friendly game and as normal we got picked up, met and end up being dropped off outside The New Inn on Ham Common, in these days with few people had phones and away games had set times to be there. So, us four lads are excited about going away for the first time as hormonal teenagers with a few pennies in our pockets, one car, a van and a tent, no work and no adults telling you what to do! Talking about what we are going to do to have a good time, without anybody telling us what to do. Jim Lee, heard what we have planned a holiday over that Bank Holiday week and as we were dropped back to the pub, beckons us four over in that circular motion with his hand, finger up, meaning 'you boys, come here, we need to chat'. Thinking it's just a debrief about training or the match, clearing his throat, looks at us individually for a second each and says, "I know you boys are planning to go away, just the four of you, on your own, is that right?". We all nod and wonder where this conversation is going, he continues "I was young once, having a holiday with mates is great fun, hopefully some sun, fish and chips wrapped in newspaper, music, dancing, beer – perhaps having a little too much to drink and of course meeting new young ladies for the first time and putting IT out there!" We nod in agreement nonchalantly as we know what 'IT' is, but inside excited about the week to come and saying 'bring it on!'. He places his hands in his pockets, thinking he is going to give us a contribution of a ten bob note or something, his face goes serious, asking directly "What would happen to your life, if you got a girl pregnant, at your age?". We all look down at our feet, hoping we didn't have to answer, as normal I go crimson with embarrassment. Danny says jokingly "I am hoping they are all on The Pill!". Jim follows up with "Just be careful, Boys!", removing his hands from his pockets and says "Hold your hands out!" and places a 'Rubber Johnny' - as we called condoms then - in each of our hands, very carefully like a priest placing a communion wafer in your palm! Now it's the first time, I have seen the packaging close-up as always too scared even to think about using one and how you use it, in the heat of passion, but we get the message! To be honest I can't remember whether any of the other boys were 'going steady' or out with anybody at that time, we were wishing 'hopefully' just to meet some girls!

The next weekend arrived, we pack our gear, our 'suedehead kitbag' making sure we got our Ivy League look going on, button down Bennies, Levi jeans and Sta-Prests, Fred Perrys, loafers, shorts and t-shirt, cut off Levis as swimming trunks, toiletries and of course aftershave. Our stuff, which consisted of a borrowed four man tent, groundsheet, sleeping bags, a primus stove, cutlery and not a lot else, most of us had been Scouts, still owning some camping gear. In our world, where no one seemed to pre-book anything, we decide to leave at the crack of dawn and head to Portsmouth to seek out our tickets to Ryde, which we had remembered was a main town on the Island. However, it was extremely busy, but was offered tickets later to Fishbourne, a smaller town and more further from Sandown and Shanklin and its night life. But it meant we had to drive, quickly to Southampton, further along the coast. The ferries did seem very busy with hippies and brightly painted old coaches and VW vans, we were looking at each other thinking about the music clubs and what did they play – Drongoe stuff? We arrive on the island and head for Sandown to look for a campsite. Even then, four lads on their own looking for a good time and any potential trouble, it wasn't easy to find a site that welcomed us.

We notice the amount of Hippies, Drongoes and even people were calling them 'Freaks' now, unbeknown to us it was supposed to be the final Isle of Wight Festival, that used to grow the population of the island by five fold, hence the difficulty in finding camp spaces. Held on the western side of the island, it was stated later, over the five days and nights that it attracted more people than Woodstock, fuelled by the popularity of hippie music, word of mouth of the festival successes of 1968 and 69.

Artists appearing were Chicago, Lighthouse, Jethro Tull, Emerson Lake and Palmer, Joan Baez, Joni Mitchell, Jimi Hendrix, Ten Years After, Free and many more to be honest we wouldn't have minded seeing The Who, Sly and The Family Stone. Redbone were scheduled but never appeared, even Richie Havens and Miles Davis performed. Planning permission and local residents limited the numbers of festival goers from 1971 onwards. We must have tried three or four places and found one that was more expensive but had washing facilities and a big clubhouse and bar. As it was late afternoon we took it and were shown a pitch at the perimeter, but not far from the clubhouse. We pitch the tent, set out our stuff and head to the bright lights of Sandown and Shanklin, taking our change of clothes, washing gear and getting dressed and washed in the public toilets. Splashed on some late 60s aftershave classics of perhaps Brut, Tabac or Aramis.

We head to a pub with the loudest music first, this lead to chatting and finding out where the best club was. After having something like a Wimpy, a local Cafe or fish and chips sitting on the sea wall or promenade, with the sun going down and a warm night. Strange days, like alcohol, food wasn't the most important thing to us as long as we had something and just enough.

The clubs were great and everybody was in a great mood, because of our clothes and our accents most groups of young ladies thought we were Londoners or Cockneys at the time, our main competition from other lads from Birmingham, Manchester and other UK towns and cities, but we were streets ahead, with our clothes. Those summer sounds in the clubs, still resonate with me, although we were into Motown and soul most clubs were very middle of the road then, trying to attract a wider group, but most locals DJs would be guided by requests and a bribe of a pint of beer, asking constantly "Have you got......?". As the clubs tried to attract all types of youngsters that summer DJs would spin popular sounds from the charts, ones that I remember from that holiday are Mungo Jerry's In The Summertime, Spirit In The Sky by Norman Greenbaum, The Kinks and Lola, Badfinger, Come and Get It, Blue Mink's Melting Pot, Groovin' with Mr Bloe and a new band T-Rex with Ride A White Swan. The following February in 1971, Hot Love on TOTP, Marc Bolan appearing on TV after dipping into his wife's make up bag, with eyeliner and putting glitter under his eyes, wearing a sparkly silver sailor suit, reputedly inventing Glam Rock!

Soul plays, seem to be chosen by popular request, with lack of choice in record shops, generally only stocking the Top 30, even DJs would have trouble getting the latest sounds outside of major cities. That summer, The Temps, Cloud Nine and Psychedelic Shack, Motown's past and present hits, youngsters loved them, Smokey Robinson, The Supremes, Up The Ladder To The Roof, that distinctive voice of Jimmy Ruffin, Stevie Wonder with Signed, Sealed, a few slowies, Diana Ross, I'm Still Waiting and Reach Out and Touch, It's All In The Game, Still Waters by The Four Tops and of course The Jackson 5's ABC and The Love You Save, along with Edwin Star's War.

A song Sweet Inspiration, from a London based US group called Johnny Johnson and His Bandwagon who were frequently to be seen around the country (still to this day!), in working men's clubs, halls and US bases in those days. Chairmen of The Boards great first hit single, Gimme Just A Little More Time got to No 2 in the UK Charts and Clarence Carters, Patches, I'm depending on you son!

The weather being great that holiday, ie no rain, but a little cool at night when getting back to the tent! After a night out and a couple of drinks, we would make our way back to the camp site, perhaps one or two of us would go missing after meeting some young ladies, without any thought or concern of how we would get back, in the hope that something may happen after a lingering kiss. I think anybody who had late nights camping and wants to lie in the following morning knows that if the sun shines, that it can be hot and uncomfortable at 10am under a strong sun. My memory recalls two events out of many, Danny and I chatting to two girls in a night club, after a couple of stolen snogs and being gents we offered to walk them home to their guest house. Convincing them it would be a good idea to invite us back for a 'coffee', but in those days 'the landladies' would stipulate, 'No guests!' and they would lock the door at a certain time. As it was after 11pm the girls had to knock on the door to be let in, the idea being that they would go in, leave the door open and when the landlady went upstairs, we would take that opportunity to gain entry. I think the landlady was used to this type of behaviour because as we were hiding behind the garden wall, we heard door being locked for the night, sadly! Thinking we had missed out, I turn to Danny and say 'That's that then!' and resign myself to walking back to the campsite! Danny, always on the trail of young ladies, has a better idea dragging me to the back of the building, from a window on the first floor up, we see the same giggling girls, beckoning us up to an open window. We climbed fences, dustbins and drain pipes to try and scale the walls. As we held tight, in fits of laughter, we notice the landlady in the next window with broom in hand, ready to break our grip on the drainpipe and a threatening to call the police. We retreat and walk back to the campsite dejected, wondering what would have happened if we had ever gained access. In my case probably nothing, that condom in my wallet would still have to wait!

We decide towards the end of the holiday, to try the clubhouse that night, they have a DJ playing and we have to leave very early for the ferry the next morning. After a visit to the shower block, the cold water, spiders and with mildew and moss growing on the walls. We are ready for the clubhouse, laid out with those tables with red vinyl seat pads, around a dance floor. A dodgy patterned carpet smelling of spilled ale, brown wood surrounded bar area, but with temporary membership for the week, beer and drinks were cheap. We comb our hair, now sharing the last few drops of Brut, as went mad with it, we are off to the clubhouse. As we enter, our pubescent antennae's pulse and scan the room, noticing lots of attractive young ladies! We look at each other, in that way of 'We should have tried this earlier!'. Again, the girls think we are

Cockneys, as they are from The Midlands and North West and like the way we talk. Unlike the other lads on the campsite were from 'T'Up North' and are boring as they told us. One problem though looking around the room as most of these girls were with their parents sitting at the tables on the edge of the floor, looking very bored, this led to feeling - the protective glare of the father or mother, in that 'keep away' look, as though we were some mountain men from some dodgy 'B' movie had entered a diner in the Appalachians.

As the night goes on, we again house arrest the DJ, buying him drinks and ask what's in his collection of boxed 45s and choose the plays. He had Desmond Dekker's, You Can Get It If You Really Want, Bobby Blooms Montego Bay even.

Danny always the insensible one, easily intoxicated on two pints of lager top and now feeling very confident, spies a very pretty girl across the dance floor. Wearing a knitted crocheted short tight fitted dress, which certainly didn't leave much to the imagination? As he looks at her, he says 'I wouldn't mind giving her one!' in that stupid way we did then. As he stands there gawping, chin on the ground, the girl and another friend make a beeline for Danny and he thinks he's cracked it, smiling enthusiastically, they stop right in front of him, her large, not so good looking minder points and prods her finger into his face and then his chest and says cruelly "You got no chance mate and by the way I can lip-read!". Us lads, just burst out laughing, it's a story that we still mention to this day, when meeting up!

What a holiday that was with new experiences, talking to girls, that would ask for your home address to keep in contact and if they 'ever came to London' they would let us know. Still have some postcards and letters from that time, with remarks like and after one night of meeting them, with mentions of 'I'm Still Waiting' or 'Someday We'll Be Together' will always remind me of you and that summer".

Something you don't think about as a lad at that time, but rock bands and their music, not my genre at all, but groups like

Creedance Clear Water Revival, Proud Mary, Bad Moon Rising, they even recorded Marvins, 'Grapevine', are etched into our memories and where and when you heard them. Any tune, that you really liked quickly builds a picture and transports you back, another song from that summer is All Right Now by Free, although a hairy group, a great song and will always recall the summer 1970 on the Isle Of Wight! I never know why, to me Joe Cocker also impresses, with 'A little help..', Sugar Sugar by The Archies, Norman Greenbaum's Spirit In The Sky, Mungoe Jerry's In The Summertime! However buying them was a different story, I never did, because they were not under the genre of soul or reggae.

In 1970, we frequent another club near Richmond and a short ride away, a sound I heard for the first time there was Band Of Gold by Freda Payne, spending six weeks at #1 in the UK charts later that September and over twenty weeks in the Top 100. It was also on that famous Invictus blue recognisable label, that Chairmen Of The Board were signed to also, along with Lamont Dozier. The name of the club, The Boathouse Kew, renowned for having young underage club goers, drinkers and most of all fighting. Factions from Hounslow, Brentford, Putney would attend, intent of taking control, particularly strong as a crew again and the name kept coming up, was the Devonshire Road Boys, from Chiswick who mostly lived in blocks of council flats located in the road of the same name. We never mentioned where we were from and never made eye contact with any lad we didn't know, trying to avoid that famous remark from a normally drunk lad with angry eyes, mumbling through gritted teeth....."What choo, lookin' at mate, wanna photo"! Frequenting The Boathouse on a mainly Monday nights, if you had the money, you could fill all the nights of the week going out. I believe the entertainment industry and breweries – had really started to recognise that yet another generation of youngsters were coming along, after the later forties born babies and its Baby Boomers in the early 1960s, we now have the another teenage mainly siblings of the 1970s.

Pubs for us, were really just a meeting place, before going out, standing around in the same location for hours on end, supping beer in a 'local boozer' is something us music lovers and club goer's just really didn't want to do, even if they had installed a juke box. Hence the popularity of establishments like The Birds Nest chain and pubs with an upstairs function room, now turned into a music venue, starting to appear everywhere, socialising and soul – a great cocktail, a great time to be a teenager.

That September, I return back to block release, three months of study, it was like going back to school. Still riding my scooter, that winter was very cold and anybody who had two wheels will know that freezing fog, rain, sleet, snow and cold wind, was not nice. Thoughts of getting 'a motor' come into my head, mainly because I am meeting young ladies, I make a promise to myself that, I will never ride a scooter in the winter again! As a group of lads, we engaged with many groups of girls, especially on our home turf of The Castle Ballrooms, it was getting a reputation of THE place to go in North Surrey, South West and West London. Youngsters would travel for miles, it was a great destination for music and fashion, thousands would attend over the weekend from Friday to Sunday and now some weeknights. Young ladies in groups, would flock to Richmond, the lads would congregate in watching these fashion conscious young girls walk from the railway station and alighting at the nearby bus stops nearby to attend, standing outside pubs like The Old Ship, in King Street and others. Chatting to these groups of young ladies was always good fun, but at the end of the night, if you 'fancied' or 'pulled' a young lady, not having 'a motor' and seeing them to a bus stop or her wanting to go home with her friends, never rounded off the night as you would want it too. On the run up to Christmas and New Year 1970, yet again The Castle tickets are in great demand, a group of about 10 of us from Ham have secured tickets. I even think the Christmas Eve night concluded at around 11.30pm or latest midnight, another good night, but haven't met any young ladies, trying to get that Christmas Kiss by holding a bit of mistletoe, courage supplied by a couple of pints of lager.

I get separated from the returning group to Ham and end up walking back with a lad called Jim McManus from Petersham, the buses have now stopped running and we have to consider, thumbing a lift or walking the two miles plus back to the village. We are both slightly merry, able to walk, but high in spirits, Jim who was a Catholic lad and thinks that Midnight Mass would be a good idea. St Elizabeth's Church is just off Hill Rise, being of Irish extract, getting sober or staying in the warm was another reason for going in. It's just after midnight, the congregation has settled down, Jim a bit unsteady pushes on the doors, as usual a bit sensible and worried I ask 'Is this a good idea, Jim?', being wary as normal with my good and bad fairy fluttering above my shoulders, not a good idea on Christmas Eve. Grabbing my shoulder, he says 'Yeh Gub, let's go in!' the large double doors swing open and we stumble in, to the dismay of the people and their turning heads. It's very busy with older families and couples, we receive a strange look from the Priest, not unlike a strict teacher, who did a lot of caning. We find two spaces towards the front, giggling we share a service sheet and sing a few hymns or carols and mumble a few prayers, the service seems very long. It's time to take Communion, Jim pushes me up, as Church of England, I now think a lightning bolt will hit me, never taken the offering in my life that I can remember at the time, I mouth to Jim, 'is this allowed?' he says 'Just copy me!'. I kneel in front of the alter, hands cupped and ready to receive the offering of a wafer, with a dry mouth it gets stuck on my pallet, not knowing what to do next, as the priest moves in front of me, I grab the chalice and take a glug of wine, hoping to dislodge the wafer, there's a tug back from the priest, trying to take the receptacle back from my grip. Jim looks at me and starts uncontrollably to giggle, as he walks back to the pews. I am so embarrassed hoping that I will not suffer any harm from any higher being, the service over we quickly leave the church and start to walk home, sobering up quickly in the cold winter air, thumbing for a lift as the cars rush by. The walk which must be nearly two miles for me and about a mile and a bit for Jim, who lives nearer in Petersham, unless we walk across the meadow and cut the bend in the river, but that would ruin your shoes and clothes with any mud, cowpats and puddles in the darkness.

Its takes me another good part of thirty minutes to get home, Mum is sitting in the front room, the dying embers of the fire and the Christmas Tree lights on, wrapping a few last presents, 'Happy Christmas Son' she says, 'Glad you are safely home, hope you had a lovely evening?' I smile and reply back 'Yes it was' with a wry smile and hope nobody from the Catholic Diocese is going to knock on our door! With my brother still not in, I sadly, never really gave it a thought to how lonely she must have been or even felt, being on her own, on these special and social nights in an empty house.

I go to bed, ears ringing as always after standing to close to the speakers at The Castle. Hoping Santa will bring me something nice, like a Cadburys Selection Box! But what is the best Christmas gift that year – 'I don't have to listen out for my father's keys in the door and any arguments'. As 1970 draws to a finish, it's over a year since I started work, clubbing and going out more regularly. 'Our' dance music is now featuring in UK charts and the musical press, The Jackson 5, Smokey Robinson, Freda Payne, Desmond Dekker, Chairman of the Board, Bobby Bloom, Edwin Starr, Jimmy Ruffin, The Temptations, The Supremes, The Detroit Spinners, Marvin Gaye, Sly Stone, Nicky Thomas, Stevie Wonder, James Brown, The Delphonics, Johnny Johnson and The Band Wagon and Steam with Na Na Hey Hey, Kiss Him Goodbye – another Chelsea Shed fans song, all appear on TOTP, in the Top 20 and are even played if you go to a 'popular music' venues, sometimes where the DJ didn't focus on upbeat soul or reggae and of course less 'Aggro'!

It seems with us youngsters, the music has divided us even more, some youngsters listening to hairy white bands, Matthews Southern Comfort, Uriah Heep, Deep Purple, Canned Heat, Black Sabbath, Three Dog Night, Ten Years After, Badfinger, Chicago, Jethro Tull, strangely they didn't enjoy the Friday nights at our youth club and we certainly wouldn't have seen them out in town. Unless they were off to Eel Pie Island in Twickenham Barnes and

The Bulls Head and Putney's Half Moon being a couple or some folk clubs.

Fashion, it seems at this time over 1971, takes a slightly different direction and a change, even for us Suedeheads. The reason being to really distance and detach ourselves yet again from The Skinhead culture and its affiliation with The National Front, football hooliganism and other factions and its direction, we grow our hair slightly longer. With some lads it look good, but for some of us it doesn't work, especially when greasy, even the girls are growing their hair longer, with a feather cuts or even perms. We still wear our suedehead staples to go clubbing but even that was slightly changing, which was quite hard if you have been doing it for over two years or more. We seem to be walking a tight line very near to a 'Semi-Hippie Look' with perhaps flares with Farah type front slit pockets, tank tops and now the Black US soul bands are wearing their hair in huge Afro Styles and loud, multi-coloured, wide long collared suits and shirts very different from those Motown, well groomed sharp suited male groups from the sixties.

Even some of the white lads are going to the hairdressers for a tight perm to emulate this cool afro look on the dance floor, I even considered it myself, with my unruly growing and lengthening hair, which now needed a hairdryer and mums hairbrush to straighten and curl it under. Over the next couple of years, higher cut flared trousers or denim bellbottoms or brushed cotton, loons, hipsters, scooped necked t-shirts and tight fitting shirts plain and patterned with long and big collars, tank tops, high roll and polo necked jumpers in various colours and some with stripes, something to make everybody think then was buying a sand, beige pair of low cut trousers and what to look out for, firstly visiting the Gents and getting water on them, from the 'flick' or even the tap spurting out, another major thing is having a couple slow dances with a young lady and perhaps a squeeze and kiss, wondering or hoping how the night will end! Boys you get my drift?

Thicker gristle soled, buck suede shoes, stack heels, start to appear in our wardrobes, even looking and shopping in such shoe shops as Ravels at the different styles. The real difference here though is the price of clothes has reduced greatly but the quality is not as good, there seems to be now more gents 'fashion' shops opening, Littlewoods and Freemans catalogues has now a large men's section. Even the famous Ivy Shop is now stocking expensive channel seamed flares, Paisley and patterned shirts, changing a little in a new fashion direction from that 'Ivy League Look' of the late sixties, although they still stocked them.

As the years click over and now 1971, many lads go steady for a time, then break up, falling in and out of the circle. But me, I am just enjoying the evenings of music, even having girl friends or knowing girls on a mate's basis and going places. It seemed to get rid of that 'relationship thing' of going out with a girl and breaking up. If I did go out with girls it wouldn't last long. However I did like the idea of a steady girlfriend probably for the company, but I had not really met anybody that I would like to spend a long time with.

For the first time, now 18 and able to vote, I am feeling quite grown up and its official. Eighteen was a time of coming of age, which for most lads, a gold signet ring with a black onyx stone from my Mum - I still wear it to this day 50 years on.

Transport wise, my brother worked part time as a driving instructor at The Ham School of Motoring in Ham Street run by Clive Pilfold in his sheepskin and Trilby, I had lessons and passed my test in a very short time, mainly because of clutch control and road sense gained with the scooter I can only presume. I am now armed with a full driving licence for a car, luckily for me, my next door neighbour, Mr Ayers worked at Sheen Lane Garage as a panel beater, by the way I gave all of my toys to his son Andy. He informs me that a trade-in is available, a clean 1962 Ford Anglia 105E Deluxe in a light blue, the 'deluxe' denotes it has a chrome radiator, the luxury of a heater and sun visors. It's nearly ten years old, but nearly new to me and would be luxury when it rained or snowed hopefully, I would be out of the elements, I sell my scooter for around £35 and buy the Anglia for £68, the registration plate, being 90 PAR. Before the term 'Pimp My Ride' was invented, it has to go through the soul boys makeover, 5.5J perhaps 6" rims and tyres using spacers of course, so they just fit under the wheel arches, finished off with mud flaps with Ford decals - however you could hear the tyres rubbing when four or five people onboard. A large exhaust that reduced power by about 20% - but who cares, it still sounded good! A small sports steering wheel, a tinny car radio with two speakers, fitted somehow mounted below that small cardboard courtesy shelf. The Anglia was a great looking car, it looked the 'Biz' when pimped, especially with wide wheels and that unique sloping rear window, but meant it had no parcel shelf for speakers. And of course matt black paint featured high at the front and rear on our cars, in the 70s, I painted the rear number plate panel to the light clusters (badly), but it looked great – to me anyway!

Somehow, needing some in-car entertainment or ICE as we called it, I managed to get - in my local pub, - a 45 record player for the car, it had the ability to play singles, which was impressive, parked up and serenading a young lady after a night out, or a ride out with mates. But driving along and hitting a pothole it would jump, skip, scratch and ruin the surfaces of any vinyl. The other problem was on a hot summer's day that year, I may take a dozen singles out, leaving them in the car to bend and warp over the seats, did no-one think that may be a problem! A great novel idea, that didn't last long as a system, very shortly to be followed up by 8 track and cassettes that were coming along.

Of course, I am now fully equipped to say to a young lady at the end of a night out, "Would you like a lift home?". One night we were 'Up The Castle', lucky enough to be 'chatting up' a young lady, she tells me her friends have left and gone to get the bus. As always slow to pick up on any signals, I ask her if she needs to catch them up, she asks if I would like to walk her to the bus stop. I say 'not to worry, I can give you a lift home, fingers crossed that it won't be a long drive. 'Only Roehampton' she replies, luckily I am parked right outside that night, there it is, my car, shiny and 'looking the business', T-Cutted and waxed in that dim light, sitting parallel to the kerb, along with the newly proudly installed by me that day, a 'short sporty looking gear stick' and centre console unit with a padded lid, that fitted between the front seats and over the handbrake. As I start to do a 'U turn', blipping the loud exhaust, my mates comes down the stairs, winking and thumbs up that that there's a young lady sitting in the passenger seat! As the first point turn begins, I go to put it into reverse, for the second point, horror - the gear stick comes off in my hand. So there we are, at a right angle and blocking the road, stranded outside the biggest club in Richmond, with all my mates watching and crowds spilling out. I am so embarrassed, she is mortified! I quickly explain this car is not going anywhere tonight in a short time and tentatively ask 'is it possible to catch up your girlfriends now?'. I get this thunderous look, she gathers her handbag and coat, slams my car door while I say sheepishly 'Bye then' and at the same time nearly crushing my hand as I reach across, she shouts, 'Thanks for the lift, then!', as she storms away. I look to see my mates laughing their heads off! I never saw her again, or she avoided me forever!

This is a big learning curve for any lad and mainly down to affordability, you must maintain your own car (especially a Ford). The tool box must contain a precision tool of a hammer, a Haynes manual, many spanners, spark plug tool, spare set of points. Common faults were.........

A starter motor jam - this meant it engaged and became stuck, the fix - take a hammer, lie under car (another issue if young lady onboard or you had a light shirt on!) and give it a hard whack. If you had mates in the car, engage a gear, they would rock it back and forward releasing the starter motor.

A missing flywheel tooth - the starter motor has nothing to engage on, fix - put gear in fourth push or rock car again.

Starting and choke control issues - if it didn't start first or second go, don't keep keying ignition until battery goes flat. Fix - wait a few seconds, hold the accelerator to the floor and try again.

If no success, lift bonnet, check distributer cap and points. Check your fuel indicator as been playing up!

Braking Issues - the car pulls to the left or right, fix one, hold steering wheel tighter on braking! Fix, check for leaking brake fluid on drum, if confirmed, buy a brake cylinder repair kit from your local motoring shop, always buy twice as many as you need and ask for a trade discount! The others will start leaking shortly anyway. Brake fluid bleeding tool also handy if no mates around on a Sunday morning to help you!

More starting Issues - Anybody who had a Ford will have suffered! Probably using your experience from scootering, pull out choke, one press of the accelerator, turn the key with fingers crossed, hopefully starter motor kicks in and the engine fired into life. Cold damp winters, hard frosts and snow, it came to a point and the need to get to work or college, that I would take the battery out the last thing every night and place a blanket over the engine compartment and newspaper on the windscreen. Take the battery into the kitchen, place on floor remove the filler caps and trickle charge until the morning and then reverse the process in the hope that a combination of a good spark, it would burst into life!

After a year and a not tested but paid for £5 MOT at Ruffells, White Hart Lane Barnes, but I am warned that the front wheel suspension was threatening to come through the body work. Quickly, Polyfilla'ing the strut tops, spraying in and throwing dirt on them, managed to sell it 'As Seen' with new MOT, to an unsuspecting innocent young lad!

Next I own, a column change 1500c Cortina Deluxe, registration 82 SAR, it had a bench seat, which made mates and especially young ladies slide towards you on the vinyl seats when turning a left and it could get three in the front officially! It had all of the above mentioned faults, however the tappets would always get very noisy, it seemed every month I would lift off the rocker cover and adjust while the engine was running, I got very good at it! All my Fords seem to steam up badly on rainy days, mainly because the windscreen leaked at the front bottom corners, that black rubber repair kit never worked!

Following that, a lovely navy blue 1500cc Cortina Super, registration DYH 141C, only six years old, famous for me getting a speeding ticket on the A3 at Tolworth on the way to The Toby Jug and blowing the engine up on the return journey, to the dismay and the hilarity of mates, until they realised and thought about how getting home! Got another engine installed for £74 (£700 today) from a dubious looking place called Madeira Motors under the railway arches in Hammersmith, which was supposed to be reconditioned, not a good deal always overheated in traffic! Ah, the joys of motoring and self maintenance, I spent many a Sunday mornings laying on freezing tarmac it seemed, fixing, replacing track rod ends and their removal with the help of my brothers brass blowtorch, once a rear leaf spring broke on one Cortina, while going around Kingston one way system, to great delight of mates, again! I clambered over many cars at Hounslow Heath Scrap yard to get spare parts and another leaf spring, using two car jacks, we managed to replace it.

Having, now a good FM/VHF/MW stereo cassette player for the car was now a necessity and called in-car entertainment. The launch of Radio London in October 1970 bought the first late night phone ins and specialist local music – a young news reporter called Robbie Vincent joined the station to forge a career on the new format of local radio. With the sad loss of pirate radio, that drew in an estimated 10-15 million young listeners in the late 1960s between them and finding the right programme with the right music wasn't easy. Emperor Rosko and Tony Blackburn, long time Motown, Soul and R&B music fans, managed to fit a few appropriate sounds into playlists on Radio 1. Our local pub on a Sunday at noon was akin to the counter of a Greenshield Stamp or an Argos Store, amid the pickled onions or gherkins and free cheese on cocktail sticks to entice the early drinkers in items were available, stepping up to the bar alongside some lads, you nod 'Alright mate?'. Step one, you offered to buy a drink for one of them, only half of course. Step two, you would ask if they could get hold of, say a socket set, a tool box, set of tyres or 5J/6J/ spoked wheel rims, but best of all a car radio or later a stereo radio cassette unit. Even asking if you wanted a certain brand, I asked about a Blauplunk stereo, the lad replies 'be here a week from now, with £25 notes, cash!'. Thinking of my father and his tricks, but there is no money upfront! 'Cheers, I reply!' and then a look and the comment from them 'Don't let me down with the cash Gub, I know where you live!' which easily translated to a threat of 'You Asked, We Deliver, You Pay or Else!'. The next Sunday, a nice nearly new Blauplunkt car radio with preset stations, in a plastic supermarket bag with the cables cut off after the connectors and obviously no instructions! – Thinking 'I wonder where that come from?', I never asked any questions, paid my £25 and left the pub premises, rushing home to try and work out how to install it, in readiness for a drive later.

You could buy anything from a pub then, either stolen or 'fallen off the back of a lorry', one night we were cruising around Richmonds one way system, after one loop Danny had seen a couple of girls from Petersham – one of which he fancied and we go around the town again getting in the lane that passes the Police Station as we slow down, a policeman steps out, puts his hand up in that Stop sign and tells me to pullover. Asking me the questions, is this your car, are you insured, licensed, has it an MOT? Not noticing 'the tax in post' note in front windscreen. Asking me politely, to turn the ignition off, get out and open the boot, before he does he asks me 'Is there anything that doesn't belong to you? I reply 'No', telling me to empty the boot. All this going outside just in view of the bus stop and a lot of villagers looking on, unloading the boot, with boxes of tools, a jack on wheels, a large socket set, I look at all this stolen stuff that I have bought in a pub at some time and obviously stolen in my head, he points to the boot - my heart thumps – 'Lift that' he says. I pick up the spare wheel, he peers under. 'OK lad, on yer way!' I stupidly reply 'You mean I can go then?', 'Yes, leave, don't go around the town again, go home!' I believe they were looking for drugs rather than stolen goods that night, but I assume tracing any of my ill gotten gains would have been difficult anyway.

Living near a town like Richmond and having a very middle class feel, The Hill and The Green with a few council estates on the perimeters, but generally the opportunity for good employment, perhaps in retail, services and the trades and a million miles from what was happening within the coal industry at the start of the 70s, the unions and the disruptions to come.

The National Coal Board - at the time, we were mostly unaware, how big the industry was and how many miners there were, even with the workers protective Labour Party in power, unrest was within their ranks in pay demands. The NUMW union began to take action, I never really knew, how strong unions were at the time and the size of the membership in the 1970s.

My job was very secure in the telecommunications industry, which is in growth and taking on more employees. We had a large union behind us, but I never attended any meetings, just paid my fees, however one Monday morning I was visited by a POEU union representative and was asked to meet him downstairs for 'a chat'. I duly go, he looks at my attendance record and asks why I have had no sick leave this year since starting my apprenticeship. I think it is a trick question and say 'Because I haven't been ill or poorly?'. With a stern look, he explains that I must take something called a 'Whitley'. Meaning, I can take 10 days off sick per year, without getting a doctors certificate. I inform him that 'I get a cold or sore throat but not enough to stop me getting into work'. He now explains in a loud voice, 'that the union fought for those days and I must take them off, they were negotiated as part of your pay agreement, next year when I check I want to see those days on your record card!' I nod my head in agreement. Thinking there are tens of thousands of engineers, the days lost in man years must have been phenomenal, although I can understand what the unions try to do for its members, but this rule seemed ridiculous. I think of my mother sometimes very poorly and making the effort to even get to work, when I was younger, if she was sick it meant no pay!

The weeks roll by, we are still going out nearly every night of the week, somewhere to listen and dance to music was like a drug. Obviously a week's pay had to last just that, so by Thursday you may just run out of money and staying in with Mum and telly, or go to the youth club, which by now had lost its wonder lust, as the younger ones had joined and running around like kids!

Towards the end of 1971, we were still going up The Castle on a Sunday night, as well as Friday and Saturday which is now even more popular as a venue. One Sunday, I notice next to us on the dance floor another group of girls, my eyes particularly catch an attractive young lady, to me quite different from the rest, very well dressed and seemingly a little older, perhaps even a little bit more mature. A slow record comes on, I try to muster up the courage, to ask those immortal dance floor words of "Would you like to dance?". To any young lad – unless you were ultra confident or just had a couple of pints, that simple five word sentence is not easy and could come out in any order, knowing the reply has the power to take your legs away, like being hit by the perfect slide tackle! Culminating in a response from the opposite sex, the worst being, like a punch in the face of "No!" without a thanks, (meaning 'why would I even consider, doing that with you!?'), "No thanks" (same thing, but a little more polite), being careful of that 'My boyfriends over there, at the bar with his mates!'. The worse thing, leaving it too late and some other lad has stepped in. Always learning the first bars of a slow record to get in quickly, was very useful! Sadly, this time I was too late and too shy.

The following Sunday, I notice her again, standing where we did in the ballroom and think I must act quickly. After a top tune that year of Curtis Mayfields 'Move On Up' that got to No 12 that July, the album version was nine minutes long and now a soul classic, the DJ announces 'it's time to slow it down a little', under the stylus goes The Temptations, Just My Imagination, I approach and ask those five words and she replies 'Yes, I'd like that and I wondered if you would try, I noticed you last week?'. To this day, when I hear that tune, I am taken back 50 years!

The night finishes, I lose track of where she went, no exchange of telephone numbers, wondering whether I would see her again or after that dance 'does she fancy me?'. The next Sunday, I see her again, I am experiencing a feeling that I haven't had before, I can't wait until a slow one comes on again, asking her to dance, I get to the next stage of the 'chat up' process and invite her to a drink at the quieter bar and she accepts! As always a big thumbs up from mates watching as they always did, when anybody left the pack, but underneath they are thinking, how they might get home that night. Our motto at the time 'All mates left behind, if you 'pulled' even if you were the designated driver!' We talk, get to know each other a little bit more and I ask her how she is getting home, because I want to say 'would you like a lift home?', but to my astonishment she has her own car! I am so used to young ladies, mostly underage going and not having transport except for a bus. Some were even still at school, which was always risky when giving them a lift home and the danger from their fathers or older brothers looking out for them from twitching curtains or even patrolling the street, especially sitting outside their house in a steamed up car!

I will call this young lady I met Susan, just to protect her identity - she is not like any girl I have ever met before. Nearly two years older than me, not really understanding at that time, that a young female and their brains act some three years older than lads of the same age! She speaks very well, seems better educated, has a job at a large well known airfreight company over at the perimeter of Heathrow, as the Managing Directors, PA – not that I knew what this meant at the time.

We start seeing each other, which I think was a dilemma for both of us as neither has had any real steady relationships before that time. We are both socially independent, but with her maturity she knew what she wanted to achieve in life, today, she would have the title of 'a career woman', I lived in the moment, more Que Sera Sera! My thoughts were that I would eventually drift into a relationship, settle down in my early twenties, get married perhaps have children later after saving a few pounds. However, my 18 year old, age 15 inexperienced brain likes this young lady, who would easily pass the 'taking home to Mum' exam, which some girls obviously didn't. It's unbelievable today to think how old you thought you were at that age and even to think about having a long term relationship. However, I was never sure whether she ever felt the same, as time went on, we used the word 'Love' only in greetings cards, never spoken, especially from me as I associated that word with 'trust' and that I found hard mentally. I am sure subconsciously, the relationship with my father was either blocking or sending any emotions to a box in my head, blocking any commitment from my side or letting anybody in. For the next two years, we develop a close relationship and because of the distance involved in where she lived - ten miles away - and the hours she worked as a PA, we only saw each other perhaps two or three times a week at each other's house, or going shopping, going for a drink or a meal, cinema or making a foursome with a mate and their current girlfriend. I think this suited both of us, with this freedom for me still clubbing, the mantra - Friday was always designated 'Boys Night Out!', going out with mates and engaging other young ladies in conversation was a distraction from wanting or needing a long term relationship. Don't get me wrong, sleeping around wasn't my thing – wasn't tall enough or good looking enough anyway and it didn't happen often, I never felt or saw it as two timing! Susan, who earned good money, in a senior position for one so young at nearly 20, she wore expensive clothes and was always generous with gifts, treating me to clothes and expensive aftershave. Buying me some new technology of a Sanyo portable cassette player and recorder, taping records with a microphone propped up near the speaker and later played in the car, before any music systems would make it easier.

One gift, was a copy of 'What's Going On' that seminal album! An album idea that Gaye took to Gordy in 1970, who believed that the music should contain relationship and love themes, not focus on the Vietnam War and letters from his brother in combat and war experiences, personal drug abuse and its addictive powers and strangely forty years ahead of its time, songs about ecology and how he saw changes – all of course very alien to many of us youngsters in the early 70s. And in a similar vein of The Beach Boys, Pet Sounds and The Beatles, Sergeant Peppers, as a concept album. Originally, Gordy saw this as a political and protest statement and a long way from his previous hits of how Sweet It Is, Grapevine, Too Busy, Lay My Hat and would alienate his crossover fan base. Marvin produced, co-wrote the songs, the in-house band The Funk Brothers are credited with the arranger David Van DePitte. Along with British Motown Chartbusters (1), Tighten Up Vol.2 (2), this makes my Top 3 albums of all time. I know, so obvious and not a rare groove at all.

When you are 18 and using the word 'Love' it's not easy, it's a little like revealing your cards and not wanting to be taken advantage of, from a weaker position. At the time Stevie's record 'If You Really Love Me', was released and peaked at number 20 in the UK charts in January 1972, when I listened to those lyrics 'be a fool who sits alone waiting for you.....'. Coincidentally this was the last time and recording, the The Funk Brothers performed on and were dismissed by Gordy shortly afterwards, with the Headquarters and main recording studio's now in Los Angeles.

I think Susan really liked me but I wasn't confident or ambitious enough for her and I didn't really want to dramatically improve or even consider any future career prospects this early. Probably like many working class lads at the time, I had a job and it was always about the take home pay and mine wasn't a taxing role. Which, for me was about getting overtime and it was plentiful, time and half on a Saturday and evenings, gave me an extra 30% of pay some weeks, I was 'life comfortable', still living at home, why would I risk that, looking for a another career?

The music and still collecting records, buying clothes and going out further afield mainly encouraged by the good crowds in Richmond and a name change to Cheekee Pete's for The Castle Ballrooms. My brother has now left home and living in Kingston with his girlfriend Shelagh. I thankfully, get an upgrade to his bigger bedroom, purchasing a stereo record player setup - well it had two speakers in cabinets anyway!

My mother is in a great place now, she has a Littlewoods Stores Kingston as a book keeper and enjoying life after all this time, she has made many friends and now goes out regular to socialise. She has also taken up smoking, as she sees this as a form of a social aid and relaxing, not a big smoker and likes to have just one cigarette a night watching her favourite telly programmes. Always sitting down, getting comfortable and lighting her cigarette, but she never did learn the art of smoking ie as most people 'taking a very big drag, cigarette glowing, taking some down and slowly releasing what's left, lifting their head into the air!'. She would just take a quick draw in and blow out straightaway, which always made my brother or myself burst out laughing, when watching!

1971 saw the introduction of the decimal coinage system and joining the European Community (EC). In sport the Ibrox Disaster where sadly 66 died and many injured. The maverick politician Enoch Powell, who in 1968 made the infamous 'Rivers of Blood Speech' that criticised immigration and opposed the anti-discrimination Race Relations Bill, Edward Heath sacked him from the Shadow Cabinet after wanting a repatriation system for immigrants, Powell denies that he was never Racist! A Postal workers strike lasts 47 days. In sport, Chelsea last year's FA Cup winners now win the European Cup Winners trophy after a 1-1 result in Greece then a replay two days later with a third of the crowd, in the same stadium and win 2-1, with Chelsea scoring two goals in the first half, Osgood scored in both games. Arsenal complete the double.

The first Hard Rock Cafe opens in the UK on Hyde Park Corner and Park Lane. In entertainment, The Old Grey Whistle Test first broadcasts and the inaugural Reading Festival takes place, I remember OGWT as the first time I saw Sly and Family Stone and Thank You in 1971, of course Larry Graham and one of the funkiest sounds of all time and Bob Marley 1973 'live' on returning from the pub one night, I couldn't believe after having hairy bands on.

A wholesale roaster coffee business was opened by two immigrant brothers called Bruno and Sergio, initially in Fenchurch Street then later relocates to Lambeth, their surname Costa, they did very well opening 3500 outlets worldwide, bought by Whitbread in 1995 and then The Coca Cola Company in 2019 for nearly £5 billion, a long way from having a 'frothy coffee' in an Italian owned sandwich shop in Richmond, ten years before.

It's now 1972, my apprenticeship finishes and I pass out from my apprenticeship as a Technician 2A (T2A), passing year 3 (just) in City & Guilds (HND). Meaning, being placed on the promotion list to be a Technical Officer and better pay, I now feel I have now 'served my time' and feel very grown up, with a man's pay-packet, three years is a long time when young

My interest in the R&B Soul Charts increases, asking constantly the DJs what 'that' record was called. More DJs moving away from the now more popular charting black music and picking up on imports. Playing them an incredible two to three months before even being released here (sometimes they wouldn't find a distribution label in the UK, making some imports very rare, expensive and difficult to get hold of). We started to ask and find out, where these DJs worked and followed their turntables around the Home Counties. There was one genre of music that started or seemed to disappear or less played as much, Reggae, a sound just four years earlier and after hearing The Skatalites Guns of Navarone for the first time, borrowed from my older brother and taken to our youth club, we were hooked, followed by a plethora of Trojan releases. Reggae and Motown had dominated my early record collection, my youth and first clubs playing Ska and Reggae. However, the more 'commercial' sounds of Johnny Nash, after Cupid and Stir It Up and his new release 'I Can See Clearly Now', so dissimilar to Return of the Django or Skinhead Moonstomp entering the charts. Was it a case of the connection between The Skinhead element, racism or fighting in night clubs that was present earlier and in many towns and DJs dropping the music from their playlists, to prevent troublemakers being attracted to venues? Who knew, I lived near a provincial suburban town and in a village in Surrey, or was it the commercialisation of reggae and the sound, or a move to heavier sounds playing in more underground clubs in London, like Brixton, Dalston or Notting Hill, that were lucky enough to still have reggae record shops and throwing house parties?

And although Motown are still charting and releasing records, they have now moved to Los Angeles and many stars are finding other opportunities, a change of location and a change in the music. That studio and productions from Hitsville USA Detroit and The Funk Brothers backing, bought a subtly different Motown sound? Although NME had a R&B, Soul column, written by Charles Shaar Murray and it reviewed new sounds, but the whole paper still leaned to rock and heavy sounds, not my choice at all, Melody Maker was similar. Even buying records now, sometimes going closer to London and The West End, where car parking after 1pm, on a Saturday was anywhere, as long as you weren't causing an obstruction. One afternoon we then found or stumbled on a small road that connected Oxford Street and Tottenham Court Road, a queue of black and white cool guys, just edging out of this doorway with a tight staircase going to the first floor. This turned out to be the famous Contempo Records at 42 Hanway Street W1. We join the queue, chatting to the lads who were asking us where we were from and many had visited The Castle/Cheekee Pete's and other clubs we knew in West and South West London. They mention strangely a club called Crackers and import night on a Tuesday night, more an underground soul venue and hadn't seen it advertised, sounds spun by Mark Roman in nearby Wardour Street.

That Saturday we were in search of The Backstabbers, as locally its been very hard to get a copy, by a new band called The O'Jays, labelled under The Philly Sound, it's now early autumn 1972, we slowly wind up the stairs, like climbing to the top of a

Helter-Skelter, approaching the counter, never seen anything like it, like a trading floor at the Stock Exchange, two cool guys, multi-processing and grabbing records, to taking money and so knowledgeable. Shelves of 45s behind them, one guy is deftly placing records on and off records the turntable, people are shouting names of bands, song titles. Like a busy bar and where I have a thirst on and trying to get the bartenders attention, he points a finger at me, I shout "Backstabbers!" he says, 'import or UK release label, mate?', I ask what's the difference, he says 'sometimes the price', I respond 'give me the cheapest?'. In one move it's in a paper bag and I notice a pile of magazines on the counter, my eyes fall for the first time on a publication called Blues & Soul at 15 pence, I pick up a copy. For the most of the 1970s, I have it delivered to my door, loved it dropping onto the doormat every two weeks! The other advantage was they offered incredibly mail order for records and interestingly Pen Pals and a Lonely Hearts column, with their actual addresses printed!

I still have that copy, issue No 92 dated 8-21 September 1972, there is an article on The O'Jays and their story of joining a new label called Philadelphia International. Working again with Kenny Gamble & Leon Huff and being recently back in the studio to finish a new album at The Sigma Sound Studio's in Philly, which will include Back Stabbers and all new material from McFadden and Whitehead, Bunny Sigler and Phil Hurtt, Oh, and the next release may be '992 Arguments', not a mention of Love Train or Time To Get Down, but as they say 'the rest is history'. The front cover features Bill Withers, who was number 2 in the UK, with Lean On Me, one behind Jackie Wilson's 'Sweetest Feeling', The Stylistics have the No1 album, in the US Still Bill by Mr Withers and top single is The O'Jays and Back Stabbers, it also spent nine weeks in the UK chart and got to number 14.

Saw them twice in the 70s and again in July 2018 in London at The Drury Lane Theatre, still grooving and belting the tunes out, fantastic performance!

There's a new chart entry of Harold Melvin & The Blue Notes with I Miss You, also on Philadelphia International and that distinctive lime coloured label we all came to recognise. Did we know then, that it wasn't Harold Melvin who was the lead vocalist, but a young 22 year old called Teddy Pendergrass and what a voice we came to love! My first copy Blues & Soul is very interesting, from a point of reference, living in the suburbs at the time it relates to a slight music change in the club scene and before we discovered the clubs of London's West End playing the right music all night. Living just ten miles away, we now had access to the capitals new emerging nightlife and the changing scene of new clubs.

Great songs seem to re-cycle then, Number 1 British Soul single by returns that week is Jackie Wilson, I Get The Sweetest Feeling, a danceable and re-release from 1968 along with Higher and Higher also released in 1969, were a very popular numbers at The Castle and other clubs in Richmond. Wilson an artist that had a first chart hit in the UK with Reet Petite in the 1950's and was born in the 1930s. Established names like Sam and Dave with Soul Man another sixties release. Jazz names like Ramsey Lewis start to enter the charts, which introduces a new smoother sound to me and will bring a greater impact to the club scene over the next few years. Powerful female vocalists like Jackie Moore's, Time or My Man's A Sweet Man from Millie Jackson and a change for Aretha with Rock Steady, a funky little number from The Queen of Soul. It also features the famous WATTSTAX '72, a seven hour $1 dollar entrance fee, charitable event which 100,000 attended at the LA Coliseum.

The words 'Funk' and 'Funky' now appears in many reviews, we first saw this used in the UK charts with Funky Broadway by Wilson Pickett in October 1967 and is believed to be the first charted single using the word Funky in the title, followed by Arthur Conley's Funky Street the year after - Rufus Thomas's 1970, The Funky Chicken (nearly a youth club soul novelty record!), 1971 heard Beginning of the End's, Funky Nassau'.

It is said Funk music originated in the mid-1960s, a word that is said to have it origins from various places, but I like the idea it could have been taken from an old German word of Funke meaning 'spark or a very lively person' because that's what it makes you! Who cares where it came from, but when it comes to the music, it was all about the beat and rhythm!

Not forgetting, that the strong influence of James Browns' development and experimenting with the emphasis on the downbeat. His release of Cold Sweat in 1967 provides that driving beat and unusual for that time together with a drum solo by Melvin Parker brother of Maceo on his saxophone, the first time I note a Part 1 and Part 2 to a song. In September 1972, we hear Get On The Good Foot, There It Is and The JBs with Hot Pants Road all in the UK R&B Charts and an advert for Honky Tonk Part 1 and 2 of course! No wonder he was THE GODFATHER OF SOUL, My Dynamite, Soul Brother No.1, Minister Of The New New Super Heavy Funk. To me he certainly earned those titles – a challenge for any soul boy or girl not to move their head when a needle rests on one of his funky records. He wasn't too bad at ballads either, listen to 'Its A Mans Mans World'.

Funky Broadway and Funky Street, were both on Atlantic and associated with the famous Muscle Shoals Studio sound run by Jerry Wexler, working with many famous names like Aretha, The Staple Singers, Dusty Springfield's 1969 'Dusty in Memphis', supposedly she was so intimidated by the artists that had recorded there, it was finished at Atlantics Studios, New York, later Rod Stewart, George Michael and Joe Cocker plus many more. The Stones recording of 'Brown Sugar' also, a favourite and earned a position on our local club scene. Rod Stewart distinctive blues vocals on Maggie May, She Wears It Well like Mick Jagger's also had a place in our local clubs, all showing their roots in Blues and R&B and very popular.

Another name appearing in that chart, I associated with primarily US TV series themes, you would say as the opening or closing credits rolled, thinking 'that's a great tune' and the name

Quincy Jones popped up. His film track score of Money Runner, coming after the release of the soundtrack album of Shaft still riding high in the charts at this time, not only bought an Oscar for Isaac Hayes, but a new type of gritty film that was given a genre name of Blaxploitation. In which black characters and communities were the focus and the heroes, rather than the perhaps villains or a dark place. Many films, great soundtracks from also Curtis Mayfield followed in both the big screen and TV.

But one of those cult films for me asked, 'Who is that black private detective sex machine to all the chicks called John – John Shaft!' That full length leather jacket and opening credits and theme tune set the bar very high for many soundtracks and opening sequences.

Bobby Womack's wrote and sung the title sound track to 'Across 110th Street' the road divides the line between Harlem and Central Park and having your picture taken there is the equivalent of The Beatles on the Abbey Road zebra crossing in St John's Wood London. It was also used again in the 1997 film Jackie Brown. While we are on soundtracks and there has been great ones from the Blaxploitation genre and social unrest and comment. Norman Whitfield who had a 25 year career at Motown from a 19 year old hanging about at Motowns Hitsville in 1959 and helped build the 'The Sound of Young America' and working with The Temptations mainly writing and producing the new sound of Psychedelic Funk, with eight albums from 1969 to 1973. Taking inspiration from Sly & the Family Stone, he added topical themes to his lyrics, beginning with Cloud Nine, leading on to Papa Was A Rolling Stone* and those opening bars – unbelievably for that time a 12 min album track! - which was initially released by Undisputed Truth, who in turn took The Temps 'Smiling Faces Sometimes' making it their own hit. Gamble and Huffs, Backstabbers was rumoured to follow the sentiment of Smiling Faces, interestingly at the time. Whitfield bought an edgier funky sound to Edwin Star's War! – a social comment on the US's ongoing involvement in Vietnam. Whitfield left Motown in 1975, followed by Junior Walker, Willie Hutch, The

Undisputed Truth, later to record on Whitfield Records, 'You + Me = Love' and also Rose Royce, later releasing the global hit and soundtrack of the movie 'Car Wash' in 1976.

Some said in the early 1970s that Motown and its geographical move was seeing the demise of the company, but with his influence and continuing high sales, adding a funkier sound.

**Papa Was A Rolling Stone for me and probably a few others could relate to anybody with a wayward and absentee father, although my 'Daddy never died', he left us alone to survive! With of course a few lyric changes, sadly and although it had one of the best intro's ever, it would always remind me of my father from that time!*

Also climbing the charts at that time was The Main Ingredient with Everybody Plays The Fool, another great male vocal group, like the The Chi-Lites, New York City, The Delfonics, The Intruders, The Dramatics, Chairman Of The Board and of course Detroit Emeralds and the Spinners, I'll Be Around, Could It Be I am Falling in Love and the classic It's A Shame, remembering young love and a song most can relate to 'sitting all alone by the telephone, waiting for your call...when you don't call at all'. Strangely The Spinners had to put the word Detroit in front, to stop them being confused with a north country folk group who had a minor hit, in case it confused the UK chart compilers on filling out returns from the record shops! One female singer and her wonderful The First Time Ever I Saw Your Face, reminds me of a local event, sitting in my car in Kingston waiting for a mate after a shopping trip, a newsflash comes on the radio – it may even interrupted The Robbie Vincent Show it's the 18th June, just after 5pm that afternoon, a BEA Trident Flight 548 following a deep stall, fell out of the sky after takeoff, just missing Staines town centre crashing into an open space, killing 118, to this day every time I travel the Egham By Pass I think of that incident, one of the UKs worst aviation accidents. After that news on the radio, Roberta Flack's record was played.

What is interesting in 1972 is the success of male singers like Al Green, I have every single release, his first in 1971 and the effect of going steady. Perhaps sitting around our houses hoping and trying to get amorous, was to listen and buy more slow records 'Tired Of Being Alone'(4) and 'Let's Stay Together'(7) and now 'I'm Still In Love With You'(35), 'Sha-La-La'(24), his six hits over four years spent 60 weeks in the UK Top 40 along with Bill Withers, 'Lean On Me' and Use Me, Ain't No Sunshine also covered by The Jackson Five. From 1978 Lovely Day that always seems to get played on warm sunny days in the UK.

⁂

The early 1970s bought both social unrest both in the UK and the US, at home the start of 1972 saw the miners go on strike for the first time since 1926. Edward Heath declared a State of Emergency and announces a three day week to save power, agreeing a wage settlement after two months, back in the 1960s there was a million miners and were the best paid industrial workers in the country, but they needing to catch up, the NUM had power. Unemployment rises to a million for the first time since the 1930s. The IRA is still active Bloody Friday, Bloody Sunday and a bomb at Aldershot saw many casualties and sadly innocent deaths, our own Vietnam dilemma it was said, would there ever be a resolution, to both 'Wars'?

Meanwhile in the US the last ground troops are withdrawn from Vietnam after 60,000 US armed forces are killed, leaving the South Vietnam Army to defend themselves. It is estimated the North and South Vietnam together lost more than 700,000 civilians and 1.2M military. As US troops return home, social unrest will dominate discussions and the treatment of the veterans, especially from the poor communities. Did the US lose the Vietnam War? If you look at North Vietnam armed forces losses it was nearly 900,000, but they overran the South Vietnamese Army, others will argue that US Forces had departed by the beginning of 1973, two years before Saigon fell on 30th April 1975 to an NVA victory.

About this time, I am amassing now a good amount of records, looking to purchase just decks, amp and speakers and advertise my services as a DJ. Many more pubs even our local village ones are hoping to attract more youngsters in, another way of getting more revenue in. Anyway, with a good amount of overtime I purchase the gear, but always shyness and lack of confidence stops me taking that next step.

Pubs with upstairs function rooms were very popular and advertising Soul and Motown nights, they could be lucrative on admission takings, but at that time it was never about 'spending money on alcohol!', you just wanted to enjoy yourself. Most of these pubs and small clubs, just had a serving hatch or small bar, just big enough for one or two bartenders, by the time you had waited and these venues were only opened for three to four hours nightly, getting a drink from a basin tap was easier and cheaper, especially if you wanted to dance to your current favourite record or a slow dance with a young lady – if you were lucky!

Often 'Kicking Off' in these venues, was still attracting what was left of Skinheads or The Bovver Boy culture, driven a lot by so-called football fans. One Thursday night, three of us went to a pub called The Wheatsheaf on New Kings Road, on the Chelsea/Fulham borders, halfway through the evening, as normal you could detect an atmosphere building up and then it would start. Who knows why, the pub was just down from Stamford Bridge. Sadly clubs and pubs seemed to drop adverts and posters using Ska and Reggae headings, leading to many DJs dropping and not buying – did this contribute to the decline of Reggae in the UK Charts of the Top 100 sales of single in the years 1972/3, the only reggae singles that seems to feature is Judge Dread, which personally for me was similar to a novelty record along with Johnny Reggae by The Piglets, a Jonathan King production which embarrassingly got to number 3 in the UK Charts! However Judge Dread was responsible for inviting and getting reggae bands to the Edinburgh Festival in 1971 - it's worth watching some clips on YouTube - and gave the artists more exposure, ironically he was the only white British artist to have a reggae hit in Jamaica and it is said that he was the biggest selling 'reggae' artist after Bob Marley.

For the youngsters at this time and like our siblings before we have a few more pennies in our pocket and more clothes and more specialist record shops – it beats hoping that your local Woollies, Boots and Timothy Whites hoping they would have that soul single you are craving for. Certainly more clubs are opening, but what I didn't like at the time and still not fond of today, is the word of "Discotheque or Disco!", entering the vernacular, which seemed to appear everywhere around this time, being used later for a particular type of dance music. It was one of those collective words that parents are starting to use like 'Dolly Birds', my Mum would say 'Are you going to a Disco tonight', I would retort "Mum, I don't go to Disco's, that's a place where they play and people dance to Pop music like Glam Rock, I go to Soul Clubs!" - although I will give a pass to the Glitter Band without Gary (an instrumental, It Makes You Blind!) and accept the word Disco in soul release titles as it continued to do, over the next few years.

We hear a rumour, like the US Blaxploitation films that came out of the US, that Jamaica has released a film, together with a great soundtrack and stars Jimmy Cliff and with the music of The Maytals and Desmond Dekker. The Harder They Come, working with Chris Blackwell, the director Perry Henzell delivers to the world visually and musically a great movie, from the island reggae and based loosely on a real life crime story. We saw the film at a midnight showing in London somewhere at a very small cinema, may have been Notting Hill, I am not sure, the audience that night were part of the film, historically it was very influential and introduced reggae globally and a landmark production from 'The Islands' along with Bob Marley. Influencing bands later and using the sound, 10CC, The Police, Blondie's cover of The Tide Is High and many more. Still worth watching today along with the soundtrack, one track Rivers of Babylon by The Melodians was covered in 1978 by Boney M – enough said!

As 1972 slips into 73, not going clubbing on Christmas or New Years Eve, when you are going steady it's just not the same, however things slightly change with our relationship. We both separately like to go out with mates to clubs and she considers taking a summer holiday abroad that year with a friend. Those early 70's, many youngsters considered and took their first trips and holidays abroad, the weather was a big bonus as tans were now very popular, strangely I don't remember many couples going abroad if going steady. I mention this to my mate Danny and suggest we should do the same?

Perhaps that's where age and thought processes of lads stood then, I think many young ladies in relationships wanted us to make the decisions and suggestions when it came to doing things together, but generally most lads like being told what to do, ie be at a pub at a certain time or let's not go out tonight? The same and a theory about music, females at very good at detail, they would know and learn the lyrics naturally to songs, lads seem to be more attuned to the sound and rhythm or just to lazy to listen and learn the lyrics. It wasn't until listening to lyrics much later that I realised what many songs were about.

Danny was up for a lot of things, but if you need to go on holiday with a mate, always full on and with little filter and he will always make it more interesting. So we look at Spain, our first time abroad together, since that fateful school skiing trip to The Austrian Tyrol in 1967. No passports though, our first ever, we make enquiries and available from your local and the strangely named Department of Employment and Productivity or the Employment Exchange or earlier the Department Of Labour Exchange previously, (using an acronym the DOLE and signing on?) which for us was opposite Richmond Station. Handy because you can get a photo in the booth, just inside the entrance to the railway station.

I thought we would get one of those nice blue hard backed ones, but it's a three page fold out card valid for a year! The other thing at that time is that you can only take £50 (£400 today) worth of foreign currency or travellers cheques with a value of £15 (£130) in sterling. The Exchange Control act of 1966, bought in by the Labour Prime Minister Harold Wilson was to stop sterling being invested in shares or property abroad, needless to say Maggie Thatcher abolished these rules in 1979. I still have that passport, looking at that photo, I am going through my long hair Apache Geronimo look, wearing what looks like a grey scooped necked t-shirt!

So there we are, travelling out of Gatwick Airport that opened in the 1930's but by the late 1960's took all charter flights out of Heathrow and was now designated London's No.2 airport. It's July 1973, we book a week in Benidorm through a holiday company called Horizon to a Spanish town on the Costa Blanca. We were told had the most clubs and discotheques and some resident British DJs playing Soul, taking advantage of living abroad for the summer, similar to Ibiza in the 1980s. The amount of youngsters now taking a week away in the sun is growing rapidly, getting that suntan was very fashionable and it showed along with your clothes that you could afford things and liked a good time!

Obviously, it's our first time in an aeroplane together and it's a Dan Air Brittania or something similar with propellers, think we were expecting some form of a jet, as they had just announced direct flights to the United States with Laker Airways. But the problem with this type of plane is speed, pressurisation and ears popping, their ceiling flight height was very low compared with modern jets that were able to fly above or around storms. Unfortunately for us on takeoff, the captain says that there are storm conditions across the channel. I was always a bad traveller unless driving, but will now add airsickness to the list, along with people smoking in the rear of the aircraft!

We step off the plane and the heat is unbelievable, even though it's the evening. A great feeling and it's like a starting gun for fun, two lads abroad, after two camping holidays on the Isle Of Wight! After a coach ride from Alicante airport we are already chatting to youngsters on the journey and getting excited about the coming days. We are dropped off, we check into our hotel, gather our room keys open the door, again the heat hits us, this was a time when only main areas of hotel, may have air conditioning, but most individual rooms didn't, especially at what we were paying.

It's about 9pm, a quick wash and brush up, splash of aftershave and then we are ready, wondering what the night will bring. Our hotel is just a short walk from the seafront and the clubs, we have something to eat, the food on the plate seemed to swim in oil, but a bonus of food and beers are really inexpensive. After a couple of beers we find a club, a few pesetas to get in and with a free drink! We go downstairs, to a very dark, freezing cold, air conditioned basement, with bright ultra violet lighting with sadly just about a dozen people in it and a couple of girls dancing on their own, in that Northern Soul way. Thinking 'is this it?!', we go to the bar and ask for a drink in our best Spanish 'Dos Beero's, poor favor, zenor?', in a London accent the barman says "Alright Boys, first time abroad?". We enquire why it's so quiet, he says 'nothing gets going until after ten, in an hours time you won't be able to move, we find out that clubs were open until 3am or later. Living in the suburbs, we had these archaic licensing rules and most clubs in the suburbs closed at 11pm, latest midnight, club nights seemed to go so quickly with only 2-3 hours of dancing and a Wimpy and Chips afterwards to fill the time. This is a completely different experience, not going home to a quiet house, everybody in a good mood, great music, yet again the London accent helps with talking to young ladies, it was purely Party Time! As both Danny and I had 'steady' girlfriends, we agree 'What happens in Benidorm, stays in Benidorm!', ignoring that it was two timing, because we were abroad and in a parallel world!

After a late night we stagger, slightly tipsy back to the hotel, as the sky lightens waiting for the sunrise, a brand new experience for us. It's so hot, as we remove our clothes, Danny is wearing a t-shirt that has stretched with his sweat, as he pulls it over his head its gets longer and longer, we fall about laughing our heads off, the room is sweltering, after a fitful sleep and the coolness of dawn we manage to get a few hours in, after being woken by the maid. We don't want to miss breakfast and it's our first experience of a Continental Breakfast, a hard roll, pat of butter, slices of cheese with holes in, some sweaty ham, luke warm boiled eggs, washed down with what seems like orange squash, the cup of tea definitely wasn't like Mum made. Every morning groups of youngsters would arrive for breakfast, who have not even been to bed yet!

⁂

What was popular on that holiday was 'Northern Soul', a term that I have seen in adverts featured in Blues & Soul being played at venues after The Watford Gap, such as The Twisted Wheel, The Torch, The Blackpool Mecca, The International Soul Club, The Wigan Casino All-Nighters spinning 'Northern Soul Sounds', I literally thought they 'must' be playing the same soul sounds t'up North as us, surely? But when I had requested my favourite sound from The Hammersmith Palais, The Elgins 'Heaven Must Have Sent You' – number 3 in UK charts in May 1971 - in a Richmond club to a DJ, he asked 'so you like Northern Soul, do you?' – I had no idea it was a different sound to our Southern Soul, skipping the northern club reviews in B&S!

Interestingly and reputedly the phrase was concocted by Dave Godin, born in Peckham in 1936, after the family were bombed out of London, he attended Dartford Grammar School, a period when he started collecting R&B records from The States. Supposedly influencing Mick Jagger, with this music genre who also attended the same school, but with the age difference of seven years, could they have been educated together? With his interest in soul music and the new popularity of the 'new sound of young America', he founded the Tamla Motown Appreciation Society in 1964, the same year Berry Gordy invited him to Hitsville USA to meet him, it is said along with Dusty and her liking for the Motown sound, they convinced Gordy to organise The Tamla Motown UK Tour in the spring of 1965, after just one hit, to release that familiar label. In 1966/7 Godin along with a partner opened a record shop called Soul City initially in Deptford, moving to Monmouth Street in the West End later, they also had a record label with the same name, releasing Gene Chandlers Nothing Can Stop Me in 1968, a youth club favourite for us! Godin, a collector of rare grooves, mostly deleted, lost and bought in through UK ports in the 1960s, realising some of these records had a 'bouncier' different sound to the funkier harder ones being played on the London music scene. Their shop in London was frequently visited by football fans from the North, on away days, to distinguish the record sound, he labelled those racks and boxes 'Northern Soul' as opposed to another phrase he used of 'Deep Soul' from the southern states (or Southern Soul) of the US, a more rhythmic sound that would contribute to the rise of Funk later. Dave Godin also contributed regularly to Blues & Soul as a music journalist in the 1970s, passing away in 2004 aged just 68.

⁂⁂⁂

Time for the beach! We wear our "Cutdown Levi's" that every lad had, instead of Speedo's, t-shirts and Adidas – five a side - trainers, but we notice youngsters are wearing strange footwear called Flip Flops, they were very cheap from a stall or market, so it didn't matter if you lost them. We take our towels and find a place on the beach, it's hot in the sun and we think about lotions. Back to the kiosk, to get some Lemon Oil, which we were told it gave you a deeper tan! Yet again we are a little too early and no youngsters are around, we start to understand, sleep late, get up late, go to the beach or someone's larger hotel pool, drink all day, sunbathe and watch the sun go down, still drinking, go back to hotel later, hoping there's some hot water left, get some food, find a bar, meet some people, chat to young ladies, find a good club, get to bed somewhere and start the cycle again! These holidays were not for a rest! The going back to hotel in bright sunlight in the morning reminded me of coming out of afternoon pictures on a warm summer Sunday afternoon at 5pm!

By coincidence we have been invited to a hotel pool by some girls and sitting around was a group of lads from Richmond which we vaguely recognised, one of the lads name is Pieter Van De Weil, we start chatting and eventually start hanging around the pool and meet in the clubs later that night. Arriving back to their hotel early one morning at about 6am, we as a group decide to take some four heavy chairs and a table and set them up in the deep end of the pool, to the amusement of guests reserving loungers at 7am, they couldn't believe their eyes and the pool attendant just scratched his head as we watched from a room on an upper floor. Boys pranks eh?

Another group of lads were from London's, Elephant & Castle, they were talking about Crackers and how good it was, they mention giving them a call once we all got back, we exchange our newly acquired home telephone numbers. Sadly can't remember their names, but I think one was Mike (to whom I later loaned a couple of albums too, one was Blowfly and never got them back!) wonder if he has still got them!

As the week goes on we start to return to the same club for a night out. The DJ is a Londoner, but has latched on to not only the Philly Sound of The O'Jays Love Train and Love Unlimited – another great new club sound. The DJ had an import copy of I've Got So Much To Give and it was constantly played with Love Unlimited and that means only one person 'The Love Walrus!' had arrived. Realising it was it was his voice on with the opening chords on "Walking In The Rain", his cover of "Standing In The Shadows Of Love" and the title track. The following year and his hits, is as they say are now just 'soul music history!' Other holiday summer sounds that year were, The Detroit Spinners and Emeralds, Stevie's funky Superstition from Talking Book kept getting the plays and for a slowy definitely Marvin's Lets Get It On and Sylvia's Pillow Talk, what a combo. The Isley Brothers are back with a stunner – Who's That Lady - after their superb funky 1969 hit of 'It's Your Thing' and those great guitar solo's, by Ernie Isley. And let's not forget "Keep On Truckin'" from Eddie Kendricks on the Motown label that year, there is just so much good music about! About halfway through the week, we meet a couple of girls from Yorkshire, impressed by our South London accents - whatever that is and any attraction it may have? - our moves on the floor. The heat in these nightclubs, overpowered the air conditioning, we got so sweaty in those clubs our shirts and trousers would be literally be soaking, it would be like taking off a wetsuit, when returning to your hotel.

One of the Yorkshire lassies and to cut a long story short and I will call her Janet, took a fancy to me and it was reciprocated and we became close in just a short time, it became the archetypical 'holiday romance'. Like many holiday romances, after spending a couple of nights in their hotel bedroom and although both of us had 'two-timed' before, for me it never went as far as this, a lovely young lady from a small Northern town on the edge of The Yorkshire Dales, it was exciting for both of us, with lots of 'if only's', we lived closer to each other and 'if only' a different time and place'. They left earlier than us that week and I thought that was the end of our brief affair and any guilt would pass, thinking she may have the same similar thoughts.

Returning home and work was like a rest, but I felt my relationship with Susan is somewhat not on an even keel, probably a sense of guilt from me or her thinking about our going out together and finishing. Caught in that 'Did you meet anyone when you were away?' and she probably didn't mean 'lads'. Not easy for me to handle, don't know how to answer and even really want too, don't want to talk about it and certainly don't like confrontation. Many of you will be familiar with the feelings around your real 'First Love' or steady partner, but trying to understand those first feelings where a long term relationship would go or end up, were so difficult at that young age. I will say though, wrestling with emotions, feelings, trust and even jealousy, could be really damaging or distracting and bring you down. Especially if that relationships was slightly one sided and had intimacy.

Again later in life, if I could have had a word with my younger self back in those 1970s, with now all my so called gathered wisdom! Relationships are part of growing up and life's learning, but being hurt and emotions are not simple things to handle. Until you find the right person and sometimes you may never, some people can be and are even happy with their own company. People and relationships will change and if it's never going to work long term and honest decisions by both parties have and need to be made. Don't waste time in hoping a relationship will work or trying to make it work, you may waste your time in hope, as I saw with my mother and fathers relationship, the pain that lingered and one sided. The expression of 'sometimes it's better to have loved and lost, than not loved at all', is a reality and a learning curve for the better.

At an early age, intimacy can be a wrong signal for any partner, is it giving or taking? In those early years, it seemed to be about asking if a girl was on The Pill, as opposed to lads carrying around condoms and taking responsibility. I was lucky and Mums words in my head about 'what happens if....?'. So with Susan, I never took chances when it came to sex and the risk - and not often - with us both living in our parent's homes, in reality there didn't seem to be a lot of opportunity, perhaps a car, which can be difficult or a disastrous experience or some other place, in fact over the time, I never remember if we ever went away together!

When a conversation talks about 'taking a break', it's painful and a knife to the heart, a gut wrenching feeling that sickens you. Going back to my childhood, I can generally accept disappointment and being let down quite easily, no pleading, no arguing, holding back any tears. Emotionally, I will cope and stick it in the back of my head and lock it up in a box. But when you have had conversations about perhaps getting engaged or even pipe dreams of marrying, you believe you may have found the right one. Even at that early age of 20 and really inexperienced emotions and the best part of a two year relationship, it seems real that you could spend the rest of your life with someone, but the words still break my heart. We probably like a lot of young couples, didn't probably want to hurt each other, but sometimes.....................? I think at this point one of us should have said 'This is not working or is it not going to work, ever' but as the lyrics go 'Neither of us, wants to be the first to say Goodbye'.

As the summer finishes we have a break, but like school 'I am easily distracted' by the music and going out and it helps. Sometimes I would see Susan in the same clubs around Richmond and later London and even talking to other lads and my mates who she knows, which again feels a little uncomfortable. But I believe you have to move on and that 'don't look back' attitude, luckily given to me by my mother. When you have broken up, why is it that, that words, programmes on the TV, lyrics and songs from your record collection or listening to the radio, really touch your emotions Al Green's, Let's Stay Together, The Chi-Lites, Have You Seen Her and Oh Girl, those Philly songs, you can name them like The Love I Lost, Motown with the Diana & Marvin album and You Are Everything, Aretha's Until You Come Back To Me, The Stylistics, Break Up to Make Up, even Harry Nielson's 'Without You', Stevie's, If You Really Love Me, keeps circling and all seems to relate to the situation and can create that lump in your throat. Even putting that thought in your head 'Will she contact me?', 'Should I contact her?', 'Perhaps she want me too?'. The best anti-dote were to listen to upbeat dancers and obviously going out and trying to enjoy yourself, luckily I could still get out and around, the music was like a retreat from any emotional thoughts.

Distractions and going out at this time, was very easy in the circle of friends that Danny and I had, concerts and live bands were plentiful, with Hammersmith Odeon and New Victoria Theatre, etc US Labels and Soul Bands were realising that the UK was a great springboard to launch into a European tour. James Brown, Chairmen of the Board, and many others, lucky enough to be able to see so many live concerts and some famous acts.

As we go into the late summer 1973, I get a phone call from Mike, who we had met in Benidorm, he suggests Danny and I, meet him at a pub near his flat at The Elephant and Castle and they will take us to Crackers, at that time not even advertised, but didn't need any promotion. Although, my Nan lived in Battersea, Clapham Junction and later Wandsworth, I was familiar with the hustle and bustle of busy London streets from the late 1950's. However, I don't ever remember going to The Elephant at that end of the A3, which we were familiar with, but didn't know it went into town that far, we have instructions to find the New Kent Road and a street just off the roundabout, with a trusty A-Z of London we set off. The blocks of flats for us are quite unbelievable, from what I describe as 1930s blocks of Peabody and London County Council (LCC) built and 1960/70s brand new tower blocks; coming from a leafy suburban village like Ham, our tallest block is no more than four floors and some of them were maisonettes. The Victorian terraced and town houses that have been converted to flats are in many streets and can be quite daunting to anybody driving about, however I have always felt very comfortable on London streets. We actually do see a large Elephant and Castle on a building and a new shopping centre, just on the roundabout, so we know we are in the right area.

It's a Friday night, we can see the pub, one of those tall community ones, that seems to stand proud on the junction of two streets, like a large wedge of cheese or slice of cake, just sitting there brightly lit. In common with most working class entertainment then, it was the end of that working week and many just wanted to enjoy themselves. It's payday and absolutely buzzing with people, a typical London Boozer, we park up and can see through the slightly opaque glass with Saloon, Public and Off Licence etched into them. The doors are those swing type, brass double finger plated that splits in the middle, the public bar entrance on the corner and a reminder of those John Wayne western cowboy saloon entrances. As we push against those sprung doors, we enter and are immediately hit by the strong smell of cigarettes that are held seemingly by anyone and everyone, standing against the bar are heavy set guys, all looking like boxers dressed in well made dark suits and booted for a good evening out with the 'Mrs'. Their wives, are all sitting nearby at the tables and chairs, drinking vodka's and lime or gin's and orange, the odd sherry it seems, holding cigarettes or cigarillos in the odd holder or between their fingers, with a large glass ashtray with the inevitable adverts on the side in the middle of the table overflowing with used fag butts, a Dunhill lighter sitting on the table, chatting away in those familiar London accents and laughing loudly.

For a moment and it felt like minutes, the pub noise just evaporates and as these faces swung around from the bar, as we stepped over the doorway, in that look of 'Who The F**k Are You Two?!!' way! Luckily, the lad we are meeting Mike see's us, rushes over and says, looking at the 'geezers' at the bar and says 'OK Gents, these boys are with us!', putting his arms around our shoulders and sweeping us away to the other side of the bar. As quick as it had gone quiet, the noise and conversations start up again. We enquire what happened then, they tell us nonchalantly that there was a shooting just a month before and any strange faces will and would always be challenged and dealt with if necessary! It's get to about nine o'clock, we think when we are going, we ask and Mike says, 'we always get there about 10, its open until 3am!'

Although we had experienced Benidorm and late nights and sunrise closing, we thought that were just for holidays! As I nearly worked every Saturday on overtime and as my football career and talent were now in decline, still the odd game of football now as a reserve, cutting oranges or running as a temporary linesman or going to see Chelsea, but even that wasn't fun anymore as the hooliganism wasn't abating.

What a great atmosphere and club Crackers was, the late openings were allowed because it served food, getting around the 'pub' licensing laws for playing music – a sausage or burger and a few chips thrown into a red plastic basket, to eat or not to eat. What a fantastic introduction to The London Club Scene, we had never experienced such music and dancing. A friendly mix of black and white groups of youngsters that created a great atmosphere – youngsters were there just primarily there for the music. Some like us, perhaps in mundane jobs earning a wage and some would be unemployed, but at night and many nights in the week, would escape and relax into a world of music and observe other youngsters dancing and would start to clear a space on the dance floor themselves. Showing us moves and for us to practice in our bedrooms or in front of your Mum's full length mirror! There was such a synergy between the crowd, the heat, sweat, in a basement that held around 300, it wasn't the biggest club, but making mental notes of what others were wearing, some outlandish and daring with their choice, becoming just as much of a challenge as to the way they moved on the floor, like so many clubs that would open in the 70s. What is interesting is that some of the plays in Crackers, some we have never even heard of, lot of imports and new sounds. DJs such as Chris Hill were promoting themselves heavily especially in Blue & Soul, whereas Crackers was initially word of mouth at the time. Mainly due to a DJ from Southend On Sea called Mark Roman, already playing in Wheatley Taverns owned venues and engaged fulltime at Crackers included that famous lunchtime slot from 1974, that long lunch break that workers and even 'bunking off' pupils would attend, while I was playing pitch and putt or snooker in East Sheen at the same time on a Friday lunch hour between work! Over the next couple of years we are regular visitors, Mark Roman was the man and the resident DJ, his format was simple, brilliantly segued new sounds, especially on a Tuesday Imports Only night and the funkiest, of course promoting the emergence of Jazz Funk! I was constantly asking 'What's that record?' and a visit to Contempo the following Saturday afternoon or evening and now opened until 8pm. What was impressive is that black, white and gay couples danced together, in co-ordinated moves, which eventually would lead to regular dance off casual competitions, before that you may dance next to your mate but not with him, that's now all dropped especially when 'The Bump' era dropped on the floor, the atmosphere and environment also broke down any cultural bias that anybody may have thought or considered in those times.

I recognise one lad instantly, young and redheaded, that I have spoken to and seen him doing his thing at The Castle Richmond now called Cheekee Pete's, The Oldfield Tavern and the Ironbridge Pub in Greenford, his name - Tommy Mack. Tommy was unique, he certainly wasn't shy, completely over the top and flamboyant, like many lads, lasses and their families at the time, relocating from Hammersmith, Fulham and West London, out to a council estate into the suburbs of Northolt, Middlesex or

Buckinghamshire. Tommy's family did just that in the mid 60s and was now part of the Hayes and Slough Soulboy Mafia. A balletic display of dancing, it's not surprising that he did not screw himself into any dance floor, he could spin as if on ice, between sounds and his short breaks from the dance floor, he would chat to everyone and anyone, carrying a towel to wipe himself down, often like the other dancing lads take their tops off before overheating. Forever on the dance floor with his mate Jabba, there were many great dancers, male and female challenging him and others, playfully into a 'dance off', trying to out manoeuvre and out move each other. Along with dancing he was a natural entertainer, no wonder he ended up in the Club Scene and Management and even taking lessons in dance studios to devise new moves from modern dance in the early days of Pineapple Studios. Like many popular, bars, restaurants, clubs and other venues, Crackers night club became the place to go and be seen for growing Funk Jazz scene, sounds and the clothes, later hints of bondage trousers and tartan, when the only 'punk', that quickly came to mind was in Clint Eastwood's Dirty Harry film, wondering whether that 'punk' had counted his bullets! After Mark Roman was reputedly forced out of Crackers in 1976, a change of management and differences, he moved onto Jaws, down in East London's, Leytonstone and took a large crowd with him, including us. The replacement DJ, George Power bought in another younger crowd and perhaps the next generation, and more vocal than Roman - except for Chris Hill of course, that could and would work a crowd, along with whistles! It is said that Crackers slowly fell out favour with many of the initial crowd from the early 70s, fashionista's and dancers, now a younger audience who were just starting out. But for me coming from a provincial town and my first foray into the West End, its legacy will forever live on, within my memory and for many.

If I am ever up in the West End, even today, I will try and sit outside the Bar Italia for a coffee in Frith Street, looking across at Ronnie Scott's then walk around to Wardour Street and the old Crackers site. Great memories of parking on a kerb in Soho, the lights and walking past or seeing the neon's of Raymond's Revue

Bar, strip joints and dive bars, still hints of the 1950s and 60s London and dodgy people, imagining a few gangsters and thoughts of protection money being collected I am sure, a few girls in fur coats hanging around the bars and clubs, brings on the nostalgia for those nights in the 70s for me.

Imports at this time were so important for any funk enthusiast, some not even getting a UK release as to late for a London crowd, from such bands as The Fatback Band's, Street Dance and Keep Steppin', Kool & The Gang's, Funky Stuff and Jungle Boogie, really hit the spot. Philadelphia International (PIR) with that distinctive lime green label, initially released here on the CBS label, that continue to get more plays and MSFB (TSOP) and entry into the charts that year.

CBS had employed a young black Grenadian, born in 1947 and raised in New York City, moving to the UK in 1971 to educate himself in Business Studies at Manchester University. While taking a break from his studies one night, he visited a club where no one was dancing and boldly asked the DJ if he could have a spin of the decks, although he had no ambition to get into music at this time. Rummaging through the DJs collection of singles he finds and spins The Foundations, 'Build Me Up Buttercup' that got people up and dancing, which soon after led to a job on local radio. One thing followed another and being in 'the right place at the right time' a CBS executive takes him on to look after their black labels of T-Neck, Invictus and of course Philly International, the blue touch paper of The Philly Sound being The O'Jays and Backstabbers. The man's name Greg Edwards! As they say, 'the rest is history'. Greg was approached by the BBC and went on to present and secure a slot on Radio 1, after initially promoting soul and jazz music. Leaving the BBC and joined the new commercial station of Capital Radio in 1973 and Soul Spectrum from 1975 on a Saturday night. To now and every cassette recorders delight, his shows timing was great, you could listen while getting ready, before you went out clubbing and then play it again in the car, one section being the famous 'Bathroom Call!'. Greg also DJ'd around the South East, a residency at The 100 Club and of course The Lyceum's 'The Best Disco In Town', a massive venue, which I visited only twice, a stone's throw from the Global Village, which we preferred across the road in the arches below Charing Cross station.

With 1973 coming to an end, my now growing record collection has new artists and labels. Tamla Motown in a slight directional change but the best selling artists are still Stevie Wonder and the start of the his historically big money album deal, now completely in control of everything he did, Wonder who signed for Motown at age 11, let his contract expire and re-signed a multimillion dollar contract with Gordy, the 1970s was his golden decade. His superb concepts of Talking Book, Inner Visions followed by Fulfillingness First Finale, Songs In The Key of Life, The Secret Life of Plants and Hotter Than July in 1980 just delivered. Eddie Kendricks, Marvin Gaye's Let's Get In On, Miss Ross's and Motown's launch into movies of Lady Sings The Blues and Touch Me In The Morning and of course their joint Diana and Marvin album, which took nearly three years to make because of their tempestuous relationship, emotions and film commitments, even recording separately. The groups, The Temptations and Norman Whitfield, Law Of The Land are changing the sounds of Motown and still riding high, chased by the new Philly sound, but there are rising stars and especially a large man called The Walrus of Love and his orchestral soul sounds!

However, one new sound is starting to attract any soulboy or soulgirl ears and moves in clubs, a man called Herbie Hancock with an album called Head Hunters – a different type of production. One track stands out, Chameleon, compelling opening bars that sounds like a bass guitar, but it's a synthesiser followed by a driving rhythm, I first heard this at Crackers. Hancock an accomplished musician with a jazz background, the sound was a fusion between jazz and funk including a driving beat, the album first appeared in the Jazz Charts and crossed over to the R&B charts as Chameleon was picked up by the DJs – I am wondering was Chameleon THE first Jazz Funk track to hit the dance floors, like James Brown's Cold

Sweat and Funk, in my personal opinion as a non-musicologist, soul music historian or DJ, it was the first one that I remember hearing, all very debateable of course to a purist.

Another band hitting the clubs and decks and gaining popularity are War, I was very interested to know and when researched, that it was Eric Burdon, the lead singer of The Animals (House of the Rising Sun fame and a great 1960s R&B band). When his group dissolved in 1968, Burdon moved to California, joined up with a new band that later changed its name to War. Touring Europe in 1970, after the release of an album entitled Eric Burdon Declares 'War', they played at Ronnie Scott's Club that September and for their last set, Jimmi Hendrix joined them on stage, a day later he was dead. The band without Burdon returned to the States, that year in a fusion of jazz, funk, latino and even hints of reggae, they hit us with the album 'The World Is A Ghetto' and a single of the same name and 'Cisco Kid'. In 1973 we heard and one of my favourites, Me and Baby Brother.

At work, my promotion to a Technical Officer comes through and better pay scales, the unions have managed to drive up pay in a now highly profitable - as no competition in a growing telecommunications industry and marketplace. Strangely in 1902 all existing telephone companies were absorbed into the Post Office Telephones except for Hull, that was granted a licence under The Telegraph act to operate it own telephone service in the Kingston Upon Hull area. I must admit, it wasn't the hardest job in the world and could be very boring, when cleaning banks of switches mainly your duties were cleaning 1930s installed equipment, unless fault tracing. My pay rises from £1483 to £2043 (still got the notification dated 11/73). Straight away, I think of more records and clothes, two weeks later I upgrade my ailing 1962 Mk 1 Cortina for a 1965 Cortina 1500 Super De Luxe with 5.5Js. I must admit, I did look at and would have loved to stretch my budget to a Mk 1 Lotus Cortina, that car with its Old English cream paintwork, distinctive green stripes and those Lotus green and yellow badges sitting on the rear panels with that racy slick look, 5.5J rims, front disc brakes, a twin cam 1600cc engine, fuelled by twin carbs' and with a rev' counter – a street racer, just pre-Capri affordability! It was the unreliability and insurance cost that slowed me down in making any impulsive decision.

Excitedly I go home that night, very pleased to be 'an Officer' and show my mother the letter. She in turn is very happy for me and instantly makes a decision to increase her 'housekeeping money' from £3.50p a week, which I have been paying for three years, to £7.50p a week! Which, at first is a shock, but then I quickly remember the situation she has been in since I was born in 1953 working many hours to scrape together the rent, put food on the table and to keep 'her boys' together! Now its Mums turn to have some treats, I am not in a position to moan.

⁂⁂⁂

1973, and the hit of 1969 Space Oddity, only three months before the memorable moon landing, bought us the establishment of David Bowie as an artist and his growing popularity. Alter ego Ziggy Stardust for me, was a more sophisticated glam rock guise, my mother watching TOTP, would certainly comment about his looks, his clothes and makeup, however, he retired Ziggy that year. It wasn't until 1975 and his visit to Sigma Studios, recording the album Young Americans, that I really warmed to him. That session he wanted to use MSFB, but they weren't available, except for one member, he then recruited a bassist from The Isley Brothers, a former drummer with Sly and a then an unknown young 24 year old Luther Vandross, to assist in the recording!

Sadly, we also hear that Innocenti, who have been making Lambretta's since 1947 made their last scooter in 1972, a GP model. The tooling was sold to SIL India in 1973. It is said, that the development of their engineering in Italy, the falling two wheel scooter market, lack of sales and a collaboration to bring in British small cars under licence, like the Morris 1100 to Europe, killed the business and we all know what happened to our own British car industry in the early 1970s, they backed the wrong automobile manufacturer.

The Saint - Roger Moore - gets the 007 role. Calls to bring back the birch for convicted football hooligans along with a spell in National Service are debated which a lot of us supported. The IRA is very active with bomb attacks across the country.

In December and as a result of industrial action, coal shortages, with a need to reduce our energy, The Three-Day Week is announced. Another blow would be the coming fuel crisis, speed limits, queuing at petrol stations became part of our life, we were even issued with petrol rationing coupons – which I still have. The local newspapers printed power outages, we prepared with stoking the fire and sitting with candles and a transistor, keeping your fingers crossed that the power would come back on, before you favourite TV programme comes on or you need to get dressed before going out. Oil price rises have a direct impact on inflation, there are goods and services price rises, along with pay caps, lead to unrest in the UK workforce.

1974 and the club scene is looking stronger than ever, - considering what's going on in the country - more clubs and venues playing Soul and Jazz Funk and the good news is that more imports and faster UK releases are being bought in by record shops in the larger towns. I think those of us who are lucky enough to have a job and miles away from any coal pits, just wanted to be distracted or didn't think about the news, we just wanted to have fun. Soul artists and bands are releasing more 'protest' songs, about the global situations, especially from The States, For The Love of Money and Give The People What They Want, Wake Up Everybody from The O'Jays as an example.

We are now regulars now at Crackers, making many friends and groups of youngsters would just invite you to parties and recommendations for other clubs. One experience I had was going to Notting Hill Gate and being invited to a house party, a couple of times. For a small white lad hanging about with Richard, who we had met at Ronnie Scott's, a black lad from Mitcham. Entering a reggae party was such an experience, a large five story house, just off Ladbroke Grove, two of the floors had been cleared of furniture. A Sound System with the biggest speakers, that I had ever seen, resting against the walls, the heat, a slight smell of weed lingering in dimly lit rooms, a mix of black and white boys and girls, just enjoying the music and scene. I can still feel the sound, not only through the floor but my body, Dub or Roots Reggae was now popular and a slight shift in what ska and reggae sounds that I had been used to in my earlier days. The most interesting thing for me that night was the welcome, Richard's friend the host and his mother were dancing, his mum came over and gave me a big hug, guided me to the kitchen and served me with my first ever taste of jerk chicken with rice and peas plated up and a bottle of imported Red Stripe. A memorable night!

This was this year that Trojan started to struggle financially, Island Records having pulled out earlier, now a slight change in popularity and sound, was leading to implications. Founded in 1968, which I believe was named after and a nod to Duke Reid, the famous Jamaican record producer, who would drive a British built Trojan truck, which he would transport his equipment and records around the Island, sadly passed away in late 1975, Trojan that year went into liquidation. The label and catalogue has been sold a couple of times and is now owned by BMG, and managed by Laurence Cane-Honeysett, who has worked with Trojan since the 1990s, Lawrence co-wrote Young, Gifted and Black, and his own The Story of Trojan Records in 2018, with more books to come.

My reggae collection reveals that my last buys of Trojan labelled singles are Ken Boothe's, Everthing I Own and Help Me Make It Through The Night by John Holt. The only other reggae purchases to come are John Holt's 1000 Volts of Holt, Bob Marley's Natty Dread album in 1974, Exodus in 1977, along with Third World's Journey To Addis 1978, Marley's Legend and Mexicano's Move Up Starsky.

Hanging about with Richard for a time, I did witness my first close-up and act of racism and ignorant behaviour, we went to either Margate or Bournemouth on an Easter Bank Holiday, not being able to get in to a places we knew as fully booked, we just drove down. Driving around looking for Guest Houses or a Bed and Breakfast and looking for that VACANCIES sign. We pull up outside one, I get out of the car, ring the bell and open the door, a woman comes out with an apron on. I ask if any twin rooms, she says 'Yes' and gives me the price and starts to read the riot act as they did 'no girls back, locking the door' etc etc, she looks to the car and sees Richard sitting in the front, her attitude changes completely, referring to her book again, she says 'Oh, Sorry I forgot, my husband took a message earlier and we have that room booked already, it went completely out of my mind!'. I am a little bemused and walk back to the opened car door to tell Richard, then the penny drops! Richard is more than aware, 'Don't worry, it's not unusual, I get it often, you can get angry, but it's a waste of time!'. As we drive away, I did get angry, should I have gone back and to call her out? I can empathise, but I never had the same experiences, luckily we found somewhere else.

Back in Richmond, drinking in a local pub and after shopping I bump into Pieter, who we had met in Benidorm. Danny 'my riding shotgun' mate is going steady and a little serious, except for our obligatory Boys Friday Nights Out. Not wanting to be a 'Johnny No Mates' and go places in the hope you meet people you know, I accept Pieter's offer to meet up and go out. Pieter, just slightly older than me is a great lad, easy going, had that shock of hair that he just ran his fingers through and it annoyingly fell in place, good looking, well dressed, loves to spend money on clothes and also worked at The Ivy Shop part time, along with Mike Dove, as well as having a full time job at Bullens in Kew. He was well connected and knew a lot of people both male and female, the great thing about him was his networking style allowed us to jump queues and get into many members clubs, like Monkberry's, Samantha's, The Blitz, The Valbonne, Tramp, The Embassy, The Zanzibar in Covent Garden. Later, nicknamed Pieter Van De Loafer, after his large collection of

Bass Weejuns and shoes, living in Mortlake opposite the brewery, conveniently situated not far from me and a quick drive to the West End. Owning a lovely green Morris 1000 convertible, which added to his coolness, not restored, so it had all those mechanical problems we all suffered with in those early days of motoring. Hanging about with Pieter took me to some interesting, pubs, bars, eateries and especially clubs. It was this year that I found what in my opinion was the best club ever and for me, Upstairs At Ronnie Scott's, - 75p to get in, chicks free as the poster said - a Thursday night excursion to 47 Frith Street – parking was easy, just bumping up on the kerb outside to park, Soho didn't seem as busy at 9 or 10pm in those days, flickering neons's and shadows in doorways as always. Ronnie's just buzzed until 3am, I must say it was difficult to get up the next morning, it was good that I didn't have to be awake to do my job! Ronnie's seemed to be more of an intimate club, a sociable crowd with its low ceiling, smaller than many, but my attendance there coincided many great tunes and dancing, choreographed around The Bump, The Hustle, Kung Fu, sounds of Crown Heights Affair with Dreamin' A Dream and Foxy Lady, Black Byrds with Rock Creek Park, Hamilton Bohannon, Gloria's Never Can say Goodbye, BT Express Do It, Kool and the Gang's Jungle Boogie, Hollywood Swinging and Higher Plane, Ohio Players, Little Beavers Party Down and many, many more. It was also about this time that Greg Edwards DJs at Bluesville House of Funk, which we all knew as The 100 Club.

⁂

My love life turns interesting, not sure whether it was out of habit but Susan and I decide to start seeing each other again, it may have been difficult for both of us to sever the relationship completely, but we probably should have at that time. I would have struggled with that famous phrase of 'Can WE still be friends?', because it would never really work for me. I wondered, does she feel sorry for me - but never asked - perhaps I didn't want to know really, thinking back, I think she should have had relationship with someone a lot older than her, not me. During this time, Janet from

Yorkshire, who I had met in Benidorm is writing to me every two weeks and with the odd phone call, about how much she enjoyed her time with me and she wished she could see me again, holiday romances eh? This is obviously great for my ego and I write back just once a month saying 'that would be nice' – but with 200 plus miles between us, it's easy to say, as it would be difficult for us to even consider meeting up. I am still going out, sometimes talking to young ladies and giving the odd lift home, it's strange, as there never was any follow up or commitment from me, but not a good way to treat people. If I saw them again at a club it became just on a social basis, or any relationship just ran its course.

At work, it's easy, with no responsibility, unbelievable to think how overstaffed it seemed to be in a telephone exchange. We were just constantly chatting and feet up at our workbenches, when bosses weren't around, reading The Sun's Page 3 and the Daily Mirror, novels, bringing in radios, vacuum cleaners and other electrical items to repair during work hours, in the car park maintaining your car, signing in and disappearing for half a day, when the Area Engineer wasn't around. I even had quite a lucrative side line of installing telephone extensions for neighbours, I knew the chaps in the nearby Post Office stores, who would supply cabling and telephones, everybody wanted now a trendy Trimphone, but were difficult to acquire. In short, I am well paid, comfortable and at that time had little ambition and devoid of it, knowing it would take years to my next promotion.

I think the majority of us saw a job as a necessary evil, pay Mum and keeping them off your back, if out of work you were labelled a 'layabout, good-for-nothing or useless', the streets in our village were deserted during the working day. Working was a real bonus if you enjoyed it, to fund going out, run cars, buy records and clothes, even better if you had some left over and could put some in your Post Office Savings book for a future treat, add a graphic equaliser to your hi-fi, buy albums, or an extra pair of new shoes. If you still lived at home, it could be really easy as long as you got on with the rest of your family and you kept out of trouble.

Clothes wise and hair wise, high streets catered very well for the young set, Saturdays out shopping at names like Mates or Chelsea Girl for young ladies and for lads in Richmond we still had The Ivy Shop, Mr James etc, further a field in Kings Road, you had Take 6, Lord John, Squire Shop, Cecil Gee and many others. There seems to be a lot of 'off the peg' buying of clothes, Sunday morning markets were also popular to pick things up, clothes and records our nearest was Brentford, Western International, even think one at Earls Court Exhibition site. The majority of youngsters go out, see what the fashions are, thinking they look great and bought similar. As long as you feel good, look smart that was good enough.

Club scene fashions were evolving at this time, Crackers and other clubs were about the look and that influenced many into some very individual fashions and away from the High Street. Pieter very much into his clothes and I see that many youngsters are wearing second hand clothing and ex-military wear. As well as going up market with expensive clothing, shopping trips to The West End, Kings Road, etc. Of course, we find Lawrence Corner Army Surplus in Euston, unbeknown to us, it had opened in the 1950s, buying up armed forces stock, from Billy Cans to a full Grenadiers Officers uniform. Many 1960s famous bands would buy ex-military wear for stage performances, The Beatles and their Sergeant Peppers clothing were sourced from there, it also inspired many new young excited designers at the time. If I remember rightly it was painted bright orange on the corner just up from Capital Radio and Euston Tower, part of our sometimes Saturday afternoon routine was for a rummage. As you opened the door to the ring of a bell, this odour of mustiness and earthiness just hit your nostrils, it was just piled high with army ephemera, clothing, shirts and trousers, it was incredible. Buying anything was a risk but also not expensive, finding a lovely pair of officers plain cap shoes, in ox-blood a great design and in nearly new, very good condition, a bargain but half a size too small, but like Cinderella's ugly sister I made them fit and suffered the consequences while going out and dancing! Army worsted and woollen shirts, that even after repeated laundering, still had a musty odour in a sweaty club, spraying with Aramis or Aqua De Selva still didn't mask it or last till the end of the night. Royal Navy square neck shirts were very popular for the summer along with officers trousers, US army combats, GI's chino's and air force fatigues, Navy uniforms, the white bell bottomed hot climate ones, that you may see on TOTP on a Thursday night, Peacoats, boilersuits, the list was endless. I even saw someone wearing a US Navy gunnery fatigues and protective headgear one night – a time when anything could be worn, the only issue being leaving your council estate house dressed in something that your neighbours and their kids looked aghast, as you stepped into your car!

The other shop that most of visited and where we bought second hand US shirts and denim Levi's, bib and brace and other outerwear was the shop Acme Attractions in Kings Road, managed by Don Letts at the time near the Chelsea Old Town Hall and The Birds Nest, Flip or Retro and others in Covent Garden were similar in clothing. Lots of American and my favourite Pendleton worsted checks and plain shirts, flat collars and button downs, US football team branded sweatshirts and Baseball jackets, college cardigans and 'Norwegian' ski style jumpers with reindeers and snowflakes or in this case Sierra Nevada's knitwear, Fruit of the Loom and logo'ed T-Shirts, they also stocked baseball and football shirts, but my favourite was bowling shirts with great logos and embroidered names on the chest, like Chuck, Sammy and advertising garage services. Oh why, oh why, didn't I keep them in store, I don't even remember getting rid of them, a warehouse and shops near Brick Lane, still has them today. Luckily I packed up and stored my vinyl in the early 1980's, not opening them until nearly forty years later!

On a Saturday, if no overtime or football and after a late night, I would start the weekend on a Saturday morning, trying to lie-in, my Mum asking 'what time did you get in last night or should I say this morning?!' as she vacuumed my bedroom, in an effort to get me up, she hated me staying in bed! The ritual of getting up meant a bath and a shave, looking in wardrobe of what to wear, because you might not come home later to change, before going out. A visit The West End, when parking a car was free after 1pm then and on a single yellow line, shopping for clothes or vinyl at Contempo, down to Kings Road for more shopping and meeting up with others at The Birds Nest, watching the Chelsea Cruise from 1975, standing on the street, then onto Hard Rock, Park Lane for your first taste of a real American burger, definitely not a Wimpy or McDonalds, meeting in a pub or bar in Soho, deciding on which club that night. Window shopping was a great past time and making purchases in such shops as Browns in South Molton Street and it's interesting row of four shops that it gradually bought out or Johnsons in Kensington Market and Kings Road, Lloyd the owner, a former employee of Cecil Gee, not the most expensive of shops but well made clothing and others recognised that, the term 'How much did you pay for that then!' banded around. I remember buying some great canvas jeans from Browns, with zipped backed pockets in black and a pair in grey, which made a big dent in my wallet along with a blouson style top, expensive and well made clothes became a thing for many clubbers on the Soul Scene. I even had a pair of low cowboy style boots, with straps coming around the ankles - not the line dancing ones! - at this time, with a second hand Pendleton worsted check shirt and a pair of second hand faded 1960s 501's from Kings Road, I thought the look was pretty cool at the time, until you saw what some other lads were wearing. A little later, buying an extremely expensive a pair of Fiorucci jeans from their Knightsbridge store and the nice glossy decorated bag you took them away in, which were cut so tight, you could trap your hand in the pocket trying to get you car keys out! Everybody seemed to have snake hips, these jeans had a brass disc on the back pocket that would constantly catch on my mother's new corduroy sofa and my car seat! The founder Elio Fiorucci was influenced by Carnaby Street fashions in the middle 60s and took ideas back to Italy.

However, Halston, Gucci, or Fiorucci, but didn't make me The Greatest Dancer! After their Mama Never Told Me, UK chart entry in 1975, the 1979 Sister Sledge hit written and produced by Nile Rogers and Bernard Edwards and the same year we were still listening to their debut band, New York City and that classic hit 'I'm Doing Fine Now' who suddenly disbanded after that hit. I wonder how their careers worked out after that?

Going to The Blitz around this time, when it was more a bar and some live music, along with a DJ, Pieter and I were dressed in baseball shirts, drainpipe jeans and both wearing AllStar Basketball Boots and topped off with baseball caps! To be honest we were the most conservative, the clothing in that place was unbelievable at the time and for the rest of the seventies and into the eighties, if you could get in.

The other big clothing influence that year was 'The Great Gatsby' movie, not only a very annoyingly handsome Robert Redford playing Jay Gatsby, the coolest guy since Steve McQueen in Bullitt and John Shaft on film, clothing styles you just had to have and wear. Cloth or worsted caps, white or cream bags with twin pleats, collarless or collared shirts with ties and a waistcoat and two-tone shoes was 'The Look' that year and set some precedence with also the young ladies, sales of second hand 20s/30s dresses looked fantastic and flapper and bobbed hair styles to match which was a cut I loved, the bars before going out and the clubs looked like a speakeasy on Rhode Island USA, from that period, a more influential look than The Godfather, the year before. The Swing period had arrived in some of the clubs at that time, tunes of Glen Miller and His Band were played in some clubs to get us 'In The Mood', more trips to Army Surplus stores for US Officers Army and Navy clothes, Soul Boys and Girls certainly knew how to dress in 1940's style! Trips to The Goldmine on Canvey Island and Chris Hill, quickly come to mind and the Lacy Lady in Ilford. I remember the round trip journey from Richmond, Kew Bridge, North Circular Road – the journey would include freshly taped sounds for the hour drive which made the time go faster, again one night my quarterlight was smashed and a box of cassettes were taken, my mate Danny again rode shotgun with me on many of these journeys. After a good night and perhaps after giving a couple of girls a lift back to Chigwell or Dagenham, he without fail would fall asleep on the way back, mind you Robbie Vincent kept me company with his very interesting late night phone ins, calls from strange night people with even stranger ideas and a link up with a New York radio station and what was happening in The Big Apple with music and its scene.

Musically 1974 was very much part of my musical journey from the middle 1960s and R&B, Britblues, blue-eyed soul to the late 60s then the established labels and sounds of Motown, Stax, Atlantic, Trojan etc. My growing collection of James Brown 45s and albums and now rebranding himself, The New Minister of the New New Super Heavy Funk could certainly knock them out, Reality and Hell albums and singles! Along with funky Maceo Parker, Fred Wesley and The JBs, Memphis Soul, The Philly Sound Stable, The Barry White Sound, The Miami Sound and other great bands and singers. The Great Plains of Funky and heading to The Foothills of Jazz Funk from 1975, with Herbie's Hancock, Mann and other great jazz crossover artists that changed the clubs, charts and dance moves. My album collections until 1979, includes Quincy Jones, Lalo Schiffrin, Seawind, Weather Report, Ramsey Lewis, Cleveland Eaton, Idris Muhammad, Jimmy McGriff, The Crusaders, Eric Gale, Maynard Ferguson, Spyro Gyra, Eddie Henderson, Herb Alpert and many jazz based artists. Ohio Players's with Skin Tight and Fire, Earth Wind and Fire, Donald Byrd and onto a mountain plateau, the club sound of that Jazz Funk explosion, for me personally was around 1976 and 77. We can all choose our own favourite sweet spot that we enjoyed on the club scene, no doubt based on your age and when you walked through the doors of youth and music clubs.

To many of us, music was a drug that didn't do any harm but did many of us a lot of good, even to this day, 1974, like 1976 a year never to be forgotten. Summer Sounds and that Disco Triangle Trio that never ages, Rock Your Baby, Hang On in There Baby and Rock The Boat.

Rock Your Baby, sold over 11 million copies produced and written by two of the KC and the Sunshine members, but rejected by the band as a release, because of the high notes and then offered to George McCrae, spending three weeks at number one in the UK charts that mid-summer, he wore the best ever brushed denim suits of every colour with his chest exposed and a prize for the worst ever in-house Top Of The Pops orchestra backing track, when he appeared, one of the records that heralded in the disco era, it is said. Hang On In There Baby, prior to this, Johnny Bristol was a songwriter and producer for the Motown label involved in many hits, not only did he get to number 3 in the UK charts that summer, but also wrote Love Me For A Reason which The Osmonds got to number 1 simultaneously in the same year. Finally, Rock The Boat, is considered to be one of the earliest disco hits, initially a slow burner, it was eventually picked up by New York and London DJs, reaching number number 6 on the UK charts in July. Another contender for the initial 'disco' hit is of course 'Loves Theme' by the Love Unlimited Orchestra, just preceding The Queen Of Disco, Donna Summer with Love To Love You Baby.

What we mustn't forget that summer was the vinyl and now more importantly, the release on my first purchase of a 'pre-recorded' cassette and K-Tel's Super Bad album, possibly the best ever compilation collection for any soul boy or girl of the mid 70s. After some great compilations to hasten our soul or reggae collection, Super Bad had 25 original tracks from Philly, Motown and many more, including Mr White himself. A must have, for the glove box or parcel tray in your motor or ghetto blaster on the beach, however I wished I had bought the vinyl and taped it as the cassette snagged later in the seventies and was virtually destroyed, I later picked up a vinyl copy in a charity shop for a pound!

Slowies of Be Thankful For What You Got, and the reissue of The Chi-Lites, Homely Girl and Eddie Holman's (Hey There) Lonely Girl, Main Ingredients Just Don't Want To Be Lonely, just evoke all those time and experiences.

1974 also set the next few years of clubbing and going out, over to Streatham and The Bali Hai, as well as the music what I remember from my experience there, we offered to give two young ladies a lift back to Sutton on the way home, parking opposite, in a residential area on a freezing night with no coats, walking back I notice, there is now a gap at the kerbside, where my Cortina was parked! Apologising to the girls, we walk to the local police station to report the theft, it took us about two hours to get home on a bitter cold night without coats (how many of us have done this?). Ironically, I receive a call the next morning from the police, it was found abandoned in Sutton, with my expensive stereo ripped out and all my cassettes missing, I was more upset about losing all those hours of recordings.

Global Village and later to be called Heaven – was under the arches beneath Charing Cross Station, where the walls ran wet with condensation, sweat and whitewash, you never touched or leaned against the walls or put anything on the floor, they would be ruined. Croydon venues like Cinatra's (Top Rank), The Orchid and Purley's Cinderella's were all very interesting and but not frequented a lot.

However, a great club that seemed to be a very long drive from Richmond (before the M3) and a ride out into the countryside, down the A316 and A30, past Virginia Water and into complete darkness to a town called Bagshot. Looking for that night club we arrive in this village or small town, Danny and I look at each other in that 'surely not here? way, in the darkness we are about to turn around and a lad from a group passing shouts 'You looking for Pantiles mate?' We nod. 'It's just around the corner back on the main road!' My memories of Pantiles are how busy it was for a club in leafy Surrey like a beacon or oasis, the way the youngsters dressed, golden bird cages with dancers in and the music played, The first time I had heard – outside of London - and the shortest record in soul club history at 2 minutes 15 seconds Act Ones 'Tom The Peeper', reputedly picked up by Northern Soulers and never a hit in the US, but let's not go there.

If you continued on the A30 further to Camberley, you will have found Frenchies Night Club which on a Sunday night played some great imports, after Cheekee's falling a little out of favour, my lasting memory of that club is winning a Frenchies t-shirt for naming the tune as heard in a London club that week. The name of the record 'I Thought It Was You' and Herbie Hancock in 77/78, in videos you would seem him using a vocoder to distort his voice, wearing a headset and a keyboard around his neck! One of my last trips to Bournemouth that year or the next I wore the t-shirt and still have the photo.

Frequent trips over to East London and which was always an interesting drive and Jaws nightclub just off Leytonstone High Street. With DJ Mark Roman now installed, a great club, with many first time plays from albums and imports. Believe Roman had had taken the crowd as many faces and their dancing were recognisable from early Crackers nights.

Life outside the music and clubs had to go on. Workwise for me I was called into the Area Engineers Office to have a career review, I am told I have a new posting to Kingston Automatic Telephone Exchange (546/549) on Birkenhead Road, a large building with about four times the staff than my current location. When I arrive, I am greeted by the Union representative, who yet again has a go at me for not taking my sick leave, as I am told again that the union worked to get and I can take 10 days off with no questions asked! I am also handed a form with a list of personnel names and seniority numbers, this list denotes my next promotion to Senior Technical Officer, after seeing my name on the fourth sheet of paper, 'I ask what does this mean?'. He explains, 'all those people before will get promoted, which is alright because some will leave or even die!' Liking the idea of more salary, I work out that it will take five to eight years to get my next promotion. Now, I am not really concerned and at that time about being ambitious, but to think working here, within these walls for many years, may drive me crazy! It was then I decided to think about my future, given my qualifications, should I now start to look for other opportunities in other workplaces?

Feeling this transfer was like working in a factory and very noisy, I think about a role that would see me travelling around, the Post Office would not let me transfer back into external maintenance or installing phones as I was now 'over qualified'. I also looked at joining British Rail as a signalling engineer, they used similar equipment and their own telephony systems at the time, a lot of shift work, which does have financial advantages, but that had very unsociable hours. After the deregulation of the telecoms industry starts in the 1970s, private companies are now springing up and installing equipment and switchboards but don't pay as much. I failed one interview for a new telecoms company and that knocked my confidence slightly.

By luck, I see an advert in the London Evening News, advertising for Customer Engineers, to maintain and repair electromechanical and electronic equipment within London postcodes, it's a company called IBM UK Limited, with a head office on Chiswick High Street - I have never heard of them, but mustering up some courage, I ring the number and ask for an application form.

⁂⁂⁂

In the meantime my love life yet again is on a very bumpy road with Susan, I start to think 'is it me?', 'am I doing something wrong in this relationship?'. I still see her but my heart is not really in it and I believe neither was hers, we never really plan anything, but still go out socially with other couples. I tell her about work opportunities and advises me 'Perhaps you should be more ambitious', which at least makes me think about it. I am sure at that time I still lacked confidence and have this shell of not letting anybody in, I really struggle to have empathy with anyone, I am not very loyal to anyone or anything, except the music, did I sometimes use people or did they use me? – or am I just worried about getting let down by any type of relationship. Still trying to compartmentalise with everything going on, I am sure it wasn't good, but it seemed to work for me. When I was younger and found out about my father I was such an angry young boy and held things in, not liking confrontation, easier to turn my back and ignore many issues. I feel deep down inside, perhaps I know, I should just walk away from this long term relationship.

I am still getting letters and phone calls from Janet in Yorkshire, her letter drops onto the front door mat, I recognise the writing. Peeling the flap back, I start to read, that she has some exciting news for me, managing to get a job with one of the major banks and will be moving to London, hoping we can make OUR relationship more permanent! My mind races, how is this going to work, I have this relationship, albeit a bit shaky, but I have one! Why oh why, did I get myself into this mess?

That following night she calls me, Susan is around my house, we are in the lounge, as soon as I hear the phone, I rush to pick it up in the hall, trying to nonchalantly to close the lounge door behind me, as I hear Janet's voice. Asking 'did you get my letter?', she is so excited about coming to live in London, telling me when she is arriving by train and can I to meet her at Kings Cross the following Saturday, gulp! After a couple of minutes of one word answers, I make my excuses and pretend I am going out and will call back tomorrow. As I return to the front room Susan says 'Who was that?', sheepishly, I say 'Oh, it was Danny, seeing if I want to go out next Saturday, is that OK?.'

⁂

Meanwhile my mother is in the best place mentally in her new full time job as a book keeper at Littlewoods. She is now part of her offices social scene, with other single younger ladies and divorcees. Every Tuesday night she meets up and they take themselves to a pub in East Molesey and a new concept of a Divorced, Separates and Singles, a gathering known as a DSS Club or to the odd predatory young lad who also signed up – a 'Grab A Grannie Evening!' as it was called at the time.

It was my 21st birthday, she tells me to meet her after work and we will go out for a meal. She presents me with this lovely gold Tissot Seastar self winding watch – she is just as happy to give it and I am to receive it, never seen her so happy and positive, it's great to see. That watch is still in my possession today, I think of her when I wear it or see it in my drawer.

Receiving a letter and seeing an IBM logo on the envelope, it's not a rejection but an invite for an interview, the following week. Now in those days, researching a company wasn't easy, went to the public library and index cards, an encyclopaedia, Kelly's or other business directories. It's a US company, that manufacturers and has been providing computers and office equipment since the 1960s, providing NASA with high performance computing for the moon landing and before that, time keeping products, my only knowledge of that type of equipment, was perhaps from a James Bond film or watching The Man From Uncle, with flashing lights and spinning tapes.

Taking a day's sick or a 'Whitley' as they called it, on the day of the interview, I am so nervous, Mum wishes me good luck and as always told me, 'You can only do and try your best, listen to any questions, take your time to answer. I arrive in Chiswick and see this skyscraper of a building above Gunnersbury Tube Station, walking into the reception; the company is not on one floor but all 17 floors! I am led to a room and initially interviewed by this smartly dressed lady, my application form in hand, she notes that I am 'single', asking whether I am 'engaged' and or if I have a long term relationship and 'courting', thinking this may impact my flexibility on travel or relocation I say NO. A frown appears on her face and she says 'That's a shame, first of all looking at your age of just 21, you are so young, we generally like to take people on, who are settled in their home life, preferably married, around their mid-twenties.' I enquire, 'Why?', holding an employee's handbook up, she explains, 'We pride ourselves at IBM, being a cradle to the grave type organisation, we are non-trade union, we offer a great deal of benefits, not only to our employees, but extended to their families, with sports and social clubs, family dinners, children's Christmas parties, generous pay packages, pensions, death in service payments, shopping, holiday and hotel discounts.'

'That's nice', I say not really understanding any of it.

I am led to another room, now feeling very nervous, first to take part in an aptitude written test for 45 minutes and then a practical test in the next room displaying boards with an array of electro-mechanical equipment, containing wiring, relay switching, feeler gauges. The task was to go through these boards and identify any faults or issues, something that I should understand, hopefully.

Being sent to a room to wait afterwards, after a short time, two out of six of us are asked to go to another room to be interviewed again. A Customer Engineering manager is sent in, asking me various questions, car, driving licences, he explains that the role will include travelling to offices to fix typewriters and dictation equipment, around London post codes, he notes where I live and that IBM has an office above Richmond train station.

With four years a working in a telephone exchange and college, he asks whether I have dealt with the public. Referring back to my greengrocer delivery boy days and working on the engineering desk answering and helping subscribers, I confirm I have and just 'blag it' being asked more questions, as many a council house lad did then! As he wraps up the interview, he looks at me, I have a shirt, cardigan and trousers on, along with my loafers. He asks, 'do I ever wear a suit, shirt and tie?'. Thinking of my tonic mohair suits I used to own, I say 'Yes'. Now if anybody remembers this period of the mid 70s, you will recall, we grew our hair slightly longer, some lads looked good with it and some looked a bit iffy, as always mine could be better! I have some photo's from that time and my hair styles are something to be laughed at, basically!

He asks, 'How would you feel, we have strict guidelines, about dress and being smart, you will represent IBM in front of all of our customers, we will require you to wear a navy blue suit, keep the jacket on at times in customers offices, a white shirt and tie, polished black shoes and looking at my hair, 'it has to be off the collar'. As any Soul Boy would know, we don't mind smart and we do it well, any excuse to dress up! 'Not a problem, I say'.

He shakes my hand and says, 'We don't keep people waiting, you will know by the end of the week if your application was successful'. 'Any questions?'. I am so shy, I should have asked about salary, holidays allowance and training, damn I think, has that spoiled my chances?

⁂⁂⁂

1974, also gave us some interesting soulcial history, a band had formed in 1972, some as sessions musicians on Chuck Berry's 'My Ding A Ling' and with various bands, playing together at local colleges. Moving separately to London and meeting by chance at a music concert, they decided to arrange a get together with their instruments and jam. It's said, that a friend who was listening to them play, remarked, "This is too much for an average white man!", the band name was born, AWB had arrived. Their initial first break came, when supporting Eric Clapton, even after their first album sold badly, Clapton's tour manager Bruce McCaskill liked the sound and with borrowed finance took them to The States, where they signed with Atlantic Records. Relocating to Los Angeles and working with the famous music producer Arif Mardin and recording in New York City and Miami produced that other plain covered 'White Album', along with The Beatles and Donald Byrd's covers! As history showed, 'Pick Up The Pieces' reached No 1 on the US Hot Billboard Chart and No 6 in the album and singles UK charts in early 1975. In respect of that success of that six man white Scottish band from around Dundee, James Brown's backing band, The JBs recorded a 'reply' song called 'Pick Up The Pieces – One More Time' under the cheeky name of AABB - Above Average Black Band. That AWB album also saw The Brecker Brothers and Ralf McDonald contributing. Sadly, in September 1974 just a month after the album release, Robbie McKintosh died of a heroin overdose at a LA party.

For me, Average White Band are one of the original Brit Funk bands along with The Equals and their 1970 hit, Black Skinned Blue Eyed Boys, from the music I had access too. Another Brit band, The Olympics Players also surprised us with club sounds and in that year they kicked off with Do It Over followed by Grab It and had UK and US hits for the rest of the 1970s. One band member Pete Wingfield, soul reviewer at Melody Maker, producer and musician had a hit in 1975 with 'Eighteen With A Bullet', making number 7 in the charts. He also worked with BB King, Patti LaBelle, Van Morrison, Colin Blunstone, The Dexy's and the song Tribute by The Pasadena's was written by Wingfield, not bad for a lad from Liphook In Surrey.

In October 1974 and after signing the famous yellow form of The Official Secrets Act, I resign and released from Post Office Telephones, to start with IBM. An organisation I joined in 1969, eventually became British Telecom (BT), formed in 1980 and now independent of The Post Office in 1981. Being privatised in 1984, when 50.2% of its shares (3000 million) were offered to the public and employees, institutions and the general public. At one stage a £500 investment gave you a £4000 return, igniting people's interest in holding stock and shares in the booming early 1980s, much promoted and spoken about by Mrs Thatcher. Privatisation saw advertising from Buzby and Beattie.

In November 1974, I start at IBM, dressed in a white button down Ben Sherman, that I haven't worn for some time, striped tie, navy blue suit, a pair of Ivy Shop Royals, I report to an IBM office in St John's Wood for three months of training, very near to Lords Cricket Ground. Using then state of the art training aids, we have our own cubicle, a mini-projector and headphones, a film shows and describes the equipment and how it works and what we will repair, dissembling, assembling and adjusting you also have the ability to shuffle back, using a foot control. The word 'nomenclature' in an American accent still makes me chuckle - the meaning, the scientific or laboratory naming of things; every part had an interesting name. We learn about two types, one the famous 'golfball' typewriter, a head that spun around up and down using clever fly by wire engineering, the second one a 'typebar' style, powered to the paper with a spinning rubber roller. Also dictation equipment that used magnetic belts for recording, mostly used in London solicitor's officers both desktop and portables.

Over my time as an IBM Customer Engineer from 1974-83, I was trained in various desk top, typing pool, print shop equipment, all on its way to using and experimenting with technology, magnetic tape, floppy disks and drives, that would eventually involve into IBM Desktop PC's and electronic office equipment for small and medium businesses – the level of training was intense and always thorough with IBM.

If I tell you that a Self Correcting IBM Selectric 82C Golfball Typewriter was £875 in 1976, the value in today's money it's over £5000! On the computing side a mainframe could cost the equivalent of £10 million today, water cooled and could fill a basement, the profits were huge from the hardware and especially software and licensing costs at the time. Interestingly, you may have more processing power on your smartphone today, than some of those mainframe computers from the early 70s. At that time computing was very profitable, but it did change dramatically the administration environment of many companies and allowed them to work more efficiently and save costs. IBM would bundle their software and it would be very expensive, a legal challenge was bought by other hardware manufacturers at the time, but it was difficult to find a lawyer or a judge who didn't have IBM shares! The Anti-Trust action from the US Government lasted for some 13 years and was eventually withdrawn as 'without merit'!

Those increasing IBM profits were reflected in the way they looked after their employees, with a great basic salary and in a time, the 70's saw growing unemployment, unrest and other social issue's coming to the fore. Pay rises were generous, they used this system, of giving you targets at the start of the year, which you discuss and agree on, they used a merit rating system between one and four. If you reached your targets and even over performed, you could achieve 10-15% pay rise each year along with promotion levels with higher pay bands! They worked you very hard with long days but you were rewarded for the effort, throughout my career of 32 years and going into midrange computing sales, other projects and worldwide travel, I never stop thinking how lucky I was to take up a career at IBM at that time of growing technology within the business world and at sometimes even believing I had 'imposter syndrome' and someone would catch me out one day. In 1997, IBM were preparing for the Millennium Change or 'Bug' as it was nicknamed, unbelievably I was given the role of leading a project and setting the strategy to make sure our base of installed mid-range computer businesses didn't suffer from any non-information from IBM. Basically we didn't know and couldn't test it, with internal clocks in hardware and software changing from '99 to '00, would systems believe its 1st January 1900 when it was 2000? Not being grammar, privately or Oxbridge educated, my council house training turned a confusing, complicated or difficult situation into simple form by breaking down the processes. The campaign was adopted by other countries and successfully rolled out across the America's and Europe. I even presented to Senior Vice Presidents in IBM offices on Madison Avenue, New York and two nights in a hotel on Fifth Avenue – to me, the epitome of 'Imposter Syndrome', I thought, as I received a Global cash award, presented to me by Fiona Bruce at a Top Performers event in Morocco! A simple council house case of just 'blagging' it?

⁂

The IBM car allowance of £25 a month together with a rate per business mile to offset running costs, was good but in '74 my Mark 1 Cortina was on its last legs. As you probably remember at this time, the British Car Industry is beset with engineering, assembly, component and material issues, quality control, strikes, and union disputes. The UK Government were propping up the industry financially needing to drive more sales and registrations. Tax benefits on leasing charges made it easier for companies to lease or buy fleet vehicles at large discounts, known too many of us a 'company car scheme'. I am given a letter by my manager John Howe (the same nice man who interviewed me) at the IBM Office in Richmond saying they are introducing a company car scheme and I would qualify. A new car every two years and free, only got to pay for personal petrol usage – a dream situation for any 21 year old. I choose a royal blue Triumph Toledo – reg. JLH 640N – one of the main reasons, that I liked the wood effect dashboard and instrument panel, it reminded of my brothers Triumph Spitfire and came with a radio cassette player! I could have also chosen a 1.3 Cortina Mk 3 but wasn't even a 'L', plastic everywhere, steel wheels and hideously under powered for a big car, a Fiat Miafiori, nice exhaust sound, but nothing else as it fell apart, or the new Vauxhall Cavalier based on the Opel – but didn't like the brand or the new Austin Allegro, badly built and 15 miles to the gallon (so bad had its own average mileage rate after complaints).

My territory, was based on postcodes from starting at Putney Bridge, SW3,5,6,7,10,W2,W5,W8,W9,W10,W11 and NW2,6,10. Park Royal NW10 trading estate was the busiest, big industry names, one being Guinness, the UK headquarters outside of Dublin, with the smell of burning roast barley, hops and ale yeast at 8.30am in the morning is not good on the nostrils and stomach, the benefits of looking after this company was the large typing pool and staff shop. There were about 150 to 200 women and girls in a large room in rows of desks. I am still very shy, especially if an attractive young lady looks at me I go will go scarlet. The typing pool supervisor or 'Matron' as they called her, would report any faults sitting at the front, I would have to walk between all these tightly packed desks. Not only would I get some remarks about anything, but some of the older ladies, would put handbags in my way, trip or nudge me, as I slalom my way through their desks and ask me to look at their typewriter. Strangely, I would meet some of these girls in London nightclubs over that period.

London SW6, W11, W14 and Kensal Green W10 had lots of record companies, Trojan being one of them just before it closed. They were all so exciting and such young staff and always good fun calling on their offices and given promotional merchandise. Virgin Records and Tapes on Notting Hill Gate starting a record company later, the Virgin name came about as they were all 'virgins in business' at the time and a 'startup' company. I believe, they had an office just off All Saints Road, fewer yellow lines and easier to park then, little kids would surround my shiny new car as pulling up and ask if 'Do you want your car looking after, Mister, because things happen!', 'What things?' I replied, "Cos hub caps and wheels disappear Man!". They were so cheeky I offered them 20p, they said 50p!

One record company or office in the area and it might have been Island Records was staffed with which seemed mainly Rastafarians, one late afternoon after being called to a typewriter fault, I entered to a fug of weed, that was the most happiest I have been trying to fix a fault, but wasn't good for my concentration!

The postcodes, many of them are were where many social and TV celebrities lived, the start of gentrification in the 70s, especially around SW3, SW5, SW6 and SW10, the closeness of the river, BBC and London TV Studios. An IBM Golfball typewriter was like having latest smartphone for typewriter technology, ease of use, speed and branding all contributed, it even had a ribbon cassette that clipped in, to keep fingers clean. Even to this day you will see the product in 70s dramas and films, sitting on desks. I have been in the house of Janet Street Porter, James Hunt, Zandra Rhodes studio's in W14 in the Depository on the A4 Cromwell Road, many authors and writers around Parsons Green, Fulham and Chelsea like Penny Vincenze, a famous society chronicler and story teller. A&M Records in New Kings Road was really a good customer, one office covered PR and often had bands in, one day in 1977, I am fixing the PA's typewriter and some young guys come in, I nod as they go through to an office, I ask who they were and she replies they are called The Police, she hands me a promo single, you know with a big A printed on it, I said 'Doesn't sound as if it's my type of music?' She asks me, what I like and I say 'Soul, R&B, Jazz Funk', from under her desk she pulls a pre-release copies of a new band called The Brothers Johnson and one from Herb Alpert, holes punched in sleeve and a label saying – Promotional Copy Only, not for resale, a quick look through Blues & Soul, I would check releases on A&M, she would reserve one for me for the rest of the 70s. Little did I know at that time, the A in A&M stood for Alpert and M for Jerry Moss founders of the label.

So many factories around Park Royal had staff shops, they would always give me access to products, another being Walls meats and ice creams, lager beer from Harp, brewed by Guinness, biscuit factories, anybody living in that area, will remember the aromas of baking and food factories during the day. Mulliner Park Ward were coachbuilders who finished Rolls Royce and Bentley interiors, along with Wood and Pickett who customised Mini's mostly for celebrities and the new money. Electronics Companies galore with some later growing into global industries.

What I enjoyed at that time was the company's senior managers always asking me what it's like working for IBM as its roots were in the Mormon culture and what that meant. However we did have alcohol in our subsidised Social Clubs at Syon Lane and Greenford, even a nine hole golf course! For a few years I was the IBM London Golf Society Club Captain in the 1990s, the power of the brand would allow us to play at some of the most prestigious golf clubs around the home counties.

One of the more interesting calls I had and still remember it well, was to a Mr Nicholas Henty-Dodd at a small top flat in Edith Grove, SW10, opposite number No.102, where The Rolling Stones first lived in the London Swingin' 60s, buzzing me in, I climbed the stairs of these impressive white Stucco houses of five floors, mostly then all converted into flats. He has a Golfball typewriter and is writing a memoir, I start conversing asking about the subject and he says 'Don't you recognise me?', not wanting to sound rude I say 'You look very familiar' "I was...I am Simon Dee". Remembering, Dee Time on a Saturday evening and his popularity in the late 1960s, but I should have asked about him opening the early Birds Nest locations, if I had known. He told me about a few job offers and perhaps finding fame again, but it was quite sad in a way, he looked like life had been drained from him. Not having a contract with us and I had to give him a bill, he never ever paid it, we gave it to debt collectors and I wasn't allowed to attend after that.

You could have five or ten calls a day, it was mad sometimes, driving around looking for parking spaces and meters, I always put a sign in the car window "IBM Engineer on Emergency Call". Even around Knightsbridge and then of course then Traffic Wardens worked for the local councils and were not on any form of targets and just kept the traffic moving, issuing tickets on expired parking meters. And I got to know them by name in some areas, chatting often.

Still going out a lot in the week and my workload, it was always very tiring especially after a late night, at lunchtimes I would recline the seat and have a nap in the car. Always parking just off Ladbroke Grove in Elgin Crescent on most days, I was friendly with the local Traffic Warden, who never gave me a ticket on a yellow line. We had a deal, if he sees me sleeping in my car after 2pm, he must wake me up, by tapping on the car window! At that time IBM issued phone cards to use in telephone boxes to use and pick up your calls, you didn't insert it, you just read out numbers to the operator. When you got through to the call dispatcher and no calls on my territory, the options were to do maintenance or help other engineers, but I would take this opportunity to hot-foot it, parking outside on a yellow line and run into All Ears Record Shop on Library Parade, Craven Park, Harlesden NW10, to see what new imports they had or chosen that week from playlists. A rubber stamp on my import 45s shows the shop as being All Ears, which a fellow Soul Boy called Jerry Pike co-managed! Jerry along with his partner at Elite Records and an original member of Atmosfear, who he also produced. Sadly, Jerry passed away in early 2021, he thankfully convinced me to buy many 45s and 12"s. The import albums were always shrunk wrapped, being £3.50 or £4, as well as using Contempo in Hanway Street, it was a good source of collecting from around 74-78 for me. Always a good selection and sounds from that week that were playing in the London clubs, I would go in for one and get upsold to three or four!

⁂

My love life is now getting very complicated, mostly from a point of burying my head and probably not being honest to anyone. After meeting the girl from Yorkshire at Kings Cross and settling her into her flat in Holborn, I meet her sometimes midweek at a Birds Nest (Hunters), North Kensington and she even stayed at my house for the odd night, to the anger of my mother, wondering what's going on! I am now juggling two relationships, as well as nights out, with Pieter or Danny or both, chatting to young ladies in clubs and we arrange to meet them on nights out.

Now as I said previously, I am just an average lad, I am not tall, not one of the Faces, - Pieter was one of those, I like to think I dress well and was affable. But I am obviously making things difficult, by not thinking, not just for myself but for anybody around me and any relationships. I am good at making friends, but will also keep them at arm's length and committing.

My new job is intense; the amount of learning, administration and along with keeping your customers happy, you need to 'fix' their typewriter first time, you could not afford to get a 'callbacks' or 'recalls' or callout a Senior Engineer to help you resolve that fix or repair. You ran your own territory as a small business and if you get it right, your personal performance has financial rewards and benefits are huge. They also had incentives, one example was called and strangely named 'A Dinner For Two' which was a £20 (around £100 today!) payment into my new first ever account at National Westminster Bank, a treat for your partner for working hard and the long days, or getting a letter from a customer to say how polite or you did a good job. My first one was from Samuelson Film and Lighting in Barlby Road W10, a company that had been in the studio business and run by the camera man who filmed the Queen being crowned in 1953.

Additionally, around every Christmas time, you were invited to a 'Family Dinner', an overnight stay in a hotel with a dinner and dance, which you took your long suffering partner too and used as a networking session with senior managers and advancing your career and always interesting to see other workplace colleagues partners! All these benefits really worked, staff mostly, would always go that extra mile, were duly rewarded and worked a lifetime at the company before retirement. When I moved into IBM Sales in the early 1980s the incentives and rewards were unbelievable – obviously in a time that there was hardly any competition and the company dominated the commercial computing marketplace and was very profitable. The IBM brand was proven, their research and development delivered innovation and gave businesses a competitive edge – similar to the Apple brand and their tremendous growth in the first twenty years of the Noughties in a very profitable telephony and computing industry.

Juggling two relationships was very stupid, to my mother's displeasure, Janet from formerly Yorkshire but now London, would stay the odd weekend - as long as in the spare bedroom, Mum always insisted! - long term Susan lived ten miles away, so it didn't seem to be a problem or a chance of being caught out. My mother became very angry with me at that time, about how I was treating people and told me 'make your mind up!?', 'it was unfair and that's not how I bought you up to treat young ladies!' and 'it won't end well!'

Trying to rectify things, I avoid contact by phone from Janet, now getting letters asking "what am I (is she) doing wrong, there seems to be something stopping you (me) from committing to this relationship and she just doesn't understand – only you know, the sacrifices I made by moving down to London for you". The most gentlemanly thing to do, was to respond and to be honest, but as always, I just bury my head, hoping it will just go away. A couple of months pass, my long term relationship also becomes difficult and she delivers the news and I should have known it would eventually happen – we part company. As anybody knows, a very painful experience, you never really forget your real 'First Love', even if one of you or better still the both of you know, when going your separate ways and know it's the right thing to do.

Another few weeks pass, we do meet to give back items of clothing, personal belongings and loaned records etc, something inside of me hopes that it will perhaps work again one day and her feelings for me will come back as when we first met....but this time, it's not going to happen. I write to Janet to apologise for my behaviour in the hope now I can revive that relationship, however a few weeks later, a letter returns, postmarked Birmingham, saying that after the way I treated her, she 'decided to not wait anymore'. Meeting a lad in her accommodation in London she has moved back North, to be closer to their families and is now 'engaged to be married' the following year. My mother bit her tongue, trying hard not to say 'don't say, I didn't warn you!', as always she was right 'it didn't end well'. Shot myself in the foot twice!

⁂⁂⁂

It's strange with music and definitely the lyrics which match your situation and mood, with the relationships and breakups that bring in the emotions when you hear it and you probably have your own. The O'Jays, The Love I Lost and the lyrics really resonated with me at that time, 'We love each other, but just can't get along, you go your way, I'll go mine....' - but did we ever make the right decisions in our relationships at such a young age, I believe we probably made more wrong than right choices.

1974, was a year that saw the three day working week, Britain entering the first post war recession and two general elections, a state of emergency in Northern Ireland is declared. The first McDonalds opens in Woolwich SE London to challenge the Wimpy Bars when peckish. More IRA and the Guildford Pubs bombings. ABBA won the Eurovision Song Contest with Waterloo, taking place at The Dome, Brighton and hosted by Katie Boyle. In politics a narrow win for Harold Wilson and the Labour Party, the growth of The National Front, catching 10% of the votes in some parts of London and Enoch Powell joining their ranks and became a candidate. The final episode of Month Pythons Flying Circus was aired. In sport, Manchester City's Dennis Law goal sends United to the second division, Bob Latchford becomes the most expensive player at £350,000 and Bill Shankly retires after 15 years at Liverpool after winning the FA Cup for the second time. The speed limit is reduced to 70 miles an hour to save fuel in the crisis.

Now single and throughout 1975, 76 and 77, my social scene is all, dating with young ladies now and again, more like 'just friends'. Invites to the cinema, a drink, a day out shopping or to the coast (reliable new car!) etc but also deciding that going out long term or trying to find the right person is perhaps something that I struggle with. Lucky enough, I am part of a wide group of people, with new work and previous friends from youth club days, so meeting up with someone is now relatively easy for me.

At home, my Mum is very happy that I that I am not 'two timing' anyone, anymore, but hoping that I will eventually meet a lovely young lady one day (her words!). However, we get a letter from Richmond Council, that our home is under occupied and that we will be offered alternative accommodation within the borough, anywhere from Barnes to far flung Hanworth! My mother must have had many memories, some good of raising her 'two boys' and some bad with my father's antics, but now in these later years, she is happy and content but to receive this letter, still must have come as a shock. The final paragraph says we will offer three places, if you do not accept any of these choices you will be evicted! My Mum inside must have been devastated, she loves her garden, her dear neighbours and friends, location and cannot imagine what it would be like, living somewhere else, especially across the river as Richmond is the only new London Borough to be divided by water. But as always Mum likes to be positive in life and doesn't let it show. I will also miss having memories of my 'box bedroom' above the stairwell, sitting on the windowsill looking out at the older kids playing outside on a summers night when younger, the lamp post outside, with an old bicycle tyre hanging on it, that allowed me to create finger shadows and 'Bunny' images on my wall, the weather forecast outlook, fog and snowflakes being highlighted in its street light glow, my Santa's Sack at the bottom of the bed at 5.30am on a cold Christmas morning, with ice ferns on the glass, my first record player and transistor. As for taking over my brothers 'Big Bedroom' for two years was a treat, a big wardrobe for my clothes and shoes, all my Hi-Fi equipment, Garrard turntable, Audiotronics amplifier and tuner, cassette deck, large Wharfedale speakers. A Realistic Graphic Equaliser from Lasky's that worked a treat on Donna Summers I Feel Love and Georgio Moroder's synthesiser introduction and the bass and for some reason of The Commodores Slippery When Wet album.

In a way, we ignore the letter and hope the council will forget us, but the council, delivers a second warning letter and another offer of a flat in Twickenham. However, by luck and going around to pick Danny up one evening, I realise that the two bedroom, third and fourth floor maisonette has just been vacated next door to him. Luckily my brother, who works for the council and knowing the housing manager and its officers, was able to get the keys for us to view. Thinking back, I must have sold the idea of a newish 10 year old flat with electric fan central heating downstairs, nearer the shops and now a London transport big red 71 bus now goes through the middle of the village, to her workplace in Kingston and park views from the kitchen, but selfishly it was handy being next door to my mate. Sad to think after nearly thirty years of moving into her brand new council house, with an inside toilet and a fireplace back boiler, which she moved into just before Christmas 1947, it must have been luxury with a garden, best friends and all the support given since the late 1940s. I would like to think it was the right thing to do hopefully, she lived there for a further 30 years, developed more close friendships especially with Norma Stacey next door, supporting each other in times of need later and Kit and Pad Mahoney, Danny's parents. It was literally a ten minute walk away from our old house I just hope she was happy with the relocation at the time, she never mentioned she wasn't, but that was my Mum, always finding the brightside!

We leave 2 Murray Road on the 21st October 1975, moving to 34 Bowes Lyon House Ham Close the rent and rates being £8.68 per week, (about £50 into today's value). Another link to myself, as a baby born then in Coronation week of 1953, that Queen Elizabeth The Queen's Mother, was born in 1900, into the Bowes Lyon family, reputedly in the original Forbes House on nearby Ham Common and just 300 yards from where my Gran Gertie was born on the same day, 3rd August 1900 in Evelyn Road. Forbes House was then the home of her maternal grandmother, her mother descended from a former Prime Minister William Cavendish-Bentinck, giving these three names to blocks of flats on Ham Close, built in the mid 1960s.

Our old house will always remind me of my Mum of course not for the bad times, but for the happy times we three shared in the 50s and 60s, but seeing her a lot happier in the mid-70s in her new flat sitting in the front room and relaxing, watching TV or reading now the Daily Express – she thought it was a little bit posher than the Daily Mirror.

When I did invite young ladies to our flat, it would always be around 11pm, after the pubs closed and playing my standards of Major Harris's 'Love Won't Let Me Wait', Donner Summers 'Love To Love You..', Bloodstones - 'Natural High' or another appropriate track on my in-car entertainment, driving back to mine 'for a coffee'. As we went into our 'lounge', with polite introductions to Mum, but she would always like to chat and ask lots of questions, where do you live, where do you work, where did you meet? My eyes would be rolling in that 'stop it, Mum' way. Next, I would be looking at Mum over the girls shoulder in that 'When are you going to bed!?' as you did or in hoping she would take the hint to leave us alone.

Offering a coffee to the young lady, Mum would say 'Can I have one also, please Graham?', sometimes changing her mind and saying 'No, it's OK I am going up now' and reminding me, 'Don't be late, you have work tomorrow!'. I am sure that she did it to wind me up, she had a wicked sense of humour - strange, I never ever remember taking a girl up to my bedroom when Mum was in the house, never seemed the correct thing to do, she coached me well! The following morning I would always have a review with my mother whether she liked the girl or had some reservations about any future relationship.

Giving a young lady a lift home, whether you were with a friend or on your own and pulling up outside their house or flat, was always an experience. You would stop, pull the handbrake on, switch the ignition off and of course with that backing track on car stereo still playing, especially now girls I am dating are a bit older, moving into flats and living alone or with friends was with hope and anticipation of that phrase, 'Do you want to come in for a coffee?'. Or the reverse of that in 'I would invite you in for a coffee, but my Dad wouldn't like it!' or 'Goodnight then, perhaps see you out somewhere next week?' followed by a light kiss on the cheek or some other rejection idiom! Let me tell you, that opportunity never happened many times, but you certainly remember those rollercoaster emotional experiences.

Everybody, now seems have a car, we may go out as a group, but would take two or three cars for more flexibility, this allowed you as a designated driver to give young ladies a lift home on your own and the others could get home in someone else's car. One night in a club, I met this lovely naturally attractive looking girl, well dressed and with a great Afro, after chatting for some of the night and having a couple of slow dances, I ask, fingers crossed 'Would you like a lift home, after?' Always a gamble, because like a London Cab driver who doesn't want to go the suburbs or South of The River, because it's impossible to get a fare back to Central London, you await the reply. To my surprise and talking to her friends she thankfully replies, 'Yes please, if you don't mind?' I follow this up again with, 'Where do you live?', 'Just off Kensington Road' she replies, I thought she had said 'Kennington', which is OK. But Kennington always bought back memories of when Danny and

I were invited 'back for coffee' to a tower block and when we went into the flat, looking like a squat, there were dirty knickers draped over radiators and piles of washing up in the sink, as we spied from the hallway, we looked at each other in that flick of the head 'let's get out of here now' and made excuses about starting an early shift, making our exit, making some hygiene assumptions! As we sit in the car, I check the address again, 'Kensington Road, SW7, just near Knightsbridge' she replies, as it's my work patch I know the area very well and we head off, loaded the stereo with my 'seduction' cassette of Major Harris etc, she gives me more directions, pulling into Ennismore Gardens. In the 70s many celebrities of stage and screen and TV lived in and around this area with its mansion flats and grand houses - I was so impressed, she might be sharing a flat there. 'Ava Gardner lives alone, over there' - famous for being married to Frank Sinatra - she says nonchalantly. 'Do you want to come in for a coffee?' Trying not to rush the answer, I say 'That would be nice, if you don't mind?'. It's the early hours of the morning about two or three, we walk up a sweeping flight of steps to a massive front door and into a hallway the size of my former house, its five floors with a flat on every level, up one flight of stairs and she opens a front door. Trying to act cool and stop my jaw dropping, looking at lovely wooden floors and size, I ask 'Do you share, your family live here?'. 'No' she says, it's my father's London flat, the family home is just outside Guildford in the Surrey Hills'. This property was something else, high ceilings, massive windows, well decorated, great lighting, furnishings and a 26" TV! She prepares the coffee, not Maxwell House Instant like normal people, but freshly ground coffee beans, spooned into a percolator, you know the one, that was really posh then, brushed aluminium and sits on the stove, with a glass domed top and its bubbles when ready! We chat for an hour, she advances for a kiss, I respond of course, always a bit slow to read the signs!

She asks 'It's getting late, do you want to stay?'. Now I must be honest, besides it feeling like a scene from Candid Camera, I get very nervous and thinking 'have I got a condom in my wallet (the one from 1970!), or shall I ask if she is on The Pill?', the good and bad fairy are observing me from my shoulders, in a squeaky and swallowed voice I say 'Yes, that would be nice!' WHAT a response, WHAT a Twat! Still looking for the cameras, she says 'Must take off my makeup, got an early start in the morning'. Now being a little shy, I don't know if this is an invitation or am I going to be handed a blanket and pillow for the sofa, after a while, she asks me to switch off the lights and come into the bedroom. Saying she is very tired and must get some sleep, as working in Harvey Nichols, Knightsbridge and it's the start of the sales. For the next 30 minutes, I sit on the edge of the bed, not knowing if she wants me into jump in bed or what!? If I do approach her, will she push me away or will she make the first move. Very tired, I open one of my eyes, she looks asleep, my upright position turns into lying next to her on top of the bedding. I doze, then fall asleep, I wake as it starts to get light, I just quietly slip out of the flat and drive home, not understanding how it was supposed to end. We never exchanged phone numbers and I never saw her again.

The music, choice of clubs and record collecting seems to grow all the time, top tunes from the year 1975 for me are Shirley Browns 'Woman To Woman', 'Hello, may I speak to Barbara?' and the 'answer' song by Barbara Mason 'From His Woman To You' and that first line 'Barbara, this is Shirley'. Kool and The Gang just riding high, with Barry White, along with BT Express, War, The Ohio Players, EWF. The soul charts were Bumpin', Hustling, Ku Fu'ing, Getting Down, Boogie'ing. Entering the R&B Charts, The Glitter Bands, It Makes You Blind, even Errol browns Hot Chocolate's with You Sexy Thing, Elton John's Philadelphia Freedom arranged by Gene Page and a nod to the Philly Sound and its talents, People's Choice and Do It Anyway You Wanna. Another all time classic, Van McCoys The Hustle, Ben E King, the co-composer of Stand By Me and that funky Supernatural Thing.

About this time we are told that Sutton Scamps, 'buzzes' on a Tuesday night, positioned above a large shopping complex, chatting to some local ladies and word of mouth tells us about a pub in Cobham, The Running Mare well attended by likeminded youngsters and played great music. Scamps, would be remembered the following year for how many times the DJ spun the classic Candi Staton's 'Young Hearts Run Free'. Travelling with Pieter or Danny to 'The Runner', a largish family pub overlooking a green, surrounded by houses, not the sought of gathering place that you would expect in a small Surrey town, just off then the A3. Made up of lots of mixed groups of Soul Boys and Girls, Alan Attree, the publican and music played by his son Steve. Many would start the evening there for a quick refreshment before going out to London or any other club choice around the south east that night or just stay there for the evening.

Driving miles then just seemed to be the natural thing to do then in search of music and a good time. Everybody at 'The Runner' was very friendly, one evening we stand at the bar, a young lad starts chatting, asks where we are from and we are instantly welcomed into the group. This was the first time I met Malcolm Critchley who lives in nearby Epsom, a good looking lad with a blonde shock of hair cut in a wedge, that many of us have now and the odd moustache starts to appear, wasn't sure what look we were going for, with hair above your top lip! Malcolm was very affable and a mate to everyone it seems, who could certainly chat up the ladies and liked a good time. A couple of weeks later, he even volunteers to go on a double date with me, after taking a fancy to a young lady from Ripley called Gilly. That North Surrey, South London area also had so many venues, The Marquis of Granby, Scilly Isles roundabout, Esher, was another one nearby.

Meeting another young lady there and later in a music club on Wimbledon Broadway or The Hill, we dated a few times and we really getting on well together, cinema, drinks etc – taking her to see A Star Is Born around 1976, she lived just a tennis ball's throw from the famous All England Ground, in a massive detached house, inviting me for coffee one night. As we chatted, I asked what her father did, telling me he was a famous Iranian surgeon and her mother was also a renowned medical consultant. Her parents came in from a night at a West End theatre and dinner, the father immediately interviews me, about what my profession is and where I am from, he liked the idea of Richmond and my newish company car on the drive, but it quickly became obvious, that I would never ever be in a position to be a future son in law! The young lady was totally embarrassed, sees me to the hall and the front door, apologises profusely – I never hear from her again. The reason I remember this is because I rarely felt awkward with parents of any of the young ladies I dated from the council estates, calling or picking them up they were always very pleasant, besides the odd and sometimes rightly unhinged protective father or brother of course, from a previous experience that his daughter may have had. I learned a trick of being polite, complimenting and talking to their mothers initially, calling them by Mrs Surname and how lovely the house was decorated, or how nice they looked, 'is that your normal lipstick?', 'it's a great on you, that colour', or 'what a pretty daughter you have just like you', which always went down well.

Hanging about with Pieter was always good fun, he liked to do unusual things on a Saturday or Sunday daytime, if it wasn't shopping or record hunting. We both invested in Peter Powell Kites, a fad at that time, controlled by two strings for stunt flying, you could make it dive and then take it up again before hitting the ground, we would go to Hyde or Richmond Parks. Also Frisbee's were just arriving in the UK, championship and professional models were available, taking them on weekends away or days out on the coast. I am sure we even saw the first early imported skateboards being used on the South Bank or Kensington Palace Gardens, Albert Memorial and South Carriage pathways. But, of course always a game of football, somewhere in any London Park. Those days seemed to be about getting around and constantly being out, sometimes not getting home for one or two nights, if the mood took us, as many of you will remember. Talking to my mother in later life, when I asked her how I annoyed her, she mentioned the worry about where I had slept and wasn't home in the morning and how nice it was to hear 'my key' in the door on return.

Top tunes around that time was Double Exposure's, Ten Per Cent on Salsoul, one of the first commercially available 12" 45rpm single's pressing in volume and my first 12" purchase, a near ten minute version, remixed by Walter Gibbons and in my top ten all time favourites with Crown Heights Affair's, Dreamin' a Dream, that will always remind me of Ronnie Scott's along with The Blackbyrds, Walking In Rhythm and Kool and the Gang's Spirit of The Boogie.

12" Singles were to me an interesting and an unusual media, the ones to have and to buy, like the first EPs of The Beatles and the brightly coloured glossy sleeve of The Equals, Baby Come Back. 12" 45rpm pressings were originally and professionally mixed as promotional material for DJs and perhaps radio stations who wanted to play a longer version. Before this, a DJ might acquire two singles say, Ultra High Frequency's, 'Were On The Right Track' and segue together giving you eight minutes of play, switching from vocal Part 1 to instrumental Part 2 on two turntables, the advent of 'Disco', drove these sales and the need for longer cuts. Technically a 12" single spaces the grooves wider, giving a louder sound and a wider overall dynamic range and amplitude, perfect for dance floors and the music club environment.

In the late 1960s a young man called Tom Moulton, played taped and edited recorded tunes, thus extending the plays, for a trendy bar called The Sandpiper on Fire Island just off Long Island New York, a hangout for music loving well-off youngsters and Ivy Leaguers. Developing his skills into later mixing the 1975 debut album of Gloria Gaynor and its 'A' side into a nineteen minute Honey Bee, Never Can Say Goodbye, Reach Out I'll Be There, although devised by Moulton, along with double drum beats, but not credited to him at the time. Donna Summer's "Love To Love You Baby" was extended to nearly seventeen minutes, Double Exposure and the backing of The Salsoul Orchestra, followed up with My Love Is Free. Ten Per Cent strangely never made the popular UK charts, but a massive play in the clubs and topped the B&S charts. The Fatback

Band's, (Are You Ready) Do The Bus Stop then followed it up with Spanish Hustle reaching number 10 in UK.

Another artist got our attention that year and had four entries into the Top 100 UK Chart in 1975, an usual funky, driving beat sound with his first hit, South African Man which reached No 22, his second release Disco Stomp got to No 6 and Foot Stomping Music – of course, Hamilton Bohannon. A UK hit that got to No 6 was Shame, Shame, Shame by Shirley & Co, that went right across Europe, supposedly the first Pan-Euro Disco hit and produced by Sylvia Robinson using influences from a 1956 US and UK hit in 1963 of Bo Diddley's 'Pretty Thing', who also had a solo hit 'Pillow Talk'on that famous All Platinum Label that many of us have the compilation album in our collection somewhere. Sylvia is also reputed to be the driving force behind the later Hip Hop genre releases and hits by The Sugar Hill Gang with 'Rappers Delight' and Grandmaster Flash, she is credited with the title 'The Mother Of Hip Hop'. Sounding like a US performer, a female British soul artist has a massive hit after being getting noticed for her vocals on Al Matthews 'Fool' and that was Maxine Nightingale and 'Right Back Where We Started From' getting to number 8 in the UK and 2 in the US charts and in 1977 'Love Hit Me' making number 11, you could say all those three tracks sounded a little 'Northern' but it's great to see British artists have US success.

After the loss of Trojan, the famously recognisable 'clicking fingers' yellow label of Stax also goes out of business that year, even the success of Isaac Hayes and many other great artists at that time couldn't save it, the magnificent Woman To Woman was their last significant hit ever! It was a label that many a Soul Boy and Girl, looked for and had in their early Seventies collections and of course early compilations, like Soul Explosion from 1968 and Taking Your There in 1972, in my own collection. The Stax label was named after Jim Stewart and Estelle Axton, using the first two letters of their surnames in 1961, founded in 1957, their house band being Booker T and the MGs. In 1967 at the height of the Stax label success, many artists were to influence 70s Funk, 1968 saw Johnnie Taylor give them their biggest hit of 'Who's Making Love'.

Another year, the music of this genre just continues to improve. I am spending so much on vinyl, wanting the albums for the longer tracks, especially the Jazz Funk and the jazz influenced releases.

What can I say about the coming year of 1976, not only did it deliver the longest hottest summer ever for a generation, but the sounds and memories delivered with spending more time outside and driving to clubs with the sun going down and leaving and coming home when the sun was coming up, when the air was cooler. All this really added to the atmosphere of anybody spending time with fellow clubbers, whether you went to Margate or Bournemouth or both for bank holiday weekends and meeting in pubs before going out. Crackers, Jaws and Upstairs at Ronnie Scott's, were my go to clubs in London, mainly because of the amount of imports, looking through my personal collection, 1976 has some of my most memorable releases and tunes.

The great thing about the mid-70s, was the now more relaxed atmosphere of clubbing, being able to walk in, enjoy the sounds, know and chat to many people, so different from the late 60s and early 70s, where the tension of it possibly 'kicking off', hovered in the air most nights. Always on high alert to potential troublemakers and not even making eye contact, with lads you didn't know, there was the odd occasion where you just left a venue, because of tension, or a 'Crew' had arrived!

Personally what I remember from the mid-70s is that the soul crowd is very mixed, multi-racial, multicultural, along with more freedom to express yourself, certainly with an anything goes fashion period, it didn't matter what colour, creed or gender you may be, the gay scene was completely absorbed into the soul boy and soul girl culture and we conversely in theirs, all 'For the Love of Music' mainly and what it brought from fashion and its experiences and that meant hunting out clothing apparel, from charity shops to high end purchases.

For me, born in the early 1950s and very young in the early 60s, I was told homosexuality was illegal according to the law, naively not understanding anything, that is today categorised as LGBT+. We were told to keep away from men we saw in our nearby bushes and fields, men offering you sweets or even money in or near any public conveniences, you were instructed to run away and find a policeman! It wasn't until 1967 that the Law changed, it legalised homosexual acts, on the condition it was consensual, in private and between two men, aged 21 and over! Doesn't even mention women, - Dusty Springfield had to keep her private life hidden because of the impact on her fans and popularity, sadly – surprisingly, it was called the Sexual Offences Act 1967, even using the word 'offence', that meant an illegal act or a breach of the law, surely wasn't a good idea! Not only this, but the law only covered England and Wales, Scottish laws not until 1980 and Northern Ireland 1982!

Living in a village, of now some 6000 plus people at this time, with large council house estates and now a Wates private housing estate and younger families. In the 'older' part of Ham, there were adults whose grandparents were probably born just at the end Victorian times, when even piano legs were covered up and prudeness reigned and were so naive as to think other people should be as 'normal' as them – whatever 'normal' was or is. Literally nothing was talked about or explained, when it came to the body and mind, my mother once told me that she thought my brother would be delivered through her belly-button, before experiencing childbirth in the late 1940s! Like so many in communities then, set in their ways and thoughts – some didn't deliberately take a liberal approach (now the phrase unconsciously biased) to many things and followed their parent's attitudes, if any at all.

My mother had always said 'it doesn't matter about what other people thought and did, make up your own mind when it comes to judging people, but don't forget, everybody is human and has failings and feelings just like you'. We as a family, certainly knew with an absent father with a substantial criminal record, we were certainly subjected too and experienced forms of prejudice, the verbal views and glares of disdain from people in the village. I was even told later by an ex-classmate and a fellow youth club goer, that her father didn't like her being around me as my father was an 'ex-convict' or 'jailbird'! I cannot even try to understand and what it would have been like to be gay in those times and unable to be yourself, or come-out to your friends, let alone your parents.

Going to night clubs in the early 70s, meant that people were still being stopped at the door by bouncers, for not liking your face, your gender, the way you dressed, the colour of your skin or gay. But astute club owners and entrepreneurs, even DJs recognised that there was a place for Gay Clubs and its audience it would attract. The music was picked up, especially Disco and some now labelled as Gay Soul, bands like Dr Buzzards Original Savannah Band, Kid Creole and The Coconuts, Coati Mundi, El Coco and many others. A blend of Latino American rhythms, with some lyrics supporting multiculturism and ethnicity. Along with Disco Tex and The Sex-O-Lettes, Manhatten Transfer, Silvetti's Spring Rain, a twin set with Walter Murphy's Fifth of Beethoven, The Hustle, that reached number 3 in the UK charts and those big arrangement sounds of Van McCoy, who sadly passed at the age of 39 in 1979, after having a string of club hits and great success in the same decade, the Best of Van McCoy definitely found its way into my collection and many others that year.

But my memories really link the great established female vocalists, Gloria Gaynor, earlier with 'Never Can Say Goodbye' and that year 'How High The Moon' and of course another anthem track 'I Will Survive', two years later, endorsed by the gay scene and feminism. Renewed success for one lady in clubs, after taking to the big screen as Billie Holliday in Lady Sings The Blues and Mahogany, with residences at Caesars Palace in Las Vegas, made sense with her following and more beloved ballad renditions. Motown's move to get into film productions led by Berry Gordy and his promotion of Miss Ross globally and now as a film star. A new album, simply titled 'Diana Ross', initial track release of 'I Thought It Took A Little Time' and on its the way to being chart hit.

At the same time, what I would say, is a 'middle of the road' band who had a hit called 'Up, Up and Away' and other chart entries in the late 1960s, The 5th Dimension - of which two members were called Marilyn McCoo and Billy Davis Jnr, a married couple whose 'You Don't Have To Be A Star' got to number 7 in the UK later that year – had taken and recorded a track from her album called 'Love Hangover'. This track had already been picked up by DJs from Ms Ross's album, needless to say it was released for that performance, being nearly 8 minutes long, building up slowly until three minutes it kicks in, to establish itself as a favourite club and disco anthem that year along with many music industry awards, shaking Donna Summer's 'Queen of Disco' throne. Towards the end of the that year Motown, a Gamble and Huff cover, originally offered to Diana Ross as a follow up to 'Hangover' is reassigned to Thelma Houston 'Don't Leave Me This Way' reaching number 13 in the UK charts.

Coincidentally, the first time I heard both of these tracks was in Jaws night club, just off Leyton High Street in The East End, spun by Mark Roman, who had now left Crackers after a management change. Jaws, another great club and a very interesting place to park and leave my shiny new company car of a Ford Capri at last! Again cheeky young entrepreneurial lads asking for money to look after it and would even offer reserved car parking places outside using dustbins! These were all club sounds that promoted partner dancing or just pure Disco tracks, contributed to that scene unlike raw Funk or big baselines, that saw male club goers dominate the dance floor, unlike the Gay clubs.

As most people found out then, it was 'word of mouth' that suggested a new club to visit, our form of social media, your new telephone in the hall and handbills given out to crowds leaving clubs, following DJs and more adverts in Blues & Soul. We were told to 'check out' The Sombrero in Kensington High Street, the next Friday night we decided to go, lucky enough just the two of us and easier to get in, a bunch of lads would have no chance on first approach, if they didn't split up.

Now the great thing about this club was it was very relaxed for both the gay and also young ladies, most clubs had groups of young lads - some fuelled by alcohol or just being 'mouthy' - that would simply annoy the females who just wanted to dance with their friends, left alone and with gay couple's coming under verbal fire by some ignoramus. If two lads started to chat to two ladies in the Sombrero it was always interesting, it was like a guessing game, if they were or who was straight or gay. The first time we visited this club with its small blue lit dance floor and lots of seating around if I remember rightly. Danny went looking for the 'gents' that night, coming back, aghast he tells me there is only one toilet or 'unisex' that now hairdressers labelled their services, it was such an experience, the clothes, the style, the music and the dancing were certainly different, but what a great club. One of the biggest dance floor club hits was D.C. LaRue's Cathedrals a Disco track popular in the gay clubs of the US and then onto London by import, another early commercially available 12" single at the time. The lyrics pick up on urban sexuality of the time and the risk of one night stands, as always liked the tune, but didn't take in the lyrics at all then.

With Jazz Funk dominating many clubs and dance floors, 1976 seems like it's up there in my memories for someone who started their clubbing life slipping into The Castle Ballrooms post youth club, underage and seven years earlier. About this time, fashions around the London clubs were so diverse to a point of 'everything and anyone' can be fashionable, by wearing something that cost pennies to expensive Kings Road and Knightsbridge purchases, the more unusual the better.

Another subculture emerging, with its clothing roots at the lower end of Kings Road at Worlds End, the previous year Malcolm McLaren had returned from the US after briefly managing The New York Dolls and together with his partner, the daughter of a greengrocer from Derbyshire and born in 1941. After her family moved to Harrow, Middlesex in the late fifties, she completed just one year at the local Art College on a jewellery and silversmith course, she left to retrain as a primary school teacher. Earning income by making her own jewellery, selling from a market stall on Portobello Road, her name Vivienne Westwood. MacLaren born in Stoke Newington in 1949, raised by his grandmother after his parents divorced, when he was two, his mother re-marries into the rag-trade business in the East End, leaving school at 16 and over the next seven years, attended various art colleges, including St Martins, studying fashion and fine arts.

Westwoods outspoken words, "Seeing if one could put a spoke in the system", combined with McLarens, "To be bad is good, because to be good is simply so bloody boring", led to them opening their first shop Let It Rock in late 1971, in 1974 it was renamed SEX. With a combination of two of his customers and a shop assistant, he managed and formed the Sex Pistols, famously known for John Lyndon's 'Johnny Rotten' and Simon Ritchie's 'Sid Vicious'. Provoking reaction, shock and to inspire change in society, Westwood and MacLaren designed clothing for the bands stage wear and shows. Their shop that would include, mohair jumpers, slashed t-shirts and artwork, tartan wear with perhaps a hint to his Scottish heritage, reverse clothing with seams and large zips, footwear and much more - as anti-fashion statements? So very different to that Ivy League and College Boy look of the late 60s and early 70s, that many of us knew and certainly wore. Their shop became a meeting place for the early UK punk scene, gathering on the pavement and an opportunity for tourist's cameras.

For me, 1976 is a year of Anthems, a new band, Brass Construction releases the album 'Movin', now if those opening chords doesn't sound like a signal to hit the dance floor, then you should check your hearing and your coordination, unless it's been damaged by standing to close to speakers for many years! Followed by Changin' and a second album, their first album got to number 9 in the UK charts and the single number 23 in early 1976. Led by Randy Muller, a nine piece funk band heavy with the brass section, hence their name. Randy had previously arranged strings on BT Express's, Do It and Express and that success bought a signing to the United Artists label. Memories of The Bali Hai Streatham come to the fore. And of course from that year Crystal World, a real funky sound and dancer.

That summer two records stand out for different reasons, like AWB in 1974 we had another Brit band this time from Liverpool called The Real Thing reaching number 1 in the UK charts and number 28 in the US R&B Charts, making them the most successful British Black Soul band in the 70s with more hits. Married to both Clarence Carter and Jimmy James, the wonderful Candi Staton and important message in the lyrics for any young lady in that hot summer with Young Hearts Run Free and not forgetting that initial slow burner of Gil Scott-Heron's, The Bottle, which makes a social comment on alcohol and drug abuse, an infectious groove and a great flute solo by Brian Jackson and covered by Joe Bataan in 1975, Scott-Heron was said to influence many Rap and Hip Hop artists. Two records held hands in the UK chart at position 1 and 2, away from the heavy funk and jazz funk, sing-along records. Tavares's Heaven Must Be Missing An Angel and Dont Take Away The Music, a certain floor filler at the Sombrero. Scamps Sutton comes to mind, with these three great songs and those hot summer nights, all your windows open in your car and the stereo playing loudly on the way there and home.

Rose Royce's, Car Wash took us all to the 'pictures' again that year. I remember going to the Curzon Chelsea with a young lady from Camden and a group of lads were down the front singing along to the soundtrack. Should have been annoying, but was very funny, with the usherettes trying to make them be quiet, insisting she should dance with them to 'I Wanna Get Next To You', not to be confused with 'You Gonna Get Next To Me' by Bo and Ruth, when requesting to a DJ. A great music score Car Wash was written and produced by Norman Whitfield.

Arriving from a different planet came George Clinton and Parliament, any concert of theirs had to be seen, steam, rockets, mad scenery and the costumes, associated acts were Funkadelic and later Bootsy's Rubber Band with many famous names as members. The Brothers Johnsons Get The Funk Out Ma Face hits the clubs, followed by I'll Be Good To You, for me free from A&M's A&R people. Now and again a white rock band will cross over, with disco becoming increasingly popular, one night in a Pittsburgh music venue an audience member yells out, to the band on the stage, 'Are you white boys gonna play some funky music?!'. Rob Parrisi, founder, lead vocals and guitar took that thought away and ended up with topping both charts in the US and number 7 in the UK, with 'Play That Funky Music', Wild Cherry never had a hit again but left a goodie behind.

Two male artists with literally voices sound like warm runny chocolate and as smooth as velvet, from the Chitlin' Circuit, Arthur Prysock and his When Love Is New and Lou Rawls's, You'll Never Find Another Love Like Mine, a must to be included on a cassette recording to drive a lady home – my mother loved these two tracks, she described both voices as like a cup of warm chocolate. More and more Jazz artists are crossing over to the Funk and the dance floor, commercially driven in some cases, it sold more vinyl more lucrative in terms of financials and of course got them more touring gigs in the US, UK, Europe and globally.

The UK charts are now peppered with good music from soul and R&B, James Brown after a quiet period comes back with 'Get Up Offa That Thing!', the great Isley Brothers from 3+3, Live It Up, The Heat Is On and Harvest For The World that year, I keep asking myself, was 1976 the best year for this genre and for any Soul Boy or Girl, nearing their mid-20s? With existing artists like Stevie etc, making more great records and a plethora of new bands, artists and sounds, they just kept coming. Looking at my collection and research, I could just go on just listing popular sounds, you will have you own memories from this particular summer and a year of soul music excellence.

Those Sounds of 1976, make you feel good even now, like the warmth and sunshine we all shared that year!

⁂

Home life means we are now settled in to our new top floor maisonette flat. Unfortunately, I now go back to a very small bedroom, with only enough room for a single bed, my hi-fi and collection of records, which seems very cramped Although my mother, I think was missing our house and her garden, she seems to be very happy and sometimes now going out more than me! My bedroom overlooks the flats car park, being very tired and going to bed sometimes earlier and my mother not home after an evening out, I notice she is now being dropped off regularly by the same car. I challenge her often and ask is she now is 'courting', all she did was look at me and tap her finger on the right hand side of her nose in 'that's my business' way! I am now nearly 25, a very busy but great job, new all expenses paid Ford Capri, financially comfortable enough to pay my Mum's £40 a month council rent for her. Not bad, in exchange getting a great deal, I am living at home, on an all inclusive meals basis, heating, hot water, full laundry service, however my mother, who trained me early in life to do my own cooking and ironing, especially with five works shirts a week. I am now thinking 'the last thing I need is to have another man, rocking the boat' and perhaps muscling in, three's a crowd you know!

My best friend Danny, who I have been know since primary school, joining Cub, Scouts, football, youth club and going out clubbing from 16, always rode shotgun and now I have moved next door to him, it is very convenient. Besides other mates, I still go out two nights a week with him, locally to Richmond clubs, Cheekee Petes, The Madingley in Twickenham during the week or the Twickenham Birds Nest and to the West End, with Crackers, Global Village, Canvey Island, Lacy Lady or Jaws on a Friday. Named after Ritchie Family tune in 1976? The Best Disco In Town, The Lyceum.

In fact around this time, it was sometimes very hard to make our minds up where to go! 'Kit' or Mrs Mahoney to me, became my second Mum, always thinking I needed a good feed, every Friday night before going out she would make us her Big Fryday Up as we called it, an all day breakfast even down to fried bread and baked beans along with a choice of red or brown sauce. If driving to Canvey we probably wouldn't be home till about 4 or 5am, so the sustenance was great, although we may stop for a Kebab from a stall on Kew Bridge or failing that, a bowl of Kellogg's Cornflakes and cold milk or buttered toast on our return, in Danny's flat or mine. Again so tired, but trying to get a good lie in, before mum started vacuuming in my bedroom! That drive to The Goldmine could be at least a good hour plus, depending on the North Circular and its traffic, I had taped and we seemed to play every road trip that spring and summer, George 'Bad' Bensons album Breezin', entering the British Soul Album charts at number 50 and after topping the US Soul, Pop and Jazz charts, it would go on to be a triple platinum and a best seller Jazz album of all time. A new B&S review stated 'although George has been around for some years, I think this will help him breakthrough into the UK....'. 'Breezin' was composed by Bobby Womack, whose guitar work was not used on that final Benson recording. The album was bought some critical remarks from the jazz purists at the time, Gabor Szabo, who also covered it in 1971, intimated that Benson had left his jazz routes behind and sold out commercially, with his style of play! Breezin' was Bensons, unbelievably his fifteenth studio album. We were all blown away by the sound and that jazz guitar skill, I even purchased some of his previous albums because of that release.

Using self recorded tapes was now more common place, you would buy you album, instantly record it and listen mostly to the tapes in your car or your stereo on the cassette player. We are now seeing more soul sounds released on pre-recorded cassettes, some record companies are experimenting not even pressing a vinyl version, being told that this new medium will take over, like compact discs ten years later, However 8-track didn't seem to catch on from the early 70s being bulkier and more expensive and was superseded by cassette although the sound seemed better. Especially with the need for music on the move, portable and personal cassette players, the Sony Walkman was first announced and hit the marketplace in the late 70s. I couldn't afford the Sony one at the time, mine was a Sanyo!

That Summer of 1976 was so warm, it just went on and on. Most days my work entailed driving over Kew Bridge most days to get to the North Circular, at around rush hour, the traffic was always bad, exhaust fumes, hot blasts from lorry exhausts. Capital had Chris Dean hosting the morning show, he played the odd soul chart entry and of his choice, early mornings when slightly cooler, you hear might play The Isley's Harvest For The World and replays of Summer Breeze, from the Deniece Williams album, 'Free', from the year before Minnie Rippertons 'Lovin' You' all still remind of those hot sweaty days travelling around London. And even our British Disco, Princess shall I say - Tina Charles, got plays even in the clubs!

At IBM we had to wear our suits to every customer call and were never allowed to take the jacket off, many offices pleaded with me to take it off, with sweat running down my face standing over a typewriter, going back to my parked car at 80 degrees and opening that car door, a blast of hot air, the seats scorching your backside along with what it seemed were burns from a very hot steering wheel! At the end of July, we all received a memo, saying we could now remove our jackets, with the customers permission!

The heat wave of'76, was the second hottest on record for 350 years, a severe drought, water rationing in homes, June, July and August was the driest, sunniest and warmest in the 20th Century. London saw 15 consecutive days and nights it seemed of over 90F degrees, the top recorded temperature being nearly 97F. Tarmac melted on our streets, stand pipes were installed and heavy lorries created grooves in the road, we saw news clips of eggs being fried on car bonnets and cracked reservoir beds. Walking around London, carrying a tool case and wearing a suit was sometimes unbearable. We lads escaped a few times to the coast at the weekend, Bank Holidays in Bournemouth and for 'a days out', one memorable trip was West Wittering, being quite close, and a straight line at the end of the A3 and turn left. On one visit a terrific swarm of millions of ladybirds settled on the hedgerow in front of the beach, in an orange/red glow. It was unbelievable people panicked and locked themselves in a car or ran into the sea, like a scene from Jaws, on claims that they were being bitten! Just as the heatwave broke that September, the government appointed, laughingly a 'Minister For Drought', the rain then went on through until November!

The word 'Disco' now starts to appear everywhere in record titles, more disco entering the UK charts, more cross over from the Soul Clubs those bands we sort out as early imports, are now quickly released in the UK, with more bands touring and backing them up. Even Blues & Soul number 208 in September 1976 the sub-title is changed to - & Disco Music Review!

Dorothy Moore's, Misty Blue on the Contempo label, originally recorded in 1966, on a request from Clint Eastwood was used in that 1971 thriller Play Misty For Me and now a big hit reaching number 5 in the UK charts. Along with some top club sounds that week in December's Blues & Soul, issue number 215, best sellers in Hanway Street that fortnight was The Sex Pistols 'Anarchy in the UK'! Not sure if it was a joke, but they had already two gigs nearby at The 100 Club and The Marquee, changing the way bands acted on stage and the audiences reactions to their performance. I can only assume that Malcolm McLaren, their manager and well known around the West End clubs may have used Contempo as an outlet for their record and ticket sales, with some younger soul clubbing goers were picking up on the Punk Scene with it's fashion and music? Their single was banned by the BBC and many independent radio stations. They also appeared on early evening TV programme that December, attacking the Queen and conformity, obscenity ruled, declaring that teenagers and youngsters believed they had been let down by the state, investment was needed, bin-men on strike with rubbish piling up in the street, the education system failing many and a 'what's the point of trying attitude' building this new subculture - The Punk Movement. The band members hung about regularly on the

Kings Road, Chelsea, Westwoods and McLarens Too Fast To Live, Too Fast To Die shop, had crowds of Punks and tourists standing outside, on a Saturday afternoon as we passed. Setting the trend of the Punk Rock scene and anti-fashions. McLarens influence and The Sex Pistols became huge in this period, I think you know what happened to the members of the band, they were together for just thirty months – many bands followed in the same musical genre.

Now, I will be very honest and at nearly 25, being bought up in Richmond with the Mod, Ivy League, College Boy Look and 'The Ivy Shop'!. We liked a smart, neat, clean and sharp look, the right shoes, sharp creases in trousers and even wearing suits when going out. Now shopping at Stanley Adams, Johnsons, Katherine Hamnett, Browns, Fiorucci, and many other popular clothing shops in Oxford Street or Kings Road, Squire Shop, Village Gate, Cecil Gee, Just Men, Lord John etc. Punks use of Tartan, ripped t-shirts, S&M wear, safety pins, zips, interesting hair, seemed totally anti-fashion to me, now working for a very corporate IBM, alien and something, I never warmed too! Assume it might had been different if younger, no track record of clothing over the last decade, just wanting to look different or support a different way.

However the styles and spin offs of those fashion did enter the soul and reggae scene, youngsters who saw this anti-socialism followed the counterculture. Interestingly Bob Marley released 'Punky Reggae Party' after hearing The Clashes cover of Police and Thieves, Marleys song mentions The Damned, The Clash and The Jam, as well as The Wailers and Maytals. I can't remember owning a pair of plastic sandals, (Royal Navy issue, from Laurence Corner and were very popular) the main thing being, I wore them as a toddler and they gave you terrible blisters on heels and toes! Mind you I did buy and where leather and suede sandals at the time, to wear with denim from OshKosh B'Gosh and Smiths workers jeans or bib and brace, with the hammer loop and handy pockets, stripy tea shirts and blouson light jackets.

Punk music didn't do anything for me either, just sounded similar to untrained musicians, shouting at the top of their voices, with no skills at all. But for many they saw punk as hopefully the death knell of Pop and the arranged Disco music sound, bringing basic and raw music back to life, from what they perceived as homogenised new sounds and perhaps raising a finger or two to the establishment. For me personally, a million miles from The Salsoul Orchestra, Van McCoy or Tavares 'Don't Take Away The Music!' and those soulful classics.

My record buying seemed to have moved to more Jazz based funk even taking me into purchasing smoother vibe albums with dance tracks of Weather Report, Seawind, Alphonse Mouzon, Cleveland Eaton, Maynard Ferguson, Ronnie Laws, Donald Byrd, Blue Note, Tommy Stewart, Jimmy McGriff, Idris Muhammad, Eric Gale, Lalo Schiffrin, The Crusaders, even purchasing Miles Davies's Kind of Blues etc. Female vocal artists such as, Lolleata Holloway, Jean Carn, Randy Crawford, Deniece Williams and our own British Soul Lady Maxine Nightingale. a former session singer.

⁂

In 1976, the IRA bombings are still being felt around London and in Northern Ireland, direct rule passes to The British Parliament. The first commercial Concorde flight takes off from Heathrow to Bahrain. Music and The Brotherhood of Man win the Eurovision Song Contest with 'Save Your Kisses For Me' with six million copies sold worldwide it remains one of the best selling Eurovision singles ever! Sadly!

I wonder what would of happened, if a new British based funk band called Heatwave, who were just compiling their album, had been chosen that year to represent Britain. Of course, one of their band members, Rod Temperton from Cleethorpes, went onto write and work with such names of Rufus, The Brothers Johnson, Herbie Hancock, Quincy Jones and contribute to three numbers on Michael Jacksons, Off The Wall album in 1979 and Thriller in 1982. In January 1977 Heatwaves, Boogie Nights made it to number 2 in the UK charts and stayed around in the R&B/Soul charts for over three months. Another band like AWB, who deserve that early 'Brit Funk' recognition and applause.

On the back of this dance music, ranging from balladeers like Lou Rawls, Jazz Funkers like Roy Ayers, dancers like Vicki Sue Robinson's who recorded one of my early favourites of The Foundation's 'Baby Now That I Have Found You' and releases 'Turn The Beat Around', covered 20 years later by Gloria Estefan. Film soundtracks like Car Wash and Jaws from 1975, a great edge of your seat film and Jaws themed club sound releases. The TV themes composer Lalo Schriffin and his version of Jaws being one.

Soul music and the sounds are becoming more diverse and accepting of this genre, more entries into UK charts, like Jazz, Jazz Funk, new bands like Brass Construction to El Coco and many new venues are opening and the choice is becoming overwhelming amount of where to go. Pubs are having their functions rooms turned into clubs and a must have at the time was to have a DJ at any wedding, especially if a soul girl and boy were tying the knot, with a 'Evening Disco' reception.

⁂

As 1977 goes on, I think my mother is having more of a social life than me, she now brings a 'steady boyfriend' home, called Frank, for a coffee after a night out, he lives in Twickenham. The tables are now turned, if I am watching late night telly, she comes in and is now giving me the eye to go upstairs to bed, prompting me by saying 'busy day, you look tired, get some rest, why don't you go to bed?'. 'What's happening here?' Not sure that I was happy seeing another man in our home. Thinking it was *my* flat! I look at Frank, nice enough, smart, suit and tie, they had just been dancing – a Scotsman, about 6 foot 5 inches – at least some height would enter the family, my Mum is now 55 years old and her 'decree absolute' is now through, very happy with her lot and about time. It's great to see, but to me 'three's a crowd!' and I don't want to see her let down or hurt ever again.

In March that year, my Mum wants to have a 'serious' word with me, I wonder what it is, has she been recently diagnosed with an illness or some other issue and takes me back to being told off and about being grounded and sent to bed early for a week. She sits me down, in one way asking me, but in another way telling me, explaining that it's a serious relationship she is having, after eighteen months of seeing Frank and telling me that she loves him and they are thinking of getting engaged to be married in the not so far distant future!

There's a silent pause and my mother announces she needs me to and hesitates before saying 'Graham, I want you to think about leaving home, no rush but Franks lease runs out on his flat towards the end of the year and we have talked about living together?'. Now imagine my reaction, first of all, my thoughts are, 'where would I live?' swinging to, is he a 'confidence trickster?' and 'do you REALLY know him?'. Thinking selfishly, I want to 'kick off' and it's only costing me £40 a month, all inclusive!'. I think about putting some doubt in my mother's head about 'you've got a council flat and is he just using you for somewhere to live and get his feet under OUR table!' But then again, reluctantly, I think 'if he is genuine, Mum deserves to and should be happy to experience things she has never had, but always wanted with my old man. But, where the hell am I going to find a flat in an expensive town like Richmond in South West London. Staying in our village there would be few rentals if any, would I qualify for a one room council flat, should I look for a room to lodge in? Should I use this opportunity to make a change in my life? However, if I am really honest, I couldn't see myself remaining in a small village of Ham and setting up a home long term then, my feet are now starting to itch and now thinking of London. Convincing myself that having a 'bachelors' pad, could be quite cool. I start dreaming of parties with mates and/or inviting young ladies back for a coffee or even fine dining them, with the Capri parked outside!

But then I woke up to the reality - it's not going to cost me £40 a week! What would the sacrifice be? Buying records, clothes, going out? My dream turns into a sort of nightmare, but I am aware that lots of youngsters I have talked to in clubs and bars in town have now left home. For many and for some far worse off than me and associated reasons, losing their parents, abusive or a relationship where they didn't get on with family members or even their parents that had bought them into this world. As always, a little of burying my head, I kept quiet for a time and hope it was just a whim, but quickly my mother asks again the next weekend, 'have you looked into any rentals or made any enquiries yet?', I shrug my shoulders trying to look sad, but I know she is serious! I am now in my mid 20s and have been looked after by my mother domestically and emotionally for all of my life.

The following Monday morning I go to work and see my manager John, for a review. He quickly notices, I am a bit down and asks what's wrong, I explain the story, I tell him I have no savings or any money, even for a deposit. Smiling, he reaches to the bottom drawer of his desk and pulls out the Employees Handbook and says read the section on the IBM House Purchase Scheme. As I mentioned earlier, benefits in IBM were plentiful, the one reason they wanted to encourage and were 'a cradle to grave' organisation, as it would tie you in and you would be rewarded if you worked hard and delivered results. It's not rocket science, but if you wanted to improve yourself and get on, move up the social ladder by owning your own property at a relatively young age, it was a big advantage going forward, financially then getting into entry level purchases, especially one or two bedroom flats and to take a step on the housing ladder, seemed a great way to start. Let's face it, at that time, a young lad from a council estate, is not going to have much delivered on a silver platter, a trust fund or inherit an any estate is not guarantee! You will and should get out there and give it a go, something my Mum has always tried to instil into my brother and myself, being positive can sometimes bring luck. The more learn, practice and try things, the luckier you get!

The House Purchase scheme was relatively simple, IBM partnered and had investments with financial institutions like banks and Building Societies and insurance companies. You initially found a property, guided by a mortgage that you could afford, based upon your salary. If your multiplied annual income did not cover the mortgage advance or purchase price, IBM would act as guarantor and forecast your salary the next three to five years, along with taking out a life insurance policy to cover value of property, should something happen. There are up and down sides to this, committing medium and long term to IBM and monthly costs will stretch you in work rate, in trying to take on more responsibilities and workload, resulting in good pay rises.

Dilemma now, where to live? Always fancied living in London, Fulham, Parsons Green for Chelsea and the West End, but so expensive. Then looking in the local paper one week, I see a property, advertised as a top floor apartment, centrally heated, two bedroomed (mate or lodger thoughts?), balcony, carpeted, separate kitchen, garage, private estate with laundry room, gardens and porterage – sounds like a 'pad' to me – location Sheen Court, Sheen Road, Richmond, a couple of miles from Mum (food/ laundry?) just over Richmond Hill. The price £12,950! Outrageous!

About this time, the average UK house price was around £13,000 (£60,000 today) in the UK, average weekly pay £72 (£300), a loaf 19p (90p), gallon of petrol 77p (£3.50) and a pint cost 32p (£1.50)! A report, the year before said that UK life had improved by affordability, lower crime rates, investment and a narrowing wage gap between the sexes. A new Mk 4 Ford Cortina was nearly £2000 (£9000) but affordable on monthly payments for a lower middle class family.

Not sure at that time that I knew anybody that owned their own property at my age and still going clubbing, perhaps maybe a village lad that got married earlier and moved to up North. My brother, now a Supervisor had moved from a council owned flat on the Lower Richmond Road above the offices to the council yard. He had now got a mortgage but now had two children, making me an Uncle to Lisa born in 1974 and Joanne in 1976, but he had a family and now stability and moved to York Road Kingston – then more affordable than Richmond.

Chapter 12 – A Place of My Own

So in the summer of 1977, and to the background music of Deniece Williams' Free, ironically, I complete on my flat and leave home and I am now definitely in control of my own future. That summer and the Queens Silver Jubilee you would have listened to singles or albums, such as The Brothers Johnson Right On Time, Marvin Gaye and a rumour he may leave Motown after his Got To Give It Up album and didn't want to go the 'Disco' route, compounded by his divorce from Anna Gordy, tax problems, alimony, child support, its not a good time, but sets off to the UK and a concert at The London Palladium (and records his Live album), Marvin is seen in many London clubs while on this leg of his tour.

The Floaters, Players Association, Idris Muhammad, Slave, Wayne Henderson, Ramsey Lewis, Bootsy, Stevie, EWF, Jean Carn and the great sound of Bo Kirkland and Ruth Davis's 'You're Gonna Get Next To Me' very much a favourite in the clubs.

I never had many chattels, except my Garrard deck, amp, graphic equalizer, stereo radio/cassette recorder player, speakers, transistor radio and around 600 45s and albums, self and now even more pre recorded cassettes for the car (a bad choice later on in life as their ageing process and non-readable sleeve notes, should have bought the vinyl at the time!) oh, and my pile of Blues

& Soul's. Toothbrush, toiletries, a bottle of Aramis, Tabac and Aqua De Selva and of course a wardrobe of clothes, shirts, shoes, belts, suits, knitwear etc – but no wardrobe to keep them in!

As a moving out present, my mother gave me a canteen of cutlery and her utility furniture set of an extendable dining table and four chairs that she had saved up for an bought in 1950! A bookcase built at school and a lathe turned wooden fruit bowl, I had made in the woodwork lesson in school circa 1967/8, along with a pottery ashtray – with my name and Class 4AC written in pencil on the bottom (if you didn't do this, some scally lad might swap it for his!), some self-help books, one being How To Win Friends and Influence People and Beating Shyness and Self Assertiveness - yes still trying to overcome it! - two other school prize books and my school first year issued school Bible and a copy of a 1965 Guinness Book Of Records! Why?

Inventory of what to get. A TV, fridge, bed (first double of course!), wardrobe, plates, cups and saucers, a telephone line, settee or was it called a sofa then and couple of matching chairs. Kettle, tea pot etc etc. And add food to this - nightmare! This is not going to be financially easy, also waiting for me and nobody mentioned it but you also have to pay rates (council tax) and a service charge for hot water and heating, an extra £250 (£1100) a year! That night, I settle down on a borrowed Lilo, blankets and sheets from my former home, wondering how this is going to work out, but there's no going back now!

My outgoings from living at home go from 10% to now a huge 80%, things will have to change. At least I have a company car, no insurance, road tax, repair bills and I can claim back some fuel costs.

My buying records starts to slow down enormously, in a way I am more selective, the 12" Singles are more interesting from a length and musical sound, the wider grooves throwing out a better sound, smoother Jazz and Funk albums and female artists. My favourite 12" purchases after Ten Per Cent are Crown Heights

Affair's Dreamin' A Dream, Lenny Williams's Choosing You, La Pamplemousse, and Get Your Boom Boom – a French disco band.

Another club we visited was Roxy's in Covent Garden a bar and club, later changed to Chaguaramas and had a lot of live music also, some Punk bands if I remember rightly, Mark Roman attracting followers from Crackers to Jaws and other clubs.

George Power's lunchtime sessions are now very popular in Crackers, drawing many youngsters that bunked off from or work and they also had a night called Vortex (I think) where Punk bands would appear.

Down the A30 to Pantiles on a Friday night in Bagshot, after the odd trip to the Agincourt on a Thursday and made it regularly to Frenchies on a Sunday, both in Camberley. If you lived in the corner of North Surrey you also had Slough and The Cat Balou and many others.

The word Disco, really starts to take a grip and it seems everywhere, even a snack name! It's a thin line between soul dance sounds and dance music, mainly influenced by The Disco Scene in New York and London, for many R&B/Funk artists/bands this was and could be a money spinner, especially if the releases crossed over and charted.

In New York, earlier that spring of 1977, two guys receive financing to take over an ex-radio studio from CBS, named after their 52nd premises purchase in 1943 and called it Studio 52, the building originally opened in 1927 as the Gallo Opera House. Steve Rubell and Ian Strager renamed it Studio 54 after the street it stood on. Becoming famous, a venue for dressing up outrageously and a modern drug culture, it became slightly hedonistic and the place to go and to be seen. Gaining entry to any club, has always had it's issues, but if you were a well known celebrity it was easier to get in. Renowned for open drug use, the police sort ways to have it closed down.

On New Years Eve 1977, Grace Jones had invited Niles Rodgers and Bernard Edwards to Studio 54, but they are refused entry. This led to them later, writing 'Le Freak' because of its long waiting times to get in and the door being slammed on them, the bouncers shouting F*ck Off! A term that was replaced by 'Freak Out!' on the recording and lyrics of "Just come On Down, to Fifty Four". The owners boasted that the club, with its specially designed lighting and dance floor, had a turnover over of some $7 million dollars, causing the IRS to investigate, why such a large sum in such a short time, this lead to them finding that they had hidden some £2.5 million between them! In early 1980, Diana Ross and Liza Minelli serenaded the owners on its final closing night, Rubell and Schrager were later to be convicted of tax evasion and were sentenced to thirteen months in prison. It was sold and re-opened again in 1981. In 2017 Barak Obama granted Schrager a presidential pardon, Rubell had sadly passed away at age 45 in 1989 with AIDS.

1977 was a strange year for me, still going out, but friendship circles tend to breakdown in a way that people settle down, changing circumstances like careers, moving location, a long term relationship, club scene change, getting married or just getting older and tired, those late nights finally taking their toll, especially if you have a job that needs concentration, attention and never stops. My life was now affected by low finances, affordability and available cash.

One of the benefits of the soulboy and girl scene was that you made lots of friends, weekends away and clubbing you just got to know like minded people. I guess it goes back to my childhood, don't get me wrong I also like to chat and mix with a group of people, but I am also very happy with my own company - think it was a childhood thing - and also don't find being and living on my own an issue, in fact, it's easier nobody tells you what to do.

Thinking back, I believe I always had an issue bonding with others and was really bad at saying 'Let's meet up again, for a night out' and not following it up. That would even go for young ladies, I had met and perhaps would see them for a couple of weeks and for some reason I wanted out of any long term or close relationship, thinking I always needed an escape route from any emotions and was terrible at explaining my reasons for any breakup. Sometimes it was the young lady who recognised this trait and gave me the 'elbow' first – or got tired of me or the way I was. Today I might be considered 'Cold' and with little feelings

I would often go to a local pub, The Lass on Richmond Hill or even a club on my own and meet up with people from my village and Richmond and people you had met before. Later that summer, I really needed a holiday, my mother who since her divorce had taken a couple of coach touring breaks in the UK on her own and being very sociable, had always made friends and was invited by other couples to join them. I decide to follow her lead.

My mum is now acting like a Jewish Mother – but thankfully so happy in her new relationship – now desperate to see me settled down with a young lady, to get married have children and make her a grandma again, 'especially now you own your own property and have a good job, any girl would think you were a good catch!'. 'Why don't you join a social club or even The Young Liberal Party, you will meet lots of young single ladies or a DSS club, there were some nice girls there about your age and on their own!'.

Last minute holidays were just becoming a thing then, Bucket Shops and cheap unsold airline seats, they would list last minute foreign holidays that were unsold and at very keen prices, think it was called Martin Rooks. Below a hundred pounds half board and in Spain! Paid for with my newly acquired Access credit card or company American Express card! I book seven days in Majorca. I don't know if you have ever taken a holiday abroad on your own, if you are lacking confidence, but it can be quite scary, especially if you are on the shy side of things. However as I arrive in Palma, there's a group of five lads behind me that are quite noisy and excited to be going away, they were talking about clubbing and getting around. As I wait and told which coach to get on, and that phrase from the holiday rep of 'Just the one person travelling in your party, Mr Clark?', I board the bus and make my way to the back, the same lads are in the back row, acting as if on a school trip. One seat was remaining, next to one of them, he did that

"Awright mate!?" the thing that normally only London lads did. We start chatting and he asked where I came from, I say Richmond and he immediately says 'Have you been to Cheekee Pete's then?'. They came from Croydon I believe. It's now about 3am, picking up our room keys, I find my 'single' room that are always notoriously bad, this one in the basement, which looks like they had bricked up a corridor at one end, installed a shower and squeezed a camp bed in and so, so, so hot and next to the hot water boiler room!

Going down to breakfast the next morning, the lads are sitting down and looking at their sad first experience of a 'continental breakfast' sitting on a table, they invite me to join them, now guessing and knowing I am on a 'Johnnie No Mates!' break. They propose finding a cafe or restaurant where you can get an English fry up and kindly invite me, realising that I am on my own and not meeting up with anybody, then later to the beach and hang around with them for the rest of the week, real 'Souf' London hospitality.

What a great week I had, the clubs or should I say the Euro Disco's played some good stuff and obviously some euro trash. DJs from the UK were common and talked about the growing club scene in Ibiza – I wonder what happened to that! Like clubbing in town, groups of boys and girls mix, bought together by the music. One night we chatted to a group of six very attractive French girls with accents to die for, obviously impressed with a 'groupe de six garcons de Londres' and our accents and hang about with them for the remainder of the week. Turned out to be another very good lad's holiday.

On my return, my nights out are still happening, with local pubs and a weekly Friday Night Out with mate Dan or Pieter to Canvey or Ilford and other clubs but also The Running Mare in Chobham, where Malcolm and his friends always made us welcome, or a trip to Sutton Scamps.

I seem to really be buying less 45s now albums and cassettes occasionally, the main reason is that many artists, tended to release at least four tracks from the album, especially if it was a goodie, it seemed the most economical thing to do, with my new found low finances.

Spending more nights in because of the lack of money, after buying a three piece suite on interest free credit over three years, a double bed and a trip to MFI to buy a really badly made and self assembled flatpack wardrobe, that needed an engineering degree to put it together, with plenty of wooden dowels, screws left over, it still wobbled! I also return to MFI to buy a flatpack kitchen, with half the screws missing this time and bits left over after installing myself along with tiling!

Visiting Granada TV Rentals to hire a 22" television, really wanted but couldn't afford the 26" screen, which would have been a dream! Working as an IBM engineer there were some clever people around me, one lad (Ian Nutton) would make a box up with an old TV tuner and dial installed in it. The benefit of this is that you could watch, say TOTP or a film and play the sound through your stereo speakers in the same room! The first ever surround sound for me and so simple!

The late 70s, and staying in for more nights, the TV bought us loads of what I would say are great dramas and I think appealed to younger viewers especially my generation of lads having a massive following. From the UK, programmes like The Sweeney (from Sweeney Todd) based upon then the uncovering corrupt real life Flying Squad of the serious and organised crime, driving Ford Cortina's and Granada's and of course those now familiar Transits smashing into cardboard boxes around West London, stitching criminals up, using excessive force and firearms. At the end of the programme, our heroes DI Jack Reagan or DS George Carter shouting 'Your Nicked!!'. In real life, the Commander of The Flying Squad Kenneth Drury was imprisoned for eight years after being convicted on numerous counts of corruption, planting evidence at scenes of crime, false statements and much more. George Carter would later change his name to Terry McCann an ex-con, former boxer released from Wormwood Scrubs and employed and manipulated by Arthur Daley as a 'Minder'. Arthur -

and we all knew someone like him!, - ran a second hand car lot and part owner of The Winchester Club, again with similar locations and premises in West London, driving a Jaguar XJ6 and Terry and a white Ford Capri!

Now, talking about Capri's, The Professionals were the ultimate lads watch, loosely based on the real life MI5 they were agents for CI5. With Bodie and Doyle chasing and racing about in RS 2000 and a Mk ll and later Mark lll Capri 3.0S. My company car a blue 1.6L with spoked wheels was now fitted Pye two-way radio and a big whippy aerial on the roof, my mate Danny and I would pull alongside the odd young scally drivers in a car at the traffic lights, we assumed a Bodie and Doyle style and I would flash my photo work ID, that looked very official. Danny would pick up the handset of the radio, indicating to the 'perp' to pull over, looking shocked they slowed up, we accelerated away laughing our heads off! Childish for 25 year olds but good fun!

Most lads loved a 'motor' or a 'set of wheels'! These cars were featured and favoured by many. My mate Danny even had a Mark X Jaguar for a time and an American Muscle car – a Chevrolet Camaro, all very affordable at the time, not on fuel obviously at 10 or 12 miles to the gallon, but the ladies loved them. Malcolm, who we had met at The Runner in Chobham was in the car trade, I remember seeing his Camaro also. These TV programmes certainly came along way from one of my mother's favourite programmes of Dixon Of Dock Green that ran for over 20 years, depicting George Dixon, a kindly character and a local Bobby who you would like on your street and part of his 'beat' where you lived. He always opened the programme with an 'Evening All' and then the end standing outside Dock Green police station with a little moral statement and a sign off 'Goodnight All', tapping his helmet, we all felt that we could sleep safer in our beds that night. Unlike anything that was happening in some towns and cities in the late 70s, relationships with respect and policing were breaking down, further fuelled by government policies and perceived rightly in some cases with the lack of opportunity for work, a dislike of the police and much use of the 1824 Vagrancy Law, or 'Sus Law', stop and search process.

Many US mini-series are on our TV Channels now, often theme tunes would make it to playlists', covers or originals from Barretta and SWAT by Rhythm Heritage.

One that picked up a cult following, fuelled I remember by Chris Hill in the clubs and Greg Edwards on the radio at the height of its popularity was Rich Man, Poor Man based on the Jordache Brothers played by Peter Strauss and Nick Nolte, one a successful businessman and one who had turned to boxing to survive. However, their nemesis Falconetti is intent on murdering them. Campaigns of "I Hate Falconetti" with bumper and window stickers featured in the Lacy Lady car park! It had a massive following, Chris Hill even mentions as part of his playlist favourites that week in Blues & Soul tucked between Idris Muhammed's Could Heaven Ever Be Like This and Keep On Keeping On by Wayne Henderson – Falconnetti Lives by Annie Adams and Billy Jordache!

One series that really that had an impact on me and very much a learning curve at the time was the TV adaptation of Alex Haley's 1976 novel Roots: A Saga of an American Family. Putting it down to an embarrassing and my naive mindset at the time, the subject of the slave trade, sugar, cotton production and the labour required, it was the first time that I had an understanding of those times in the 17th Century. My only knowledge of slavery and suppression was gleaned from novels and films, such as Gone With The Wind, Too Kill A Mockingbird, Tom Sawyer, Huckleberry Finn, even Disney's Song Of The South, but I never really understood the situation some 300 years earlier. This mid 17th century time in history, just wasn't on our timetables or sadly the curriculum, although my knowledge of The Civil War from 1642-1651 is quite good, but from this period, you have to ask 'Why?' wasn't this used or included in any education then, perhaps things would have been different now if had, from an understanding point of view.

Trading triangularly and efficiently across the Atlantic and transporting 'goods' from England ports such as Bristol and in exchange for human cargo via the West Coast of Africa to the Americas and The West Indies, to cruelly work in cultivating, producing and the 'business process' of sending sugar, cotton and other commodities back to England making stake holders extremely rich, literally on the back of what was initially called 'indentured servants' under contract!

Sadly, estimates of over 12 million slaves made this journey with over 3 million dying on the journey or in holding compounds. Although the Slave Trade Act of 1807, prohibited the trading in The British Empire, however, it did not abolish the practice of slavery altogether, that wasn't until 1833. Sir William Wilberforce, a British politician and philanthropist who from 1787 was prominent in this first human rights campaign. Wilberforce died in 1833, the same year The Slavery Abolition Act stopped this barbaric trade within most of the British Empire.

In 1834, 800,000 slaves around The British Empire were deemed property, some 50,000 'Slave Owners' were shockingly paid out for their 'loss of property' receiving in compensation some £20 million – nearly £17 billion in today's money, since some of the payments were converted into government annuities, they lasted until 2015! Ironically, this 'compensation' literally financed, paved and built large houses and the streets of The West End and others parts of London and the UK where we clubbed, shopped and entertained ourselves in the 1970s.

As I grew older and hopefully gained some wisdom and empathy, I would like to think I understood a little more about this time in our history and what it meant to a future black generation. Being able to put myself in the place of a white working class lad from a council house, bought up by a single parent who tried to do her best in the 50s and 60s, with a jailbird father and all the issues and name calling that bought. But I will never understand what is was like and still be like, being bought up, in say Peckham, Shepherds Bush or Hackney in similar circumstances with black skin, or anybody that didn't look 'white normal' at the same time in the 1950s and 60s as me and in similar circumstances.

That period of Colonial History was embedded in our society then and today, whether in Britain or the US and what that resulted in, the awareness that Roots gave to me in the late 70s certainly helped me and many others to understand that period. Over the last few years, this knowledge has been supplemented by David Olusoga, a Professor of Public History at Manchester University, he has written some great books and its worth watching his documentaries, all very informative of those times.

⁂

About this time, my father who I have not seen each other for about seven years, contacts me out of the blue. He has found out that I work from an IBM office in Richmond, approaching the building and the receptionist, makes up a story and they thinking it is an emergency they give him my home phone number. One evening, I am shocked to silence, when I hear 'Hello Son". Honestly, if I ever saw him in the street, I would have crossed the road to avoid him, instead of slamming the phone down, I listen, as usual talks to me as if we are on good terms and have spoken just a week ago. But when you have those deep seated feelings that verge nearly on hatefulness, I am sick to my stomach, I answer, yes and no's to his questions and blurt out "What do you want, Dad?!". Asking me to meet up, telling me what a fool he has been all his married life and now he has heard that Mum is happy and enjoying life with someone else, he now wants to have a proper relationship with his sons. He asks and pleads, 'Let's meet up, just once, ten minutes in a pub near you, come on?' I relent and we meet in the Kew Gardens Hotel Pub, I enter, look around and see this man sitting at the bar, grey complexion, lined face, unshaven and a little unkempt, looking 70 not 55 years old, not the image I had of him from the past, he was always smart, suited and booted. He looks around, see's me as I approach him and says 'Buy us a drink, son, you look like me when I was your age' laughing, which immediately annoys me, NO 'Nice to see you', 'Sorry about the way I have treated your Mum and not being the best Dad', 'How are things?', 'What's happening in your life?'.

The last time I saw him, his fist was clenched and threatening to punch my mother, after that, he broke into our house he was locked out of, stole our Post Office Savings books, after forging cheques from his own Mother. He makes the conversation all about himself, not really listening, I offer to buy him a sandwich and another drink and say my 'Goodbye's'. He asks one more thing 'Any chance of lending me a tenner, Son?'. I reach for my wallet, take a twenty pound note out and slap it on the bar without any regret or remorse, I turn, don't look back and leave the pub. Forgiveness Last Finale, I wondered?

The next time I see him, is sixteen years later, the afternoon of 18th March 1993. My brother had called me to say he has been admitted to Kingston Hospital and is in serious failing health. I visit him, hooked up to monitors, I am not sure if he was looking for forgiveness of his wrong doings, but my emotional wall is in place. After some small talk, I leave to go home, he asks me if I will visit again, I don't directly answer.

At 5.30am the next morning, I get a call from my brother to say it won't be long before he passes, as I drive the sun is rising in that early spring morning with a covering of frost on the verges and trees, I watch the road with watery eyes, my mind takes me back, not to any happy times with him, but just to being constantly let down and never feeling that father son relationship that I saw my mates had in the village. I arrive at the hospital an hour later, he died at 6am, 30 minutes before I had arrived. I stare at his body lying in bed, I did share a tear, not really sure whether it was for him or for what we lost as a family and a husband to our Mum what should have been in our lives. He was 69, the death certificate states: heart and liver failure along with prostate cancer. His funeral had just three attendees, my brother and I and a man he drank with and lived next door in his bedsit on Kingston Hill.

He did leave us with one more final thing, a funeral bill of £1447!

***

At the back end of 1977, I will still take any opportunity to stand in any record store, Our Price, Tower Records or HMV - a huge selection - and check out the Soul/R&B labelled sections, now we have Jazz Funk and Disco Compilations added (I now will finally accept the word Disco, can be generally aligned with soul dance music as a genre), flipping through dozens of imports and UK released albums.

One album catches my eye, the tracks include Walter Murphy's Fifth Of Beethoven, MFSB's K-Jee, Disco Inferno by Tavares, Kool and The Gang's Open Sesame, KC and The Sunshine Band, a track called Salsation – Salsoul Orchestra?, no, but David Shire along with Ralph MacDonald. However, there are other tracks from a group that nearly had the right vibe for me and took me back to soulful, earlier R&B sounds that my brother had in 1967, with 'Massachusetts', The Bee Gees, what is this album?! Tracks Jive Talkin' and You Should Be Dancin', a couple of records that entered the R&B and UK charts previously.

Looking at the front cover 'The Original Movie Sound Track', Saturday Night Fever – not heard of that, or any film to hit the cinema of the same name!

1977 saw the emergence of Punk Rock, many bands from The Clash who headlined at The Roxy, The Stranglers completed a ten week tour. The Sex Pistols EMI contract is terminated and they sign to A&M, being terminated six days later after a visit to their headquarters in Fulham. In June, they try to interrupt the Silver Jubilee celebration from a boat on the Thames by performing "God Save The Queen". Now signed by Virgin Records, they release Never Mind the Bollocks, Here's The Sex Pistols, their only studio album but considered as one of the most important albums of all time – for some! It spent two weeks at number 1 in the UK Charts that November.

A 29 year old Marc Bolan of T.Rex is killed when his Mini, driven by his girlfriend leaves the road and hits a tree, after driving over a humped back bridge in Barnes SW13, very near where I lived. Seven IRA bombs explode in The West End. British

Leyland threaten to dismiss 40,000 toolmakers that are on strike, foreign cars outsell British cars for the first time. Firefighters go on their first ever strike asking for a 30% increase, we see the Army's Green Goddesses on the streets. Liverpool are Division 1 champions for the tenth time, Manchester United win the FA Cup for the fourth time, stealing the English double from Liverpool, who go on to take their first European Cup. Virginia Wade wins the Ladies Wimbledon title in a Jubilee year, that August Elvis Presley, dies of a heart attack at the age of just 42.

The National Front attempt to march from New Cross to Lewisham, bringing counter demonstrations and violent clashes.

In travel, Freddie Laker launches his Skytrain service to New York at a seat price of £59 (£400 today), nearly 25% of the normal cost, British Airways first Concorde service to New York commences. That Christmas, The Morecambe and Wise Show attracted some 28,000,000 viewers, more homes are watching it now on colour TV, than on black and white. I queue for hours in Leicester Square to get tickets for Star Wars for my mate Danny and I, being a fan for the rest of his life. Another movie, like Jaws that started initiated a Disco hit, like Meco's version of Star Wars, nearly 16 minutes long, from an album called Other Galatic Funk.

Chapter 13 - The Beginning of The End

As I go into 1978, going out seems to have slowed down, now in my 26th year of life, nearly ten years of working and having enough cash in my pocket for anything within reason, but now having a mortgage, bills and other financial commitments and making life tough to have a full social life.

Of course, there was no financial safety net for many who take on a mortgage, the phrase 'The Bank Of Mum & Dad' hadn't been invented yet, unless you had a trust fund, 'You have made your bed, now lie in it!' seemed more apt then. Even getting my head around paying for mortgage over 25 years, raised questions about finances and paying it off as a 50 year old, seemed and was a lifetime away!

So fortunate that there were heavily subsidised restaurants at many IBM locations, as I was driving around London, also at Chiswick (two locations), Park Royal, Greenford, Rayners Lane, St John's Wood and many others made a welcome lunchtime stop. A bigger territory now as trained on more advanced pieces of kit like IBM Composers, used in the print shops, both mechanical and electronic. Magnetic card media to store word processing and floppy disk technology, the advancement of technology that would announce the office personal computer in a couple of years.

In 1974 Arthur C Clarke of Space Odyssey fame predicted that by 2001 everyone will have a console in your home, with the use of a keyboard and will able to leave messages, access bank accounts, read the latest news. It will change the way we communicate in our personal lives and change business forever, earlier in 1964 he talked about the conducting business anywhere in the world by 2001, replacing commuting with communicating.

Still managing to get out now and again, the Jazz Funk just kept coming, another sound, not out of the US but North West London (another AWB moment?!), a blend of jazz, funk, soul, mainly instrumental and dance. A genre, labelled BritFunk, being played in the clubs. In 1978 we see Hi-Tension on TOTP with a record of the same name and shortly after the great title of - British Hustle and reaching No 8 in the UK charts and no doubt where it originated from, followed by Light Of The World, many on the Ensign label, a collaboration by DJs and names that you be all familiar with.

Courtney Pine and Phil Fearon were Hi Tension band members who went on to have their own personal success later.

These band members were young lads, along with female vocalists who went to, liked the same clubs and music as us, they are now in a position to form bands and a write music, not really trying to imitate or emulate US funk bands, but putting their own twist on things, one being the speed of delivering in beats per minute. Many of these releases made it across to The States and became hits.

When I think about this period, its similar to fifteen years earlier in the early 60's and it seems to have gone full circle, British blue eyed soul and multicultural bands, influenced by R&B, Soul, Funk and Jazz Funk, these bands sprung up after enjoying the music club scene and records from the US. After the success of The Stones, The Beatles, Spencer Davis, Chris Farlowe, The Equals and many others and later the Average White Band, The Real Thing, Heatwave etc, it would continue for another new generations and their interest in music.

Lads and sometimes young ladies, that visited music venues in the 1960s, also longed to take up instruments and make music, forming bands. They bought guitars, a drum kit and even better and more fortunate if got access to a Hammond Organ and practiced in their bedrooms, Dads garage, hoping to get gigs, make the big time or even a record deal. But this time, it's not a majority white working class, it's the first generation of Black British born youngsters that have the same drive and needs, being influenced by the music of the 1970s.

BritFunk was said to influence many other bands like Haircut 100, Dexy's Midnight Runners, Culture Club, Bow Wow Wow, Pigbag, in the 1980's and Spandau Ballet using the musicality of Beggar & Co and again these were club goers in the decade and then New Wave. These BritFunk bands are still around today, perhaps with different band members, under The British Funk Association banner.

There is also now a trend for more All Nighters and All Dayers in the South, born out of that all day music experience of Bank Holiday events that were more common in the North earlier in the 70s with the likes of The Wigan Casino and The Twisted Wheel. Many coach parties and carloads of youngsters travelled beyond, to take the floor, with Southern funk dancing and perhaps even taking their own records.

More and more Soul, R&B artists enter the charts that year, again after a hit in 1973, The Detroit Emeralds Feel The Need gets to number nearly the top ten in June 1977, can't keep a good tune down! From the clubs, Manhattan Transfer's Chanson D'Amour, Marvin, Stevie, The Floaters, The Jacksons after Motown, Heatwave, Van McCoy, The Bluenotes's, Thelma's Dont Leave Me This Way, Rose Royce, The Moments, Odyssey, Chic, Shalamar, The O'Jays, The Commodores, some reggae from Barry Briggs, and many more.

From the ladies, The Emotions, Candi Staton, Deniece Williams, Donna Summer, Millie Jackson, Natalie Cole, Chaka

Chan, Odyssey, Dorothy Moore and Aretha, still The Queen of Soul, 1942 – 2018 RIP.

⁂

I also notice towards the end of this decade, that women are starting to take more control of their lives. Born into families in the 1950s, where 'The Man Of The House' was 'The Bread Earner', most mothers were at home, or in low paid part time jobs, just to cut that 'earned bread' and make provisions for their children and take responsibility to manage the house with daily chores, but many working class families had a mother who both juggled a job, the home and sometimes their husband.

With no access to transport, many spent many hours at home and carried out these duties, but in this period now finding jobs and careers in professions, to give them some financial independency. Any young lady leaving a state school in the 1960s at 15, knew what the career and advice guidance would be. Now in the 1970s, more opportunities appear, rejecting the guidance from the decade before. With the school leaving age increased in 1972, staying on at school, qualifications, perhaps even going on to university, it drove more ambition and an 'I can do that also' philosophy.

1970, bought us the passing of the Equal Pay Act, sowing the seeds and highlighted by the famous earlier Ford Sewing Machinists strike and the following demonstrations and marches in 1968. The Sex Discrimination Act of 1975, that covered employment, training, education and even harassment. I believe at this time, more are women are driving cars, getting mortgages and developing careers independently.

Female workers were pressurising company leaders to look at their positions within organisations, where women could do the same job, for the same salary but even better, in many cases given the opportunity! What I notice is that, many young ladies are delaying settling down, they are enjoying their social lives with their girlfriends, just like the lads. Even to a point that I received calls from young ladies who might want to see a film or go out for a drink just as friends, they would take the initiative to call you, not waiting by the phone hoping that someone would call them!

There were no unions in IBM, they developed practises that aimed for 50% of the staff to be female from the bottom to the top, along with diversity, with a Rainbow Society that covers the LGBT+ employees. I worked for many female team leaders and managers within my 32 years in IBM.

My own career ironically, saw me as a Sales Leader in The Women In Business sector for small and medium companies, driven mostly by the dotcom boom in the late nineties and a Year 2000 strategy of change in that sector. IBM partnered and sponsored Everywoman.com, founded in 1999, in 2017 the co-founders Karen and Maxine received MBE's for services to and for the advancement of women in business. At their seminars, the opening and closing music was a blast of Chaka Khan's, 'I'm Everywoman'!

Margaret Roberts, a Lincolnshire daughter of a grocer, a bright pupil and head girl of her grammar school, winning a science scholarship to university, an alumni of the women's college Somerville Oxford, graduates with a Chemistry degree who later turned to law and politics. A brilliant orator and fearless, she runs as a Conservative candidate against the Labour seat in Dartford, losing but with a greatly reduced majority. Rising through the Conservative Party and later becoming MP for Finchley. Famously, as Secretary of State for Education and Science, she took away, like it or loathe it, warm or better cold - school milk - earning the nickname 'Maggie Thatcher, The Milk Snatcher!' and took over as Leader of The Conservative Party in 1975.

Earning the title of The Iron Lady, after her style and defeating Labours James Callaghan to become our first women Prime Minister in 1979 and a role model for many. Implementing policies, now known as Thatcherism, reviewing Trade Union powers and the coalminers, the financial sector deregulation, 'the right to buy', home ownership and taking action in The Falklands, which gave her another term in office 'this Lady was never for turning!'

she retorted. She spent nearly 12 years as Prime Minister, being replaced by a rather grey in comparison, John Major.

The Death Of Disco as we knew it?

It's strange and the use of the word 'Disco', is there any difference between say a Teena Marie or Tina Charles record being played across a dance floor or The Bee Gees versus Earth Wind & Fire?, all very debateable. Rock music fans, tried to create a Disco Demolition Night in July 1979, blowing up a crates of Disco records on a baseball pitch in Chicago, it was supposed to be a promotional night, but resulted in Rock fans invading the pitch and making a large hole in the playing surface.

It is said that Disco declined as a trend in the late 70s, the very early 80s leading and the next stepping stone to hip hop, electronic dance, house, new wave, neo and progressive soul and other genres in the post-disco era. But as George 'Bad' Benson sang 'Everything must change, nothing stays the same, everyone must change, nothing stays the same, the young become the old....'

Like most things you can categorise, to this day people still ask me what music I liked, what I listened to as a youngster and going out nights. My reply, simply 'R&B, Soul, Reggae or just Black Music and still do!' which to me covers many genres for me culminating in Jazz Funk of the 70s. Defined it as any music that gets to your soul, including reggae, many of us who clubbed in the 70's, enjoyed not only the music, but the life style that went with it. A lifestyle that delivered clothes, music, dancing, the atmosphere of great clubs, like minded mates, exploring and crossing borders with a nice set of wheels and of course that preparation and anticipation of going out. Wondering whether it's going to be a great night, good night or an OK night or a complete letdown? Nothing better in the memories and the feeling of walking through the doors of a club with your mates, with the tune of the day playing as you make your way to the bar, looking around to see if there's people you know and people you might meet!

⁂⁂⁂

1978 bought us that movie, cleverly and originally preceded by the soundtrack album with some familiar great tracks on it. But strangely added to, by a group that did have hits in the late 60s and floundered in the early 70s, even playing at working men's clubs in the North after a fall in their popularity.

The plot of the story is based around a lad who likes to dance, go out, mix with his friends and loves a night club atmosphere. Typically working class, has perhaps a job that he doesn't enjoy or is just really hard work, living for the weekend or a weeknight, is what keeps him going from month to month, year to year and all the ups and downs it bought. Sound familiar?

The idea came from a British writer born in London, called Nik Cohn who in 1975 researched the New York club scene and was struggling to understand what was going on. Writing an article in 1976 'Tribal Rites of the New Saturday Night', he pens a story, not based upon a boy from Brooklyn and any research carried out there, but as he admitted in 1996, a Mod soul mate from London ten years earlier! I think the London club scene at the time would have had lots of similar people and their stories perhaps they should have filmed it here, calling it 'Friday Night Funk (In London Town!)' could have been the title and as a soundtrack, Light of The Worlds, London Town?! It is also rumoured that Cohn's book 'I Am Still the Greatest' inspired David bowie's album 'The Rise and Fall of Ziggy Stardust' and his criticism of a rough mix of The Who's Tommy rock opera needed a top single, inspiring Townsend to write and add 'Pinball Wizard' to the opera.

The 'Tribal Rites...' story was picked up by Robert Stigwood, an entrepreneur, film maker, music impresario and manager of the Bee Gees. The album Saturday Night Fever, remains one of the biggest selling soundtrack albums of all time, selling some 40 million copies worldwide. It spent 18 consecutive weeks at No 1 in the UK album charts and 24 weeks in The States, after selling 16 million copies and didn't leave the charts until 1980!

Interestingly, there are two versions of The Bee Gees, More Than A Woman on the album and both are featured in the film,

Tavares cover reached no 7 in the UK charts in May 1978, The Bee Gees never released it as a single. SNF, like it, as a guilty pleasure or loathe it as a Disco film. There are two great scenes from the film for me and I know it's Brooklyn, Hispanic and Italian dance rivalry. But the opening shot could be a lad in London, at the end of his work week and the walk home and the soundtrack, the bounce in his step and picking up a MacDonald's or a Wimpy, instead of that pizza! And later the dressing scene in his bedroom, preening and grooming himself to go out could have been us in our council house bedrooms, whilst playing records – that we were all doing this at one stage, I believe!

In 1979, another film, that touched many of us, if old enough, or had an older sibling in the middle 1960s. Again based on a young working class lad, frustrated by his job as a postboy in an advertising agency and anger towards his parents. Partying hard, popping amphetamines, drinking, fighting with bikers and riding his Lambretta alongside his mates. It shows the clothes of the time, the live bands, the excitement of a club and a house party scene that some of us would have experienced along with a bank holiday trip to the coast. Jimmy, would like to be noticed or to become 'A Face' and with a crush on a young lady, which also sounded familiar, especially for me! The film gained a cult following and spawned - to me - a Third Generation of Mods, their clothing, the revival of Fred Perrys, music, two-tone (after the tonic trousers), ska revival, this time new bands from Birmingham and Coventry and of course a revived interest in scooters.

I think there was a lot of Tony Manero and Jimmy Cooper in many of us!

My nights out are now reduced to perhaps one or two nights, record purchases are now very low, but I am still taping Soul Spectrum and keeping in touch at a distance of that great music and club scene that lasted a decade for me.

Did I morph into inviting people around, nibbles, glasses of red wine, wearing Lacoste, Polo Ralph Lauren, Tacchini, Kappa and dodgy double breasted suits to work etc. Listening to Sade,

Hall & Oates, Simply Red, Al Jarreau, Teddy Pendergrass, Luther Vandross, Lisa Stansfield, Rick Astley from t'up North with Kenny Thomas – a North London council estate boy and many, many more on my Fisher Micro Hi-FI System. Now talking about how much my property is worth, comparing our shares portfolio and what car are you driving now, a Beemer or Merc? Yes, of course I did, I had entered the 1980s!

Nostalgia, and as I get older, I don't think one day passes without a thought of those times, the memories from childhood in the 50s, the early and late 1960s, the crushes when at school and youth clubs, falling in love momentarily, the relationships and of course the music of the 1970s, will never be forgotten and still uplifting to this day, forever date stamped with a tune! The music must have been good, look at how many samples have been used in the 80s, 90s, 00s, 10s and 20s from music of the 70s. Like the '66 World Cup squad, we have lost so many DJs, blues, soul, jazz, reggae artists and musicians in the recent years, RIP all, I am looking forward to the sets up there. Thank you, for the music of great and good times.

Oh, by the way. If you are wondering about my love life and any relationships I may have had, I did meet a girl in these final years of the 1970s, moving in with me for a time. Unfortunately, it didn't work out, at that time I really wondered whether I could ever have a 'normal' long term relationship and would ever find 'the right' partner. I am sorry it's not you, it's was always me.......

PostFace

'Without the following people, I don't know what I would have done'

Murray Road and Stuart Road neighbours, my young street mates, Rob and Paul (what fun we had at a young age!)

Neighbours Anne and Brian Cottee, Auntie's Joan and Mary

Grey Court School and Miss E Lewis for recognising something

Youth Club Leaders John Saville and Jim Lee

The Ham Lads and Lasses, 'it takes a village to raise a child', reconnecting some 30 years later and those memories. The H&P Memories FB Group and John and Mick and Keith with his research. The Soul Boys, Soul Girls FB Pages for jogging the memories.

Friends - Jane and Patrick O'Connor - thank you for having faith in me so many times, when I could have hesitated, you encouraged, building my confidence.

Work - John Howe, Lionel Beckett, Alison Mathers, Julian David, John Hopwood - my IBM Managers. And of course my Mum with the help of my brother Keith, who pointed me in the right direction, I'll Always Love My Mama.

"And last but never least my soulmate KC – no words can ever convey what you truly mean to me."

Lightning Source UK Ltd.
Milton Keynes UK
UKHW021129020122
396453UK00005BA/167

Christopl